Futures of Comparative Literature

Futures of Comparative Literature is a cutting-edge report on the state of the discipline in Comparative Literature. Offering a broad spectrum of viewpoints from all career stages, a variety of different institutions, and many language backgrounds, this collection is fully global and diverse. The book includes previously unpublished interviews with key figures in the discipline as well as a range of different essays – short pieces on key topics and longer, in-depth pieces. It is divided into seven sections: Futures of Comparative Literature; Theories, Histories, Methods; Worlds; Areas and Regions; Languages, Vernaculars, Translations; Media; Beyond the Human; and contains over 50 essays on topics such as: Queer Reading; Human Rights; Fundamentalism; Untranslatability; Big Data; Environmental Humanities. It also includes current facts and figures from the American Comparative Literature Association as well as a very useful general introduction, situating and introducing the material. Curated by an expert editorial team, this book captures what is at stake in the study of Comparative Literature today.

Ursula K. Heise is the Marcia Howard Chair of Literary Studies at the Department of English and the Institute of the Environment and Sustainability at UCLA, USA. Her books include *Imagining Extinction: The Cultural Meanings of Endangered Species* (2016) and *The Routledge Companion to the Environmental Humanities* (2017).

Editorial Board: Dudley Andrew, Alexander Beecroft, Jessica Berman, David Damrosch, Guillermina De Ferrari, César Domínguez, Barbara Harlow and Eric Hayot.

Futures of Comparative Literature

ACLA State of the Discipline Report

Edited by Ursula K. Heise

with Dudley Andrew
Alexander Beecroft
Jessica Berman
David Damrosch
Guillermina De Ferrari
César Domínguez
Barbara Harlow
and Eric Hayot

Routledge
Taylor & Francis Group

LONDON AND NEW YORK

First published 2017
by Routledge
2 Park Square, Milton Park, Abingdon, Oxon OX14 4RN

and by Routledge
711 Third Avenue, New York, NY 10017

Routledge is an imprint of the Taylor & Francis Group, an informa business

British Library Cataloguing-in-Publication Data
A catalogue record for this book is available from the British Library

Library of Congress Cataloging-in-Publication Data
A catalog record for this title has been requested

ISBN: 978-1-138-29333-5 (hbk)
ISBN: 978-1-138-29334-2 (pbk)
ISBN: 978-1-315-22740-5 (ebk)

Typeset in Galliard
by Apex CoVantage, LLC

MIX
Paper from
responsible sources
FSC
www.fsc.org   FSC® C013056

Printed and bound in Great Britain by
TJ International Ltd, Padstow, Cornwall

Contents

Areas and regions   169

Media 237

Beyond the human 291

Facts and figures 327

Figures

Editorial board

Contributors

Jonathan E. Abel is Associate Professor of Comparative Literature and Asian Studies at Penn State University. His current project is a history of new media in Japanese culture from late nineteenth-century stereoscopic photography in Yokohama to post–March 2011 disaster Twitter novels.

Avram Alpert is a 2016–17 Fulbright Scholar at the Federal University of Bahia, Brazil. His writings have appeared in *diacritics, Postcolonial Studies, Theory, Culture & Society, Third Text*, and elsewhere.

Aaron Bady earned his PhD from University of California, Berkeley, in 2013, and was a postdoctoral scholar in the English department at University of Texas, Austin, from 2013 to 2015. His interviews with African writers are available online at *The New Inquiry* and *Post45*; he blogs and tweets as zunguzungu.

Antonio Barrenechea is Associate Professor in the Department of English, Linguistics, and Communication at the University of Mary Washington. He is the author of *America Unbound: Encyclopedic Literature and Hemispheric Studies* (U of New Mexico P, 2016).

Thomas O. Beebee is Edwin Erle Sparks Professor of Comparative Literature and German at Pennsylvania State University. He is the editor of *German Literature as World Literature* (Bloomsbury, 2014), and his recent books include *Transmesis: Inside Translation's Black Box* (Palgrave Macmillan, 2012), *Citation and Precedent* (Continuum, 2011), and *Millennial Literatures of the Americas, 1492–2002* (Oxford, 2008).

Timothy Brennan is the Samuel Russell Chair in the Humanities at the University of Minnesota. His most recent book is *Borrowed Light I: Vico, Hegel and the Colonies* (Stanford UP, 2014). *Borrowed Light II: Imperial Form* is forthcoming.

Christopher Bush is Associate Professor of French and Comparative Literary Studies at Northwestern University. His research and teaching focus on transnational and interdisciplinary approaches to literary modernisms, especially the interactions between Euro-American and East Asian aesthetic theory, avant-gardes, and media. His book *Ideographic Modernism: China, Writing,*

Media appeared in 2010, and his current book project is titled *The Floating World: Japoniste Aesthetics and Global Modernity.*

Rey Chow is Anne Firor Scott Professor of Literature and the director of the Program in Literature at Duke University. Since 1991, she has authored nine monographs, including, most recently, *Not Like a Native Speaker: On Languaging as a Postcolonial Experience.* Chow's work has appeared in over ten languages; *The Rey Chow Reader* was published in 2010 by Columbia University Press. In 2016 Chow was elected to the American Academy of Arts and Sciences.

Marcel Cornis-Pope is Professor of English and Media Studies at Virginia Commonwealth University. His research interests include literary theory, post/modern American literature, British Victorian literature, and new media. He has been president of the ICLA Coordinating Committee. He coedited the four-volume set of the *History of the Literary Cultures of East-Central Europe.* He has also published the edited volume *New Literary Hybrids in the Age of Multimedia Expression: Crossing Borders, Crossing Genres* (2014), which emphasizes recent trends in literary and multimedia publications.

Mara de Gennaro is Visiting Fellow of the Committee on Globalization and Social Change at the Graduate Center, CUNY. Her current book project, *Modernism after Postcolonialism*, brings the study of Francophone literature and theory to Anglophone transnationalist debates over the cultural politics of modernism. Recent work has appeared in *Comparative Literature Studies*, *Textual Practice*, and *Paideuma.*

Ivonne del Valle is Associate Professor of Spanish and Portuguese at UC Berkeley. She has written on the Jesuits as an influential politico-religious order that served modernization and the expansion of the Spanish empire, as well as several articles on water and politics, and the rule of law in Mexico. Her research and teaching try to show the relevance of the colonial period for an understanding of contemporary times.

Jacob Edmond is Associate Professor of English at the University of Otago, New Zealand. He is the author of *A Common Strangeness: Contemporary Poetry, Cross-Cultural Encounter, Comparative Literature* (Fordham, 2012; honorable mention for the ACLA Harry Levin Prize and the Association for the Study of the Arts of the Present book prize), and has published essays in such journals as *Comparative Literature*, *Contemporary Literature*, *Poetics Today*, *Slavic Review*, and *The China Quarterly.*

Nergis Ertürk is the author of *Grammatology and Literary Modernity in Turkey* (Oxford UP, 2011), the recipient of the 2012 Modern Language Association Prize for a First Book, and the coeditor (with Özge Serin) of a 2016 special issue of *boundary 2* entitled *Marxism, Communism, and Translation.* She is currently working on a book project on early twentieth-century Turkish and Soviet literary encounters.

Charlotte Eubanks is Associate Professor of Comparative Literature, Japanese, and Asian Studies at Penn State, where she teaches courses in world literature, literary Buddhism, Japanese culture, book history, and visual studies. She is the author of numerous articles and the monograph *Miracles of Book and Body: Buddhist Textual Culture and Medieval Japan* (U of California P, 2011). She is currently working on a book manuscript titled *Crossing the Red Line: Akamatsu Toshiko/ Maruki Toshi and the Visual Cultures of Transwar Japan* and is associate editor at the journal *Verge: Studies in Global Asias* (University of Minnesota Press).

Gail Finney has been Professor of Comparative Literature and German at University of California, Davis, since 1988. She has published books on the nineteenth-century European novel, on turn-of-the-century European drama, and on Christa Wolf. In recent years she has been exploring the staging of family trauma in contemporary American cinema.

María Andrea Giovine Yáñez works as a full-time professor and researcher in the Institute of Bibliographical Research at the National Autonomous University of Mexico. Since 2013, she has been a member of the Laboratory of Extended Literature and Other Materialities (lleom.net).

Susana González Aktories is Professor in Comparative Literature at the National Autonomous University of Mexico and has published and edited several books on the relations between literature, music, and fine arts and on musical semiotics. Since 2013, she has been a member of the Laboratory of Extended Literature and Other Materialities (lleom.net).

Erin Graff Zivin is Professor of Spanish and Portuguese and Comparative Literature at the University of Southern California. Her most recent book is *Figurative Inquisitions: Conversion, Torture, and Truth in the Luso-Hispanic Atlantic* (Northwestern UP, 2014), winner of the 2015 Award for Best Book, Latin American Jewish Studies Association. She is author of *The Wandering Signifier: Rhetoric of Jewishness in the Latin American Imaginary* (Duke UP, 2008), as well as the editor of *The Ethics of Latin American Literary Criticism: Reading Otherwise* (Palgrave Macmillan, 2007) and *The Marrano Specter: Derrida and Hispanism* (Fordham, forthcoming 2017).

Yucong Hao is a graduate student in Asian languages and cultures at the University of Michigan. Her research interests include modernism, socialist realism, and literary institutions in East Asia.

Waïl S. Hassan is Professor of Comparative Literature at the University of Illinois at Urbana-Champaign. He is currently writing a book on Arab-Brazilian literary and cultural relations and editing *The Oxford Handbook of Arab Novelistic Traditions*.

Jarrod Hayes is Professor of French in the Department of Romance Languages and Literatures at the University of Michigan. His books include *Comparatively Queer: Interrogating Identities across Time and Cultures* (Palgrave Macmillan, 2010), coedited with Margaret R. Higonnet and William J. Spurlin, and *Queer Nations: Marginal Sexualities in the Maghreb* (Chicago UP, 2000).

Margaret R. Higonnet is Professor of English and Comparative Literature at the University of Connecticut. She has taught at George Washington University, University of Santiago de Compostela, and Munich. She has been president of the ACLA and the ICLA Coordinating Committee. Her theoretical interests range from the Romantic roots of modern literary theory to the intersection of feminist theory and comparative literature.

Neville Hoad is Associate Professor of English and Women's and Gender Studies at The University of Texas at Austin. He is the author of *African Intimacies: Race, Homosexuality and Globalization* (Minnesota UP, 2007) and coeditor (with Karen Martin and Graeme Reid) of *Sex & Politics in South Africa: Equality/Gay & Lesbian Movement/the anti-Apartheid Struggle* (Double Storey, 2005). He is currently working on a book project about the literary and cultural representations of the HIV/AIDS pandemic in sub-Saharan Africa.

Jeanne-Marie Jackson is Assistant Professor of English at Johns Hopkins University and the author of *South African Literature's Russian Soul: Narrative Forms of Global Isolation* (Bloomsbury, 2015).

R. A. Judy is Professor of Critical and Cultural Studies at the University of Pittsburgh, and a member of the *boundary 2* Editorial Collective.

Lucas Klein is a father, writer, translator, and editor whose work has appeared in *LARB*, *Jacket*, *Rain Taxi*, *CLEAR*, *Comparative Literature Studies*, and *PMLA*, and from Fordham, Black Widow, and New Directions. Assistant Professor at the University of Hong Kong, his translation *Notes on the Mosquito: Selected Poems of Xi Chuan* won the 2013 Lucien Stryk Prize, and his *October Dedications*, translations of the poetry of Mang Ke, is recently out from Zephyr and Chinese University Press.

Adam F. Kola is Assistant Professor at Nicolaus Copernicus University, Toruń, Poland, and president of the Polish Comparative Literature Association. His research has been focused on Slavic World Literature and East- and Central European intellectual and literary history of the nineteenth and twentieth centuries.

Susan S. Lanser (Brandeis University) is most recently the author of the award-winning *The Sexuality of History: Modernity and the Sapphic 1565–1830* (Chicago UP, 2014) and the coeditor with Robyn Warhol of *Narrative Theory Unbound: Queer and Feminist Interventions* (Ohio State UP, 2015).

Jos Lavery is Assistant Professor in the Department of English at the University of California, Berkeley, where he teaches Victorian literature and critical theory. He is currently completing his first book, *The Sword and the Chrysanthemum: Victorian Theories of Japanese Aesthetics*, and has work published or forthcoming in *Comparative Literature Studies*, *Novel: A Forum on Fiction*, *English Literary History*, the *Journal of Modern Literature*, and *Studies in the Novel*.

Francine Masiello holds the Sidney and Margaret Ancker Chair in the Departments of Comparative Literature and Spanish and Portuguese at University of California, Berkeley. A Latin Americanist who works on North/South issues, she is most recently the author of *El cuerpo de la voz* (2013), winner of the LASA Southern Cone best book prize, and has just completed *The Senses of Democracy*, a book on the sensorium, politics, and culture, forthcoming in 2017.

Sophia A. McClennen is Associate Director of the School of International Affairs and Director of the Center for Global Studies at Penn State. Her most recent book is *The Routledge Companion to Literature and Human Rights*, edited with Alexandra Schultheis Moore.

Wander Melo Miranda is Professor of Literary Theory and Comparative Literature at Universidade Federal de Minas Gerais, and principal investigator at Conselho Nacional de Desenvolvimento Científico e Tecnológico. He is the author of *Corpos escritos* (1992) and *Nações literárias* (2010), among others.

Adam Miyashiro is Assistant Professor of Medieval Literature at Stockton University in New Jersey. He has published articles and reviews in *Neophilologus*, *Notes and Queries*, *Comparative Literature Studies*, and the *Journal of Law and Religion*. He is currently working on a book manuscript on race in medieval literature.

Christian Moraru is the Class of 1949 Distinguished Professor in the Humanities and Professor of English at University of North Carolina, Greensboro. His recent publications include the monographs *Cosmodernism: American Narrative, Late Globalization, and the New Cultural Imaginary* (U of Michigan P, 2011) and *Reading for the Planet: Toward a Geomethodology* (U of Michigan P, 2015) and essay collections such as *Postcommunism, Postmodernism, and the Global Imagination* (Columbia UP/EEM Series, 2009) and *The Planetary Turn: Relationality and Geoaesthetics in the Twenty-First Century* (Northwestern UP, 2015, with Amy J. Elias).

Franco Moretti is the Danily C. and Laura Louise Bell Professor and Professor of Comparative Literature in the Department of English at Stanford University. He is the author of *Signs Taken for Wonders* (1983), *The Way of the World* (1987), *Modern Epic* (1995), *Atlas of the European Novel 1800–1900* (1998), *Graphs, Maps, Trees* (2005), *The Bourgeois* (2013), and *Distant Reading* (2013). He writes often for *New Left Review*, and has been translated into over twenty languages.

Mario Ortiz Robles is Professor of English at the University of Wisconsin, Madison. He is the author of *The Novel as Event* (Michigan UP, 2010) and *Literature and Animal Studies* (Routledge, 2016) and coeditor of *Narrative Middles* (Ohio UP, 2011).

Jessica Pressman is author of *Digital Modernism: Making It New in New Media* (Oxford UP, 2014), co-author, with Mark C. Marino and Jeremy Douglass, of *Reading* Project: *A Collaborative Analysis of William*

Poundstone's Project for Tachistoscope {Bottomless Pit} (Iowa UP, 2015), and coeditor, with N. Katherine Hayles, of *Comparative Textual Media: Transforming the Humanities in the Postprint Era* (Minnesota UP, 2013). She teaches in the Department of English and Comparative Literature at San Diego State University.

José Quiroga, Professor of Comparative Literature at Emory University since 2003, has published extensively on literatures, art, gender/sexuality studies, and cultural projects of the Americas, from the early avant-gardes to the present. He has published, among others, *Tropics of Desire* (NYU P, 2001), *Cuban Palimpsests* (U of Minnesota P, 2005), and *Mapa Callejero* (Buenos Aires UP, 2010). He is presently working on *The Havana Reader* for Duke UP, and a longer manuscript, *The Book of Flight* (2017).

Brigitte Rath (pseudotranslation.org) is Senior Lecturer in Comparative Literature at the University of Innsbruck. She has published a book on narrative understanding, *Narratives Verstehen* (2011), three edited volumes, and several articles on pseudotranslation, and is currently finishing her book *Original Translation: Imagining Texts in Other Languages.*

Sangeeta Ray is Professor of English and Comparative Literature at the University of Maryland. She has written two books and numerous articles and coedited an anthology. Most recently she coedited the three-volume *Encyclopedia of Postcolonial Studies* (Wiley-Blackwell, 2016).

Michael Rubenstein is Associate Professor of English at Stony Brook University, where he teaches classes on Irish, British, Anglophone, and postcolonial literature and culture, environmental humanities, and cinema. His first book, *Public Works: Infrastructure, Irish Modernism, and the Postcolonial* (U of Notre Dame P, 2010) won the Modernist Studies Association Prize and the American Conference for Irish Studies Robert Rhodes' Prize for a book on literature. He is coeditor of the Winter 2015 special issue of *MFS Modern Fiction Studies* dedicated to the topic "infrastructuralism."

Mohammad Salama is Associate Professor of Arabic and Chair, Department of Modern Languages and Literatures, San Francisco State University, and Associate Editor of *SCTIW Review.* He is the author of *Islam, Orientalism and Intellectual History* (I.B. Tauris, 2011). He has a forthcoming book, *The Qur'an and Modern Arabic Literary Criticism* (Bloomsbury, 2017), and is currently completing a monograph on Islam and the culture of modern Egypt.

Haun Saussy is University Professor at the University of Chicago (Comparative Literature, East Asian Languages and Civilizations, and Committee on Social Thought). His most recent books are *Introducing Comparative Literature: New Trends and Applications* (with César Domínguez and Darío Villanueva, Routledge, 2015) and *The Ethnography of Rhythm: Orality and Its Technologies* (Fordham UP, 2016).

Corinne Scheiner is the Maytag Professor of Comparative Literature and Judson M. Bemis Professor of Humanities at Colorado College. Her research and publications focus on translation studies, Samuel Beckett, Vladimir Nabokov, and the practice and teaching of comparative literature. She is the editor of the ADPCL and ACLA's 2005 Report on the Undergraduate Comparative Literature Curriculum.

S. Shankar is a critic, novelist, and translator. He is Professor of English and Director of the Creative Writing Program at the University of Hawai'i at Mānoa. His most recent book is *Flesh and Fish Blood: Postcolonialism, Translation, and the Vernacular* (U of California P and OrientBlackswan India, 2012). He is co-editing a special issue of the journal *Biography* on caste and life narratives and has a novel entitled *Ghost in the Tamarind* forthcoming.

Snehal Shingavi is Associate Professor of English at the University of Texas, Austin, and the author of *The Mahatma Misunderstood: The Politics and Forms of Literary Nationalism in India* (Anthem Books, 2013). He has also translated Munshi Premchand's Hindi novel *Sevasadan* (Oxford UP, 2005), the Urdu short-story collection *Angaaray* (Penguin, 2014), and Bhisham Sahni's autobiography, *Today's Pasts* (Penguin, 2015). He has a forthcoming translation of Agyeya's *Shekhar: A Life* (Penguin, 2018).

Mariano Siskind is Professor of Romance Languages and Literatures and of Comparative Literature at Harvard University. He is the author of *Cosmopolitan Desires: Global Modernity and World Literature in Latin America* (Northwestern UP, 2014), two edited volumes, and several academic essays.

Joseph R. Slaughter is President of the American Comparative Literature Association (2016–17). Associate Professor of English and Comparative Literature at Columbia University, he teaches and writes about ethnic and Third World literatures and international law.

Gayatri Chakravorty Spivak is University Professor at Columbia University and a founder of the Institute for Comparative Literature and Society. She runs six elementary schools among the landless illiterate in western West Bengal and has won the Kyoto Prize (2012) and the Padma Bhushan (2013).

Shaden M. Tageldin is Associate Professor of Cultural Studies and Comparative Literature and Director of the African Studies Initiative at the University of Minnesota. The author of *Disarming Words: Empire and the Seductions of Translation in Egypt* (U of California P, 2011), awarded an Honorable Mention for the 2013 Harry Levin Prize of the American Comparative Literature Association, she is completing a book provisionally titled *Toward a Transcontinental Theory of Modern Comparative Literature* on a 2016–2017 Frederick Burkhardt Residential Fellowship for Recently Tenured Scholars from the American Council of Learned Societies.

Dennis Tenen's research happens at the intersection of people, texts, and technology. His recent work appears in *Computational Culture, Amodern, boundary 2,* and *Modernism/modernity* on topics that range from book piracy to algorithmic composition, unintelligent design, and the history of data visualization. He is Assistant Professor of English and Comparative Literature at Columbia University, co-founder of Columbia's Group for Experimental Methods in the Humanities, and the author of the forthcoming *Plain Text: The Poetics of Computation* (Stanford UP, 2017).

Rei Terada is Professor of Comparative Literature at University of California, Irvine, and author of *Looking Away: Phenomenality and Dissatisfaction, Kant to Adorno* (Harvard UP, 2009) and *Feeling in Theory: Emotion after the "Death of the Subject"* (Harvard UP, 2001; winner of the ACLA's René Wellek Prize).

Mads Rosendahl Thomsen is Professor with Special Responsibilities of Comparative Literature at Aarhus University, Denmark. He is the author of *Mapping World Literature* (2008) and *The New Human in Literature* (2013), coeditor of *World Literature: A Reader* (2012), and editor-in-chief of *Literature: An Introduction to Theory and Analysis* (forthcoming 2017).

Karen Thornber is Professor of Comparative Literature and of East Asian Languages and Civilizations at Harvard University, Victor and William Fung Director of the Harvard University Asia Center, Chair of the Harvard University Council on Asian Studies, and Director of the Harvard Global Institute Environmental Humanities Initiative. Thornber is author of two multiple international award-winning scholarly monographs – *Empire of Texts in Motion: Chinese, Korean, and Taiwanese Transculturations of Japanese Literature* (2009) and *Ecoambiguity: Environmental Crises and East Asian Literatures* (2012) – as well as close to seventy articles and book chapters. She is also coeditor of four volumes and an award-winning translator.

Rebecca L. Walkowitz is Professor of English and Affiliate Faculty in Comparative Literature at Rutgers University. She is author of *Born Translated: The Contemporary Novel in an Age of World Literature* and *Cosmopolitan Style: Modernism beyond the Nation*, and coeditor, with Eric Hayot, of *A New Vocabulary for Global Modernism*.

Ban Wang is the William Haas Professor in Chinese Studies and Comparative Literature at Stanford University. He is the author of *The Sublime Figure of History, Illuminations from the Past*, and *History and Memory*. He has written widely on Chinese literature, aesthetics, cinema, and intellectual history.

Sarah Ann Wells is Assistant Professor in the Department of Comparative Literature and Folklore Studies at the University of Wisconsin, Madison. She is the author of *Media Laboratories: Late Modernism in South America* (Northwestern UP, 2017) and coeditor of *Simultaneous Worlds: Global Science Fiction Cinema* (Minnesota UP, 2015).

Jennifer Wenzel is Associate Professor in the Department of English and Comparative Literature and the Department of Middle Eastern, South Asian, and African Studies at Columbia University. She is the author of *Bulletproof: Afterlives of Anticolonial Prophecy in South Africa and Beyond* (Chicago UP and KwaZulu-Natal, 2009) and coeditor (with Imre Szeman and Patricia Yaeger) of *Fueling Culture: 101 Words for Energy and Environment* (Fordham UP, 2017).

Introduction

Comparative literature and the new humanities

Ursula K. Heise

The bylaws of the American Comparative Literature Association mandate a report on the state of the discipline every ten years, but what this report should look like and who should write it has changed considerably over the last five decades. This volume and the website from which it emerged (stateofthediscipline.acla.org) make up the fifth decennial report, and the large number and diverse formats of the contributions already indicate how much the shifting forms of ACLA reports themselves track changes in how comparative literature conceives of itself. It is what the reports say but also how they say it that traces the discipline's dynamic evolution.

The Levin Report from 1965 and the Greene Report from 1975 were summaries written by a single researcher and emphasized the standards and boundaries that should define the discipline. After a hiatus in the 1980s, the Bernheimer Report of 1993 included in its published version not just Charles Bernheimer's ten-page assessment of how comparative literature should reposition itself in relation to cultural studies, media studies, and more generally the "broadened scope of contemporary literary studies" in its "multicultural, global, and inter-disciplinary" dimensions (47), but also sixteen responses and position papers. Clearly, what the report should deliver had metamorphosed from a set of diagnoses, standards, and prescriptions to a lively and at times controversial dialogue among a variety of researchers. This model also informed the nineteen contributions to the 2004 Saussy Report, *Comparative Literature in an Age of Globalization*, which sought to re-envision the discipline in view of changing geopolitical constellations in the aftermath of 9/11. They also highlighted the diffusion of comparatist concepts and methods into other departments of literature. "The premises and protocols characteristic of our discipline are now the daily currency of coursework, publishing, hiring, and coffee-shop discussion. . . . Our conclusions have become other people's assumptions," Haun Saussy observed in his lead essay (3). He added that this broad acceptance has not necessarily helped the institutional profile of comparative literature, and has in some sense even made it appear superfluous (4–5).

The 2017 report continues the ACLA's efforts to include the voices of an increasingly diverse array of contributors from different types of academic institutions, home departments, and career stages in its reflections on the development of comparative literature. But it breaks with the assumption of previous reports that conceptions of the discipline, however much they might differ in content, should inevitably be expressed in more or less the length and format of the usual academic essay (see Hayot, this volume). The ACLA Executive Board designated a team of eight editors and myself as managing editor to oversee this effort. To reach out to a greater number of comparatists than our team of nine already knew, we created a website that was open for submissions and comments by ACLA members between the 2014 and 2015 conventions, and explicitly designed to accommodate a variety of lengths, formats, and styles: short essays of under one thousand words on keywords of the discipline, slightly longer reflections on practices and possible futures of comparative literature, and more formal essays on emergent and continuing theoretical paradigms, along with a section on facts and figures about comparative literature departments and the ACLA. After the end of the open submission period, we selected a set of pieces from the website to transition into print and added five conversations and interviews that were initiated by members of the editorial team and carried out either via e-mail or in person: Jessica Berman's conversation with R. A. Judy and Rei Terada on affect theory; Guillermina De Ferrari's conversation about comparative literature and Latin America with Ivonne del Valle, Francine Masiello, Wander Melo Miranda, José Quiroga, Mariano Siskind, Sarah Ann Wells, and Erin Graff Zivin; César Domínguez's conversation about comparative literary history with Marcel Cornis-Pope and Margaret R. Higonnet; Barbara Harlow and Neville Hoad's interview with Aaron Bady about African literature; and my own conversation with Franco Moretti about computational criticism.

Clearly, a discussion that includes two different media (web and print), over fifty texts, and sixty participants pushes the boundaries of what is normally called a "report." As it should: neither literary studies in general nor comparative literature in particular can today be described as anything other than a diverse constellation of theoretical and analytical approaches to questions of languages, literatures, and media. We hope that the mix of formats and styles both on the website and in the print version of the report in and of itself helps to convey a sense of the lively spectrum of possibilities that comparative literature encompasses today. From this constellation of surveys and surveyors, a rough map of our discipline's current conceptual topography emerges: its major theoretical commitments; its conflicts over how to negotiate the global, regional, national, and local scales of literary production and reception; its engagement with old and new media; and its position in a matrix of new interdisciplinary research areas, many of which involve science or technology.

Three interrelated but different theoretical orientations run through many of the contributions to this report. One is the continuing interest in literary theory in its interconnections with philosophy, which runs the gamut from aesthetics (Wang, this volume) to poststructuralism. Poststructuralist philosophies, which departments of comparative literature played a crucial role in introducing to the United States in the 1970s and 1980s, have in recent years helped to shape new areas of study, such as object-oriented ontology, affect theory (Berman, "Conversation," this volume), and human-animal studies (Ortiz Robles, this volume). Postcolonial theory, with its roots in work by distinguished comparatists, such as Edward Said and Gayatri Spivak, has also developed into new directions through its connections with human rights (McClennen, this volume; Slaughter, this volume) and with ecocriticism (Nixon; Wenzel, this volume), even as it retains its foundational interest in how cultures and literatures are shaped by global power differentials (see Ray, this volume). World literature, the third theoretical axis, is of more recent vintage as a shaping influence on comparative literature. Debates over how to globalize and democratize the study of the world's many literatures – and concurrently, how to loosen the hold of the nation, of written language, and of high culture on the study of literature – erupted in the responses accompanying the Bernheimer Report in the early 1990s. They led Franco Moretti to call, in 2000, for "distant reading" as a way of approaching world literature – in its original formulation, a method related not to computational tools but to the synthetic reading of literary genres and themes through the analyses produced by comparatists with expertise in specific languages and regions ("Conjectures"). David Damrosch, in *What Is World Literature?* (2003), redefined world literature as "a mode of circulation and of reading" (5) rather than a particular canon, a way of reading that pays particular attention to the reception of a text beyond its culture of origin (4).

Following the analyses by Moretti, Damrosch, and Pascale Casanova in *The World Republic of Letters*, world literature has arguably become one of the most generative concepts for comparative literature over the last decade, as the founding of the Institute of World Literature and multiple publications on the topic demonstrate (see, e.g., D'haen, Domínguez, and Thomsen; D'haen, Damrosch, and Kadir; Prendergast; Thomsen). This body of theory and analysis has contributed much to the understanding of the production, migration, translation, and cross-cultural reception and valuation of literary texts, whether it focuses on world literature as an encompassing system on the model of Wallerstein's economic theory, on the migration of genres such as the novel or the haiku, on patterns of canonization, on the politics of translation, or on the economies of publications and awards. But the world literature paradigm has also given rise to skepticism and fierce rebuttals that often go to the heart of what can or should be compared in comparative literature. Emily Apter, for example, has criticized translation studies and world literature studies for assuming that most or all texts can be translated, and for imagining that translation furthers transnational communication, understanding, and world peace, without paying due attention to the untranslatable as an important form and even a right in literature. Postcolonial critics have expressed reservations about the way in which world literature elides geopolitical differences of class, wealth, and power (Nixon 38), while ecocritics are concerned about its lack of attention to the material conditions and costs of text production and distribution in a resource-strapped world (Wenzel). Some comparatists have foregrounded the importance of national and cultural differences in any construction of "the world" (Wang, this volume; see also Damrosch, this volume; Moraru, this volume), while others call for a diversification of theoretical sources for comparatist approaches that might equal the diversification of its objects of study (Beebee, this volume). And the emphasis of world literature studies on transnational patterns, let alone systems, has sometimes met with renewed insistence on the importance of the unpredictable and nonsystematic in literary creation, scholarship, and pedagogy (Alpert, this volume), and more generally, on the centrality of philology (Brennan, this volume) and close reading for comparative literature.

These conflicts over what methodological innovations a truly global object of study requires are neither limited to comparative literature nor entirely new in the discipline. Similar debates over new forms of universalism and their relation to the study of cultural and historical differences have arisen across the humanities and qualitative social sciences in response to theories of cosmopolitanism since the 1980s, and since 2000 in discussions about the Anthropocene, the hypothesis that we now inhabit a new geological epoch due to the transformative impact of the human species on planetary ecosystems. In comparative literature, the Bernheimer Report triggered fierce debates over how to approach a truly global literary canon through its call to free the discipline from lingering Eurocentrism and to include more national literatures from around the globe, more literatures that are not dominant in their nations and sometimes not written in the same language (e.g., Quechua orature and literature), literatures that are not linked to a national territory (e.g., Kurdish or Palestinian literature), and popular forms of literature and culture. Jonathan Culler, Marjorie Perloff, and Mary Louise Pratt, for example, took widely divergent positions in response to this challenge. Such questions also resonate in the current report – for example, when Waïl Hassan and Adam Kola reflect on how the increased interest in Arabic and East European literatures challenges the familiar comparatist geographies of East-West studies and global South-global North postcolonialism. In this context, it is unsurprising that the world literature paradigm, as one approach to globalizing the literary object of study, would be met with resistance and alternative proposals.

What is more problematic is that the challenge of scale presented by the study of literature as a global phenomenon sometimes gets conflated with the emergence of new quantitative tools and methods meant to address "big data" in literary studies and other humanities disciplines (cf. Abel, this volume; Tenen, this volume; Thomsen, this volume). Both of them may appear to conform at first sight to some version of the "grand narratives" that literary researchers have usually been skeptical of since the 1980s. Yet the two are by no means identical or even closely associated. "Global literature" or "world literature" describes an object of study that has to date typically been approached without the help of digital tools: neither Casanova nor Damrosch nor Thomsen employ digital methods in their influential analyses of world literature, and even Moretti, well-known for his experiments with computer-based analysis, has to date seldom used them to approach global literature. Indeed, in the conversation included in this volume, he highlights the difficulties of digital approaches to comparative literature and the "reprovincialization" that has accompanied computational criticism. Conversely, some of the studies that have most persuasively applied digital methods to large text archives – Jockers's analysis of themes in the nineteenth-century novel (*Macroanalysis* Ch. 8) or Archer and Jockers's *The Bestseller Code*, say – are focused on English-language texts. Saussy's diagnosis that comparatist assumptions have spread to many areas of literary studies, therefore, does not yet hold true for computational criticism. One of the challenges that this new area holds out is how it might be used for comparatist analyses, and how comparatist frameworks might transform its premises and methodologies.

The specific debate about the role of computational methods in comparative literature, however, is only one part of the discipline's broader engagement with the landscape of new, digitally supported genres and media that has arisen over the last few decades. Indeed, one could argue that one current understanding of comparative literature revolves not so much around the study of different languages and cultures as of different media. Long-standing intellectual investments in the comparative study of texts, sounds, and (moving) images have in recent years combined with an explosion of interest in the history of the book (an area of research that is not as well represented in the contributions to this report as it should be). In no small part, this interest has emerged out of the increasing transformations of writing, publishing, reading, and text archiving into digitally based activities. The currently unfolding conflicts and convergences of print culture with electronic culture – including the "social media" that have taken on such importance over the last decade – take quite different shapes in different regions, languages, and cultures. Comparatists are uniquely positioned to understand and intervene in the making and unmaking of media cultures whose rapid transformations sometimes outpace social, legal, and knowledge innovations.

The new objects of study, historical archives, methodologies, and technological tools that are usually lumped under the label "digital humanities" – that is, the study of new media texts with the means of conventional literary and rhetorical analysis, as well as the study of literature with computational means – form part of a larger panorama of emergent research areas (Fitzpatrick; Heise, "Conversation," this volume; Pressman, this volume; Tenen, this volume). Many of these fields, typically labeled "x studies" or "y humanities," signal by their very names that they seek new convergences between disciplines in the humanities, social sciences, and natural sciences. Women's studies, gender studies, and queer studies as well as various types of ethnic studies have of course operated on a similar model for several decades already, and many of the contributions to this volume demonstrate not only how comparatist perspectives deepen and diversify analyses of gender but also how queer thinking might reshape the terms of comparative literary history and analysis (see, e.g., Berman, "Trans," this volume; Hayes, this volume; Lanser, this volume).

Many of the new interdisciplinary fields now connect to medicine, technology, or the natural sciences. Disability studies, narrative medicine, and the medical humanities, for example, link the study of culture, history, and rhetoric with human biology, public health, epidemiology, and medical imaging to explore discourses of body and health standards, diseases and cures, childhood and aging. Food studies explore the complex interface of agriculture, economy, and culture in the production, distribution, consumption, and representation of food. Human-animal studies, sometimes also called critical animal studies, draw on ethological research about the cognition, perception, communication, and skills of individual animals as well as the culture and politics of animal communities to investigate humans' interdependence with nonhumans, along with historically and culturally shifting conceptions of the human subject in its variously construed differences from animals and plants. Some strains in this field emerged from and explicitly link back to poststructuralist critiques of the human subject (de Gennaro, this volume; Ortiz Robles, this volume). Ecocriticism, which started out its exploration of environmental themes in North American and British literature in the 1990s and paid a great deal of attention to ecological science, has in the last ten years turned comparatist under the influence of postcolonial ecocriticism and eco-cosmopolitanism. In the process, it has veered away from biology and ecology in favor of closer associations with disciplines such as environmental history, environmental philosophy, environmental anthropology, and cultural geography, in a matrix that has recently come to be called "environmental humanities" (Heise, "Environmental Humanities," this volume). Most recently, the urban humanities have begun to emerge as a new effort to explore the culture, history, infrastructure, and representations of cities by drawing on architecture, design, geography, and urban planning as well as literature and film studies. The public humanities, in addition, aim to connect humanistic research with public debates and policy-making.

In contrast with the pioneering role that comparative literature played between the late 1960s and the early 1990s in introducing various strains of theory to literary and cultural study – to the point of sometimes becoming identified as the theoretical branch of literary studies – it has not protagonized any of these more recent innovations in the humanities in general and literary studies in particular. Even in those new research areas where comparative literature has by now had a major impact – ecocriticism, for example – it arrived belatedly, and in other areas such as the medical humanities, comparatists are only beginning to weigh in. Since the history and development of these new research areas are quite heterogeneous, it is difficult to generalize about the reasons for this belatedness: in ecocriticism, it had to do with the origins of the field in the study of American literature; in the digital humanities, with difficulties of copyright, translations, and technological tools; food studies and the medical humanities have paid a good deal of attention to cultural difference, but due to the contributions of anthropologists and geographers more than literary comparatists (but see Thornber, this volume). Because of this diversity of research trajectories, comparative literature's belated or, to date, minor role in these new research areas may not be any particular reason for disciplinary anxiety – especially since innovation tends to be overrated and elaboration or modification underrated in many academic disciplines.

But the current scenario of new interdisciplinary research clusters does hold out the challenge for comparatists to foreground how relevant and indeed indispensable their multilingual and cross-cultural research is for determining the scope, the limits, and the historically and culturally divergent implications of these emergent paradigms. This diversification of cultural horizons may matter more, over the long term, than having pioneered particular disciplinary innovations. Comparatists should, in theory at least, be well positioned to stake these claims, since so much comparatist work has been interdisciplinary all along: it has interfaced with art history, film studies, gender studies, history, musicology, philosophy, and translation studies. The emergent interdisciplinary humanities call on comparatists to show how their work on languages, narratives, and images modifies and challenges the often universalizing discourses of science, medicine, technology, and media.

Stories about the biological, social, psychological, and spiritual causes of individual and collective illness, for example, vary widely across cultures and historical periods, as do those about cures and the responsibilities of the patient and the physician: this matters for the medical humanities. Ideas about human identity in its relation to other species – and the more basic question of what taxonomy should account for the varieties of visible and invisible life – diverge in similar ways when historical, linguistic, and value frameworks come into focus in ways that are crucial for human-animal studies; and these ideas are shaped by different traditions of song, performance, narrative, and image creation. Questions surrounding the nature of tools and technologies – who has or should have access to them, what uses are appropriate and which ones not, how they might be reappropriated for varied cultural and political projects – have been given a wide spectrum of answers in texts ranging from indigenous cosmologies to speculative fictions. This spectrum is important to grasp in media studies and computational criticism. In all of these contexts, comparatists have the potential to transform emergent humanities fields.

Staking the comparatist claims in the study of new media cultures as well as in emergent interdisciplinary research areas is important for intellectual reasons, but also for institutional ones, because it entails the most realistic and perhaps the most exciting possibilities for growth in our discipline. Universities all over the United States are investing in new majors and programs in fields such as disability studies and food studies, and in the digital, environmental, medical, and urban humanities. The creation of new programs or departments of literature, by contrast, seems unlikely in the foreseeable future, except as a result of departmental mergers and consolidations. Comparative literature will no doubt continue to have an institutional presence and trajectory of its own, as it has over the last sixty years of disciplinary crisis rhetoric (René Wellek published his essay "The Crisis of Comparative Literature" in 1959). But one of its most important tasks in the years ahead will be to ensure a diffusion of comparatist theories and methods to the emergent interdisciplinary areas in the humanities where it has not yet made the kind of impact Saussy outlined in 2004 for other literature departments. Many of the contributions to this report demonstrate comparatists' beginning engagement with these areas. Re-envisioning comparative literature as part of this rapidly changing map of the humanities is comparatists' most immediate and most exciting disciplinary challenge.

Works cited

Apter, Emily. *Against World Literature: On the Politics of Untranslatability*. London: Verso, 2013. Print.

Archer, Jodie, and Matthew L. Jockers. *The Bestseller Code: Anatomy of the Blockbuster Novel*. New York: St. Martin's, 2016. Print.

Bernheimer, Charles, ed. *Comparative Literature in the Age of Multiculturalism*. Baltimore: Johns Hopkins UP, 1995. Print.

Culler, Jonathan. "Comparative Literature, at Last!" *Comparative Literature in the Age of Multiculturalism*. Ed. Charles Bernheimer. Baltimore: Johns Hopkins UP, 1995. 237–248. Print.

Damrosch, David. *What Is World Literature?* Princeton: Princeton UP, 2003. Print.

D'haen, Theo, David Damrosch, and Djelal Kadir, eds. *The Routledge Companion to World Literature*. Abingdon, UK: Routledge, 2012. Print.

D'haen, Theo, César Domínguez, and Mads Rosendahl Thomsen, eds. *World Literature: A Reader*. London: Routledge, 2012. Print.

Fitzpatrick, Kathleen. "The Humanities, Done Digitally." *Chronicle of Higher Education* (8 May 2011). Web. 10 July 2016.

Jockers, Matthew L. *Macroanalysis: Digital Methods and Literary History*. Urbana, IL: U of Illinois P, 2013. Print.

Moretti, Franco. "Conjectures on World Literature." *New Left Review* 1 (2000): 54–69. Print.

Nixon, Rob. *Slow Violence and the Environmentalism of the Poor*. Cambridge, MA: Harvard UP, 2011. Print.

Perloff, Marjorie. " 'Literature' in the Expanded Field." *Comparative Literature in the Age of Multiculturalism*. Ed. Charles Bernheimer. Baltimore: Johns Hopkins UP, 1995. 175–86. Print.

Pratt, Mary Louise. "Comparative Literature and Global Citizenship." *Comparative Literature in the Age of Multiculturalism*. Ed. Charles Bernheimer. Baltimore: Johns Hopkins UP, 1995. 58–65. Print.

Prendergast, Christopher, ed. *Debating World Literature*. London: Verso, 2004. Print.

Saussy, Haun. *Comparative Literature in an Age of Globalization*. Baltimore: Johns Hopkins UP, 2006. Print.

Slaughter, Joseph R. *Human Rights, Inc.: The World Novel, Narrative Form, and International Law*. New York: Fordham UP, 2007. Print.

Thomsen, Mads Rosendahl. *Mapping World Literature: International Canonization and Transnational Literatures*. London: Continuum, 2008. Print.

Wellek, René. "The Crisis of Comparative Literature." *Comparative Literature: Proceedings of the Second Congress of the ICLA*. Ed. W. P. Friederich. 2 vols. Chapel Hill: U of Carolina P, 1959. Vol. 2:149–59. Print.

Wenzel, Jennifer. "Turning Over a New Leaf: Postcolonial Environmental Humanities and the Grounds of Comparison." *ACL(x) Conference*, Penn State University, September 2013. Conference Presentation.

Futures of comparative literature

Institutional inertia and the state of the discipline

Eric Hayot

What's good about institutions is what's good about concepts: by excising from the realm of consciousness the immense diversity of the possible, they allow one to concentrate on a small enough set of mental data to begin the process of acting, or thinking. The negation at the heart of the concept and the institution is the negation of any form: a bracketing that opens up, paradoxically, the possibility of a certain freedom, a possibility whose exemplification in literature includes not only the self-aware jokers of the Oulipo school but also anyone who has ever written a sonnet, a one-act play, a novel.

Or for that matter a piece of literary criticism. For criticism, writing, too, has its forms; it is, also, an institution. Though we do much, together and separately, that is not writing, the profession's most prestigious economies flow through the institutional and formal structures that govern its published prose. The process whereby those structures shape our writing begins before the university, in the reproduction of national rhetorical styles. The tendency of different linguistic and state formations to generate their own rhetorics of academic nonfiction is perhaps something those of us in comparative literature know especially well, since we encounter it in the work of our colleagues and our students. Anyone who has ever had to unteach a graduate student the normative rhetorical formalities of his or her home culture, and thus to inculcate a new embodiment of the particularly American style – different, let us agree, from the styles in other Anglophone spaces, most obviously those in the UK – has immediately understood the way that writing consolidates itself as an institutional form.

The institution has media-specific forms. You cannot, most of the time in comparative literature, have a fifty-page idea. Almost no one will publish a fifty-page idea. You can bring it down to thirty pages or so (*PMLA*'s limit is nine thousand words); or, if you are famous enough, you may bring it up to ninety, and make it into a small book. For everyone else fifty pages makes at best a book chapter – but of course that assumes you are willing to write the other one hundred and fifty pages that it would take to publish the fifty-page idea as a chapter, and that the fifty-page idea would not be changed by that context, becoming, in effect, no longer a fifty-page idea. And so what you write, when you write, is *before the fact* operating within a set of constraints – the constraints of the article format, yes, the constraints provided by the rhetorics and logics of writerly practice, also – but here minimally a set of constraints that say: ideas can be this long, or that long; otherwise it is too long, or not long enough.

Do we really think that ideas come in only a limited number of sizes? Obviously not. And yet . . . it would be perfectly reasonable for someone from the outside to accuse us of so thinking. These are the constraints of the institution, and we reinforce them constantly: in, for instance, our evaluations of journal articles, including the ways we count them for tenure; but also, say, in the normal length of the normal end-of-term graduate seminar paper, which is merely a proxy for its potential future as a journal article. Like all forms, these mediatic restrictions come to us from an outside that is also, like all outsides, an inside. Indeed, the institution always comes to us that way, which is why the institution is so often the site of our feelings of historical helplessness, or worse, complacency; why so often the institution appears the immutable nature or ground of the rhetorics, logics, and patterns of action we, in its indifferent embrace, deploy.

The institution of writing in literary studies is, therefore, what Christian Jacob has called a *lieu de savoir*, a site of knowledge. Not a site in which knowledge is produced, but an aperture, a context, like all apertures and contexts also shaped by the things that pass through it – but which tends to appear to us in a simple, fixed form, as the natural framework for the production and consumption of humanistic knowledge. The only thing I want to ask is: is it too much to spend some of the same attention we spend on literature on the institutional, rhetorical, and logical parameters of our own prose? Is it too much to spend time wondering whether, in fact, knowledge about literature is best produced in nine-thousand-word chunks, or what it means that we have built ourselves an institution that acts, most of the time, like it is? Would it be crazy to wonder what would happen if we treated ourselves with enough respect as writers to imagine that our prose was capable of more, sometimes, than the communication of the results of our research? Do we really think – as we honestly seem to, if you look at the way we behave – that our writing is somehow exempt from the theories of language that we apply so easily to literature? Is it because we think that we're doing "science"? We mostly do not believe *science* is doing "science" . . .

Listen: I am not saying, let's all do collaborative writing online, let's blow up the tenure system, let's have the blog post I write on the new *Dungeons and Dragons* rule set count the same as my article on enjambment in Celan, or whatever. All those ideas are fine, but they miss the point, I think, by being too big, too "revolutionary" to notice that even the most minimal change to the system within which we write might alter the kinds of things it is possible for us to talk about and know. The dramatic is the enemy of the simple. What if, in the context of the work we do now, we could also publish five-page or ten-page articles? What would knowledge look like in that context? What if, likewise, an edited collection did not include only one type of essay – that is, what if what one imagined as the totality of a work could be composed of material in different genres, and not just a string of thirty-page essays? What if a single-authored book were so composed?

Listen: I am not saying, either, down with all institutions, let's make every project a nonce project; let everyone invent her own form; let everyone set down, as though for the first time, the uncreated conscience of his race. I am asking what would happen if we had more than the three or four institutional forms we have now. Like six, or seven.

The critique goes for historical periodization, as I have shown elsewhere (see Hayot); it also goes for graduate education. It is not clear to me that the best way to teach someone how to become a professor – and these remarks are directed mainly at my colleagues in the United States – is to have them take courses in groups that last between ten and fifteen weeks for two to three years. Maybe it is. And I certainly understand that there are some logistical conveniences here. But why is that the best way to do things? Is it the best way to do things? Again, listen: I'm not saying that every student needs a uniquely tailored plan of study, that we have to reinvent the pedagogical wheel anew each time; just that it would be nice merely to have a few different systems at work, or to imagine what it would look like if you said, "Okay, we've got six years to get this person a PhD and make them eligible for employment: what's the best use of his or her time?" Instead of what happens now, which is that more or less every school runs more or less the same pedagogical system. What has determined that inside the nation the pedagogy of the graduate program ought to look more or less everywhere the same? Is that good for students? Is it the product of serious thinking or the perpetuation of habits from another time?

All this amounts not to a critique of institutions, of form as such, then, but merely to a critique of *bad* or *impoverished* institutionalism that does not think much about itself, that does not have much truck with experiments, that complains about institutions in general so as to avoid thinking about them in particular. That such an institutionalism – by which, I should be clear, I mean not the institutions as such but the ways in which we think about and respond to institutions as academics and university professors – is at some level inevitable, the product of having institutions, of having forms at all, is true enough. But it does seem especially ironic that several generations of intellectuals weaned on Foucault have not for all that integrated a kind of self-reflexive practice into their own institutional patterns, into their production and reproduction of epistemologically and pragmatically determining sites of knowledge.

We need to institutionalize institutional innovation.[1] Such a proposal feels contradictory only if you have a bad theory of institutions – if you imagine, that is, the institutional as somehow *hors-texte*, as something that you have no duty toward because it is either (a) too big and too impossible to change, or (b) too dirty or too stupid or too restrictive to be worth changing at all. How can we proceed so that we can be certain that we have figured out the best ways to produce knowledge, either as teachers or as writers? And would that certainty be more or less sure of itself – would it be more or less theorized, more or less the product of a certain close reading, or of a serious philosophical consideration of the concepts involved – if it were subject to the same levels of intensity and thoughtfulness as the forms of culture studied elsewhere in the building?

Some twenty years ago, Tobin Siebers wrote an essay I very much admired. In it he wondered if any of us really knew what we were doing in the classroom, if in fact what we are doing is in any serious way knowable. He said that it was not clear to him whether in fact he would not just be better off reading to his students aloud, that it might be that the latter was just as good as discussing a text (199). Since then I have on occasion simply spent a class period reading aloud to students. I have no idea if it works, but some of them seem to like it more than regular class, which is not, I suppose, nothing.

Siebers's essay appeared in *Comparative Literature in the Age of Multicultural-ism*, the third major report on the state of the discipline commissioned by the ACLA, published as a collection edited by Charles Bernheimer. The structural differences between that report and the two that preceded it can be read as products of an institutional step forward. While the previous two reports, from 1965 and 1975, were issued as single-authored documents signed by a committee, Bernheimer's report (1993) is best known via its inclusion in the edited volume from 1995, which includes not only the committee-generated report but also a number of responses to it. In some respects the "report" that came from Charles Bernheimer and his committee included, then, not only a series of definitive statements about the field but also the responses to it. In this way it became something more like a conversation.

That conversational model held for the report that succeeded Bernheimer's, though again we can observe institutional differences at work. Haun Saussy wrote not a report but a forty-page essay on the history of the field; it was one of twelve essays collected under the book's "Part I: The State of the Discipline, 2004." These twelve were followed by seven more essays, designated "Part II: Responses." Though there is some tendency to refer to Saussy's essay as the "report," the book allows it to occupy that position only formally, by virtue of its scope, its position as the first essay in the edited volume. Like Bernheimer's, the report oriented itself toward the present with a title that imagined comparative literature as the potentially beleaguered occupant of an age that was not exactly its own: *Comparative Literature in an Age of Globalization*.

It was with these things in mind that the ACLA Board came, two years ago, to the consideration of the latest report on the state of the discipline. The decision to do things this way, this time, came out of the Board asking itself some of the questions I have asked here about the nature of institutional form. What after all, is a "report," and what parts of the discipline do we refer to? The 1965, 1975, and 1993 reports treat at length the expected structure of graduate and undergraduate programs – students should know this many languages, should take a survey of literary theory, and so on. But in the responses to the 1993 report, we see a model developing that comes full flower in the 2004 report: pedagogy disappears, the undergraduate program disappears (or is relegated to a single section of the whole). This happened not, I think, because the report is dismissive of teaching but because the only mode in which teaching had been discussed in the earlier reports was via a series of prescriptive recommendations. But the result of this understandable discomfort with prescriptions is that the 2004 report treats the discipline as primarily an act of scholarly research, and imagines the state of the discipline largely as an effect of the intellectual history of the field.

The current report attempts to alter or undermine those patterns. We have done so not by excluding them but by making a place for them amid a wider umbrella of formal structures. I will point out, as only one example of the way things have already changed, that the report you are currently browsing includes for the first time contributions from people located professionally outside the United States. Second, it includes, also for the first time, contributions from – gasp! – assistant professors, and only for the second (and third and fourth times) contributions from associate professors as well (until now the only associate professor who had participated in the report was Rey Chow, who was still an associate in 1994). It does seem to be a fairly clear instantiation of the kind of institutionalism I have been criticizing so far that the previous two reports, both written in the throes of any number of claims about the need for comparative literature to reach out to its others, to expand its global reach, to help resolve problems of classism and injustice, did not manage to include anyone who was not already at or near the peak of the profession. As though the *state of the discipline* were somehow visible only from, or only taking place in, the ethereal reaches of its institutional mountaintops.

This is not class warfare. This is epistemological warfare: I am talking about how institutions make truth possible. How is it possible to say true things about the state of something if one talks only about, or includes only the perspectives of, its smallest, most powerful part? It is not. That is all I am saying. It is not a question of affirmative action for the benighted and the impoverished, but of actually trying to understand what this discipline is in all of its forms of practice – *all* of them.

We know this when it comes to literature – in fact it is perhaps the most basic thing we come to understand through the serious practice of literature, or the reading of theory. And yet we do not know it when it comes to our institutional practice, neither in the reports nor in the modes of writing that we teach and enforce. Neither in the graduate programs nor in the periodizing structures of the undergraduate curriculum, nor in the structure of the job market.

Note

1 Echoes here of "Crisis-obsessed humanists characteristically fail to appreciate the extent to which institutionalization and experimentation are interlinked" (Cooper and Marx 131). The relationship between the kind of institutionalism I am describing and the more general announcements of a crisis in the humanities is too large to be taken on here. Reading Cooper and Marx has given me some sense of its likely parameters.

Works cited

Cooper, Mark Garrett and John Marx. "Crisis, Crisis, Crisis: Big Media and the Humanities Workforce." *Différences* 24.5 (2014): 127–59. Print.

Hayot, Eric. "Against Periodization; or, On Institutional Time." *New Literary History* 42 (2011): 739–56. Print.

Jacob, Christian. *Lieux de savoir.* Paris: Albin Michel, 2007. Print.

Siebers, Tobin. "Sincerely Yours." *Comparative Literature in the Age of Multiculturalism.* Ed. Charles Bernheimer. Baltimore: Johns Hopkins UP, 1995. 195–203. Print.

Performative scholarship

Avram Alpert

Contemporary scholarship has a content problem. I do not mean that there is anything wrong with the actual contents of academic criticism. Rather, I mean that the academy focuses too narrowly on innovations in content. We assume that advances in modern scholarship will arrive as content-ideas and not as form-ideas. This state of affairs is endemic to an academic situation that privileges publication over pedagogy, knowledge of smaller periods over broad-based investigation, and that allows an economy of information to dictate an increasingly unjust labor market.

We should rethink academic labor as constituted by innovations in form, remapping scholarship as per*form*ance. If we value scholarship as the creation of aesthetic experiences of information, as much as the creation of argumentative turns, it becomes easier to see why constructing an expertly conducted, interactive, digitally enhanced lecture course should count as much for *scholarship* as a new argument about the literature of any given period. Furthermore, such an attention to form increases theoretical pressure on the research-driven, two-tiered academic world that benefits an increasingly small percentage of faculty.[1]

What might such scholarship look like? Consider, as an example, the academic cabaret organized by the academic-artist hybrid group Our Literal Speed at Princeton in 2012, which included "super-live performances" and a "theory installation" entitled "On the Aesthetic Education of Man, 2011." At one point in the evening, art historian Claire Bishop was slated to give a talk, "Delegated Performance: Outsourcing Authenticity." Bishop walked up to the podium, put down her lecture notes, and returned to her seat. A hired performer dressed in a burlesque costume took Bishop's place and began to *perform* the lecture. As Mashinka Firunts wrote in her review of the event,

> The performer gingerly sips a glass of white wine. She transitions to drinking straight from the bottle and swaggers into the audience. She announces, "We must therefore ask, what is the relationship of outsourced performance to the market?" She removes her pumps and absentmindedly spreads her legs. She assaults a politely obliging Princeton professor with her décolletage. She requests assistance pronouncing "fetishistic."[2]

When, following the outsourced lecture, artist Theaster Gates pounded rhythmi-cally on the lectern and chanted, "I want the value of my labor, artistic labor," the audience saw that this was not mere self-reflexivity but part of a battle cry for a new aesthetic education: one in which the content and the form of our intellectual labor in fact work toward the social conditions that would give it meaning. Such a collective, organized performance may be beyond what most of us can reasonably accomplish, but even simple gestures of formal innovation can advance our scholarship. For example, Margaret Price, a scholar of disability stud-ies, passes out notecards for people to write questions and comments on during her lecture, so as to interrupt the presumed orality of academic interaction, which excludes any number of physical and mental dispositions.

Such activities require time and collaboration; they also require being brave enough to risk looking foolish. But the form-content of aesthetic experience is always a part of the work we do, and it is time to engage it more broadly and more conscientiously. Performative scholarship calls upon us to think beyond the restriction of our scholarship to pure content, and invites us to make the presen-tational and formal varieties of teaching, political organizing, database-making, and creative writing, among others, equal aspects of our scholarly careers.

Notes

1 This is not at all to suggest that full-time faculty are responsible for the corpora-tization of university life, but it is to insist that in such a context we need to find more robust vocabularies to defend the value of non–tenure track faculty.
2 My interest in performative scholarship has grown through my collaborations with Firunts and Danny Snelson (cf. "Research Service"). I owe my claims here to many conversations with them over the past few years.

Works cited

Firunts, Mashinka. "Our Literal Speed: Doing Things with Words in the Vicinity of Art." *Culturebot.* 30 Apr. 2012. http://www.culturebot.org/2012/04/13318/our-literal-speed-princeton/
Our Literal Speed. "Our Literal Speed." Lecture-Performance. Princeton. 2012. http://www.ourliteralspeed.com/19april2012princeton.html
Research Service. "About." *Research Service.* Web. 15 February 2014. http://researchservice.info

The reign of the amoeba
Further thoughts about the future of comparative literature

Gail Finney

No one has a crystal ball. If a single stockbroker were to get his hands on one, he could make billions. But if we are to look ahead and attempt to predict what the discipline of comparative literature might look like around the year 2025, we do well to assess what has happened during the past ten years and to examine recent trends. In a paper presented at the ACLA Convention in 2005, I suggested that the ways in which comparative literature is taught in the United States can be described in terms of four dominant structures or models: the wheel, the tandem, the umbrella, and the grab bag.

Probably the most common of these is the wheel structure, in which comparative literature constitutes the hub and national literary traditions the spokes. In this model, a student receiving a degree in comparative literature at the graduate or undergraduate level draws on courses from the spokes, possibly specializing in one or two of them, and takes courses in theory and comparative literature from the hub. This has served and still serves to some extent as the model for numerous comparative literature programs, such as those at Harvard University, UC Berkeley, Stanford University, Indiana University, and UC Davis. In the tandem structure, comparative literature is paired with another national literary tradition, most often English, resulting in a Department of English and Comparative Literature, in which the two programs supposedly exist on more or less equal footing with varying degrees of integration between them. If we conceive of this metaphor as a bicycle built for two, however, comparative literature often takes a back seat to English. Examples of this structure are found at Columbia University, the University of North Carolina at Chapel Hill, and San Diego State University. The umbrella or blanket model is often employed at schools that do not offer the PhD in smaller national literary traditions, such as German, Russian, or even French, but instead offer the doctorate in comparative literature with an emphasis in German, Russian, or French.

The first three models are predominantly literary, regardless of which program – English or non-English – is administratively combined with comparative literature. The fourth model for comparative literature programs, which I have rather colloquially termed the grab bag, is interdisciplinary, exemplified by the practice of combining comparative literature with film studies, as in the case of the Department of Cinema and Comparative Literature at the University of Iowa.

This last model underlines the fact that much comparative work of the past decade is characterized by the destruction of walls or boundaries: boundaries between periods, between national traditions, between media, and between disciplines. One finds productive exchanges not only between comparative literature and film but also between comparative literature and art history, cultural studies, philosophy, television, and of course an array of national literary traditions, to mention only a few of the relevant fields. This eclectic process of drawing on other disciplines and traditions, so nourishing to comparative literature, is likely to continue and grow – hence the metaphor of my title. Just as an amoeba feeds itself by assimilating other tiny organisms, skillfully enveloping them with its single-celled, permeable body, practitioners of comparative literature take in other fields of knowledge that nurture and enrich their literary studies. It is my prediction that comparative literature will keep moving in this direction and will therefore continue to change. Like the amoeba, whose etymology – from the Greek *amoibè*, "change" – reflects its protean nature, the discipline of comparative literature will persist in evolving, eschewing stasis.

Because comparative literature is likely to continue the practice of interdisciplinary nurture, I maintain that by 2025 a more apt term for the discipline may well be comparative literature studies. This designation evokes an association with cultural studies, a field to which comparative literature is increasingly indebted. This linkage has also made its way into departmental administration, as in the case of the Department of Cultural Studies and Comparative Literature at the University of Minnesota. Some comparatists, perhaps frustrated with the highly historical or literary emphasis of comparative literature (such as in the first three program structures I outlined), have moved into the field of cultural studies. Just as cultural studies, with its interest in social transformation and cultural change, has focused on popular and contemporary culture, the assimilation of comparative literature into cultural studies can lead to an opening up, in terms of both genre and level of discourse, of the material studied. Products of visual culture, theater, and film – which are also frequent objects of investigation by literary scholars – could be very useful in strengthening the relationship between comparative literature and cultural studies.

The extent to which the two disciplines are intermeshed is perhaps epitomized in the online journal *CLCWeb: Comparative Literature and Culture*, edited since its inception in 1999 through 2016 by Steven Tötösy de Zepetnek and described on its masthead as a "peer-reviewed, full-text, and open-access quarterly in the humanities and social sciences [which] publishes new scholarship following tenets of the discipline of comparative literature and the field of cultural studies designated as 'comparative cultural studies'" (*CLC Web*). The March 2014 issue is characteristic of the wide range of national literary traditions and authors represented in the journal, including articles on African, Irish, Turkish, French, Hungarian, American, Korean, Chinese, Russian, Persian, Italian, Romanian, and German-language writers.

Taken alone, this list would announce a fairly traditional, if impressively international, journal of comparative literature. But the journal goes on to issue a number of calls for conference papers or contributions to collections that point to its interdisciplinary orientation, including announcements of conferences on literature, culture, and the arts and on the aesthetics of emotional restraint, as well as calls for papers on technology and literature/culture, science and literature/culture, the other arts and literature/culture, and new developments in ecocriticism. These conferences and collections signal the wide-ranging disciplinary possibilities available to comparative literature scholars. In sum: comparative literature and the arts, comparative literature and aesthetics, comparative literature and technology, comparative literature and science, comparative literature and ecology – these interdisciplinary fields of interest, all growing, can be seen as predictors of what lies ahead for the discipline, indicating the degree to which – to return to my title metaphor – the amoeba of comparative literature is nourished by the manifold other fields assimilated into its permeable body.

The interdisciplinary direction in which comparative literature continues to move is likewise evident in volume 66.1 of *Comparative Literature*, the flagship journal of the discipline, which features several essays from an ACLA forum devoted to the topic of remediation. Defined as the process of remedying or correcting something bad or defective, the term was coined in its media-theoretical sense by Jay David Bolter and Richard Grusin in their study *Remediation: Understanding New Media*. Comparatists traditionally use remediation to refer to "literature's incorporation of and incorporation into other media and modes" (McClennen 1). In the essays in the special issue of *Comparative Literature*, the concept of remediation is broadened and explored in a variety of its nuances. The contributors engage nonliterary fields – media studies, ecocriticism, the law, disability studies, and education – in order to rethink the concept of remediation in comparative literature. Especially because this interdisciplinary work is showcased in the exemplary journal of the discipline, these essays can be seen to forecast what lies ahead.

In light of the proliferation of interdisciplinarity in the field at large, a workable and productive comparative literature graduate program of the future promises to be a hybrid program, combining seminars on primarily literary topics with the study of literary theory and another discipline. Such interdisciplinary study is available in the graduate curriculum at UC Davis in the form of designated emphases, which are tantamount to graduate minors in that students typically take four seminars in each area. Designated emphases in which comparative literature graduate students have participated include critical theory, feminist theory and research, second language acquisition, social theory and comparative history, studies in performance and practice, and classics and classical receptions. In addition, graduate student instructors should be trained in pedagogy, whether in the teaching of a foreign language or in the instruction of writing and composition. A tall order – but comparative literature students tend to be prepared for the challenge.

Foreign language study remains paramount for graduate studies in comparative literature. As I reported in an article in *symplokē* in 2008, when I polled the twenty-four students enrolled in the comparative literature graduate program at

UC Davis in 2006 about their wishes concerning the future direction of the field, all of them emphasized the importance of studying foreign languages, and all felt that the study of literary texts in the original, from more than one national tradition, belonged at the center of the discipline. Yet students also noted the practical difficulty of learning several languages within a reasonable length of time, and I mentioned the phenomenon whereby a comparative literature student who learns a language as a non-native speaker is sometimes regarded with skepticism by students and faculty in the department representing that language. In this connection, I would endorse the suggestion made by one student in our program that graduate students receive credit for study abroad.

The issue of foreign language study is complicated by what I termed in the *symploke* article the "paradox of globalization" (Finney 222): the increasing ease and scope of international travel reveal the degree to which English has become dominant around the world, yet the growing prominence of the Middle East and South Asia as crisis zones, along with the looming power of the Internet, has heightened awareness and popularity of "critical" languages. The addition of Arabic and Hindi or Urdu to the foreign language curriculum at UC Davis in 2006 mirrors similar developments around the country. The rising importance of non-European languages has led and will continue to lead to changing attitudes toward the role of translation. In the 1993 *ACLA Report on Professional Standards*, published two years later as part of *Comparative Literature in the Age of Multiculturalism*, Charles Bernheimer could scarcely have realized the prescience of his recommendation that in the era of multiculturalism, comparatists should re-evaluate their definition as scholars and their standards for comparative work. "It may be better, for instance, to teach a work in translation, even if you don't have access to the original language, than to neglect marginal voices because of their mediated transmission," he points out (44). This expanding receptiveness to minority literature in English translation inclines comparative literature in the direction of world literature as this concept has come to be defined in the United States in recent years by David Damrosch and others – most simply, as the reception and circulation of texts from around the globe in English translation. Yet the study of literature in the original whenever possible is likely to remain a hallmark of comparative literature.[1]

Since our subject is the future of comparative literature, I would like to introduce a translation model devised by an inhabitant of that future, Jordan A. Yamaji Smith, a junior scholar whose research focuses on the relationship between translation and world literature. His concept of "translationscapes" demonstrates the extent to which literary translation is culturally, historically, and politically inflected and hence subjective or perspectival. As Smith explains, this concept is indebted to Arjun Appadurai's notion of "global cultural flows" and ethnoscapes, mediascapes, technoscapes, financescapes, and ideoscapes as formulated in his *Modernity at Large* to convey the "historical, linguistic, and political situatedness of different sorts of actors: nation-states, multinationals, diasporic communities, as well as subnational groupings and movements" (Appadurai 33). Smith writes that "translationscapes can be thought of as global flows of language-based culture via translation, something that forms a selective, metonymic, partial picture of a 'national culture' for the target language community" (1). Smith cites as examples of comparative translationscapes those

> of obscured literary histories through Octavio Paz, of ideological barriers to translation of "invisible" texts from Oe Kenzaburo, of Upton Sinclair across iron curtains, of Shel Silverstein in global children's literature, and of "translation-resistant" poetry by authors such as Yoshimasu Gozo.
>
> (1–2)

Demonstrating the ways in which texts are filtered through manifold cultural influences in the process of translation, Jordan Smith's concept of translationscapes exemplifies the practice of interdisciplinary nurture that increasingly characterizes comparative literature. Metaphorically speaking, there is no end in sight to the reign of the amoeba.

Note

1 For a critical examination of the disservice often done to language by translation, see Apter.

Works cited

Appadurai, Arjun. *Modernity at Large: Cultural Dimensions of Globalization*. Minneapolis: U of Minnesota P, 1996. Print.

Apter, Emily. *Against World Literature: On the Politics of Untranslatability*. London: Verso, 2013. Print.

Bernheimer, Charles. "The Bernheimer Report, 1993: Comparative Literature at the Turn of the Century." *Comparative Literature in the Age of Multiculturalism*. Ed. Charles Bernheimer. Baltimore: Johns Hopkins UP, 1995. 39–48. Print.

Bolter, Jay David, and Richard Grusin. *Remediation: Understanding New Media*. Cambridge, MA: MIT Press, 1999. Print.

CLCWeb: Comparative Literature and Culture. Ed. Steven Tötösy de Zepetnek. Web. 25 Nov. 2015.

Finney, Gail. "Elitism or Eclecticism? Some Thoughts about the Future of Comparative Literature." *Symploke* 16 (2008): 215–25. Print.

McClennen, Sophia A. "Introduction to Remediation: An ACLA Forum." *Comparative Literature* 66 (2014): 1–4. Web. 27 Dec. 2015.

Smith, Jordan A. Yamaji. "Excerpts from working draft of *Translationscapes: Language, Ideology, World Literature*." Typescript, two pages.

Comparative literature
The next ten years

Haun Saussy

We can confidently predict that ten years from now, comparative literature will be in a state of crisis. It is always in crisis. In 2004 I ventured that nothing has ever defined comparative literature so well as the search for its own definition, a search conducted between and against better-established fields (Saussy). *That* continued sense of crisis, however, is one we make for ourselves. External conditions impose another shape on comparative literature's sense of crisis.

In my 2004 essay I also claimed that because of its lacking a definite subject matter or methodology, comparative literature was doomed to improvise and to proceed fitfully, occasion by occasion (Saussy). That concession, however, was meant to flip over into a compensating strength. If comparative literature lacked the solid boundaries of other academic specializations, it could avoid being walled in by them too, and so could welcome unlikely topics, disciplinary collisions, things without a name, art forms without a nation. It could take on such present-day dynamics transcending national and linguistic boundaries as growing inequality, the prevalence of information, and the transformation of institutions under market pressures. It could range into the past to recover the means of production and circulation of knowledge in societies differently organized from our own, while being protected from the provincialism and triumphalism that sometimes affect scholars who possess only one language or culture. And it could do these things more readily than disciplines that had been built up to serve a particular nation, language, art form, or period.

These are hopes based on a theory of what the field should be doing, or at least a theory of what the field is not hindered from doing by any internal logical obstacle. From its nineteenth-century inception, comparative literature has imagined itself as the locus from which it would be possible to describe and relate the literary productions of all times, peoples, and languages.

> The modern spirit, that is, rationalism, criticism, liberalism, was founded the same day philology was founded. *The founders of the modern spirit are the philologists* . . . The task of modern scholarship will only be accomplished then when all the facets of humanity, that is, all the nations, have been explored definitely . . . Then and then only, the reign of criticism will be inaugurated. For criticism will only proceed with perfect surety when the field of universal

comparison shall be thrown open to it. Comparison is the great instrument of criticism.

(Renan 133, 277; original emphasis)

One of our contemporaries who wears without shame the label of "philologist" and has contributed greatly to enlarging "the field of universal comparison" available to comparatists is the Sanskritist and literary historian Sheldon Pollock ("Future Philology"). When I invited him to give the plenary speech at the 2010 ACLA meeting in New Orleans, I expected to hear an account of poetics and literary history from the Indic world, perhaps a short version of the argument of Pollock's *The Language of the Gods in the World of Men* (2009). Instead he gave us a scolding. Although we claim to be limited only by the dialectical conditions of possibility and to welcome works from every imaginable language, time, and tradition, Pollock showed, numbers in hand, that the great majority of doctoral dissertations written in the field and a similar share of the articles in our main journals deal with English, French, and German literature between 1800 and 1960. It was with a sheepish look that I went on to the next part of the program, the announcement of the annual prizes, which – although they recognized excellent work – only confirmed the modernist and European center of gravity of the ACLA.

There is nothing wrong with writing about canonical authors in easily accessed languages, as long as you do it well and inventively, but the writers who are the subjects of such research have so much in common with each other and with us that they can yield only a little of the strangeness, of the unexpected, that ambitious comparative projects seek out. The choice to write yet again about Proust and Joyce and Woolf and Kafka, about Freud and Benjamin, signals respect for the layers of meaning yet to be discovered in these authors, but it also suggests that these are the right authors to be investigating and that others do not repay close scrutiny – an attitude that proves convenient when, in order to test those assumptions, it turns out that one would have to learn not only difficult languages but also the rules of a different social order, the conventions and allusions of a different literary tradition, and much else besides.

Pollock's challenge instantiates one of the recurrent crises in comparative literature, the rebuke to our provinciality. The obvious answer – that we need to recruit and reward scholars who are ready to range far afield and dislodge our inveterate modern European–centered scale of value – sends us to the other type of crisis, where external pressures shape our ends. For many years now, but in North American institutions most acutely since 2008, teaching and research in the humanities have been performed in the face of shrinking budgets, declining student numbers, and diminishing faculty positions. All language and literature departments today are on short rations, a situation not conducive to bold experimentation. Like a freezing mountaineer, institutions reduce the supply of blood to the extremities (or what they perceive as such) in order to keep the core warm. The consequences are not hard to anticipate. If teaching positions go to reward conventional work on canonical subjects, students will be discouraged from doing work that mixes genres, periods, and languages, or invokes complex theoretical frames. Comparative literature, one function of which has always been to disturb the reigning order of priorities, will then increasingly align itself with the disciplines that have the greatest investment in the current local cultural canon.

The emphases of the moment in comparative literature seem to me to bend to the same pressures. Approaches to comparative literature that offer a historical narrative of the diffusion of cultural capital (e.g., the novel) from Europe to the less fortunate areas of the world find a hearty welcome, because such globalization stories, although eminently questionable on historical grounds, comfort the biases of our institutions and our public. Globalization stories as the new form of modernization narratives end up being about us. World literature, taught predominantly in translation, adapts to the new order by lightening up the language requirements and the corresponding cultural information. Present-ism allows us to minimize the fact that the greatest variety of recorded human experience relates to the past. "History is bunk," said Henry Ford, and "There is no alternative [to neoliberal policies]," said Margaret Thatcher (*New York Times*; McPherson). They had definite motives for wanting to limit reflection on the possible shapes a state, a culture, an economy, could take. But it is our job as scholars to guard against the attitude attributed to a nineteenth-century Oxford don: "I am the master of this college,/And what I don't know isn't knowledge" (rhyme cited in Foster, 765).

The ambition to write literary histories of regions outside Europe, showing their internal organization and development – which are often instructively different from what is seen in the European example – is one way of resisting the triumphalist urge. I see Pollock, in *The Language of the Gods in the World of Men*, as taking a subversive pleasure in using the Sanskrit model to "provincial-ize" and question the standard-setting function of Roman precedents, all the more in that a reconstituted "Romania" was the not so obscure object of our comparatist ancestor Ernst Robert Curtius's philological desire (Curtius; see also Chakrabarty). Other literary networks distinct from the Greco-Roman axis and the modern chain of transmission become legible, for example, through the recent *Cambridge Histories* of Chinese and Arabic literature, Ronit Ricci's *Islam Translated*, and the vast archive of folklore research, usually ignored by literary comparatists (Chang and Owen; Beeston et al.; Ricci; Reichl). Specialists have of course for generations written literary histories of their own or other nations, but the comparative perspective frames these histories differently, not foregrounding progress or identity but testing the causality and the cross-cultural plausibility of the links they assert.

Literary histories are, however, histories, and call on the theoretical connectors common to all historical writing: cause and effect, influence, documented relationships, chronology, geography. That which makes a history comparative may be, for the historically minded, what makes it less of a history. Everyone remembers Borges's Tlön, where

> [t]he concept of plagiarism does not exist: it has been established that all works are the creation of one author, who is atemporal and anonymous. The

critics often invent authors: they select two dissimilar works – the *Tao Te Ching* and the *Thousand and One Nights*, say – attribute them to the same writer and then determine most scrupulously the psychology of this interesting *homme de lettres*.

(Borges 13)

Fashioning connections across places and times requires some kind of theory – at the very least, a sensibility. But we often hear that scholarship has entered a post-theoretical age. If this is the temper of the times, it wonderfully corresponds to the imperative of efficiency, for the point of theoretical investigation is to look beyond the immediate task and raise questions of principle, implication, or relation.

An analogy, most instructive where the parts fail to correspond, may help to show where theory belongs in the articulation of comparative literature. There have always been people studious of their own language: grammarians, philologists, lexicographers. In the field of linguistics today there may be researchers whose interest lies exclusively in one particular language, but to describe the features of that language they must resort to terminology and models from the toolkit of general linguistics. (Naturally, data from specific languages can and always will be used to challenge the applicability of received general theories.) The fairly ready recognition given to general linguistics as a central conceptual clearinghouse and domain of theorizing results, for linguistics, in a social organization in which all linguists have something in common: the body of concepts and practices that shape linguistics as a field. Beyond that, most have a more concrete interest in some particular language or language family that they share with a smaller group of fellow specialists. The construction of the commons (e.g., transcription systems, nomenclature for grammatical features, and methods of geographical surveying) can be seen in the making if one will only open the volumes of proceedings from the early international linguistics conferences (see, e.g., Congrès).

Despite the wide circulation of a number of technical terms, available to any comparatist wishing to describe an unfamiliar work, the domain of comparative literature is not organized in the same way as that of linguistics. Two linguists discussing a language known to only one of them will chiefly be discussing that language as a system (roughly: a grammar), not as a corpus and not as a history, whereas two comparatists discussing a work in a tradition with which only one of them is familiar must talk about the work, about the literary system that produced it, and about the literary and cultural history surrounding it. Moreover, the theoretical language that, among linguists, makes possible agreement and disagreement about the data is, for us, a realm of unsettled debate and incompatible assumptions. It can be said that, just as every language is an object for general linguistics, so too every literary work is an object for comparative literature (under the aspect that in French is called "littérature générale"). Yet working out how unfamiliar works are to be interpreted and valued, with what they are to be compared and along what lines, demands the comparatist's greatest effort and is inherently controversial.

In such projects, the ongoing "crisis" finds a home. Comparatists should support the members of the profession who are taking the greatest intellectual risks, those who fit together unaccustomed bodies of work in ways not predicted by our ready-to-hand theoretical vocabularies, because it is these and not the ones doing "safe" comparisons who will advance inquiry. When adventurous projects and adventurous young people find little support, the discipline is impoverished and loses its way.

The crisis we make for ourselves – both by venturing into factual realms where we are not at home and by raising theoretical questions we cannot expect to see solved by consensus – is our greatest resource; the crisis outside of us is a matter of resources denied. Comparatists will have to stand up for themselves in the next ten years, first by championing the so-called national language departments without which comparative literature will not survive except as a label for general-education literature-in-translation courses; second by reminding the culture around us of the value in being able to synthesize complex and discrepant information that was never designed to be drawn together; and third by demonstrating new ways of making sense exactly where existing canons and methods fail us. That is how we can keep comparative literature's specific difference open in an increasingly consolidated and shrinking humanities domain.

Works cited

Beeston, A.F.L., T.M. Johnstone, J.D. Latham, R.B. Serjeant, and G.R. Smith, eds. *The Cambridge History of Arabic Literature*. 6 vols. Cambridge: Cambridge UP, 1983–2006. Print.

Borges, Jorge Luis. "Tlön, Uqbar, Orbis Tertius." *Labyrinths: Selected Stories and Other Writings*. Trans. James E. Irby. New York: New Directions, 1964. 3–18. Print.

Chakrabarty, Dipesh. *Provincializing Europe: Postcolonial Thought and Historical Difference*. Princeton: Princeton UP, 2000. Print.

Chang, Kang-i Sun, and Stephen Owen, eds. *The Cambridge History of Chinese Literature*. 2 vols. Cambridge: Cambridge UP, 2010. Print.

Congrès international de linguistes. *Actes du premier congrès international de linguistes à la Haye, du 10–15 avril, 1928*. Leiden: Sijthoff, 1928. Print.

Curtius, Ernst Robert. *Latin Literature and the European Middle Ages*. Trans. Willard Trask. Princeton: Princeton UP, 1953. Print.

Foster, Joseph, ed. *Alumni Oxonienses: The Members of the University of Oxford, 1715–1886*. 4 vols. London: Foster, 1888. Print.

McPherson, Fiona. "The Iron Lady: Margaret Thatcher's Linguistic Legacy." *Oxford-Words Blog*, 10 April 2013. http://blog.oxforddictionaries.com/2013/04/margaretthatcher/

New York Times. "History Is Bunk, Says Henry Ford." 28 October 1921. Print.

Pollock, Sheldon. "Future Philology: The Fate of a Soft Science in a Hard World." *Critical Inquiry* 35 (2009): 931–61. Print.

———. *The Language of the Gods in the World of Men: Sanskrit, Culture and Power in Premodern India*. Berkeley: U of California P, 2009. Print.

Reichl, Karl. *Singing the Past: Turkic and Medieval Heroic Poetry*. Ithaca: Cornell UP, 2000.

Renan, Ernest. *The Future of Science: Ideas of 1848*. Trans. Albert D. Vandam and C. B. Pitman. London: Chapman and Hall, 1891. Print.

Ricci, Ronit. *Islam Translated: Literature, Conversion, and the Arabic Cosmopolis of South and Southeast Asia*. Chicago: U of Chicago P, 2011. Print.

Saussy, Haun. "Exquisite Corpses from Fresh Nightmares: Of Memes, Hives and Selfish Genes." *Comparative Literature in an Age of Globalization*. Ed. Haun Saussy. Baltimore: Johns Hopkins UP, 2006. 12–54. Print.

Theories, histories, methods

Periodization

Adam Miyashiro

Over the past decade, challenges to traditional periodizations have flourished as a self-reflexive form of critique in medieval and early modern studies, as critics trace the foundations of our fields alongside the growth of European nationalisms and empires. These studies have had broad implications for other literary fields, including postcolonial theory and transnational studies. "Periodization" is "a template for dividing up not only time but also place," as David Wallace and Jennifer Summit suggest (447). A period label such as "the Middle Ages" or the adjective "medieval" conjures up images and ideas that are perceived as antithetical to the definition of modernity and can also be attributed to non-European cultures. Modern deployments of the terms "medieval" or "feudal" as rhetorical tools to signify the "backwardness" of Eastern and Southern cultures recycle the most basic elements of Orientalist and colonialist representations of Muslims going back to the twelfth century and expose the Western eagerness to impose European origins onto colonial subjects and geographies. Kathleen Davis, in particular, has argued that categories which postcolonial theorists have usually taken for granted, such as feudalism and secularism, should be understood as bound up with concepts of sovereignty and political shifts between the seventeenth and nineteenth centuries toward a "secular" and modern English state. In this historical imaginary, according to Davis, "Europe's 'medieval' past and cultural others – mainly colonized non-Christians – were defined as religious, static, and ahistorical – thus open for narrative and territorial development" (77).

The projection of Europe's medieval past onto its colonial modernity also underlies the idea that Islam historically bookends the beginning and end of medieval Europe. The Belgian historian Henri Pirenne (1862–1935) argued in his thesis that with the appearance of Islam in the seventh century, the Western Mediterranean was "closed off" from the wider Mediterranean world, forcing Europe to withdraw into itself and thereby creating a hermetically sealed-off space in order to generate a sense of a distinctly European and Christian identity. He suggests in his final book, *Mohammad and Charlemagne*, that

> Islam had shattered the Mediterranean unity which the Germanic invasions left intact . . . It was the end of the classic tradition. It was the beginning of

the Middle Ages, and it happened at the very moment when Europe was on the way to becoming Byzantinized.

(164)

For Pirenne, the western Mediterranean was a "Musulman lake" (162). He quotes, via secondhand reading, the fourteenth-century historian Ibn Khaldun as saying that "the Christians could no longer float a plank upon the sea" (166). At the end of the medieval period, the fifteenth-century conquests of Constantinople by Ottoman Turks and of Granada by Catholic Spain become two markers in the early modern period that redraw Europe's periodized geography: in this modernity, Iberia becomes wholly "European" and Byzantium ceases to be Europe and reverts to "Asia."

Postcolonial medievalist criticism of periodization highlights Western assumptions about secular modernity that structure discourses about contemporary globalization and transnationalism. An emergent field, for example, of "global medieval studies" attempts to challenge dominant Western narratives of modernity by rereading the premodern age against Eurocentrism. When they globalize the "medieval," though, medievalists should beware not to repeat the colonial narratives that defined European empires in the Americas, the Middle East, and Central and South Asia. In understanding both the medievalisms of the world outside Europe and the margins of medieval Europe itself in places like al-Andalus, Sicily, the Maghreb, Russia, and the early Ottoman Empire, we may come closer to understanding how our current geopolitical imaginaries shape our ideas about premodern temporalities (Davis and Altschul; Mallette).

Works cited

Davis, Kathleen. *Periodization and Sovereignty: How Ideas of Feudalism and Secularization Govern the Politics of Time*. Philadelphia: U of Pennsylvania P, 2008. Print.
Davis, Kathleen, and Nadia Altschul, eds. *Medievalisms in the Postcolonial World: The Idea of "The Middle Ages" Outside Europe*. Baltimore: Johns Hopkins UP, 2009. Print.
Mallette, Karla. *European Modernity and the Arab Mediterranean: Toward a New Philology and a Counter-Orientalism*. Philadelphia: U of Pennsylvania P, 2010. Print.
Pirenne, Henri. *Mohammed and Charlemagne*. Trans. Bernard Miall. Mineola, NY: Dover, 2001. Print.
Summit, Jennifer, and David Wallace. "Rethinking Periodization." *Journal of Medieval and Early Modern Studies* 3 (2007): 447–51. Print.

Comparative literary history
A conversation with Marcel Cornis-Pope and Margaret R. Higonnet

César Domínguez

Comparative literature as comparative literary history

DOMÍNGUEZ: In contrast to mainstream narratives of comparative literature, which stress the emergence of transnational literary comparisons as a disciplinary field in its own right, the earliest manifestos and programs show that comparative literature was first conceptualized as a subdiscipline of literary history. During the 1830s, when lectures focused on such transnational literary comparisons attracted wide (male) audiences and this kind of study started the transition from para-academic milieus to the university, Jean-Jacques Ampère – a disciple of August Wilhelm Schlegel – argued in "De l'histoire de la poésie" that literary science comprises two branches, *philosophie de la littérature* and *histoire de la littérature*. Both are closely interlinked to the point that without the latter, understood as "histoire comparative des arts et de la littérature chez tous les peuples" (3), it's impossible to formulate any theory at all. Ampère's program resulted in a myriad of *histoires comparées*, from Abel-François Villemain's 1830 *Tableau de la littérature au Moyen Âge en France, en Italie, en Espagne et en Angleterre* to Ampère's own 1841 unfinished project of a *Histoire de la littérature française au Moyen Âge comparée aux littératures étrangères* and Louis-Adolphe de Puybusque's 1843 *Histoire comparée des littératures espagnole et française*, to name but a few.

Once comparative literature became a discipline of wider horizons and comparative literary history was one of its subfields, interest in the latter lay dormant for more than a century until 1964, when, during the Fourth Conference of the International Comparative Literature Association (ICLA), Jacques Voisine advocated that a *histoire comparée* of literatures in European languages be carried out by international teams. An ad hoc committee (Coordinating Committee for the Comparative History of Literatures in European Languages, CHLEL) was created three years later during the Fifth ICLA Conference in Belgrade. And in 1973, the first volume – *Expressionism as an International Literary Phenomenon* – was published under the leadership of Ulrich Weisstein. Today, the CHLEL's project comprises around thirty volumes, from the Renaissance to postmodernism, and more are in process on topics such as medieval literatures in Latin, literatures in the Scandinavian region, transatlantic literatures, migration literatures, and literature and slavery.

How do you see the project's main tenets fifty years later? What to you have been crucial developments of this project as a whole?

CORNIS-POPE: In the aftermath of the political changes of 1989, most of us working in the field of literary and cultural studies have become mindful of the need to provide new ways to conceptualize and relate cultures – comparing, translating, and interfacing traditionally separate entities. Focusing on "cultural contacts" continues to be important today as a corrective to both narrow ethnocentric treatments of culture and the countertheories of globalism that erase distinctions between individual cultures.

Recent comparative literary history has been illustrated by comprehensive multicultural works like the *New Literary History of America*, edited by Greil Marcus and Werner Sollors (2009), and the four-volume *History of the Literary Cultures of East-Central Europe*, edited by myself and John Neubauer (2004–2010; hereafter shortened to *East-Central Europe*). In addition to offering transnational studies of literary regions that stretch across continents, both works have challenged traditional literary histories based on national and even text-oriented premises, focusing also on other media, such as theater, opera, and occasionally visual art. Moving beyond the boundaries of national literatures, historical trends, and generic divisions, these histories seek those "junctures" that bring together various traditions, allowing for a cross-cultural interpretation. For example, *East-Central Europe* is organized around five kinds of "nodes" – temporal, generic, topographic, institutional, and figural – at which various literatures, genres, and historical moments come together, transcending national definitions.

A more recent project, *New Literary Hybrids in the Age of Multimedia Expression: Crossing Borders, Crossing Genres* (2014), is informed by a similar desire to cross not only geo-cultural boundaries but also genres and in this case even media. A major emphasis in this volume is on literary production in multimedia environments and on genres that break down boundaries between the arts, allowing the interpenetration of various discourses.

HIGONNET: Whereas Ampère postulated that a comparative history of the literatures of all peoples must ground the construction of theory, today we are more likely to understand theory and history as a dialogue. A theory of hermeneutics informed the reverse chronology in the first volume of *East-Central Europe*, which underscored the circular movement in interpretation from the present to the past and back. Ampère's vision of a literary history of "all peoples" reminds us of the limits of CHLEL working on "the Comparative History of Literatures in European Languages," which precludes the broad metahistory and theory that might be propelled by a consideration of the literatures of India, China, or Mesoamerican codices. Nonetheless, the project includes the diffusion of European literary movements through regions outside Europe, such as colonial and postcolonial literatures in Africa and the Americas.

One factor manifest in the emergence of nineteenth-century comparative literary histories was a nationalist expectation that comparisons would reveal national character in the realm of literature, a contrast, for example, between German *Kultur* and French *civilisation*. Yet after World War II, scholars turned toward the international perspective stressed in the CHLEL series, whose history traces phenomena across national boundaries. The first in the series, Weisstein's *Expressionism*, foregrounded questions about genre and media such as painting and music and also took care to address national and regional variants, such as American or South Slav expressionism, apologizing for unavoidable "gaps." Now, the impossible goal of coverage or completeness no longer dictates the volumes in this series.

Fifty years on, recent volumes have sought to interrogate basic premises of literary history. As Mario J. Valdés and Linda Hutcheon explained in "Rethinking Literary History – Comparatively," the "literary" itself has evolved to include many categories of discourse, "oral as well as written, vernacular/popular as well as canonical/'elite,' " and we must add new media to our list of examples. The two most recent volumes in the series exemplify the innovative turn to include material overlooked by literary historians: Daniel F. Chamberlain and J. Edward Chamberlin's *Or Words to That Effect: Orality and the Writing of Literary History*, and *New Literary Hybrids*. Where the eighteenth century sought to distinguish disciplines in order to develop scientific methodologies, recent literary historians have shown the importance of cross-fertilization in the interplay between disciplines. A volume of *Comparative Critical Studies* devoted to "Gender in Literary History" (Higonnet 2009) pointed to conceptual challenges brought by feminist and queer theory to comparative literary history, starting with Mme de Staël's *De la littérature considérée dans ses rapports avec les institutions sociales* (1800). Such thinking from the margins can be found in the prizewinning pair of CHLEL volumes on *Modernism* (2007), which include a study of modernist children's literature and call attention to neglected contributions of women to the modernist "revolution" (4), following the lead of coeditor Vivian Liska's volume *Die Moderne – ein Weib* (2000).

International teamwork and comparative literature

DOMÍNGUEZ: Since the first working papers of CHLEL, international teams of scholars working in collaboration have been considered essential for this project: the prefaces to the volumes state that no researcher can deal with all the facts. Teamwork isn't very common in the humanities or in literary histories. What's been your own experience in this regard?

CORNIS-POPE: Both *East-Central Europe* and *New Literary Hybrids* foreground various examples of creative "entanglements of the global, regional, national, and local" (Chopra and Gajjala 11), emphasizing the hybridity of the European media and their messages, especially evident in subregions such as Scandinavia, East-Central Europe, and Southern Europe. The multicultural expertise of the various contributors has helped in this sense. The first volume of *East-Central Europe* featured fifty-six contributors from different countries and cultures; volume two, fifty-one multinational and multicultural contributors; volumes three and four each around thirty-five contributors. Similarly, *New Literary Hybrids* included twenty-seven contributors from twenty countries around the world, emphasizing the intercultural hybridity of most of the works discussed.

Both volumes develop a more flexible understanding of the interplay between global and local, national and transnational, challenging the lingering construction of a unidirectional world system that relays advanced Western multimedia technologies to non-Western and postcolonial peripheries. The end of the Cold War challenged the grids used by writers to make sense of an ideologically polarized world. Emerging hybrid identities and narratives have filled the vacuum created by the collapse of the bipolar world. A postnational space has been created as nation-states have been weakened by transnationalism, identities have been hybridized, and languages have been deterritorialized in cyberspace. The volume *New Literary Hybrids* employs the concept of "intermediality" to describe the literature emerging after 1989, emphasizing its complexity of form, medium, and technology. As several essays in this volume suggest, not only literature but also some of the other arts have moved toward intermediality. For example, inspired by cubism, expressionism, and futurism, both theater and film have experimented with several media (dance, music, improvisation), providing models for modern intermediality.

HIGONNET: César is right that teamwork is much more common in scientific research than in literary scholarship, where collaboration may instead find expression through coauthorship or editorial suggestions. One reason to work as a team is obviously the desire to address a broad range of cultures, including "small" literatures whose languages are not widely spoken. Few of us are familiar with more than a handful of European languages. We might also think of teamwork as a kind of "translation," which permits us to discover commonalities across cultures. A third model of teamwork is offered by the CHLEL Romanticism series, whose five volumes on four genres and the mode of irony were edited by different scholars.

At several points, CHLEL has held brainstorming meetings that were critically important for the exchange of ideas and debates over the directions a project would take. The concept for *East-Central Europe* was initiated at a small meeting in Bellagio, organized by Mario J. Valdés in 1993, and further developed at meetings in Kingston and the Netherlands, where unforeseen topics, such as the institutional roles of censorship and dictionaries, sprang into being. The ultimate editors, Neubauer and Marcel, played a critical role in weaving together separate contributions from scholars, some of whom had little knowledge of other national literatures in the region; they deftly helped make manifest parallel institutions and experiments. A similar editorial practice of regular consultation is underway for the large network on

"Landscapes of Realism," led by Dirk Goettsche, which is holding regular meetings to elaborate structural models across periods and media and to examine local case studies that both exemplify and test our ideas.

Target languages of the project

DOMÍNGUEZ: As CHLEL's name clearly indicates, it focuses on literatures in European languages, both inside and outside Europe, but the 2006 revision of the bylaws states that "non-European languages may be considered in conjunction with European languages if such inclusion is deemed essential for the scientific integrity of the project." And yet this inclusion has not taken place so far. What's the reason for that? In what situation are languages such as Arabic and Hebrew placed in relation to European languages? Moreover, as in the ICLA, the primary working languages of the series have been English and French. What are the difficulties for publishing the volumes also in the languages that they address?

CORNIS-POPE: While it is true that European languages dominate in the two projects described, it is important to note that especially the volume *Literary Hybrids* proposes a regional mapping of the recent multimedia cultures of Europe that often oversteps the boundaries of Europe. East-Central Europe and Russia are a particularly strong focus because of their alternative mapping and rewriting of paradigms from Western Europe. Other essays (e.g., Pedro Andrade's) emphasize the role that hybrid literacies play in a postcolonial redefinition of Europe. Eva Midden brings together transnational digital networks, migration, and gender in relation to the performance of religious identities. Her example is Muslim women in the Netherlands who use digital media to negotiate their religious affiliations and multiple belongings. Călin-Andrei Mihăilescu proposes an "intercolonial" approach to the digital literatures of Europe, arguing that such an approach undermines old habits of thinking and forms of writing. My own article picks up the inter/postcolonial paradigm and applies it to East-Central Europe, suggesting that the recent hypertexts, hypermedia installations, and animated works produced in this region stretch the definition of textuality, moving beyond the verbal to the visual, aural, and kinetic. Several other projects echo Salman Rushdie's celebration of hybridity, impurity, intermingling in the *Satanic Verses*, the transformation that comes from new and unexpected combinations of human beings, ideas, politics, movies, and songs, and which rejoices in mongrelization and fears the absolutism of the Pure (Rushdie 52).

HIGONNET: To answer your second question first: in today's marketplace, the language in which scholarship is published depends less on its subject than on the interested readership. The digital age has brought a crisis to publishers who invest in huge projects, such as the CHLEL volumes, and e-books and e-articles have not yet compensated for the cutbacks by libraries. "Open" publication, sponsored now by the ACLS and the MLA, also poses a problem for presses, in terms of copyright and loss of royalties. We hope that digital access to translations may overcome the problem of the target audience in the near future.

The question of which languages qualify as "European" should undoubtedly be examined in a "problem" volume on the question, what is Europe? In practice, A. James Arnold's volumes presented not only Spanish, English, French, and Dutch literatures of the Caribbean but also Creole literature, an offspring that is neither European nor indigenous. A sophisticated theoretical analysis of bilingualism and multilingualism in the first volume of Cabo Aseguinolaza, Domínguez, and Abuín González's *A Comparative History of Literatures in the Iberian Peninsula* (2010) presents a major contribution to the work of comparative literary history on issues of language. Hebrew and Arabic texts figure, of course, in this volume. In the case of medieval al-Andalus, where Arabic, Romance languages, and Hebrew coexisted, inhabitants were probably bilingual orally but literate (if at all) only in Arabic, according to Roger Wright (332). At many times and in many places, patterns of conquest and migration have produced linguistic hybridity and code-switching, linked to playful satire in second-generation Turkish and other migrant literatures – the topic of a volume that is underway in the CHLEL series.

Comparative literary history and comparative literature: a difficult relation?

DOMÍNGUEZ: Of the thirty-two editors who have coordinated volumes so far, twenty were or are affiliated with European universities. Does this fact explain the striking absence of any discussion on comparative history at North American universities? What role do macrosociological studies and the pervasive importance of the national play in the neglect of comparative history at US universities? While there is no doubt about the vitality of comparative literature in the United States, comparative literary history doesn't seem as active, at least in comparison to Europe. Is it possible that the poststructuralist discrediting of literary history and, more recently, the emergent role of world literature play any role in this situation?

CORNIS-POPE: Poststructuralism has no doubt had a significant impact not only in Europe but also in the United States. Poststructuralism has made us all more skeptical about the possibility of articulating comprehensive, quasi-global critical narratives. But it has also made us aware of provisional local and regional narratives in their interplay across geo-cultural areas and historical periods. These local and regional narratives are to a great extent "unfinished," dynamic, even self-questioning. They are also prone to revision and even self-deconstruction as they are confronted with other provisional interpretive narratives. The ample transnational projects I have been involved in have problematized the conceptual frameworks of more traditional literary and cultural history (Cornis-Pope; Cornis-Pope and Neubauer). Especially the volume *New Literary Hybrids* treats literary history itself as one of these "hybrids," emphasizing its continuous conversation – and often conflict – with other paradigms. In *Literary History*, these other paradigms include popular culture, political history, nationalism, and transnationalism; in *New Literary Hybrids*, literature is confronted with a range of transverbal multimedia. In both cases, the discussion of literary cultures emerges enriched through the problematization of the historical and cultural frameworks.

HIGONNET: You observe correctly that only one-third of the scholars who have shaped the ICLA series taught at American universities. One might be concerned if the number were higher! The wealth of comparatists in the United States returns us to the themes of diaspora and emigration, responding to historic catastrophes in Europe from which American universities profited. This having been said, there does seem to be an emphasis today on the "global," which may correspond to the shift to teaching literature in translation in the United States. In contrast to European schools that provide language instruction at early ages, languages in American schools have languished, and with them perhaps the study of literary history as a standard academic topic has yielded to "theory" – although Ampère might question that term. The loss of prestige for comparative literary history several decades ago might be traced to formalist rejection of methods of contextualization that translated literary texts into vehicles for political and social concerns. The first volume of the CHLEL Renaissance cluster specifically addressed this issue, advocating new methods of historical contextualization. Precisely that problem has been foregrounded in recent CHLEL volumes.

Regional study has also been attacked for its political baggage. Gayatri Spivak has called attention to the Cold War mentality that attracted CIA funding for interdisciplinary regional work, rather than the study of literary history, for ideological reasons (Ch. 1). An accomplished comparatist as well as a deconstructionist, she has also advocated "close" reading of the text – in the original, naturally – for its specificity. Rowing against the globalizing tide, Werner Sollors has edited two literary history volumes (Sollors 1998; Marcus and Sollors 2009) that range across Comanche, French, Russian, Ladino, Yiddish, Norwegian, and even sign language, reminding us that the comparative impulse can turn inward to examine the subnational frame of intercultural networks of expression. Reaching back a couple of centuries, we find that in an age of digitization we can recover items such as literature painted on bark or printed in newspapers on disintegrating paper, and return them to the historian's gaze.

Comparative (literary) history

DOMÍNGUEZ: When we think about how comparative literary history works, an evident referent is comparative history. And yet, both (sub)disciplines seem to have been working in isolation from each other. Why? Comparative historians claim that the main four functions of comparison in their field are heuristic, descriptive, analytical, and paradigmatic. How do they apply to comparative literary history?

CORNIS-POPE: The four functions apply to any form of history, but in the case of literary history we need to allow for a certain variance, even self-contradiction. Given the material that comparative literary history works with – literary texts that often overstep their boundaries, adding new implications in the process of translation and interpretation – we need to allow our process of description and interpretation to be recursive, unfinished, open to new articulations. History in the broad sense often surprises us, breaking patterns and turning in paradoxical directions. Literary history is even more unpredictable, creative, and informed by contradictory trends and interests. Each new literary work rereads preceding works in often surprising ways.

HIGONNET: The ideas of historian Fernand Braudel and the *Annales* school were highly influential for the series, and also for the volumes that Valdés and Djelal Kadir edited, *Literary Cultures of Latin America: A Comparative History* (2004). Some of the most interesting work done by comparative historians has been at a crossroads between *histoire des mentalités* and the "emplotments" of literary history. Comparative literary history is necessarily a metadiscourse, self-conscious about its choices and about the social and political as well as aesthetic hierarchies that frame the meanings and value of texts. Like the volumes of *East-Central Europe*, Valdés and Kadir's comparative history of Latin America probed institutions of production and reception that endow cultural forms with meaning. Unlike earlier formalist literary histories that tended to focus on high art, these newer comparative histories have chosen a broader base that includes oral forms, such as folklore, popular theater, graphic novels, and new digital forms. Rather than adopting a singular methodology, these projects map multiple patterns of interrelationship and historical turning points that trigger cultural exchanges and developments. The kinship with the "linguistic turn" in historiography is obvious. As Hutcheon, Kadir, and Valdés put it, the task of "collaborative historiography" required an embrace of open-ended, "comparative interdisciplinarity."

The spatial turn in comparative literary history

DOMÍNGUEZ: Some say that Cornis-Pope and Neubauer's first volume of *East-Central Europe* inaugurated a new subseries on regional histories in the CHLEL project in 2004. However, a geographical domain had already been selected as a historiographical object in previous volumes, such as Albert S. Gérard's 1986 history on sub-Saharan Africa and A. James Arnold's 1994–2001 history of the Caribbean. What is the main rationale for this history of East-Central Europe in contrast to the time-oriented ones? In what ways has this history of East-Central Europe led the way for other geography-oriented histories?

CORNIS-POPE: *East-Central Europe* seeks to replace organic conceptions of literary history with an understanding of cultural evolution as open to potentially limitless "mappings," to borrow J. Hillis Miller's term. As Miller puts it, a given mapping is always provisional, "infinitely variable, always open to revision." The different mappings can be thought of as "superimposed on one another and on the landscape, like different navigations through a hypertext" (281). While we do not understand "limitless" in an absolute way, we do share Miller's "not so totalizing or totalitarian" view (281), which replaces organic narratives of national cultures with open-ended "hypertexts" that interplay different interpretive perspectives. Such an approach, illustrated through the four volumes of *East-Central Europe*, is particularly important in today's political climate, in which resurrected nationalist and ethnocentric concepts of culture vie with globalist ones. Though seemingly opposed, both the globalist and the ethnocentric models encourage "organic" narratives, unified either by some Romantic notion of ethno-linguistic purity or by uncritical trust in global markets. What we have proposed is to rearticulate East-Central European literary history around a transnational approach that foregrounds *dis*junctures as much as junctures, emphasizing the interplay of specific regional features without dissolving them in a universal melting pot.

In the process, we brought national histories into dialogue with one another, foregrounding minority literatures and the transnational German and Yiddish traditions, as well as multilingual texts, translations, and other modes of cultural mediation. In practice, our history consists of many *microhistories*, of localized, perspectival, and situated stories that cannot be read as simple illustrations of an overarching organic system.

HIGONNET: The CHLEL editorial group obviously took an early interest in a "spatial turn" toward regional study in the volumes edited by Gérard on Africa and Arnold on the Caribbean. Moreover, the spaces they turned to lay at least in appearance far from the mandate to study the languages of Europe, allowing them to explore a contact zone with a doubled comparative task, that of juxtaposing colonial cultures that were themselves caught up in the conflicts of imperialism. It may not surprise that Arnold's project continues to attract interest and is being translated into Spanish. In retrospect, it may be convenient to think of the volumes dedicated to regions as a subseries, but the differences we can observe in more recent volumes should be underscored. Whereas Gérard broke up the analyses of African colonial literatures by language, and Arnold organized three linguistically separate volumes corresponding to patterns of colonization, more recent projects have mapped their materials in a different fashion. One metaphor to suggest the coexistence of discontinuous analytic sections is a set of transparent maps – for social institutions like the opera, or the movement of linguistic groups such as the Romany along the Danube, or the invention of national icons and poets at the moment of struggle for nationhood. In the first volume of the *Comparative History of Literatures in the Iberian Peninsula*, the geo-literary spaces of an expanded "imagined community" were scattered across a literary archipelago, a spatial topic that led to other themes, such as peninsular languages, forms of orality, and temporal frames at different moments. In the second volume, images of cultural identity, genres, and forms of intermediation create a sequence that is neither chronological nor spatial. If we compare the study by Sollors of polyglot American literatures to the multilingual situation of Iberia, with its evolving political regions, or to the Scandinavian case, we may be struck by the different functions of languages spoken by minority peoples, sacred languages preserved through ritual use, dialects preserved by geographical features of separation, and the emergence of distinct languages in support of political claims of independence. Their various functions oscillate between connection to the land and mobility, prior cultural attachments and assimilation.

DOMÍNGUEZ: While the *découpage* of the *East-Central Europe* may be read as a response to other poetics (*Mitteleuropa*, *Zentraleuropa*, Eastern Europe, Central Europe) and other choices seem to depend on natural borders (Iberian Peninsula, Scandinavia), would a geographical delimitation such as the *hautes terres du centre* between France and Germany be equally acceptable for a comparative literary history? What kind of "experimental" comparative literary histories would you like to see?

CORNIS-POPE: In the nontraditional approach we have taken, we "scan" the last two centuries of literary production five times, considering the region's literary cultures each time from a different angle or through a different "node." In Part I, the nodes are crucial dates or date clusters in political history. Deployed in reverse order to avoid the impression that the region's history unfolded in a predictable way, the temporal nodes (1989, 1968, 1956, 1948, 1945, 1918, 1867/1878/1881, 1848, and 1776/1789) emerge as "nonhomogeneous" entities that connect cultures across national boundaries while at the same time allowing them to experience similar events with different rhythms and directions of development. In Part II, traditional concepts of literary history – genre, movement, and period – serve as nodes, though we regard them as temporary crystallizations of literary life and focus on their transformations instead of their imagined essences. Instead of seeking the "core" of a national or regional genre (e.g., the "essence" of Polish lyric poetry or the Romanian realist novel), we focus on boundary transgressions, highlighting the emergence of new cross-genres, like reportage, the lyrical novel, and the fictionalized autobiography, or examining literature's interplay with other media in the subsection on opera and film.

In Part III the nodes are topographic: we focus on the literary culture of multinational cities, border areas, (sub)regions, and the Danube corridor, emphasizing the fact that shifting ethnic identities yield hybrid literary phenomena. By remapping the literary production across traditional ethnic and national borders, as we do in our discussion of Ashkenaz culture, we emphasize the role that these hybrid sites have played in diversifying and pluralizing national literatures. Part IV, subtitled *The Making and Remaking of Literary Institutions*, considers the impact of theater, folklore, universities, multicultural magazines and journals, translation, and literary history as a genre on the development of East-Central European literatures. Finally, Part V, entitled *Types and Stereotypes*, focuses on the representation of real and imaginary figures, such as the national poet, figures of female identity, figures of others, figures of outlaws, figures of trauma, and figures of mediators. Many of these figures have been historically challenged by hegemonic groups (in the case of national minorities), or have been excluded through an arbitrary process of othering (the Romany).

Volume 4 ends with an epilogue that pursues the region's history beyond 1989, highlighting the movement of writers across borders, as new forms of exile and cultural mobility emerge after 1989. To a large extent, the history of literature in East-Central Europe has alternated between exile and problematic returns: from the exodus of the great Polish romantics of the nineteenth century to the writers who left Hungary in fear of the white terror in 1919, the refugees fleeing Hitler, and the exiles fleeing Communism. After 1989, renewed anti-Semitism and violence against minorities forced a number of writers to move to the West. In the current context of lingering interethnic conflicts and divisions around the world, our work challenges the isolation of national literatures, relativizes national myths, and recovers texts, writers, and minority literatures that have been marginalized or ignored.

HIGONNET: Why has an "hautes terres" study of the mountainous region often bypassed in European wars not been proposed? Perhaps the key lies in the need to extend Benedict Anderson's "imagined communities" beyond the nation and its print culture to incorporate traditions of oral self-representation and a working paradigm of center and periphery. By contrast, the spatial frame of the Mediterranean, as a vehicle of transmission and contamination as well as conflict, seems to call out for a comparative literary history, perhaps at a precisely provocative moment.

A decade ago, the CHLEL committee proposed that problematic terms such as "Europe" be made the focus of short volumes focused on the theory implicit in our methods rather than on sweeping comparisons. Paradoxically, one of our largest current projects is devoted to an extremely problematic term, "realism."

Nationalism and comparative literary history

DOMÍNGUEZ: It's well known that one of the basic aims of national literary history has been – and still is – to legitimize the identity of the human community in question by highlighting its linguistic and cultural commonalities in contrast to other communities. In the case of comparative literary history, is this aim simply transferred to an international and interregional domain? In what ways is this project still indebted to comparative literature's activism in the aftermath of WWII?

CORNIS-POPE: Boundaries, their challenge and extension, are very much part of our focus. Our "activism" as comparativists has called into question the idea of a self-contained work, secure in its boundaries, emphasizing instead the notion of an open-ended text whose boundaries are continually expanded through the collaborative work of writers and readers. These shifts have been aided by the new hypertext and networked communication technologies over the past three decades. The new electronic technologies have allowed us to interact more closely with the text, highlighting its associative or dissociative impulses and adding layers of annotations, linked intertexts, and "winding paths" of signifiers. "The writer and the reader do not discover or recognize a preexisting pattern; rather, they make patterns possible" (Travis 9).

The new reading and writing technologies are in many ways liberatory, enhancing the interplay of literature and other media; they have also challenged the very definition of verbal literature. A major emphasis in our volume *New Literary Hybrids* is on literary production and expression in multimedia environments. Literature remains an important focus, even as its modes of manifestation expand to include new hybrids that stretch the definition of what is "literary."

HIGONNET: National identities may seem ineluctable, in part because the linguistic inflections of our literary categories (e.g., *modernisme/modernismo*) carry a burden of cultural difference. Thus the wide-ranging volumes of *Modernism*, edited by Astradur Eysteinsson and Vivian Liska, explore broad topics such as irony, Bakhtinian theory, myths of rupture, trauma, and acoustic space – topics that play across national boundaries. Yet they also analyze eighteen different modernisms, including those of Catalonia, Spanish America, Russia, and six Nordic countries. It seems, however, that when we relocate our focus to an earlier period, such as the Renaissance or the high medieval age, travel, the physical movement of texts, and new means of copying texts displace and undercut the importance of political boundaries. Marcel is right also that the new technologies for reading and writing transcend older boundaries anchored in concepts of group identity. Instant transmission and translation do build a larger international community, not necessarily with a recognizable geo-literary identity. But we must keep in mind that cultural reception is highly variable, as witnessed in extreme cases, such as violent reactions to satiric cartoons and texts that violate cultural values. As a result, the growing attention to reception as a feature of comparative literary histories has a significance not imagined in an earlier era of formalist internationalism.

The future of comparative literary history

DOMÍNGUEZ: One of the most recent CHLEL developments is a new series called "Problem Series." What are the main tenets of this series and how does it differ from the traditional CHLEL series? What are the main areas that you see as possibilities for comparative literary history in the next ten years?

CORNIS-POPE: As per our description, the Problem Series should be devoted to shorter volumes (around 250 pages) that problematize specific themes and structures. Possibilities that I see: a volume that will problematize the concept and strategies of realism (or representation, more broadly), moving from traditional forms to postmodern and antirealist ones. This would complement the volume on realism as a literary and cultural trend that is currently part of the chronological series. Similarly, we could devote a volume to the very notion of literary history, to question our traditional frameworks (e.g., linear ascending or descending plot; teleological structures; distribution of roles – "heroes" vs. "opponents"; organic narrative).

HIGONNET: At a meeting in Amsterdam in 2002, CHLEL proposed that future projects turn from monumental, encyclopedic paving stones (as the French would put it) to shorter, selective, and problem-oriented book proposals. Such issues might include not only the meaning of "Europe" but also the term "periodization" as "naturalized chronology," translatability in the formation of international canons, or basic cultural mechanisms in the transmission and adaptation of texts. The lively interest in adaptation might form the core of a volume about transmedial adaptations across linguistic cultures. The possibilities seem open-ended, especially at a moment when volumes like *Iberia II* and *Landscapes of Realism* are turning to metacritical reflections rather than conclusions as symptoms of closure.

Works cited

Ampère, Jean-Jacques. "De l'histoire de la poésie." *Mélanges d'histoire littéraire et de literature.* Vol. 1. 1830. Paris: Michel Lévy, 1867. 1–50. Print.

Ampère, Jean-Jacques. *Histoire de la littérature française au Moyen Âge comparée aux littératures étrangères. Introduction: Histoire de la formation de la langue française.* Paris: Just Tessier, 1841. Print.

Arnold, A. James, ed. *A History of Literature in the Caribbean.* 3 vols. Amsterdam: John Benjamins, 1994–2001. Print.

Association Internationale de Littérature Comparée. "Coordinating Committee By-Laws." 2006. Web. 17 Feb. 2016.

Cabo Aseguinolaza, Fernando, Anxo Abuín González, and César Domínguez, eds. *A Comparative History of Literatures in the Iberian Peninsula.* Vol. 1. Amsterdam: John Benjamins, 2010. Print.

Chamberlain, Daniel F., and J. Edward Chamberlin, eds. *Or Words to That Effect: Orality and the Writing of Literary History.* Amsterdam: John Benjamins, 2016. Print.

Chopra, Rohit, and Radhika Gajjala, eds. *Global Media, Culture, and Identity.* New York: Routledge, 2011. Print.

Cornis-Pope, Marcel, ed. *New Literary Hybrids in the Age of Multimedia Expression.* Amsterdam: John Benjamins, 2014. Print.

Cornis-Pope, Marcel, and John Neubauer, eds. *History of the Literary Cultures of East-Central Europe.* 4 vols. Amsterdam: John Benjamins, 2004–2010. Print.

Eysteinsson, Astradur, and Vivian Liska, eds. *Modernism.* 2 vols. Amsterdam: John Benjamins, 2007. Print.

Gérard, Albert S., ed. *European-Language Writing in Sub-Saharan Africa.* 2 vols. Budapest: Akadémiai Kiadó, 1986. Print.

Higonnet, Margaret R., ed. *Gender in Literary History.* Spec. issue of *Comparative Critical Studies* 6.2 (2009). Print.

Hutcheon, Linda, Djelal Kadir, and Mario J. Valdés. "Collaborative Historiography: A Comparative Literary History of Latin America." Occasional Paper No. 35. N.p.: American Council of Learned Societies, 1996. Web. 17 Feb. 2016.

Liska, Vivian. *Die Moderne – ein Weib: am Beispiel von Romanen Ricarda Huchs und Annette Kolbs*. Tübingen: Francke, 2000. Print.

Marcus, Greil, and Werner Sollors, eds. *A New Literary History of America*. Cambridge, MA: Harvard UP, 2009. Print.

Miller, J. Hillis. *Topographies*. Stanford: Stanford UP, 1995. Print.

Puybusque, Louis-Adolphe de. *Histoire comparée des littératures espagnole et française*. 2 vols. Paris: G.-A. Dentu, 1843. Print.

Rushdie, Salman. "'In Good Faith.' Pleasures and Popularity." *Newsweek* (1990): 52. Print.

Sollors, Werner, ed. *Multilingual America: Transnationalism, Ethnicity, and the Languages of American Literature*. New York: New York UP, 1998. Print.

Spivak, Gayatri Chakravorty. *Death of a Discipline*. New York: Columbia University Press, 2003. Print.

Travis, Molly Abel. *Reading Cultures. The Construction of Readers in the Twentieth Century*. Carbondale: Southern Illinois UP, 1998. Print.

Valdés, Mario J., and Linda Hutcheon. "Rethinking Literary History – Comparatively." Occasional Paper No. 27. N.p.: American Council of Learned Societies, 1994. Web. 27 Jan. 2016.

Valdés, Mario J., and Djelal Kadir, eds. *Literary Cultures of Latin America: A Comparative History*. 3 vols. Oxford: Oxford UP, 2004. Print.

Villemain, Abel-François. *Cours de littérature française: Tableau de la littérature au Moyen Âge en France, en Italie, en Espagne et en Angleterre*. 2 vols. 1830. Paris: Librairie Académique Didier, 1875. Print.

Weisstein, Ulrich, ed. *Expressionism as an International Literary Phenomenon*. Budapest: Akadémiai Kiadó, 1973. Print.

Wright, Roger. "Bilingualism and Diglossia in Medieval Iberia (350–1350)." *A Comparative History of Literatures in the Iberian Peninsula*. Eds. Fernando Cabo Aseguinolaza, Anxo Abuín González, and César Domínguez. Vol. 1. Amsterdam: John Benjamins, 2010. 333–50. Print.

Petrocriticism

Michael Rubenstein

Amitav Ghosh coined the term "petrofiction" as the title of his review of Abdel-rahman Munif's quintet of novels *Cities of Salt* in the March 1992 issue of *The New Republic*. Ghosh pointed out just how few novels about the "oil encounter" between the United States and the Middle East had up until then ever been written. Munif's novels were, in Ghosh's view, the exceptions proving the rule that "the history of oil is a matter of embarrassment verging on the unspeakable, the pornographic" (29). But if in 1992 Ghosh meant by petrofiction simply a fiction directly concerned with the oil industry, Imre Szeman would argue in a 2012 issue of the *American Book Review* that "petrofiction" ought to be construed far more capaciously – and controversially – as a grand new periodizing gesture. Munif's *Cities of Salt* and Upton Sinclair's *Oil!* are self-evidently petrofictions in Ghosh's sense, because they are explicitly about oil. But if, as Graeme MacDonald speculates in the same issue, "all modern writing is premised on both the promise and the hidden costs and benefits of hydrocarbon culture," then "is not all fiction from, say, *The Great Gatsby* (1925) to *The Corrections* (2001) 'oil' fiction?" (31).

What prompts Szeman and MacDonald to reposition petrofiction as a literary period instead of a genre? In the two decades between Ghosh's petrofiction and Szeman's, the oil era became retrospectively more visible as a result of the growing public awareness of, and scientific consensus about, the link between carbon dioxide emissions and global warming. By the turn of the twenty-first century, the consequences of the productive and demographic explosion of the "Great Acceleration" since 1950, enabled largely by the burning of hydrocarbons, became much clearer and more disturbing (Steffen et al.). With the popular introduction of the concept of the Anthropocene in 2000, a new environmental awareness emerged: that petroleum is not an infinite energy resource, and that, even if it were, it could not continue to be burned at the current rate without causing the earth's climate to change in ways we are not fully able to predict, and to which we may not even be able to adapt. Oil, to borrow a phrase from Timothy Mitchell, could no longer "be counted on not to count" (234). What will it mean to the way we read cultural works that they were created under the shadow of a global ecological transformation – wrought and accelerated by the widespread burning of hydrocarbons, and, crucially, felt most by those least responsible – of which they were largely unaware, but in which they were wholly imbricated?

Petrofiction therefore is not only fiction that explicitly represents oil. It is any fiction that can be read to reveal our modern entanglement with oil, an entanglement that Stephanie LeMenager characterizes, in figurative language redolent of drilling and pumping, as "ultradeep" (11). Petrocriticism, then, is that branch of literary criticism specializing in petromodernity for which the concept of the "energy regime" is the most significant mode of historical and literary-historical periodizing; to paraphrase Patricia Yaeger, instead of the political unconscious, petrocriticism supposes the energy unconscious. We might say that petrocriticism is a name for the intersection where climate change (Wenzel, this volume) collides with literary criticism by way of the hermeneutics of suspicion (Felski). A petrocritic may be someone looking to say something about texts about oil; she may also be looking for oil in cultural places where it is otherwise unspoken or unspeakable, at once too close, too far, and too immense to be immediately perceptible; and she may be looking, in fictions, for the profoundly uneven distribution of oil's benefits and consequences to peoples and territories around the globe.

Works cited

Felski, Rita. *The Limits of Critique*. Chicago: U of Chicago P, 2015. Print.
Ghosh, Amitav. "Petrofiction." *The New Republic* (2 March 1992): 29–33. Web. 27 Apr. 2014.
LeMenager, Stephanie. *Living Oil*. New York: Oxford UP, 2014. Print.
Macdonald, Graeme. "Oil and World Literature." *American Book Review* (March–April 2012): 7 and 31. Web. 27 Apr. 2014.
Mitchell, Timothy. *Carbon Democracy*. London: Verso, 2011. Print.
Steffen, Will, Wendy Broadgate, Lisa Deutsch, Owen Gaffney, and Cornelia Ludwig. "The Trajectory of the Anthropocene: The Great Acceleration." *The Anthropocene Review* 2.1 (April 2015): 81–98. Web. 5 Mar. 2016.
Szeman, Imre. "Introduction to Focus: Petrofictions." *American Book Review* (March–April 2012): 3. Web. 27 Apr. 2014.
Yaeger, Patricia. "Editor's Column: Literature in the Ages of Wood, Tallow, Coal, Whale Oil, Gasoline, Atomic Power, and Other Energy Sources." *PMLA* 126 (2011): 305–26. Print.

The politics of the archive in semi-peripheries

Adam F. Kola

Although the First World, seen through the lens of academia, seems to be prospering, and the Third World has found its own place in the postcolonial intellectual order, the post–Cold War world of semi-peripheries in East and Central Europe (ECE) has largely disappeared from the discourse of comparative literature (with few exceptions: Cornis-Pope and Neubauer; Tötösy de Zepetnek). It sometimes appears as a convenient intellectual counterpoint or is included in postmodernist or postcolonial narratives; in both cases, however, it does not convey regional specificity or allow local voices to speak. Both strategies – a focus on the core or postcolonial literatures – expropriate the semi-peripheral realm of Second-World nonplaces.

Second-World memory has been blurred and occluded in academic neocolonialism and the politics of the archive. Often the semi-peripheries do not even possess their own archives. Their archives were frequently destroyed – burned during historical upheavals, stolen, dispersed, or not preserved by elites who were continuously exterminated over the course of centuries. The history of growing disproportion between Western and Eastern Europe thus reaches centuries into the past. This memory is often not preserved and kept alive by oral culture either because of the lack of a formalized oral tradition – for example, in the Balkans. With significant migrations and interregional mobility, as in Poland and the Ukraine, oral memory serves no important social purpose, while the disruption of transgenerational relations has impaired traditional forms of cultural transmission. Memory is kept by ashes and ruins, tortured biographies, unfinished stories and, in the postsocialist period of transformation, by buildings stripped of memory for the sake of neoliberally perceived modernization.

Individual writers' archives and some larger collections have sometimes found more secure homes abroad. Yet recorded memory remains caught up in a power game between inaccessibility in the East and the subordinate status of ECE archives when they are located in the West. Regaining archival knowledge is a necessary process in building one's own semi-peripheral identity. Power over archives and the knowledge they deliver becomes, in the global game, a condition of speaking with one's own voice. This is the politics of the archive.

The archives are often stored in territories of the core rather than the periphery, but their accessibility has been limited in the past for geopolitical reasons.

They can now at last be accessed, even if only in part. The politics of the archive, then, discovers unknown worlds, and recreates relations between the core and the semi-periphery of the Second World, but also acts the other way round, by uniting the Second and Third Worlds, beyond the unnecessary burden of earlier Communist propaganda in ECE. Searching for real world literature therefore requires the completion of a missing semi-peripheral link. The near absence of representatives of the Second World in today's globalizing discourse of comparative literature results from this understated position of semi-peripherality, which, like every in-between existence, causes the disappearance of our object.

Another consequence of History with a capital H in ECE, and a reason for the sorry state of its archives, is the fact that in reconstructing this history "we need to concentrate on the precious little that has not perished in the turmoil" (Kola and Ulicka 64). But thousands of documents have been lost forever. That is why I would call this kind of reconstruction a "presumptive history" (Kola and Ulicka 63). Simone Osthoff writes about the "unstable boundary between artworks and their documentation" (44). Second-World records that have found themselves in the core territories, particularly in the United States, have often survived better than archives at home, and this in itself constitutes their great value.[1] Here I would like to focus on archives of individual writers, which allow for detailed examination at a manageable scale of material. Complete collections of documents by Czesław Miłosz and Roman Jakobson, whom I will discuss here, and also such writers, scholars, and translators as René Wellek, Józef Wittlin, or Manfred Kridl offer unique examples of the unstable boundary between literary and theoretical works and their documentation. It is a challenge to place these materials in a new light, changing categories of thinking about the original cultures of particular immigrants (Poland and Russia), their transfer cultures (Czechoslovakia, France, and others), and finally, their destination culture (the United States in these cases).

Ann Laura Stoler turns our attention not only to colonial archives as a source of knowledge but also to the power relations that emerge from "particular archival forms" (20). As she explains, "[b]y 'archival form' I allude to several things: prose style, repetitive refrain, the arts of persuasion, affective strains that shape 'rational' response, categories of confidentiality and classification, and not least, genres of documentation" (20). In this sense, she concentrates on "archiving-as-process rather than archives-as-things" (20). The processual character of literary works in the ECE context is especially salient when it comes to the practice of universalizing language in migrant situations. The materiality of these documents (and other sources such as radio interviews) highlights the struggle with translingual writing, which might be overlooked in classical textual studies.

Philology and translingualism

Processual archives and the semi-peripheral context can give an introduction to translingualism and philological issues. "The Golden Age" of philology in the nineteenth century has passed and will probably never come back.

In the twentieth century, linguistics sidelined philology, which became largely restricted to the study of classical languages and literatures. Philology stayed on a bit longer in textual practice, but was also pushed out in this field by editing and publishing. Linguistics, especially in its structuralist form, tried to take over the whole field, as Roman Jakobson states in his "Closing Statement: Linguistics and Poetics" (1960). This text was in fact a manifesto for the domination of linguistics not only over poetics but also over literary studies as such, including comparative literature. Of course this was only Jakobson's wishful thinking and attempted disciplinary coup d'état. Literary studies were already well developed at that time and were independent enough to resist such an attack. Even though literary scholars sometimes still collaborate with linguists, they have more connections today with other fields, like cultural studies, anthropology, postcolonial studies, and philosophy. Philology exists on the margins of other disciplines, and continues to have a kind of schizophrenic identity between linguistics and literary studies.

On the other hand, philology is winning favor in the humanities more generally (Hartog). Hans Ulrich Gumbrecht writes about "the powers of philology," focusing on philology as textual practice (Ziolkowski, "Metaphilology"; see also *On Philology*). James Lockhart and other historians in the field of Mesoamerican studies, especially the Nahuatl language tradition, use the term "New Philology" or "Philological Ethnohistory" to describe a kind of subaltern history, based on the written sources of colonized people rather than Spanish conquerors (Lockhart).[2] From this perspective, the problem of translingualism is or should be one of the crucial issues of philology as well as of comparative literature.

The main focus of this chapter is on the materiality of translingual migrants' writing, which is a bridge to the archive-as-process. By translingualism I mean, following Steven Kellman, "the phenomenon of authors who write in more than one language or at least in a language other than their primary one" (ix). Suresh Canagarajah underlines the difference between multilingualism and translingualism: "The term *multilingual* typically conceives of the relationship between languages in an additive manner" (7), and, importantly, this "is still somewhat influenced by the monolingual paradigm" (7–8). In multilingualism "the languages are kept separate" (8), whereas "[t]he term translingual conceives of language relationships in more dynamic terms" (8). This dynamism of languages is very important for my approach and examples. Canagarajah adds that "[t]he semiotic resources in one's repertoire or in society interact more closely, become part of an integrated resource, and enhance each other. The languages mesh in transformative ways, generating new meanings and grammars" (8).

Why is this problem not a key issue for philology and comparative literature as such? Pascale Casanova uses the notion of the "Herder effect" in *The World Republic of Letters* (75–79). For her this means, among other things, the growing nationalization of literatures in nineteenth-century Europe. This tradition is connected, inter alia, with Johann Gottfried Herder, Johann Gottlieb Fichte, and Jakob Friedrich Fries. The nationalization and ethnicization of literature and culture were predominant in the German and other ECE nations. This was the reason Casanova wrote her book:

> The purpose of this book is to restore a point of view that has been obscured for the most part by the "nationalization" of literatures and literary histories, to rediscover the lost transnational dimension of literature that for two hundred years has been reduced to the political and linguistic boundaries of nations.
>
> (xi)

According to the classical, nineteenth-century paradigm, this difficulty is insurmountable because the domain of literature is language in the national rather than the universal or global context, even when a language is shared by several nations.[3] Hence, whether we follow Immanuel Wallerstein and Andre Gunder Frank or Casanova, we should admit that our knowledge and understanding of language are shaped by nineteenth-century scholarship. Wallerstein and Frank build their theories on unthinking nineteenth-century social science, whereas Casanova constructs her interpretation on a critique of the Romantic-nationalist paradigm of literature and literary studies. The point is that modern philology arose at the time of the domination of the "Herder effect" not only in literature, language, and politics but also, obviously, in academia (for the ECE context, see Kamusella). That is one of the reasons why philology concentrated on monolingual texts, eventually with some exceptions, like studies of intertextuality.

Historical linguistic research proves that bilingualism or even multilingualism was, and in fact still is, the norm in many parts of ECE, and even characterizes nearly the entire world (see Dev for India). As Kellman points out, "[m]ost inhabitants of this planet are at least bilingual" (viii), and Canagarajah emphasizes that translingual practice is not new or recent (9). This makes the category of the national language – so popular in the nineteenth and twentieth centuries as a basis for literature and "high culture" among intellectuals and scholars – almost unnecessary (objections see Damrosch 282–283; Saussy 5–24). Multilingualism is significant when it comes to both spoken and written language, everyday and literary language. What is more, "permanent multilingualism often causes reciprocal influence and constant fluctuation between languages" (Sawicka 98). As a result, there is an unstable and indefinite language norm for literature and literacy, or rather – from the viewpoint of classical literary studies – an antinorm. Hence, a multilingual situation is fully correlated with literary forms and literary languages, and the multilingual upbringing of the ECE immigrants I will discuss here shaped their translingual practices in the United States.

In the case of "high culture" in ECE, more variables should be taken into consideration. The language of the elites was either French or German in the nineteenth and twentieth centuries. That is why in a letter dated April 17, 1971, Jakobson says that "French is my childhood language, second after my Russian mother tongue" (Jakobson, Papers Box 4, Folder 13). Almost all of the ECE intellectuals who became so important for postwar American comparative literature used two or more languages as their mother tongues or childhood languages. In that sense it was easier for them to adapt to their new American milieu. But two other factors should be taken into account. First, none of these scholars had English as their second mother tongue or childhood language, and what is more, no one except René Wellek used English as an academic language in the initial context of interwar Europe. Second, during the first stage of their stay in the United States they were often working in languages other than English – for example, Jakobson in Francophone New York, at the École Libre des Hautes Études at the New School for Social Research (this school was advertised as "French University Courses in the French Language by French and Belgian Professors," even though some of the professors were in fact from ECE; Jakobson, Papers Box 2, Folder 5).

Roman Jakobson's American career

The case of Roman Jakobson is instructive for our purpose. I would like to focus on his important first years in the United States. In the early 1940s, he focused on Native American languages, comparing them to Paleosiberian languages. His American research was largely based on materials compiled by the late German American ethnographer and anthropologist Franz Boas. However, Jakobson's Siberian contribution is much more interesting. His research was possible thanks to rare fieldwork data collected in Siberia by the Russian American ethnographer Vladimir Ilyich Jochelson, whose materials wound up in New York after his death in 1937. Jochelson had Jewish roots and hailed from Wilno in prewar Poland (today Vilnius, Lithuania), so his collection is itself an example of semi-peripheral politics and the politics of the archive. Jakobson had access to his data, and I would argue that his American (and probably also global) career started at that time, as he established his reputation as an excellent scholar. He combined his linguistic skills, knowledge of Russian, the American tradition, and crucial Native American topics with an interdisciplinary perspective and the ability to work on the margins of a newly developing discipline – linguistic anthropology. He was able to focus on one of its most prominent and authoritative representatives, Boas, and finally to adopt a comparative approach as an ordering principle. He published his results in the prestigious journals *American Anthropologist* and *International Journal of American Linguists* (Jakobson, Papers Box 10, Folder 28–30; Box, Folder 60; "Paleosiberian;" "Franz Boas"). His notes from this period are in various languages: Russian, French, German, and English, as well as occasionally Czech, in the versions of each text published in the Czech immigrant journal *New-Yorské Listy* (Jakobson, Papers Box 9, Folder 77; "Fr. Boas").

At the same time, he was also working on a patriotic book for his second country, Czechoslovakia: *Moudrost starých Čechů* (*Wisdom of the Old Czechs*; Jakobson, Papers Box 10, Folder 1–24; Box 9, Folder 79–83; see the seventeenth-century *Wisdom of the Old Czechs* by Jan Amos Komenský). The book, prepared during World War II as an encouragement in the fight against Hitler and published in Czech in the United States, is a cultural history of the Czech nation, starting in the Middle Ages. The idea of the book is simply to demonstrate that Czechs are Slavs and that their culture developed in isolation from German culture. In fact, Czech and German culture developed in interaction, and the two "nations" intermingled. But if we look at Jakobson's notes, the galley proofs of the text, and his remarks and corrections, this political aim becomes even more obvious. Most of the notes and quotations he selects are anti-German, or present Czech culture as purely Slavic and antagonistic to German culture. At the same time, in the book's galley proofs, Jakobson softened his arguments, making them more precise and – in a way – academic. Due to the topic, the language of the published text, its potential readers, and his political engagement, Jakobson wrote the book in Czech, sometimes using German, less frequently other Slavic languages, especially Old Church Slavonic for the earliest history. He almost never used English, even though he was working on the text in the United States, or French, as one might have expected given his other works and the Francophone intellectual milieu he was part of. This text, like other writings in Czech published at the same time, shows that he was seriously considering the possibility of returning to Czechoslovakia after the war.

Czesław Miłosz and translingualism

In contrast to scholar-linguists and literary theorists such as Jakobson, the position of immigrant writers in the American milieu differed from their European status as they were now also often connected with academia. This marriage of art and the academic world was an interesting effect of the transatlantic transfer of knowledge. A writer's reflexivity and creative use of languages in translingual writings and bicultural literature can be read as a metacommentary on this process, sometimes even more perspicacious than that of literary theorists. The best-known case is Vladimir Nabokov, but here I would like to focus on Czesław Miłosz, whose case is similar to other writers from ECE, such as Witold Gombrowicz or Leopold Tyrmand. On the one hand, these writers often do not change the language of their creative literary output, especially poetry. But they do, on the other hand, switch the language of their academic work, journalism, and commentaries, seemingly without difficulty. What is especially interesting in this context is that they translate and often control the translation of their works into other languages, especially languages that they know and use.

However, even in the case of Miłosz, the process of writing lectures or speeches in English was a multistage one. Often he prepared the first draft in Polish with quotations in the original languages. In the cases I have analyzed, these were French, English, Russian, and Polish. He would then look up existing English translations of selected excerpts, but would often improve them; he rarely produced his own translations, even though he was a prolific translator from different languages into Polish. We therefore find several English versions of each text with multiple remarks, corrections, and modifications that sometimes alter the text significantly, though without substantially transforming its structure. We may thus say that the structure and idea of the text were prepared in Polish, while serious modifications were introduced in the course of translation. In all of Miłosz's huge archival collection, we can find texts to which he added pages or notes, in the English manuscript or even the typescript version, but these still do not modify the text substantially. The last possibility, especially after Miłosz received the Nobel Prize in 1980, was that his manuscript would be typed on a typewriter or computer by others with empty spaces for indecipherable words, which were then filled in by Miłosz on the typewritten copies, which he continued to work on. For instance, one assistant writes, "I have marked places where words are difficult to read. Molly. 5/7/93" – a fully understandable remark, because Miłosz's handwriting is extremely difficult to read (Miłosz, Papers Box 156, Folder 2546). It is significant that I did not find any texts where this typist had made any substantial corrections and modifications.

Conclusions

Even though the archives of Roman Jakobson, Czesław Miłosz, and other figures that I have examined are exhaustive, with several copies for each text from the original writing to the final version, we are not sure if these archives give us a full picture of the writers' creative process. The materiality of these texts uncovers for us the writing mechanisms in translingual situations, but cannot be treated as a complete picture. We have to remember that like all creative works, including autobiographical texts, diaries and memoirs, journals and registers, letters and notes, archival sources and materials are an effect of someone's well-considered, intentional, and creative work. We will never be sure of the scope of the changes, interventions, and intrusions by authors themselves or their families and heirs. However, work in these archives can uncover the language mechanisms, real work, and struggles of each author in a translingual situation. And if philology – both in its linguistic and literary dimensions – offers us tools for analyzing such situations, this archival methodology of working with a text on different levels and at different stages of the process of its composition can make the practice of meaning-creation visible, opening up words and worlds alike.

I would also like to emphasize that translingualism is highly context-dependent, in each case determined by crucial factors, such as institutions, readers, topics, problems, fields of interest, potential influences and reactions, interpersonal relations, and the writer's network of allies and associations. Translingualism is not a simple transition from one language to another, but a series of steps, forward and backward. It is more like dancing with languages than a straight path forward in that the process does not simply lead from an initial Slavic language (Russian, Polish, or Czech) to a new English language. The story is usually much more complicated. However, my archival research has revealed what I call the shifting the authority of language: from the peripheral Slavic languages to French – somewhat passé but still current for these writers – and finally to the domination of global English. We can observe this process on both the individual level of each biography and writing practice and on the supra-individual level of the cultural shift of languages on the global scale.

Third, the new philology can encompass the study of translingualism in two ways. First, together with historical linguistics, it highlights multilingualism as a linguistic norm and standard, which is a good starting point for the discussion on translingualism, as well as for comparative literature generally. Second, archival research on the real history of philology as an academic discipline and a political practice of nationalization goes beyond the false self-image of the discipline toward a new philology and comparative literature.

A fourth point is connected to the very deep need felt by writers to control their language production, even if the writer's language skills are far from native-speaker level. Often, scholars as well as creative writers have tried to control the whole process of creating each text, including in translingual situations. An archive as a work of creative art that documents someone's entire literary life is part of writers' control of their self-image, even after – or perhaps especially after – their death.

A fifth problem is the valuation of translingualism. Translingual in-betweenness produces linguistic hybridity (Canagarajah 3) and constructs new norms for each language. In that sense, translingualism is positively valued as a chance for global, truly cosmopolitan relations. I have no doubt that this is true. However, my analysis here points to all kinds of problems, struggles, and failures in such linguistic situations. What is more, a translingual situation could be exploited with good or bad intent – for example, to produce gains in the field of political engagement, sometimes by manipulating translanguages.

Finally, a last remark related to philology. Traditionally, the limits of philology were determined by relatively stable knowledge production and the stable objects constructed by this knowledge. That is why we need a more dynamic and processual new philology; it is the only way to research translingualism from a philological and comparative point of view.

Notes

1 The case of Zbigniew Herbert's archive and debates after his death about where it should be stored are an excellent example of issues related to the politics of the archive. Herbert's inheritors, his wife, Katarzyna Dzieduszycka-Herbert, and sister, Halina Herbert-Żebrowska, couldn't decide whether the materials he left should be sold to one of the American university archives (Herbert's will was to send them to Beinecke Rare Book and Manuscript Library at Yale University) or stay in Poland. Finally, after two years of discussion, all materials are now available at the National Library of Poland. Aside from financial considerations, the geopolitical safety of that archive was crucial. This situation goes to show that the division of the world into core and semi-periphery – as well as the risks and threats, or even state of emergency, it entails – is permanent in this part of Europe.
2 Sheldon Pollock has used the term "New Philology" in the context of the South Asian philological tradition, referring to "commentarial work as well as grammatical, metrical, rhetorical, and related disciplines" focused on early Kannada ("New Philology" 399).
3 The problem of translation, one of the most important problems in modern comparative studies, is a good example of this because it expresses our attachment to our national language and concern for what will happen with it (see Apter; Damrosch 145–205; Liu).

Works cited

Apter, Emily. *The Translation Zone: A New Comparative Literature*. Princeton: Princeton UP, 2006. Print.

Canagarajah, Suresh. *Translingual Practice: Global English and Cosmopolitan Relations*. New York: Routledge, 2013. Print.

Casanova, Pascale. *The World Republic of Letters*. Trans. M. B. DeBevoise. Cambridge, MA: Harvard UP, 2004. Print.

Cornis-Pope, Marcel, and John Neubauer, eds. *History of the Literary Cultures of East-Central Europe: Junctures and Disjunctures in the 19th and 20th Centuries*. Amsterdam: Benjamins. Vol. 1–2004, Vol. 2–2006, Vol. 3–2007, Vol. 4–2010. Print.

Damrosch, David. *What Is World Literature?* Princeton: Princeton UP, 2003. Print.

Dev, Amiya. "Comparative Literature in India." *CLCWeb: Comparative Literature and Culture* 2.4 (2000). Web. 12 May 2015.

———. *The Idea of Comparative Literature in India*. Calcutta: Papyrus, 1984. Print.

Frank, Andre Gunder. *ReOrient: Global Economy in the Asian Age*. Berkeley: U of California P, 1998. Print.

Gumbrecht, Hans Ulrich. *The Powers of Philology: Dynamics of Textual Scholarship*. Urbana: U of Illinois P, 2003. Print.

Hartog, François. "The Double Fate of the Classics." *Critical Inquiry* 35 (2009): 964–79. Print.

Jakobson, Roman. "Closing Statements: Linguistics and Poetics." *Style in Language*. Ed. Thomas A. Sebeok. Cambridge, MA: MIT Press 1960. 350–77. Print.

———. "Franz Boas' Approach to Language." *International Journal of American Linguists* 10 (1944): 188–95. Print.

———. "Franz Boas, hrdina práce." *New-Yorské Listy* (27 December 1942). Print.

———. *Moudrost starých Čechů*. New York: Nákladem Československého kulturního kroužku, 1943. Print.

———. "Paleosiberian Languages." *American Anthropologist* 44 (1942): 602–20. Print.

———. Roman Jakobson papers. 1908-1982. MC.0072. Cambridge, MA: Institute Archives and Special Collections, Massachusetts Institute of Technology Libraries.

Kamusella, Tomasz. *The Politics of Language and Nationalism in Modern Central Europe*. Houndmills, Basingstoke: Palgrave Macmillan, 2012. Print.

Kellman, Steven. *The Translingual Imagination*. Lincoln: U of Nebraska P, 2000. Print.

Kola, Adam F., and Danuta Ulicka. "From Circles to the School (and Back Again): The Case of Polish Structuralism." *Theoretical Schools and Circles in the Twentieth-Century Humanities: Literary History, History, Philosophy*. Ed. Marina Grishakova and Silvi Salupere. London: Routledge, 2015. 63–83. Print.

Komenský, Jan Amos. *Moudrost starých Čech: Dílo Jana Amose Komenského*. Vol. 1. Prague: Academia, 1969. Print.

Liu, Lydia H., ed. *Tokens of Exchange: The Problem of Translation in Global Circulations*. Durham: Duke UP, 1999. Print.

Lockhart, James. "Introduction: Background and Course of the New Philology." *Sources and Methods for the Study of Postconquest Mesoamerican Ethnohistory*. Ed. James Lockhart, Lisa Sousa and Stephanie Wood. Eugene: Wired Humanities Project, University of Oregon, 2007. 1–24. Web. 12 May 2015. http://whp.uoregon.edu/Lockhart/Intro.pdf

Miłosz, Czesław. Papers: GEN MSS 661. 1940–1989. New Haven, CT: Beinecke Rare Book and Manuscript Library, Yale University.

Osthoff, Simone. *Performing the Archive: The Transformation of the Archive in Contemporary Art from Repository of Documents to Art Medium.* New York: Atropos Press, 2009. Print.

Pollock, Sheldon. "A New Philology: From Norm-bound Practice to Practice-bound Norm in Kannada Intellectual History." *South-Indian Horizons: Felicitation Volume for François Gros on the Occasion of His 70th Birthday.* Ed. Jean-Luc Chevillard. Pondichéry: Institut français de Pondichéry/École française d'Extrême-Orient, 2004. 399–417. Print.

Saussy, Haun. "Exquisite Cadavers Stitched from Fresh Nightmares: Of Memes, Hives, and Selfish Genes." *Comparative Literature in an Age of Globalization.* Ed. Haun Saussy. Baltimore: The Johns Hopkins UP, 2006. 3–42. Print.

Sawicka, Irena. "Continuity or Discontinuity – the Case of Macedonian Phonetics." *Colloquia Humanistica* 1 (2012): 97–113. Web. 9 Mar. 2016. https://ispan.waw.pl/journals/index.php/ch/article/view/ch.2012.007/924

Stoler, Ann Laura. *Along the Archival Grain: Epistemic Anxieties and Colonial Common Sense.* Princeton: Princeton UP, 2009. Print.

Tötösy de Zepetnek, Steven, ed. *Comparative Central European Culture.* West Lafayette: Purdue UP, 2002. Print.

Wallerstein, Immanuel. *Unthinking Social Science: The Limits of Nineteenth-Century Paradigms.* 2nd ed. Philadelphia: Temple UP, 2001. Print.

Ziolkowski, Jan M. "Metaphilology." *The Journal of English and Germanic Philology* 104 (2005): 239–72. Print.

———, ed. *On Philology.* University Park: Penn State UP, 1990. Print.

What the world thinks about literature

Thomas O. Beebee

Most likely everyone contributing to or reading this report is interested in the following two questions about the "state of our discipline": one, where is the study of world literature headed? And two, where is literary theory headed? These questions converge on my thesis that the next step in world literature should be the activation of a world literary theory and world literary criticism. Those who profess world literature should be uncomfortable, as Revathi Krishnaswamy puts it, with "what we have today: world lit without world lit crit" (400). We should take cognizance, as Earl Miner did, that "critics aware of what goes on outside the European and North American parishes have taken offence at the imposition of 'western' literary culture on that variously termed 'eastern' or 'oriental'" (577), or "African," or "Latin American," and so forth. In this piece I explain the unease and the offense, adduce some examples of the kinds of thinking about literature that could be brought into the critical conversation, and in the end make a modest proposal in favor of more equal dialogue.

The unease

The heavily populated genre of reflexive writing about world literature – asking the questions of why, who (and for whom), what, and how far – has repeatedly emphasized the need to overcome Eurocentrism and to balance the playing field in terms of regions and languages considered worthy of study, translation, and anthologization. And demonstrably, the trend has been to broaden the scope of what is routinely included in anthologies, in syllabi, in published scholarship, and in MLA discussion groups. When one turns to the area of theory and criticism, on the other hand, the broadening of perspective has lagged behind in most syllabi and critical discussions; we are for the most part willing and able to engage only in "NATO theory and criticism," to coin a phrase after the acerbic epithet Werner Friederich once gave to world literature (78). We need an anthology of world literary theory and criticism that would supplement both the world literature anthologies and the *Norton Anthology of Literary Theory and Criticism*, which follows the NATO line in deciding what is of interest.

The *Norton Anthology* is designed to appeal to a variety of users and, more importantly, classroom adaptations: English professors, for example, need to be given enough material to adopt it for a course in the Anglo-American history of criticism, since such syllabi probably outnumber those addressing comparative criticism. This marketing consideration helps us understand why interest in world lit crit continues to lag so far behind the interest in world lit: literature anthologies can be adopted for undergraduate classes, which by now enjoy a long history and secure place in the North American academy. There is no such market for world lit crit. Furthermore, it can be argued that the success of world literature depends upon the development of a translational culture, resulting in a thick matrix of literary translations from which anthologizers and teachers can subsequently choose. The very first translation of a work is rarely satisfactory, but functions more like a first draft upon which subsequent translators can build, so that most later retranslations are palimpsestic. Yet with a few notable exceptions, such as the premodern Chinese poet-critic Lu Chi (also spelled "Lu Ji"), whose *Wen fu* (ca. 290 CE) has appeared in at least three different English versions, translational cultural capital has not been as heavily invested in theory and criticism over a sustained period. Even more broadly, the resistance to assembling a palette of exotic aesthetic objects pales beside the resistance to engaging with an aesthetics of the Other. There is at least some truth in Friedrich Nietzsche's critique of world literature, that it is a matter of placing ourselves as readers "mitten unter die Kunststile und Künstler aller Zeiten, damit [wir] ihnen wie Adam den Thieren, einen Namen geben" (Nietzsche 120; "in the midst of the art styles and artists of all ages, so that [we] may give names to them as Adam did to the beasts"). Rather than exercising our power of logos as Nietzsche describes it, engagement in world lit crit is a surrender of that power in favor of a dialogic process and a "thinking in radical exteriority" (Vallega x) which has been given the name "decolonial theory" (cf. Mignolo and Escobar).

Two momentous shifts in literary studies have happened at approximately the same time: Theory has been displaced as the dominant guidepost and arbiter for judging the validity of literary investigation; and world literature has emerged as an object of intense scrutiny and theorization.

The growth and expansion of world literature and of its subcategories (e.g., the Anglophone novel, hemispheric American studies, transatlantic and transpacific studies) are so perfectly timed against the shrinkage and redeployment of theory as to cause us to suspect a causal relationship. There are two possibilities for this: world literature killed theory; or theory was killed by the same cultural forces that are causing world literature to thrive (see Tiwari).

Untranslatables west and east

To speculate on the former, we may wish to consider the concept of untranslatability, central to Emily Apter's *Against World Literature*. In other words, as comparative literature enlarged its field beyond European and neo-European cultures, the concepts it deployed became less and less translatable into the languages and cultures of these new contexts. The earliest ACLA reports on the discipline of comparative literature – the so-called Levin and Greene Reports – discouraged comparatists' use of translations in teaching and research, which of course also put a damper on attempts at apprehending world literature. World literature seemed a utopian project, and was memorably belittled by Werner Friederich in his intimidating 1959 address, "On the Integrity of Our Planning," mentioned earlier.

By the mid-1990s, the who's-afraid-of-world-literature attitude, as well as the embargo on literature in translation, had disappeared from official discourse, only to resurface in Apter's critique of world literature. Apter's *pierre de touche* is the *Vocabulaire européen des philosophies: Dictionnaire des intraduisibles*, under the direction of Barbara Cassin. Now available in English translation (!), this dictionary is unusual in that it presents terms from different "Western" languages in the alphabetical order of their original language, or of their transliteration from that language in the case of Arabic, Greek, Hebrew, and Russian. This creates a kind of hierarchy of terms, and presents an interesting challenge for the user similar to navigating a postmodern narrative. So, for example, rather than English or French "image" or Greek "eidôlon," the German term "Bild" was chosen as the main entry for that concept, with its potential translations following the main entry. For some reason, French wins the battle for Romanticism with "romantique," and English for conformity with "standard." The editors wish to "constituer une cartographie des différences philosophiques européennes" (create a cartography of the differences between European philosophies) with this project. These differences arise, of course, from the untranslatability hidden in the listing of equivalent words. We know that Greek "eidôlon" is not an exact translation for German "Bild" in all situations, and the fact that four French terms (*image, tableau, figure, visage*) follow the German is also telling. At the same time, however, a thesaurus of quasi-equivalent terms in different languages is given for most concepts, which inevitably implies some degree of translatability.

One can certainly read through this lexicon with an eye to difference, but the mapping of terms and their coordination with each other also implies a certain solidarity and mutual comprehensibility. The *Dictionnaire*'s invocation of Europe is conceived with an admirable breadth: Arabic words head forty-five of the entries, for example, thus revealing the interconnections between Arabic and European philosophy – which brings me to my first example of the world lit crit shadow canon: the Greek works of Aristotle formed the basis for thinking in that language by Al-Farabi, Ibn Sina (Avicenna), Ibn Rushd (Averroes), and other thinkers of the *falsafa* who had a profound effect on European thought. Whenever I teach Aristotle's *Poetics* as theory at the graduate level, I also include portions of Ibn Rushd's *Middle Commentary* in the English translation by Charles Butterworth. When Ibn Rushd explains that tragic catharsis "makes souls become tender and prompts them to accept the virtues" (Averroes 93), or when the Arabic philosopher gives the story of Yussuf's (Joseph's) betrayals and redemption in Genesis and in the Qur'an as an example of tragedy, new possibilities inherent in Aristotle's compressed definition of the tragic genre are activated. Averroes's commentaries on all of Aristotle were translated into Hebrew and from Hebrew into Latin, in which form they influenced medieval European theophilosophy.

Returning to my discussion of the *Vocabulaire*: what if the adjective "européenes" in the dictionary title were to be replaced by "mondiales"? What if Chinese were to contribute the concepts of *li* and *wen*, Japanese the concept of *yūgen*, Sanskrit the concepts of *dhvani* and *rasa*? What would our *Dictionnaire de théorie mondiale* look like then?

Let us explore the untranslatability of a few of these terms, starting with *rasa*, an untranslatable that can be found in encyclopedias of world theater. Tom Stoppard inserted a monologue on it into his play *Indian Ink*, and it informs two essays in the collection *Suffering, Art, and Aesthetics* – one by Roma Chatterji on Bengali folk art concerned with the 2004 tsunami, and one by Michael Nijhawan and Anna C. Schultz on Sikh and Indo-Caribbean music and images of suffering. The former piece shows that *rasa* theory, despite its origins in Sanskrit classical literature, has a broad appeal to performers and artists, while the latter piece considers *rasa* to be "a rich tool for exploring the social formation of subjectivity" (197), an indication of the adaptability of the theory to contemporary concerns. A useful translation of the Sanskrit "rasa" for literature might be the word "essence," especially when used to refer to an aesthetically pleasing scent – something evanescent and volatile, much less tangible than the materials used to create it. V. K. Chari, in the book *Sanskrit Poetics*, on the other hand, translates the term as "aesthetic relish." This translation continues the implicit comparison with notions of taste, and it also corresponds to the previous meanings, given that the word "relish" is etymologically related to "release," as when the fruit under pressure releases its juice or essence.

For *rasa* theory, the essence of literature is a special kind of transpersonal emotion, and its job is to create this affect in the spectator or reader. Layering this connotation over the denotation, we conclude that *rasa* is the essence of feeling or emotion, made essential by being abstracted from reality. Thus Chari:

> As a general theory of literature, the rasa doctrine (rasa-vada) is based on two premises: (i) that literary works, as verbal compositions, express emotive meanings; and (ii) that all literature is typically emotive discourse or discourse that has to do with the portrayal of feelings and attitudes rather than with ideas, concepts, statements of universal truths, and so forth.
>
> (9)

The first explicator of *rasa* theory, Bharata, posited in his *Natya Shastra* forty-nine different human emotions, of which eight are stable, thirty-three transitory, and another eight psychosomatic (e.g., tears and goose bumps). From that point (ca. 100 BCE) forward, the dominant theory of classical Indian art has been that an artwork seeks to create in the experiencer one of the privileged eight emotions. A ninth, quietude, was added centuries later. These became, as a catalogue of a French exhibit of Indian art put it, "les neuf visages de l'art indien" (the nine faces of Indian art). There is nothing chaotic or unnameable about emotion in this system; everything can be made to fit into this complex vocabulary, and reactions to certain stimuli, called *vibhavas*, are entirely predictable. Also, certain emotions (except quietude) are complementary and can exist in tandem, whereas others cancel each other out. The Indian philosopher Krishnachandra

Bhattacharyya sought in 1930 to explain the concept of *rasa* in English, making direct use neither of the most prominent Sanskrit texts nor of the Kantian aesthetic philosophy that undoubtedly influenced his understanding of the idea, but rather speaking directly to the phenomenon with his own examples and vocabulary. Bhattacharyya gives the following example:

> I may . . . enjoy contemplating an old man affectionately watching his grandchild playing with a toy. Contrast here the child's joy in the toy with the grandfather's sympathetic joy and this again with my contemplative joy. Although the old man is not immersed like the child in the enjoyment of the toy, his feeling is not yet of the artistic character: it is still a personal, selective interest in the particular child and his feeling. My contemplative joy has no such personal complexion. I am interested in the child's feeling reflected in the grand-father's heart as an eternal emotion or value. I enjoy the essence of the emotion, get immersed in it even like the child in the toy, without, however, being affected by it and thus losing my freedom. I no longer feel the distinction between my feeling and the child's feeling, as the old man does between his feeling and the child's feeling. My personality is, as it were, dissolved and yet I am not caught in the object like the child. I freely become impersonal.
>
> (198)

We could say that in this example the child corresponds to the character in a play, the grandfather to the actor, and the observing "I" to the audience member. Bhattacharya's formulation of a nontraditional explanation of *rasa*, equally free of both the complex web of Sanskrit terminology used to anchor the term and any explicit comparison with Kantian aesthetics, is an interesting example of world literary theory, where "West" and "East" engage in dialogue.

An analogous translation difficulty surfaces in an attempt to give the Japanese term *yūgen* an entry in our hypothetical world-theoretical dictionary. The two parts of this compound word together mean something like "cloudy impenetrability," indicating the aesthetic impression of seeing the moon through clouds, or a path to the teahouse partly obscured by fallen leaves. Henry W. Wells gives the following translations: "understatement, intimation, elegance, aristocratic grace, composure, equilibrium, serenity, and quietism" (264). The options here range from the unproblematically tangible (aristocratic grace, which brushes up against the European idea of decorum) to the ungraspable – "intimation" indicates an aesthetic perception that arises when something is not stated or shown, like hiding the monster or slasher in a thriller movie, or more subtly in Zeami's instructions to the Noh actor, "feel ten while showing seven." "Grace" is the translation used by Thomas Rimer and Yamazaki Masakazu in their volume of Zeami's works (Thomas Hare, on the other hand, simply calls *yūgen* untranslatable).

The author most responsible for creating a coherent and sustained discussion of *yūgen* in Japanese aesthetics is Zeami Motokiyo (1363–1444), who shaped the Noh theater into the form still performed today. As a theatrical idea, Zeami used *yūgen* to supplement *monomane*, a term roughly equivalent to mimesis. The goal of the actor was now to intimate and to suggest, rather than simply to mime, and the highest level of performance was one where the actor's concentration was able to gather the audience's intention into a single purpose, often at a point in the performance where the actor was "doing nothing." I quote here from the opening of the "Kyūi," translated as "Nine Levels" or "Nine Ranks." That the term *yūgen* is absent from this description of the highest "flower" obtainable by the Noh actor, the "wondrous flower," is perhaps due to the fact that the concept is encompassed by the entire quotation:

> Silla, midnight: the sun is bright. What I mean by wonder pertains to the severing of the path of language, and foundering of the operations of the mind. Is the sun at midnight a matter to which language can aspire? How does that happen? So then, the sublime effect of a true master in this vocation is beyond the reach of appreciation, an excitement that transcends the mind, a vision apart effected by the caliber of no-rank must most surely be the wondrous flower.
>
> (Zeami, *Performance Notes* 193)

The opening is typical of Zen koans, the verbal puzzles or paradoxes given to students in order to free their minds from received patterns of thought. There follows the typical Zen admonishment to "sever the path of language," whose assumption that the highest aesthetic experience begins where language leaves off reminds me of deconstruction, and thus also of one of the other few attempts at linking Western contemporary theory with another part of the world, the formidable *Derrida on the Mend*, by Robert Magliola. As the levels descend from peak to more ordinary performance, the koans get easier and easier, as the acting talents become easier to achieve. Delightful as it is, the "Kyūi" shares a difficulty with much premodern criticism due to its focus on performance: it is not about how to write a poem, but how to perform a poem transcendentally.

I wish to close my examples with a very brief mention of theory from Latin America, not just for the sake of geopoetic equity but also because my examples so far may have given the impression that I find only premodern and telluric traditions to be worthy sources for the construction of world lit crit. Surveying the vast output of theory and criticism from Latin America, our eye might fall first on the untranslatable "transculturación" invented in 1947 by the Cuban thinker Fernando Ortiz, and intended to express the idea that the various acculturations carried out on such a gigantic scale and at such a rapid pace in the Americas necessarily involved an equal portion of deculturation (Ortiz 103). Transculturation has not only become a keyword in hemispheric American literary criticism but also made its way into standard dictionaries, such as that of the Real Academia Española. Transculturation then leads to other prominent themes of Latin American theory and criticism, such as the preoccupation with the role that literature might play in the imagined community of nation. We see this theme, for example, in the work of the Peruvian José Carlos Mariátegui, who argued that since *mestizaje* had failed to produce a single national type in Peru, Peruvian literature would need to move forward through cosmopolitanism. The theme of nationalism constantly invokes its dialectical inversion, whether as a plea for local treatment of the universal, as in Machado de Assis's "Literatura brasileira: Instinto de nacionalidade" (*Brazilian Literature: The Instinct of Nationality*, 1873) and in Jorge Luis Borges's "El escritor argentino y la tradición" (1951; "The Argentine Writer and Tradition") or as an analysis of the dysphoria caused in literature by weak national institutions in Antônio Cândido's "Literature and Underdevelopment." I have only scratched the surface on writing that could usefully be brought into dialogue, in my opinion, with the by-now classics of post-colonial theory and criticism. Yet not a single theorist from Latin American has been included in either the Norton anthology or in *Global Literary Theory*, not to mention in their "predecessor" anthologies, such as Hazard Adams's *Literary Theory since Plato*.

A modest proposal

To repeat the point with which I began, not a single word of any of this thinking about literature, not a single untranslatable term of world lit crit, has found its way into Leitch's *Norton Anthology* or into the Routledge compendium entitled *Global Literary Theory*, edited by Richard Lane. The idea of a "global literary theory" that reflects nothing more than the rest of the world's ability to mimic the language of "Western" theory is disturbing and worthy of counterdiscourse.

Admittedly, we cannot assess the status of a field solely by its major anthologies, and I should mention some examples of world lit crit occurring in other contexts. Major reference works, for example, have sought to be more inclusive. *The Princeton Encyclopedia of Poetry and Poetics*, in its third edition under Alex Preminger, did have an entry for "Rasa," which referred the reader to the information on "Indian Poetics," which is flanked by analogous articles on "Arabic Poetics," "Chinese Poetics," and so forth. The fourth edition, edited by Roland Greene, has gone even further in this regard, adding a full entry for Bharata's concept of "dhvani." The table of contents for the online version of the *Johns Hopkins Guide to Literary Theory and Criticism* lists entries such as "African Theory and Criticism," "Arabic Theory and Criticism," "Caribbean Theory and Criticism" (which treats the region as a plurilingual cultural space and critiques noncomparative approaches to its literatures), "Chinese Theory and Criticism," "Indian Theory and Criticism," "Latin American Theory and Criticism," and even an article on the criticism and theory of Nigerian Wole Soyinka. Nor am I the only teacher to think that comparative theory and criticism should go global, as the syllabus entitled "The Anthropology of Literary Culture" posted to the ACLA State of the Discipline website shows.

My proposal, then, makes three overlapping suggestions: one, literary theory should understand itself in the same expansive and cosmopolitan ways that world literature does. No teacher of world literature should think that the flow of literary ideas and forms in general moves only in one direction (though it may do so for particular forms or genres at specific points in time), nor that one corner of the globe has the "correct" take on a literary form – so why should we be content with allowing theory and criticism to be conceived of so provincially? Two, the vocabulary of theory and criticism should be expanded to include *rasa*, *yūgen*, and other terms. And three, the pedagogy of world literature should include some world lit crit as a metadiscourse that disrupts the homogeneity created by translation of the Babelian heterogeneity of world literature into a single language and the preformation of our interests by the predilections of a global literary marketplace.

The second part of my proposal calls for anthologies of criticism and theory that are formulated on the same ideas of balance and comprehensiveness as are our current anthologies of world literature. I admit to not being the first to contemplate such a project. Revathi Krishnaswamy, whose article gave me the term "world lit crit," tells the tale of asking Jonathan Culler why increased interest in world literature had not brought with it a concomitant interest in "world poetics" or "world literary theory"? Culler, whose bestselling *Literary Theory: A Very Short Introduction* also confines itself to European and North American contributions, suggested that Krishnaswamy write to Norton proposing such an anthology. She did, and received no response (Krishnaswamy 400). My own story is either more tragic or more hopeful than this. The humanities editor of a highly reputable academic press who visits the MLA every year expressed an interest in getting onto the world literature bandwagon, and could I help? I explained to her that my own interest coincided with hers to the extent that I have been revealing to you here. She asked for a proposal, but we appear to have misunderstood each other. I wanted to put together a truly global anthology of literature and criticism that would use the expertise of subeditors based in the various parts of the world outside of Europe and North America. My story is more hopeful in that my proposal was dignified with a reply. More tragic because in the end I was reminded of the truth of Herman Melville's useful phrase, "I am damned by dollars!" Or pounds, really, or euros, or bitcoin. My editor noted the cost of the translations and the permissions involved in putting together an anthology of this sort, which would not be justified by its sales. The immense glory and prestige of a state-of-the-art anthology of world lit crit do not compensate for the material loss incurred by the press in producing it.

But someday, somehow, somewhere, on someone's dime, I believe that this anthology, or several anthologies and intercultural dictionaries, will come into existence. I emphasize the need for an anthology of world lit crit because, while I have explicated individual lexical items in the foregoing, a lexicon does not exist in and for itself, but calls for syntagmatic embodiment. Indeed, the entries of the *Vocabulaire* consist not of simple definitions but of sustained and at times polemical philosophical argument. Anandavardhana, Ibn Rushd, Lu Chi, Zeami, and others confront their Western readers not just with additional arguments but also with alternative modalities for speculating on literature and aesthetics. What might result from this comparative exercise is hinted at, I think, in the Bhattacharyya essay mentioned earlier, but also, for example, in Hélène Cixous's theoretical exposition of the poetics of Brazilian author Clarice Lispector, and in some of the comparisons of Chinese with Western aesthetics in Li Zehou's work.

I would wager that most readers of this report would agree with the hypothesis that the world will be more, rather than less, connected one hundred years hence. And most readers of this report are aware of the contingent nature of history, which implies that the cultural scenarios a century from now will look very different than they do today. Regardless of whether the pillars of my particular modest proposal are realized, I would hope that in the future the recolonization of the mind via theory that we see today will be replaced by more balanced critical and theoretical fusions, exchanges, and mutual enlightenment, some of which are already occurring.

Works cited

Anandavardhana. *Dhvanyaloka of Anandavhardana with the Locana of Abhinav-agupta.* Trans. Daniel H. H. Ingalls, Jeffery Moussaieff Masson, and M. V. Patwardhan. Ed. Daniel H. H. Ingalls. Cambridge, MA: Harvard UP, 1990. Print.

Apter, Emily. *Against World Literature.* New York: Verso, 2013. Print.

Averroes [Ibn Rushd]. *Middle Commentary on Aristotle's Poetics.* Trans. Charles Butterworth. Princeton: Princeton UP, 1986. Print.

Avicenna [Ibn Sina]. *Commentary of the Poetics of Aristotle: A Critical Study with an Annotated Translation of the Text.* Trans. Ismail M. Dahiyat. Leiden: Brill, 1974. Print.

Bhattacharyya, Krishnachandra. "The Concept of Rasa." *Indian Philosophy in English: From Renaissance to Independence.* Ed. Nalini Bhushan and Jay L. Garfield. New York: Oxford UP, 2011. 195–206. Print.

Borges, Jorge Luis. "The Argentine Writer and Tradition." *Selected Non-Fictions.* Ed. Eliot Weinberger. Trans. Esther Allen, Suzanne Jill Levine, and Eliot Weinberger. New York: Viking, 1999. 420–27. Print.

Cândido, Antônio. "Literature and Underdevelopment." *The Latin American Cultural Studies Reader.* Ed. Ana del Sarto, Alicia Ríos, and Abril Trigo. Durham, NC: Duke UP, 2004. 35–57. Print.

Cassin, Barbara, ed. *Dictionary of Untranslatables: A Philosophical Lexicon.* Trans. Steven Rendall, Christian Hubert, Jeffrey Mehlman, Nathaniel Stein, and Michael Syrotinski. Ed. Emily Apter, Jacques Lezra, and Michael Wood. Princeton: Princeton UP, 2014. Print.

———. *Vocabulaire européen des philosophies: Dictionnaire des intraduisibles.* Paris: Le Robert/Seuil, 2004. Print.

Chari, V. K. *Sanskrit Criticism.* Honolulu: University of Hawaii Press, 1990. Print.

Chatterji, Roma. "Event, Image, Affect: The Tsunami in the Folk Art of Bengal." *Suffering, Art, and Aesthetics.* Ed. Ratiba Hadj-Moussa and Michael Nijhawan. New York: Palgrave Macmillan, 2014. 75–98. Print.

Cixous, Hélène. *Reading with Clarice Lispector.* Trans. Verena Andermatt Conley. Minneapolis: U of Minnesota P, 1990. Print.

Culler, Jonathan. *Literary Theory: A Very Short Introduction.* 2nd ed. New York: Oxford UP, 2011. Print.

Friederich, Werner P. "On the Integrity of Our Planning." *World Literature: A Reader.* Ed. Theo D'haen, César Domínguez and Mads Rosendahl Thomsen. New York: Routledge, 2013. 74–82. Print.

Greene, Roland, ed. *The Princeton Encyclopedia of Poetry and Poetics.* 4th ed. Princeton: Princeton UP, 2012. Print.

Krishnaswamy, Revathi. "Toward World Literary Knowledges: Theory in the Age of Globalization." *Comparative Literature* 62 (2010): 399–419. Print.

Lane, Richard J., ed. *Global Literary Theory: An Anthology.* New York: Routledge, 2013. Print.

Li Zehou. *The Chinese Aesthetic Tradition.* Trans. Marija Bell Samei. Honolulu: U of Hawaii P, 2010. Print.

Lu Chi. *The Art of Writing.* Trans. Sam Hamill. Minneapolis: Milkweed, 2000. Print.

Machado de Assis, Joaquim Maria. "Notícia da atual literatura brasileira: Instinto de nacionalidade." *Obra Completa.* 4 vols. Rio de Janeiro: Nova Aguilar, 1973. 3: 801–9. Print.

Magliola, Robert. *Derrida on the Mend.* West Lafayette, IN: Purdue UP, 1984. Print.

Mariátegui, José Carlos. *Seven Interpretive Essays on Peruvian Reality.* Trans. Marjorie Urquidi. Austin: U of Texas P, 1988. Print.

Mignolo, Walter, and Arturo Escobar, eds. *Globalization and the Decolonial Option.* New York: Routledge, 2015. Print.

Miner, Earl. "Why Lyric?" *The Lyric Theory Reader: A Critical Anthology.* Ed. Virginia Jackson and Yopie Prins. Baltimore: Johns Hopkins, 2014. 577–88. Print.

Nietzsche, Friedrich. 1872. *Die Geburt der Tragödie aus dem Geiste der Musik: Kritische Studienausgabe 1.* Ed. G. Colli and M. Montinari. Munich: DTV/de Gruyter, 1980. 9–156. Print.

Nijhawan, Michael, and Anna C. Schultz. "The Diasporic Rasa of Suffering: Notes on the Aesthetics of Image and Sound in Indo-Caribbean and Sikh Popular Art." *Suffering, Art, and Aesthetics.* Ed. Ratiba Hadj-Moussa and Michael Nijhawan. New York: Palgrave Macmillan, 2014. 177–205. Print.

Ortiz, Fernando. *Cuban Counterpoint: Tobacco and Sugar.* Trans. Harriet de Onís. Durham, NC: Duke UP, 1995. Print.

Preminger, Alex, ed. *The Princeton Encyclopedia of Poetry and Poetics.* 3rd ed. Princeton: Princeton UP, 2000. Print.

Rasa, les neuf visages de l'art indien: Galeries nationales du Grand Palais, 13 mars–16 juin 1986. Paris: Association française d'action artistique, 1986. Print.

Rimer, Thomas J., and Yamazaki Masakazu, trans. *On the Art of Nō Drama: The Major Treatises of Zeami.* Princeton: Princeton UP, 1984. Print.

Tiwari, Bhavya. "The Death of Theory and the Birth of New Comparative Literature." MLA Convention, Boston MA, 2013. Presentation.

Vallega, Alejandro A. *Latin American Philosophy: From Identity to Radical Exteriority.* Bloomington: Indiana UP, 2015. Print.

Zeami Motokiyo. *Performance Notes.* Trans. Tom Hare. New York: Columbia UP, 2008. Print.

Minimal criticism

Jos Lavery

Ten years ago to the week in which I wrote this, "thefacebook.com" went online, offering those with university affiliations the opportunity to craft, in prose and in lists, what Judith Butler might not call "an account of oneself." But accounts they were, initially expressed through discrete profiles to be visited, and becoming gradually more social: in "news feeds," a feature added in 2006, the profiles began to talk to each other, establishing etiquette and ethics, co-negotiators of a social contract determined less by subjects encapsulated within identities than by a flow of images, events, language. The profile mutated into a Wall, in 2008, a *tabula rasa* on which Lockean consciousness might inscribe its remarks, and then into a Timeline, in 2011, through which Shandean consciousness could broadcast the inadequacy of linear biographical narration. In 2009, news feeds became public and statuses promotable – this latter because, as everybody knows, Facebook has yet to determine how best to monetize its assets. The company's difficulty underlines what is already obvious to every user of Facebook: that, far from enabling the self-expression of its users, the news feed has acquired a life of its own – we run things, but the things also run us. It is a glossary for a text that could not exist, *un dictionnaire des idées impossibles*. More vaguely, and truer: the short-form "status updates" that it comprises feel as far away and as near as a Barthesian *haiku*:

> You are entitled, says the haiku, to be trivial, short, ordinary; enclose what you see, what you feel, in a slender horizon of words, and you will be interesting; you yourself (and starting from yourself) are entitled to establish your own notability; your sentence, whatever it may be, will enunciate a moral, will liberate a symbol, you will be profound: at the least possible cost, your writing will be *filled*.
>
> (Barthes 70)

Some thoughts emerge from this narrative that might have bearing on the discipline of comparative literature in 2025 – without it being necessary to assume that the decoupling of the profile from the news feed is irreversible. But before mentioning a few, I will just declare that I treat as axiomatic that the word "discipline," designating as it already does a socialized process of individuation, must include not just the quasi-public objects with which we are beginning to grapple (Twitter, para-academic blogs, the online version of this ACLA report) but also the quasi-private objects that we generally prefer to let rest unexpressed (Facebook, the hotel bar). This axiom might have some general applicability, but it is especially important for the discussion of comparative literature. First, the social conditions out of which our methods emerged have been privileged objects of study themselves at various points in our history. As Haun Saussy puts it, "If the specific object of comparative literature is not found in the thematic content of works, perhaps it lies in a dimension of which works and their contents are only symptoms" (14). Auerbach's *Mimesis* is not just a study of the canon but also an account of the conditions under which *any* canon might be recognizable as such – an ideological finesse that partly explains why the idea of a canon remains indispensable decades after it has been, apparently, discredited. Recent debates over world literature (Apter; Hayot) and over the viability of comparison as grounds for argumentation (Cheah; Felski and Friedman) situate the methodologies of literary studies in relation to histories of empire, emigration, professionalization.

Quite right: but in an age where those histories are lived through what I have called the quasi-private, so should be the institutional critique. The private should be especially important to members of this association because of the extraordinary recent growth of its conference (see "Facts and Figures," this volume), a source of pride and anxiety for the ACLA. The ACLA Convention brings together scholars from a variety of different fields and periods, and so, it is sometimes argued, risks losing its principle of cohesion. The growth appears to some a kind of newsfeedification of the academic conference: rendering relatively marginal discrete profiles of workshops, panels, keynotes, and other formal addresses, these events take on a life of their own in which the temporary cohabitation of social space becomes the reason for gathering. I am quite comfortable – maybe more comfortable than not – with a conference whose bonds are relatively loose, but which places me in conversation (literal, not figurative!) with scholars I would otherwise never meet. Just as well because that, I suspect, is part of the future of comparative literature.

Still, more with *a descriptive than a normative aspect*, here are some modes of comparative literary study that I take to be in the ascendency.

Distractions

We evoke delay when discussing reading practices: we "tarry," we "stay with," we "maintain close contact with"; the textual effect may "remain," may be a "trace." These words are legacies of a deconstructive critical practice that entailed (and perhaps valorized) an aesthetics of immobility, and found in various evocations of slowness a responsible textual politics. Such, in John Guillory's argument, was the rhetorical style that encoded theory-speak as professional expertise. But this style operates differently at the moment of multitabbed browsing and social media, when the difference between tarrying with something and rushing headlong into it is increasingly difficult to determine. Flipping between documents and tabs is a form of channel-surfing that in fact pulls us away from the deconstructive mode of delay-as-aporia and into a mode of distraction and disinclination. Though Wai Chee Dimock understands the "weak theory" she elaborates as an inheritance from Robert Boyle, one might see argumentative "leakiness" as a product not of seventeenth-century empiricism but of a writing subject that cannot stop itself from dissolving into Facebook from time to time. And this, too, is a comparative mode, if by "comparative" we mean nonsingular, nonsovereign: describing two leaky chains of literary-historical association (Colm Tóibín à Henry James; James à W. B. Yeats), Dimock writes,

> my hope is that, in attending to both these networks – as equal probabilities distributively scattered, not linearly entailed, and not hierarchically ranked either – literary history might be more easily conceived as a nonsovereign field, with site-specific input generating a variable morphology, a variable ordering principle.
>
> (738)

Hashtags

In 2013, the hashtag became a common function of indexical speech, but it also, in some sense, *arrived*. 2013 was not the year in which the term first appeared; Wikipedia tells me that it originates from the C programming language, developed in the late 1970s. But it was the year in which the word was spoken out loud, across a wide array of cultural spaces, and attained a highly unusual status in spoken English: from a common noun, it morphed into a punctuational phoneme, a voiced paratext. A commercial for Subway's Tuscan Chicken Melt sandwich encapsulated why this was important, for comparative literature and for the institutional structures that support it. A white, button-down-shirted Subway customer on his lunch break is so excited about his sandwich that he Instagrams it, and vocalizes his hashtags as he enters them into his smartphone. "Hashtag delicious, hashtag low-fat," he witters on for seventeen inglorious seconds, irritating both the viewer and his Asian American companion, apparently a coworker with whom he is passing a lunch break. Our annoyance is directed partly at the adoption IRL (in real life) of a glossary best suited to online discourse, but also because the character reproduces diachronically (by droning *on*) a technique best experienced synchronically (at a glance), in the process accidentally publicizing the fact that the adverts themselves are experienced as aporetic dead time, interruptions in the program you are trying to watch. The man's time-wasting phone fetishism is a good example of procrastination: hashtagging represents an activity indispensable to the reproduction of academic labor, and indeed that of the increasing number of white-collar laborers who "work from home," with whatever attendant sense of postspatial mobility, bedsit isolation, social deprivation, egoistic self-determination. Within the diegetic frame, though, the character meets a more practical comeuppance: we see, long before he does, that his Asian American colleague has taken the sandwich off the table and is eating it himself. This second man then proclaims the moral to the first, and the viewer: "hashtag you snooze you lose!"

At first glance, this was nothing but a paranoid fantasy about Asian productivity and American decline. Everything is usurped in the zero-sum game of the labor market, not only the commodity but also the textual forms of American corporate culture: "you snooze you lose." The Asian sidekick reveals himself as the sur-reptitious protagonist, just as Asian capital assumes the threatening role it did in Mitt Romney's "Stand Up to China" commercial (to take a memorable recent example of a long-standing trope of American Orientalism), in which a voice-over claims that under Obama, "China is stealing American ideas." But that first read-ing will only get us so far. What the Subway commercial formalizes is a new form of nostalgia that plays with and as the hashtag: not an imaginary nostalgia for a time one never inhabited – as with the sitcom *Happy Days* – but a prospective nostalgia that precedes, and can therefore prohibit, the pleasure of consumption. This form of longing looks a bit like Freudian cathexis: it produces high-intensity pleasure and inhibits longer-duration intimacy. But it is distinct. The glory of the commodity, crucial though it is for the Subway customer's affect, is less rich to him than the admiration that his friends (or coworkers) will express in response to the photograph, and which will vicariously transfer onto him. What he wants is fundamentally social, and closer to an anal neurosis than a narcissistic one: his <3 belongs to Instagram. Notice that from this perspective, it does not matter in the least that the sandwich was taken away. If anything, it makes his plot more interest-ing and furnishes him with more online prestige. The attention economy, with its own archive of "big data" and its own methods of generating value, refashions the desires, and so the neuroses, of its incorporated nodes.

Wikipedia

Okay, this one is normative: by 2025, I hope, we will have collectively worked out how best to use and cite Wikipedia. Our refusal to do so can be predicated only on the assumption that knowledge production requires, if not an actual author, at least a figure whose author function can be provisionally stabilized by an authority like "Oxford," "Pears," or "Webster." This assumption is no longer defensible for any humanistic discipline, but surely not for one of which "what most needs to be preserved . . . is *metadisciplinarity*," as Saussy so aptly claims (23). It was a rather depressing moment when I realized that there was almost no subject on which I knew *more* than Wikipedia. There are a handful of pages against which I would take my own knowledge over the wisdom of the crowd – those on subjects for which I have myself written encyclopedia entries, *for sure*. And then there is certainly a larger number of topics about which I know some-thing, but for which there is at present no entry. I am not overly bothered about it anymore. My disciplinary training has furnished me with plenty of advantages over an online encyclopedia, and I have learned to live with the castration of my social performance of expertise. If we play the robots at their own game, we're going to lose. But given the work Wikipedia does for me, in my research as well as my teaching, and given how rewarding and pleasurable that work frequently is, it is time to give the devil his due.

Minimal criticism

Against the minimally persuasive empiricism evoked by Dimock via Boyle, one might set the maximally persuasive empiricism evoked by Franco Moretti via Darwin. Maximally persuasive, but minimal nonetheless. Moretti says, everywhere, that change is incremental, contingent, and slow – lots and lots of work will yield precious little workable analysis. One does not find in any of his books, as is sometimes irresponsibly claimed against him, any kind of data-fitting; his Eurocentrism, if that is an appropriate term, is as critical as it is polemical. But what James F. English so beautifully calls the "Morettian picaresque" inheres in its optimistic, gamesome attitude toward data: "things can be counted on to go wrong," says English, "but never so wrong as to deter the protagonist from embarking on further adventures" (English). Moretti's *maximalism* – that sublime, exhilarating feeling he cannot not generate – derives neither from the enormity of his data sets nor from any emphasis placed on one or another claim. The claims themselves are always midpoints in an extensible series. On the other hand, I think we should also avoid simplistic oppositions of quantitative and qualitative modes of analysis. After all, Freud's "oceanic feeling" is properly speaking a feeling of quantity, an aesthetic cognition that closely relates the full experience of a perceived object to the experience of its essential irrelevance in a larger field. On the other hand, Moretti insists on the relevance of the part to the whole, even and especially as their precise relationship becomes increasingly difficult to describe.

I have been describing an institution that exists in a number of different places, and whose institutional viability derives from both its diffuseness and its tendency to become more diffuse. There are those for whom such a literary studies would be affectively marked as lethargic – as for the Bruno Latour of "Why Has Critique Run Out of Steam?" There are others, such as Lauren Berlant in "Structures of Unfeeling," for whom this minimal criticism might afford particular access to the flat political affects of the postindustrial, and indeed postfinancial, global arrangement of power. Partly in order to distinguish minimal criticism from a lack of criticism, then, let me finish with this: that there is something sickeningly loathsome about this exercise – chasing one's thoughts down another decade in which most will grow older and the rest will die. The very corporate slogans I have been evoking, the brand names I have been using, are slightly revolting to me – think of a book stitched from human faces, or imagine your voice coming from a bird's throat, a tweet from your own. Icky, though, rather than terrifying. If the first decade of the twenty-first century was, as is so often asserted, the era of apocalyptic dystopia – of *The Matrix*, *Left Behind*, and *No Future* – then this second one would be the decade of queasy futurity – of *Captain America: Civil War*, *Her*, and *Cruel Optimism*. And while the suggestions listed earlier are entirely falsifiable, I do think we overestimate the ephemerality of technological forms, the rapidity with which they are replaced. Hashtags, again, are older than me. The neoliberal narrative of permanent acceleration is one that comparative literature, with its tendencies toward recondite formalism and its intimate affective *habitus*, is capable of resisting.

Works cited

Apter, Emily. *Against World Literature: On the Politics of Untranslatability*. London: Verso, 2013. Print.

Barthes, Roland. *Empire of Signs*. Trans. Richard Howard. New York: Farrar, Straus, and Giroux, 1982. Print.

Berlant, Lauren. "Structures of Unfeeling: *Mysterious Skin*." *International Journal of Politics, Culture, and Society* 28.3 (2015): 191–213. Print.

Cheah, Pheng. *What Is a World? On Postcolonial Literature as World Literature*. Durham: Duke UP, 2016. Print.

Dimock, Wai Chee. "Weak Theory: Henry James, Colm Tóibín, and W.B. Yeats." *Critical Inquiry* 39 (2013): 732–53. Print.

English, James F. "Morettian Picaresque." Rev. of *Distant Reading*, by Franco Moretti. *Los Angeles Review of Books* (27 June 2013). Web. 1 Mar. 2015.

Felski, Rita, and Susan Stanford Friedman, eds. *Comparison: Theories, Approaches, Uses*. Baltimore: Johns Hopkins UP, 2013. Print.

Guillory, John. *Cultural Capital*. Chicago: U of Chicago P, 1993. Print.

Hayot, Eric. *On Literary Worlds*. Oxford: Oxford UP, 2012. Print.

Latour, Bruno. "Why Has Critique Run Out of Steam? From Matters of Fact to Matters of Concern." *Critical Inquiry* 30 (2004): 225–48. Print.

Saussy, Haun. "Exquisite Cadavers from Fresh Nightmares: Of Memes, Hives, and Selfish Genes." *Comparative Literature in an Age of Globalization*. Ed. Haun Saussy. Baltimore: Johns Hopkins UP, 2006. 3–42. Print.

"Stand Up to China." Mitt Romney's Channel, You Tube. 24 September 2012. http://www.youtube.com/watch?v=TRViUQntMfs

"Subway Commercial – hashtag." YouTube. 30 September 2013. http://www.youtube.com/watch?v=abkVrXLzvPU

Philology

Timothy Brennan

Theory dismisses philology with a wave of the hand for naively believing in truth, being hung up on interpretation, having the bad taste to think that meticulous reading produces specific meaning, believing authors' intentions matter. The received portrait, taken straight from Nietzsche, is unflattering: the pseudoscholarly machinery of a spent method, the tedious sifting of editions, the misguided search for sources, the vast linguistic architecture, the craze for minutiae, addiction to dead languages, documentary mastery over the soul of the Orient, talk of the vernacular hiding its real love (written documents), the literary nationalism of the "people," the pretensions to science.

But what is wrong with this picture? What did comparative literature do over the last four decades but flee philology in the foregoing spirit? And if so, then why are our dominant theories in comparative literature precisely about "linguistic architecture" – a *langue* based on dead languages, textual fixations, and the governing laws of modernist form? Why is it all about written language over a supposed bias toward the oral? About an obsequious devotion to science found in structuralism, chaos theory, rhizomatics, histories without subjects, fractals, and (more lately) distant reading and the digital humanities?

Philology, it turns out – in its modern eighteenth-century origins, its nineteenth-century putrescence, and its current resurgence – is everything comparative literature has always struggled over, failed to recognize in itself, or busily (and impossibly) tried to abandon. In Herder (*not* Goethe), philology gives us world literature and incipient postcolonial theory; in Vico, radical sociology, anthropological linguistics, and the first historical materialism; in Leo Wiener, the case for an African new world; in Gramsci, a scathing critique of calligraphic textual ontology and modernist elitism; in Volosinov, a paean to the orality of peripheral cultures; in Said, a humanistic riposte to the scientizing of the humanities where authorship matters (as *authority*) and sources are vital as consciously chosen influences and lineages rather than anonymous epistemes.

Paul de Man, in "The Return to Philology" (1986), trying to head off Said's revival, persuades theory to dispense with philology. In the early 2000s, philology is taken up again in high-profile journal articles and experimental "avant"-books as though its historical backwash were lapping against postmodern shores. Classicists, Sanskritists, and polyglots complain, territorially, that philology has been diluted by amateurs, and too freely applied to the likes of Auerbach, Spitzer, and other erudites who know nothing of textual recension or comparative linguistics. Then come the *neo*-philologists who want to get rid of philology, hating herme-neutics and critical thought, seeing reading, in a narrow "materialism" derived from the sciences, as ontological "experience" (Gumbrecht 1, 7).

But the earlier tradition (Vichian, Herderian) won't die. Like Georges Sorel against turn-of-the-century positivism, it reasserts itself, not as an anatomy of texts but as what Vico calls "the doctrine of all the institutions that depend on *human choice* . . . all histories of the languages, customs, and deeds of peoples in war and peace" (6). Philology mounts a protest against the divisions of academic labor. Auerbach's definition: "the whole story in the strict sense . . . the only sci-ence that includes a *general social theory*" (23). It forces Europe to learn modesty by studying immanently, not normatively, others' civilizations. Gramsci calls it "scrupulous accuracy and scientific honesty" in dealing with an author's writing, searching for "*the rhythm of the thought*" rather than "isolated quotations" (137). Philology in the end is what theory cannot live up to: not symptomatic reading, not "reading against the grain," not reader-response or any other alibi for mak-ing things up or appropriating authors for political purposes to make them mean the opposite of what they say – "creatively." Philology does not deny ambiguity and ambivalence, but neither does it make them its telos as theory does. It stands for the labor of learning instead of the rhetorical lure of the latest market pose.

Works cited

Auerbach, Erich. "Vorrede des Übersetzers." *Die Neue Wissenschaft über die gemein-schaftliche Natur der Völker.* Ed. Giambattista Vico. Munich: Allgemeine Verlagan-stalt, 1924. 7–24. Print.

De Man, Paul. "The Return to Philology." *Resistance to Theory.* Minneapolis: U of Minnesota P, 1986. 21–5. Print.

Gramsci, Antonio. *Prison Notebooks.* Vol. 2. Ed. and Trans. Joseph A. Buttigieg. New York: Columbia UP, 1996. Print.

Gumbrecht, Hans Ulrich. *The Powers of Philology: Dynamics of Literary Scholarship.* Urbana, IL: U of Illinois P, 2003. Print.

Vico, Giambattista. *The New Science.* Trans. Thomas Goddard Bergin and Max Har-old Fisch. 1948. Ithaca: Cornell UP, 1968. Print.

Comparative literature and affect theory

A conversation with R. A. Judy and Rei Terada

Jessica Berman

BERMAN: In the past decade, comparative literature has undergone what some might call an "affective turn" – spurred in part by Rei Terada's book *Feeling in Theory: Emotion after the "Death of the Subject."* How might we understand the importance of that turn? More specifically, given Rei's argument about the role of feeling after the death of the subject, how might we understand emotion beyond or without expression and what are its implications for reading imaginative literature from a planetary, comparative perspective?

TERADA: I'd locate an "affective turn" in the United States around 1997, in work including, prominently, Adela Pinch's *Strange Fits of Passion: Epistemologies of Emotion, Hume to Austen.* My impression is that, in recent years, affect is thought, in a Spinozan-Deleuzian way, to be the nonsubjective component of emotion, whereas my point was that in the supposed centers of humanist subjectivity – emotion and reason – there is no subjectivity, either. For me, affect conceived of as free-able from ideology and interpretation, in contrast to emotion conceived as entangled with them, is universalized and thereby removed from the political (and the more than political). Affect becomes a vital or economic flow that may cause or illuminate political friction but isn't able to be seen as itself a variably ideological construct. From the perspective of the nonsubjectivity of rationality and emotion, then, a lot of the affective turn is problematic – it recovers universalist "agency" in nonsubjective guise and leaves humanist subjectivity intact in a separate sphere. That's problematic no matter how liberatory the rhetoric – or maybe more so, the more liberatory the rhetoric. Since I was arguing that there is no nonemotional social or linguistic phenomenon, I was asking for an autocritique regarding what people were already doing (e.g., typing things as emotive or not emotive), not calling for an affective turn that would strengthen the illusory separation.

Comparative literature has more potential for autocritique than national literatures. What's useful for the field about nonsystematic "phenomenological" (small p: not the philosophical tradition) observations is the possibility of their leading to inconvenient, off-the-grid diagnoses and theoretical suggestions. One should ask what something is like, how it is experienced and by whom, as well as what it says and how it's supposed to be experienced.

That said, a lot of the following ten years in comparative literature was actively regressive – a period of universalistic reconstitutions of the subject and of Christian theology. Even the affect studies I don't much care for provided something different during that decade.

JUDY: The phrase "affective turn" has a rather broad denotation across the humanities and social sciences these days. From Antonio Negri's and Gilles Deleuze's philosophical engagements with Spinoza's ethics, which Michael Hardt has relatively recently tried to elaborate into a "new social ontology," to *The Affect Theory Reader*, it has come to designate a new way of theorizing the human being in response to the increasing technologization of life. The primary question in this regard is about the nature of human sociality. It is important to remark this when attending to the question of what the affective turn means for comparative literature specifically as a discipline because the issue of sociality is also fundamentally engaged in the problematic of subjectivity, of the relationship between subjectivity and communicative reciprocity, to invoke a Kantian concept. In that respect, the greatest importance of *Feeling in Theory*, in my judgment, is how Rei's reading of modernity's inquiry into subjectivity, from Spinoza to Deleuze, de Man, and Derrida, foregrounds the crucial importance of theories of affect to the very idea of community. In focusing attention on the way expression actively articulates the subject-in-common, she recalls another earlier turn in the field toward Peircian semiotics, which makes feelings central to the ordering of knowledge. Recall that for Peirce it is aesthetic forms – or as he preferred to term them, "esthetics" – that generate the conditions of what is possible. This is consonant with the issue of the extended mind that has been so important in the fields of cognitive science and social psychology. Except, whereas the psychophysical problem still plagues these fields, comparative literature primarily attends to the material affective agency of signification. Poetic forms engender not merely images in the mind but also the processes of imaging and imagining. This is a very old problematic of mimesis going back to Aristotle. Significantly, its elaboration as a theory of poetic expression, according to which poetry effects change in the mind and material world, was undertaken initially by the Arabic philosophers, specifically al-Fārābī, ibn Sīnā, and ibn Rushd, in their theory of الأمة الشعرية (*al-umma ash-shiʿīrīya*), "poetic community," which so compelled Aquinas. Significantly, Arabic-language morphology enables the cognate phrase, الأمة الشعرية (*al-umma ash-shuʿūrīya*), which can be rendered in English as "aesthetic community," in the classical sense of *aesthesis*.

The significance of this problematic for the field of comparative literature is the opening up of a historically fecund, as well as conceptually pertinent, line of inquiry into the continued significance of literary forms in the articulation of the world. In other words, "world" is not only a philosophical concept but also one that has been fundamental to the unfolding of global modernity, from Goethe's *Weltliteratur* and Kant's cosmopolitanism to Husserl's *Lebenswelt*. This is why the indeterminacy of the term "world" still plagues us – notwithstanding Merleau-Ponty's and Patočka's monumental efforts to elaborate it in a more dynamic manner, along with Lyotard's and Derrida's attempts to free us from its genealogy. Although I think Sloterdijk has recently suggested a way past all that. That is certainly not the case with the current conception of so-called world literature, which does not seem to take seriously enough the significance of the philosophical genealogy of "world," and so persists in uncritically presupposing the givenness of the subject of knowledge as the locus of theoretical work, preserving non-English language works, and principally those from the "global South," as objects of interpretation. And it is in this regard that the affective/semiotic turn offers comparative literature a significant role in reimagining how we might conceive the world.

BERMAN: To add a second question, Rei writes of "frailty" when speaking of the ontic, and R. A. writes of "dignity" when addressing contemporary Tunisia. Might there be a productive tension between these two terms? How might they be mobilized toward what R. A. calls a "radical humanism" that recognizes "the transformative force of poetic statement in the formation of popular imagining about our collective world" ("Introduction" 15)?

JUDY: Rei's conception of the frailty of the ontic inquires into the psychoanalytic activity of working through, which, as we all know, is a narrative activity involving the creative plasticity of imagining, or more precisely, imaging the world. The therapeutic affect in analysis has to do with coming to terms with the limits of ego in its mediating activity between desires and morality. Ego, in this sense, does not aspire to the transcendental, to the irreducible grounds or necessary logical locus of being. W.E.B. Du Bois spoke of this as the nonegotistical manifestation of intellect-in-action, discerning it in poetic expressions of Black folk, which Albert Murray subsequently characterized as representing or expressing human feeling – how humans are constituted affectively and so what they are aware of.

My point regarding poetry and radical humanism is really an elaboration of Fanon's insight that poetry is essential to thinking something different. It is not so much the case that jazz, say, or even the blues is therapeutic. It is, again to cite Murray, an attempt to order the chaos of experience without being able to, and without aspiring to mastery. Here allow me to quote Murray, who said that in chaos,

the one thing we have or the only thing we can do about it is to use that endowment that we have that Joyce was talking about when he referred to the 'ineluctable modality' of the visible, of the audible, of the conceptual. The concept is an attempt to bring some form. Without that, you just have chaos. So you've got to have some sense of form.

(Noble 130)

He meant, of course, style, which is about finding an adequate metaphor commensurate with the complexities and possibilities of our surroundings. What serious poetry – and I mean poesis in the broadest sense – tries to do is to bring the deepest, the most comprehensive insights to bear upon it.

In this sense, poetic expression activates imagination in a way that can be construed as instrumentally intersubjective, generating what I mentioned earlier as الأمة الشعرية (*al-umma ash-shiʿrīya*) – let me note that this is chiefly ibn Sīnā's designation to which I refer in "Introduction: For Dignity," and which I think is best rendered as "poetic commons," or even "aesthetic commons"; indeed, we can also take it to mean "affective commons" (الأمة الشعرية / *al-umma ash-shuʿūrīya*). The point in the Tunisia piece as well as here is that this way of thinking poetry is still very much at play in the world. Engaging such thinking seriously involves the sort of epistemological rupture Black studies in its early formation at San Francisco State set out to achieve, and which Sylvia Wynter has tirelessly been working toward.

TERADA: Reading R. A.'s response while turning toward "For Dignity," I have some questions that maybe can clarify what I was saying earlier as well. On my reading, for both of us the stakes of emotion lie in subjectivity and non-subjectivity, in the human and nonhuman, in the use of emotion and expression to establish what counts as those things. I think we agree that linguistic and semiotic systems can't be considered apart from that, which also means that they can't be emotion- and affect-poor even in their most abstract form; and that "literature" is always involved in social regulatory systems. Social and political significance is going to be stripped if you make "affect" a realm autonomous from ideology; either that, or people will back-project ideology into this "autonomous" realm. "A critique of the conception of the subject as an expression of its own intentionality" is something I value very much in R. A.'s *(Dis)Forming the American Canon* (146). That seems here with us today when you say "ego, in this sense, does not aspire to the transcendental."

But your response made me wonder, first, whether we take our perceptions of this complex in quite different directions; and second, about a tension between, on one hand, the coerciveness of "literature" that you've been concerned to bring out, and on the other, your affirmative tracking of Arabic literary forms in "For Dignity." Already in your earlier work, literatures enable (or ought to have enabled) something other than an imperative to write their histories or theories. But you also were interested in the ideological function of literacy in the United States and the fundamental insult of attaching the value of persons to their literacy, as you showed can be seen in slave narratives' treatment of the subject. I realize the historical specificity of the argument – Black slaves uniquely are forced to exhibit "humanity" through writing or count as having none. Your argument has been influential in pointing up the difficulty with the category of "literature": literature always separates what accomplishes literary legibility from that which, even in the same person, even in the same writing, does not. This resonates for me because I don't find "expression" a salvageable category. It, too, is exemplary in setting up as transparent a nonexistent match between "inner" content and language. It says: here, through "expression," the subject is accomplished and congratulates itself. I've argued variously that subjectivity, art, pedagogy, and the human are normative in damaging ways. Their institutional status is dramatically, if not completely, different from the mode of existence of, for example, perception, dream, insurrection, conversation.

So I'm worried by your emphasis that in studying emotions and signs I was focused on the production of the common. I may have focused on the production of "expression" as universal, but this is pejorative in my account, and happens with subjectivity and humanity's attachment to expression as an accomplishment of a back-projected human potential. So, my question to you amounts to wondering how you get from the damage of literacy to radical humanism – even given an Arabic tradition with a very different itinerary.

Regarding "The Frailty of the Ontic," R. A., where you associate that essay's interest in heterogeneous perceptions with Fanon's investment in poetry as a way to "thinking something different": yes. Only poetry (as "literature") isn't *especially* a means to that, because it is special only in the eyes of the institution. In that essay I wanted to see how large an ontological role could be given to fleeting perceptions of all kinds. To come at this from the opposite side, many, if not most, regular social forms operate as close to chaos – or maybe madness – as things that count as "formless." I want to say, though, that this essay is a one-off experiment, and I wouldn't overemphasize it. I wouldn't claim it as any kind of central statement.

BERMAN: Would you like to speculate on this discussion's implications for comparative literature programs?

TERADA: I'd like comparative literature to treat the "literature" in its name figuratively, and open up institutional requirements to everything known under everyday life and "cultural studies" (while remaining critical of the "culture" concept). There has also been an implicit splitting off of US ethnic literatures and continued tepid support for non-Western languages. Methodologically and generically too, comparative literature programs ought to fulfill the unfinished promise of interdisciplinarity at the level of departments – that is, with students and not just in faculty work. That doesn't mean that students shouldn't specialize, only that departments have no basis for enforcing specialization as necessarily meaning two national literatures (amid comparative literature scholarship's critiques of nationalism). Nor should programs impose "core" curricular requirements, which is literally impossible in comparative as opposed to a national literature. My program has tried to live by these ideas for a long time, with varying degrees of success. The privatization of universities makes it harder and harder. Comparative literature programs shouldn't be the only ones to care about these things, but I wish that all departments would live the principles of their scholarship institutionally.

I don't know that what people navigate was ever, or can be, a "world." I agree with R. A. about how the "world" of "world literature" takes for granted a subject of knowledge; I also think the posing of a "common," even as something never actually achieved, works to produce that subject.

JUDY: Yes, I do think the question of affect involves the issue of subjectivity and nonsubjectivity. I approach this in terms of the processes and procedures of individuation. When I say that Rei's inquiry into affect recalls semiotics, I do not mean to suggest an abstract formalism of signification to which affect is an added value, a quality, as she puts it. On the contrary, it is a process of cognition that is no more a quality than apophantic reasoning in our having and being in the world communicatively. And that is very much about the ethics of community, or as Kant would have it, the ethical basis of community in reason. As Schiller tried to show in his *Aesthetic Education*, there is no viable relationship between subjectivity and communicative reciprocity without affect. I have in mind here Hortense Spillers's long struggle with the relationship between fleshliness and persona, taken up in a series of studies on the way toward reimagining the question of community while eschewing the long-standing tradition of positing a rupture between animality and the intelligence of poesis as requisite for human sociality. In this regard, I particularly have in mind her construal of "flesh" as a primary narrative in the 1987 essay, "Mama's Baby, Papa's Maybe: An American Grammar Book." Now Rei's remark that literature is always involved in social regulatory systems – with which I agree as a matter of meaningful performance – touches directly, I think, on the problematic of the flesh put into play by Spillers's notion of "cultural vestibularity," a spatial metaphor for the biopolitical economy of what she calls the hieroglyphics of the flesh, referring to the "undecipherable marking on the flesh" resulting from the systemic physical violence done to Black bodies which carries over into our present juridical system. In describing these lacerations and tears as what create the distance between culture proper and its antechamber, the "cultural vestibularity," Spillers effectively recognizes them as indicial representations of the disciplining action of culture on the flesh. They index the action by which animality is differentiated from humanity. In her query as to whether "this phenomenon of marking . . . actually 'transfers' from one generation to another, finding its various *symbolic substitutions* in an efficacy of meanings that repeat the initiating moments" (67), I take Spillers to be referring to not only the judicial system but the entire matrix of social institutions – what we euphemistically call "institutional or structural racism." That query along with her remark that the flesh "bears in person the marks of a cultural text" (67) brings to mind Edmund Husserl's definition of culture as "nothing but the group of achievements occurring in the ongoing activities of people in a community, which have their abiding spiritual existence in the unity of the communal consciousness and its continuing tradition" (21–22). To the extent the issue is epistemological – how we know what we know about the world and ourselves – for Spillers, it is less a matter of phenomenology than semiotics. Clearly, the hieroglyphic marks are an index of some process of signification in which these markings bear some relationship to things, recognized and interpreted as such by some community. That process fixes the significance of person as a cognitive articulation of determinable sets of life practices. Cognition as semiosis is neither a priori to – as in divinely revealed – or merely an epiphenomenon of the flesh. Rather, it is in correlation with it. Person is an action that embodies this process. In my nearly completed book manuscript, "Thinking in Disorder," I call this process "grammar of sociality," referring to the action of articulating and enforcing communal intersubjectivity, in which its linkages of things and expressions constitute an assemblage of conceptual, perceptual schemata, an architectonic that achieves a type of subject and mind properly integrated into the social order. I take this to be some of what you are getting at in your examination in *Looking Away* of the relation between acceptance and experience. And I do think we concur on the shortfall of the Kantian project in this regard. Community predicated on the primacy of the transcendental ego, come upon exclusively in the action of reasoning apophantically, seems destined to a certain violence of order that is unsustainable in the world without necessarily destroying the physical circumstances of our being. As Rei correctly notes, my point in *(Dis)Forming* was to trouble the too tight identification of humanity with a specific literacy tied to the expression of a (transcendent or transcendental) subjectivity. Hence the "damage" of literacy. But it was also to trouble the deracination of literature as semiosis, which, in the case of Kant's architectonic, is an aspect of curtailing what he considered "unbridled imagination." The persistent adherence to teleology in modern metaphysics gives us human cognition as structure – the architectonic of transcendental critique – rather than a process of action. This is the erasure of semiosis I refer to. And it is significant that in the aesthetic and anthropological investigations, where Kant elaborates his regulative teleological principle, the Negro is a primary sign, one wants to say iconic, of this erasure. I think it is also significant that early on in his career, Du Bois tracks this to the continuity of scholastic theistic teleology in modern metaphysics, based on the hard distinction between mind and matter as objects of study. At stake is the question of the universal, but not the universalization of the iconic "I." The question at hand is whether universals are real; and that is a question of semiosis as a community-engendering action. And I mean something like "world-making," or in the more current parlance "worlding." In other words, I am concerned with how the representative function of a sign is something it is, not in itself or in a real relation to its object, but in relation to a train of thought.

Cognition as semiosis is neither a priori to – as in divinely revealed – or merely an epiphenomenon of the flesh. Rather, it is in correlation with it. Person is an action that embodies this process. Yet, if intelligence is always embodied, regardless of the morphology – so that intelligence is everywhere – then does "human flesh" necessarily entail "human intelligence," and if so what is the character of that intelligence? Is human flesh sentient flesh, and if it is, what makes it human? These questions are resonant with what is entailed in the events of popular insurrection that happened and are still underway in the Arab world, and there is a tradition of this kind of theorization that affords us possibilities for reimagining the work of criticism, what I call poetic criticism in relation to radical humanism.

BERMAN: You have both raised the question of the universal, the matter of community, and the problem of "worlding" in your reflections on affect. Rei has also proposed that comparative literature programs become fully interdisciplinary, resist the cordoning off of US ethnic literatures and non-Western languages, and "open up institutional requirements to everything known under everyday life and 'cultural studies.'" What might this kind of practice of comparative literature mean for our understanding of community and world? How does R. A.'s discussion of the attempt in Spillers's work to "reimagine the question of community while eschewing the long-standing tradition of positing the rupture between animality and the intelligence of poesis" or the importance of flesh, change the conversation? Does it change our understanding of the "worlding" that accompanies (or results from?) the practice of reading?

JUDY: Taking up your invitation to speculate on what implications my engagement with poetic criticism might have for the field of comparative literature, I return for a moment to Spillers's struggle with the relationship between fleshliness and persona, which will allow me to spell out a bit more what I take from Fanon's investment in poetry. The struggle, then, is not between the abstraction of person and the thing of the flesh; it is between disparate and frequently heterogeneous as well as heteronymous ways of imagining things. Fanon gave us a sense of this in *Peau noire, masques blancs* on wholly literary grounds. Upon invoking the legal battles, defeats, truces, and victories that mark the American Negro's greater recognition of freedom, Fanon gives in evidence Richard Wright's *The Twelve Million Black Voices.* "'The twelve millions black voices,'" he writes, "roar against the curtain of the heavens. And the curtain, torn from end to end, marked with teeth bites in its belly of interdiction, falls like a burst balloon. On the battlefield, its four corners marked by scores of Negroes hanged by their testicles, a monument is being slowly built that promises to be grandiose" ("'*The twelve millions black voices*' ont gueulé contre le rideau du ciel. Et le rideau, traversé de part en part, les empreintes dentales bien en place, logées dans son ventre d'interdiction, est tombé tel un balafon crevé. Sur le champ de bataille, limité aux quatre coins par des vingtaines de nègres pendus par les testicules, se dresse peu à peu un monument qui promet d'être grandiose" [Fanon 180; translation mine]). Because Fanon understands the *Negro* – this being the term he uses for what Spillers calls *the captive Black body* – to be in the confluence of biological propensities (ontogenetic), symbolic structures (linguistic, but primarily narrative), and socioeconomic institutions (by which *he* means the historical, including political and cultural/ideological institutions of society), it is a *persona*, articulating a set of roles, of life practices that are provided by the larger world of language and not the embodiment of inherent psychophysical properties. In this sense, *Negro* represents the entire semiological system, foregrounding in its very expression the activity of the process of signification.

I want to be well understood here. To the extent *Negro* is iconic, it is not in the sense of iconicity Barthes sets out in *Mythologies*. Rather, it is iconic in the sense that it perpetually puts on display in its manipulations, one way or another, the hermeneutic workings of similitude. It evidences that the relationship between perception, conceptuality, and expression is still a matter of how things are read. Put a bit more carefully, in reading, the world of language is encountered as a vast system of parts that one's self is cast in, and in accordance with whose order one's self is compelled to assume a role. When we say, then, that the Negro is both a figure and figuration of imagination, we mean the articulation of the Negro person exhibits the full range of social formations and relations constitutive of modernity. If the thoughts all humans understand when expressed in their respective languages are the same thing for them, as the long Aristotelian tradition maintains, and the sense objects and the perceptions beneath those thoughts are also common to all, then that is a formal fact. Or think of it this way: for every human, the particular discrete perception of things is a function of the combined faculties of sensation and imagination – both of which are precognitive but essential constitutive elements of cognition. "So here we have the Negro rehabilitated," Fanon states, " 'standing before the bar,' governing the world of his intuition, the Negro recovered, taken up, in demand, accepted, and he is a Negro – no, he is not merely a Negro but the Negro, activating the fecund antennae of the world, placed in the foreground of the world, sprinkling the world with his poetic power, 'open to all the breaths of the world.' I espouse the world! I am the world!" ("Et voici le nègre réhabilité, 'debout à la barre,' gouvernant le monde de son intuition, le nègre retrouvé, ramassé, revendiqué, assumé, et c'est un nègre, non pas, ce n'est point un nègre, mais le nègre, alertant les antennes fécondes du monde, planté dans l'avant-scène du monde, aspergeant le monde de sa puissance poétique, 'poreux à tous les souffles du monde.' J'épouse le monde! Je suis le monde!" [Fanon 103; translation mine]). Having this universal form of cognition is not enough, however, because how the thing is perceived plays a major role in its evaluation, which is to say in its significance. How an image is generated involves the issue of convention, of how convention articulates. And here again, Fanon's is a literary articulation with importance for how we practice comparative literature. The line *"poreux à tous les souffles du monde"* [open to all the breaths of the world] is quoted from Césaire's *Cahier d'un retour au pays natal* to state then, as he does, "Je me faisais le poète du monde" (I made myself the poet of the world [Fanon 103]).

Positing that poetic statement has such a transformative force in forming popular ways of imagining our collective reality calls us to ponder whether poetry as mimesis can foster a significant *social* consciousness. It may very well be the case that it fosters the formation of certain ways of thinking and conceiving, indeed perceiving the world – I would say, imagining the world. The question is whether those ways are, or can ever be arranged into, an aggregate integral collective, capable of articulating and sustaining a tradition of thought (ideology), a historiography of intelligence in relation to political or social institutions. This is something like the *convivir* or تعايش (*ta'āyush*) supposedly associated with al-Andalus, the material trace of which is certain rather popular poetic forms, not least of which is the *cante jondo* that so preoccupied Federico García Lorca, who heard the great Andalusian cantor Manuel Torres say that the thing to always look for in *cante jondo* is the black body of Pharaoh ("el tronco negro de Faraón" [quoted in Auclair 58–59]). For Torres, who was *gitano*, this was an explicit and emphatic assertion of the African origins of the sound he made that famously came up from the depths of his body and which he called black, the materiality, the earthliness of which is a sign of *duende*. He is reported to have said once, "All that has black sounds has *duende*" ("Todo lo que tiene sonidos negros tiene duende" [García Lorca 151; translation mine]). Torres's sense of *duende* is resonant with Fanon's sense of the Negro person. In a profoundly mundane way, the flesh is recognized as material for many personae for multiple ways of thinking. So thinking is not about the body but with the flesh that does not incarnate any particular person – this body is not Negro. The Negro is not embodied here – but rather serves as a bearer of all sorts of black sound, the sort of sound Torres and his fellow Andalusians call *duende*.

We should not forget, however, that *duende* is also a *fantasma*. Lorca writes that it "is a power, not a work. It is a struggle, not a thought. I have heard an old maestro of the guitar say, 'The *duende* is not in the throat; the *duende* climbs up inside you, from the soles of the feet.' Meaning this: it is not a question of ability, but of true, living style, of blood, of the most ancient culture, of spontaneous creation" (García Lorca; translation mine). But what can be meant by spontaneous creation except that the poetic image is a material manifestation of imagination as the faculty essential to thinking *in the world*? So the poetic image is transformative, giving shape to life's actualities while at the same time being transformed by them in a voiceless sounding, *duende*. This is what Fanon characterized as introducing invention into existence, the institution of creative imagination in the world articulating a community of feeling.

What Fanon could not do, all said and done, was to find a language of speculative theory within the dominant Western conceptual schemes adequate to giving an account of this community of feeling as a historical sociopolitical force. Thinking about poetry and imagination since Kant has taken a specific Aristotelian track, and leaving that track is, I think, the fundamental challenge facing what we have long construed as the human sciences in general, and comparative literature as a specific field. And this involves a significant departure from the received *organon*. What I suggest in "For Dignity" is a first step in that direction by exploring a different Aristotelian tradition that includes the likes of al-Fārābī and ibn Sīnā, which takes up poetry as a form of cognition that expresses an intersubjective validity based on what they define precisely as a "community of feeling." I'll not rehearse the details of that lineage here. I'll simply point out that taking up or engaging this tradition is not a matter of revivalism or quest after conceptual origins in the Arabic roots of the Enlightenment. On the contrary, it is a demonstration of how we need to recalibrate our orientation toward languages.

As a practical matter, much attention has been given to the need to not only shore up our research and teaching of European languages but also to expand our scope. While I think as a field we need to reiterate our fundamental working in as well as with multiple languages, we ought not be about expansion. What I mean is, rather than viewing underexplored languages – Arabic, Farsi, Urdu, Chinese, and Kiswahili being examples, which can mean only underexplored by the field of comparative literature, seeing that these all have long traditions of philologically based studies even in US academia – as object fields of study in which, quite frankly, old, often moribund theories of language, cognition, and society are deployed, we take seriously theorizing about these issues that has taken place in those languages. And by take seriously, I do not mean as ethnographic objects, or even as artifice of "alternative modernities." I mean that we undertake the arduous task, which will involve decades of extensive monographic work as well as speculative work, of collaborating in the instituting of what I am still comfortable calling, à la Fanon, a different humanism.

TERADA: To start with the institutional and work back to the epistemological, I agree completely that comparative literature's relation to languages can't be that of subjects of study to objects of study, and that the idea of "comparison" isn't working to get out of such a mode, any more than the coordinating "world" of world literature is, or "theory" considered as a coordination of objects that are not theoretical. There are no nontheoretical phenomena, and no object-languages or object-fields. In regard to what departments offer to and are willing to learn from students, I'd like to see faculty defend in program structure these things that many of us affirm in principle. My remarks about languages and fields don't come from the point of view of coverage, nor of expansion into hidden areas. They come from frustration that departments do so little to allow students to use any and all resources to shape what counts as questions as well as answer "legible" questions. Departments deploy field, period, and genre descriptors as pragmatic restrictions on the realities that are considered viable – viable in the eyes of some other university superego of expectations thought to be out there and not oneself. Professors need to stop writing position requests that perpetuate conventions that most people believe are only someone else's.

Even more emphatically, if possible I'd like to support R. A.'s emphasis on the force of processes of cognition – understood to include the nonconceptual, the material, and thinking with Spillers, the vestibular – to produce every possible order and self. The systematic significance of blackness, as seen in Kant's teleology, which R. A. points out, and also in every other philosophical itinerary in use in the profession, could be taken up by comparative literature as a central concern in the way that the field of Black studies points to: I mean, it indicates taking apart conceptual genealogies entirely, as Denise Ferreira da Silva, notably, has shown. Black studies' pressure on the entire mesh of critical concepts is the most important movement in the profession. For comparative literature, it's not a matter of moving into a different field, but of each scholar asking what the pressure means for her existing work. If I could turn around one of R. A.'s remarks for a moment, there's no way to study affect or emotion without relationship to the conditions of social constitution, and these are necessarily racialized from the beginning rather than as a layer of quality. It's from here that I see the Bergsonian move of instrumentalizing perception itself (for him, basic perception scans for a place to intervene) deflecting social operations in the act of hoping to get back before them. Because constitutive elements are crucial in this way, there is conflict in and over anything that seems to be a vestibule, and I have been tracking these conflicts. The political conflicts are clearer to me, and perhaps finally more meaningful to me, than the positive potentials of epistemologies. I mean "political" very broadly here – I'm not speaking only of actualized or actualizable power – and not as a single bottom line or origin.

The existence of the conflicts dominates, for me. So, what I'm examining at any given time, my relationship to grammars, and even the construction of "commons," which I see largely as a process of conflict-management, remains troubled. In a couple of places, I find myself wanting to go down the avenues that R. A.'s remarks open up by imagining their negatives: to ask what happens if the idea of any aggregate integral collective capable of sustaining tradition, for example, is not already collapsed, for better and worse; or what happens if there is indeed no viable relationship between subjectivity and communicative reciprocity at all. I don't pretend that these questions are answerable, but I can still say "if" and think ahead – there's not nothing. Rather than leading toward any deprivation, this thought imagines an almost inconceivable richness of existence that goes on with no need for ground. I hope in taking that path, I could still think with Fanon's emphasis on invention. Maybe my pessimism about the bases for community and for literature can still, in a different way, help us explore what's been missing from the conventional critical triumvirate of politics/ethics/aesthetics.

Works cited

Auclair, Marcelle. *Vida y Muerte de García Lorca*. Trans. Aitana Alberti. Mexico City: Era, 1972. Print.

Fanon, Frantz. *Peau noire, masques blancs*. Paris: Éditions du Seuil, 1952. Print.

García Lorca, Federico. "Teoría y juego del duende." *Obras completas*. Vol. 3. Ed. Miguel García-Posada. Barcelona: Circulo de Lectores, 1969. 150–62. Print.

Husserl, Edmund. *Aufsätze und Vorträge, 1922–1937*. [Articles/essays and lectures, 1922–1937.] Ed. T. Nenon and H. R. Sepp. *Husserliana: Edmund Husserl – Gesammelte Werke*. Vol. 27. The Hague, Netherlands: Kluwer Academic, 1988. Print.

Judy, R. A. *(Dis)forming the American Canon: African-Arabic Slave Narratives and the Vernacular*. Minneapolis: U of Minnesota P, 1993. Print.

———. "Introduction: For Dignity; Tunisia and the Poetry of Emergent Democratic Humanism." *boundary 2* 39.1 (2012) 1–16. Web. 8 June 2016.

Noble, Don. "A Conversation with Albert Murray (1996)." *Albert Murray and the Aesthetic Imagination of a Nation*. Ed. Barbara A. Baker. Tuscaloosa: U of Alabama P, 2010. 130–7. Print.

Pinch, Adela. *Strange Fits of Passion: Epistemologies of Emotion, Hume to Austen.* Stanford, CA: Stanford UP, 1996. Print.

Spillers, Hortense J. "Mama's Baby, Papa's Maybe: An American Grammar Book." *Diacritics* 17.2 (1987): 64–81. Web. 8 June 2016.

Terada, Rei. *Feeling in Theory: Emotion after the "Death of the Subject."* Cambridge, MA: Harvard UP, 2001. Print.

———. "The Frailty of the Ontic." *South Atlantic Quarterly* 110.1 (2011): 37–55. Web. 8 June 2016.

———. *Looking Away: Phenomenality and Dissatisfaction, Kant to Adorno.* Cambridge, MA: Harvard UP, 2009. Print.

Comparatively lesbian
Queer/feminist theory and the sexuality of history

Susan S. Lanser

For all its innovative history, comparative literature has been slow to embrace two of the most significant movements in contemporary thought. It was not until 1994 that Margaret R. Higonnet's edited collection *Borderwork* explicitly took up the question of gender within the field. It was not until 2010 that the anthology *Comparatively Queer* sought a similarly visible intervention. As the ACLA considers the state of the discipline, it is worth asking how and to what ends we might forge a queerer comparative literature. In raising this topic, I consider not only queer "content" but also approaches that can advance the comparative study of sexual discourses, texts, and representations. Such critical methods might also, if metaphorically, queer the assumptions and practices of comparative literature *tout court*.

I take the liberty to work outward from my recent monograph, *The Sexuality of History: Modernity and the Sapphic, 1565–1830*, since the book embeds itself in comparative practice. Its governing aim is to reverse the usual emphasis of sexuality studies, asking not what we can learn about sexuality from studying history but what we can learn about history from studying sexuality – or in my case, from studying representations of female erotic relations. I argue that the period of reform, revolution, and reaction that characterized seventeenth- and eighteenth-century Europe also witnessed an intensified discursive interest in lesbians. In scientific treatises and Orientalist travelogues, in French court gossip and Dutch court records, in passionate verse, in the rising novel, and in cross-dressed flirtations on the English and Spanish stage, poets, playwrights, philosophers, physicians, and pundits were placing sapphic relations before the public eye. But these sexual representations served more than sexual ends. They were entangled with core preoccupations of the times: authority and liberty, power and difference, desire and duty, mobility and change, order, governance, and, of course, the increasingly troubled place of women as persons and property. In short, a historically specific interest in lesbians intersected with, and stimulated, systemic concerns.

Because my work reads through sexuality rather than only reading sexuality, the significance I have sought in sapphic representations lies in the themes and tropes they share with other historical formations. I am thus not trying to ferret out "closeted" content, which has necessarily been the paradigmatic reading practice of queer studies; I am trying to trace the connections between erotic surfaces and other discursive spheres as a way to pull sexuality more fully into the historiographic main stream: to see sexuality as a lens for reading the past and perhaps as a factor in shaping it. To this end, I use the admittedly vexed rubric of modernity as a conceptual anchor, and I invert the conventional wisdom that modernity consolidates a heteronormative order by suggesting that modernity can be read as the emergence of the sapphic – or what I call the logic of woman + woman – as an epistemic plausibility. And in relegating a gender marker to the subtitle of my book, I claim for female homoeroticism a central place in sexuality studies as an unmarked case. My research relies for its core claims and findings on a comparative approach, but it has led me to queerer versions of spatiality and periodicity than the ones I inherited. It has also led me to privilege confluence over the more traditionally comparative project of influence, to engage in "large reading," and to see the sign "lesbian" as itself a site for comparison.

In the context of early modernity, queerness is already geographically comparative: same-sex relations are often figured as a foreign vice or import, and queer folk real and imagined routinely flee unsafe social spaces for other countries or colonies. But comparativity became a deeper project in my research when I recognized divergent national patterns in the "distribution" of sapphic representations. I found a copious public discourse around 1600 in France, England, Spain, and to some extent in the Dutch Republic, but almost none in the German or Scandinavian states, followed by a falling off in Spain by 1700 and a rise in German writings in the late eighteenth century. What began simply as a comparatist's desire to be comparative thus ended up becoming a critical methodology, leading me to speculate about the factors that may have fostered interest in female homoeroticism in some places but not in others, and tentatively to map the sapphic in tandem with other national and regional investments.

This geography suggests an altered approach to spatiality. The intersections between sapphic representations and social practices that crossed the pages of my book were neither nationally bounded nor broadly continental nor even regional, so they invited me to think more deeply about commonalities and differences among European societies. I saw a shifting middle ground in which odd national bedfellows converged as sites of sexual representation and then diverged again, in a series of temporal-spatial assemblages that defy both consistency and conventional expectation and are thus in the metaphoric sense queer. Reformation and Enlightenment, colonialism and the slave trade also, of course, involved major and minor participants, bystanders, and opponents, yielding different national clusters on the European map, in effect making Europe a shifting complex of "interest groups" and rendering it more richly and queerly comparative.

My work has necessarily departed from the comparatist tendency to privilege influence as a methodological rubric. One frustrating problem for sexuality studies is the degree to which queer texts and their travels, hence both reception and influence, get covered up. For example, a fat, anonymous, and blatantly sapphic novel, *The Travels and Adventures of Mademoiselle de Richelieu*, went through five editions between 1744 and 1758, yet its textual traces are limited to one brief notice in a journal. The 1723 *Love Letters between a Certain Late Nobleman and the Famous Mr Wilson* has left a similar dearth of traces, as have plays of the 1630s respectively by Isaac de Benserade (*Iphis et Iante*) and Cubillo (*Añasco el de Talavera*). This remainder of silence makes it difficult to pursue queer studies even at the level of the individual instance, let alone to figure out the "trade routes" by which one text might have influenced another. For all the noble intentions of the new historicisms, then, thick description may be impossible to achieve when it comes to queer texts.

Where influence falters, though, there is ample ground for what I call "confluence," the practice of exploring discrete phenomena that may be causally connected. Unlike influence or the problematic Zeitgeist, confluence allows us to study what Claudio Guillén called "genetically independent" instances in order to see whether they share a cultural deep logic (70). My model for confluence study is Walter Cohen's *Drama of a Nation*, which explores the "remarkable features of kinship" between the public theaters of Elizabethan England and Golden-Age Spain that were largely "unknown to each other" and arose in societies "far distant from one another in physical, moral, political, and religious respects" (16–17). Only in England and Spain, Cohen concludes, was there a concurrence of social and political forces, most notably the early growth of capitalism in an absolutist state, that fostered analogous "theatrical institutions, dramatic genres, [and] individual plays" (120).

That both of these theaters relied on cross-dressing starts to suggest why thinking through confluence might benefit queer comparative work. But I also find something metaphorically queer about confluence itself. Influence looks for direct and presumably linear evidence, whether textual or collateral. Confluence recognizes the rhizomatic rather than axiomatic assemblages that make odd cultural bedfellows, encouraging a speculative search for intersections between textual and material phenomena and acknowledging the promiscuity of their intercourse. For example, a cluster of texts that take Turkey as the site of lesbian "contagion" begin to connect up with anxieties about incursions from the Ottoman Empire and about what counts as European in a colonial age. And it is queer confluence indeed when notions of governance get figured through sapphic alliances, as happens both in eighteenth-century England in the wake of an incomplete Glorious Revolution and again in Revolutionary France.

Confluence may also trouble notions of periodicity and the problem of period itself. In *Why Literary Periods Mattered*, Ted Underwood argues that departments of literature built their legitimacy by reifying notions of disruption and contrast between periods. Despite some scholarly pushback, periodization remains a tight professional rubric controlling jobs, journals, and academic identities. To some extent, comparative literature has resisted periodicity, all the more as trying to date movements across national borders already disrupts temporalities. But queer studies, even in its most temporally historicist forms, offers another layer of reinvention. My own book began as an eighteenth-century project, but early on, I found compelling textual confluences that led me back to 1565, and each of my chapters ended up suggesting a somewhat different periodization for a particular generic or ideational project. If I were mapping the sapphic more boldly,

I would want to single out historically or spatially separate textual practices with shared resonance – for example, connecting representations of "political lesbianism" in the 1970s United States and England with similar tendencies in 1920s France and seventeenth-century Western Europe. One might consider renaming literary periods in queer terms: the years from 1590 to 1635 could well become the Age of Erotic Crossdressing or the Metamorphic Age, while the 1740s could be marked as a key decade of heteronormative struggle. Digital mapping might allow us to see where queer texts converge and then to see where periods emerge inductively.

In the interest of queering the field, I would also encourage what I call "large reading," a middle-ground practice that seeks cross-textual patterns in works that can productively be read together whether they cross time and place or huddle within a particular chronotope. My research surprised me, for example, with historically specific clusters of both apostrophe and elegy, on the one hand, and with recurring bouts of what we might call queer hypotheticals, utopias conditionally rather than constatively posited. To move to a later period, we might speculate about the writers who pioneered the rise of free indirect discourse, that metaphorically queer form that Frances Ferguson considers the novel's "one and only formal contribution to literature" (159). To push the demographic envelope, what might we make of the fact that so many modernist innovators of free indirect discourse – James, Richardson, Joyce, Woolf, Barnes, Stein, Proust, Gide, Colette, Mansfield, Forster – were a rather queer lot? Might the ambiguity and elusivity of free indirect discourse – whereby "nothing was simply one thing" (Woolf 277) – have been particularly appealing to writers with queer investments? A history of free indirect discourse that is at once social, cultural, and formal might well be comparatively queer.

Finally, and without rehearsing either the long-standing and sometimes contentious feminist critique of queer theory or the long-standing and sometimes contentious queer critique of feminist thought, I would press for a strategic duality that recognizes histories of dominance and difference without accepting identity categories as essential, permanent, or predictive. Modifying feminist with queer resists promoting stable or unified cross-cultural or cross-temporal categories of sex, gender, or sexuality. Anchoring queer with feminist reminds us that however we might wish literature – or the world – to operate, gender-based hierarchies, inequalities, oppressions, and suppressions are global, if diversely configured, phenomena. Queer feminism signals a conviction that gender must be theorized with sexuality whether the focus is women or men; as theorists from Eve Kosofsky Sedgwick and Biddy Martin to David Valentine and Tom King have insisted, the relationship between gender and sexuality is ethnographic rather than theoretical.

With this understanding, I would ask comparative literature to reclaim the now abjected "lesbian" from the dustheap of critical theory, with the reminder that some of the earliest queer theory arose beneath that sign. As the only word in the LGBTIQ acronym that is insistently gendered, "lesbian" – perhaps best retained as adjective rather than reifying noun – reminds us that the edifices of patriarchy persist in ways that other category-busting rubrics often overlook. As

Annamarie Jagose argues in *Inconsequence*, such a reclamation would push back against the cultural production of lesbianism as "anachronistic," "imitative," and "second-best," a position that might be understood as a defense against the difficult knowledge that all categories of "sexual registration" are necessarily derivative and belated (Jagose xi, 23, 144). In this context, "lesbian" becomes a kind of warning sign. And precisely because of its uneasy coalescence of the legible and illegible, that sign, as Valerie Traub's *Making Sexual Knowledge* sees it, provides "a point of access and leverage for reactivating historicity in queer theory" that may contribute "to theorizing how and what 'queer' will signify in times to come" (293).

But "lesbian" also needs that modifier of comparativity. A "comparatively lesbian" approach would open the relatively uncharted study of queer male and female representations in tandem and would also embrace cultural differences of concept, practice, situation, signification, and terminology. Gayatri Gopinath's *Impossible Desires: Queer Diasporas and South Asian Public Cultures*, for example, eschews the word "lesbian" for what she calls the "queer female diasporic subject," and from that position starts to provide the comparative basis for understanding how different queer female subjects can be understood. Sahar Amer writes movingly of the danger wrought by simply translating words like "gay" and "lesbian" into Arabic, where the terms unwittingly create a "culture of shame" (387). My insistence on "lesbian," then, is metonymic: I would happily see comparative literature embrace a range of words that signal the salience of gender for studying sexuality and of sexuality for studying gender.

In putting into play unlikely subjects – lesbian, comparative, queer, feminist, theory, history – I hope to suggest the kinds of queer assemblages from which comparative literature might benefit. A commitment to queering comparative literature, which is arguably also a commitment to exposing and intervening in restrictive systems of sex and gender, has a part to play in changing more than an academic field. If comparative literature is to thrive in the twenty-first century, it needs to reinvent itself as the go-to field for thinking about complex globalities both present and past. The need is critical, and critically queer.

Works cited

Amer, Sahar. "Naming to Empower: Lesbianism in the Arab Islamicate World Today." *Journal of Lesbian Studies* 16 (2012): 381–97. Print.

Cohen, Walter. *Drama of a Nation: Public Theater in Renaissance England and Spain.* Ithaca: Cornell UP, 1985. Print.

Ferguson, Frances. "Jane Austen, Emma, and the Impact of Form." *Modern Language Quarterly* 61.1 (2000): 157–80. Print.

Gopinath, Gayatri. *Impossible Desires: Queer Diasporas and South Asian Public Cultures.* Durham: Duke UP, 2005. Print.

Guillén, Claudio. *The Challenge of Comparative Literature.* Cambridge: Harvard UP, 1993. Print.

Higonnet, Margaret R., ed. *Borderwork: Feminist Engagements with Comparative Literature.* Ithaca: Cornell UP, 1994. Print.

Higonnet, Margaret R., Jarrod Hayes, and William J. Spurlin, eds. *Comparatively Queer: Interrogating Identities across Time and Cultures*. New York: Palgrave Macmillan, 2010. Print.

Jagose, Annamarie. *Inconsequence: Lesbian Representation and the Logic of Sexual Sequence*. Ithaca: Cornell UP, 2002. Print.

Lanser, Susan S. *The Sexuality of History: Modernity and the Sapphic, 1565–1830*. Chicago: U of Chicago P, 2014. Print.

Traub, Valerie. *Making Sexual Knowledge: Thinking Sex with the Early Moderns*. Philadelphia: U of Pennsylvania P, 2015. Print.

Underwood, Ted. *Why Literary Periods Mattered: Historical Contrast and the Prestige of English Studies*. Stanford: Stanford UP, 2013. Print.

Woolf, Virginia. *To the Lighthouse*. New York: Harcourt Brace Jovanovich, 1927. Print.

Queer double cross
Doing (it with) comp lit

Jarrod Hayes

A volume I coedited with Margaret R. Higonnet and William J. Spurlin in 2010, *Comparatively Queer: Interrogating Identities across Time and Cultures,* assembled essays that attempted to queer comparative studies and theorize the importance of insisting on comparative approaches to queer studies in a "double crossing" that we playfully characterized as "going both ways." Indeed, we argued, the expression "comparatively queer" would ideally become queerly redundant if our intended intervention into field-defining were successful.

Already in the 1993 report, Charles Bernheimer had mentioned the possibility of including sexuality in an interdisciplinary notion of what it means to compare:

> The space of comparison today involves comparisons between artistic productions usually studied by different disciplines; between various cultural constructions of those disciplines; between Western cultural traditions, both high and popular, and those of non-Western cultures; between the pre- and postcontact cultural productions of colonized peoples; between gender constructions defined as feminine and those defined as masculine, or between sexual orientations defined as straight and those defined as gay; between racial and ethnic modes of signifying; between hermeneutic articulations of meaning and materialist analyses of its modes of production and circulation; and much more.
>
> (41–2)

We were thus somewhat surprised that, seventeen years later, so few seemed to have taken up this suggestion. Almost immediately following the Bernheimer Report, Higonnet's collection *Borderwork: Feminist Engagements with Comparative Literature* had taken on the project of comparatively feminist studies. Why had the queer counterpart taken so long? While I am not sure I can answer that question here, I would like to make a case for safeguarding a prominent place for queer scholarship within the discipline of comparative studies.

Without claiming to be exhaustive in the possibilities that *Comparatively Queer* explored for a "comparatively queer studies," we did point toward a number of strategies for such a project. These included an insistence on, first, the importance of comparing, and second, an erotics of comparison. In relation to the writing of queer history, early lesbian and gay activists and scholars sought "to prove that lesbian and gay sexualities were not only 'natural' but also existed across broad historical, geographical, and cultural contexts" (Hayes, Higonnet, and Spurlin 11–12); they sought, in other words, gay and lesbian roots throughout history. By implication, then, much early gay historiography avoided comparison in its assumptions that a same kind of gayness could be uncovered throughout the past to reveal what had been "hidden from history" (cf. Duberman et al.). Yet, even though such research looked for proof of sameness in the past, crossing time often led to a historicization and denaturalization of sexuality and of the hetero/homo binary at its center. Lesbian and gay historians were thus forced into comparison with the object of their studies, other erotic folks from the past. If queer studies denaturalized the contemporary sexual subject in crossing time, casting queer historical studies as a comparatist practice allowed us to understand this subject, including the queer scholar him- or herself, as an object of comparison as well.

Susan S. Lanser's contribution to the collection *Comparatively Queer*, entitled "Mapping Sapphic Modernity," offers a starting point for a trajectory that Lanser describes at the end of her later book, *The Sexuality of History: Modernity and the Sapphic, 1565–1830* (2014). Acknowledging previously published parts of the book, she writes, "Most of these essays predate the 180 degree turn of my project and thus operate more fully within a 'history of sexuality' than as manifestations of a 'sexuality of history'" (303). The title of her book thus inverts the title of Foucault's foundational *History of Sexuality*. This inversion would out-Foucault Foucault if this emphasis were not already implicit in Foucault's insistence (and the insistence of many who have followed) that sexuality has a history not only in the sense that it has undergone transformations that can be traced but also in that there is a time before sexuality, that sexuality appears (not at once, of course) in a certain period, and that the history of this appearance or "invention" can also be written.

"Inversion" is a term with its own queer possibilities. It suggests not only that sexuality has a history but also that history might "have" a sexuality, might itself be thought of as being sexual, or that sexuality must be central to the writing of history rather than a peripheral concern. As Lanser puts it, "sexuality is history" ("Sexuality"). When I speak of "doing the history of sexuality," I am also indebted to David Halperin's *How to Do the History of Homosexuality*, in relation to which "doing it" for me also suggests, even here, engaging in a sexual act. Doing comparative literature, then, might be thought of as potentially being a similarly sexual act. It seems to me that Lanser's trajectory also represents a move from modernity as sapphic to a broader claim about history as sexuality, about how to "do" the history of sexuality. I suggest, then, that we think of "doing" the history of sexuality itself as a queerly comparative gesture, one with its own erotic pleasures.

When I, a contemporary gay subject, come into contact with Lanser's sapphic subject, I must cross not only time but also genders. I am forced to come to terms with the fact that my "object" of comparison is also a subject. The relation between my subject and hers is one of productive dissonance. Rather than approaching her sapphic subject in a colonizing gesture of appropriation or a masculine gesture of objectification, I am called to allow my subjectivity, now somewhat less mine, to be challenged. In this way, Lanser's sexuality of history is queerly comparative and comparatively queer. Or perhaps I should say "comparatively sapphic" in the hope that this phrase can come to resonate as generally as "comparatively queer." Indeed, the subject of comparison – in Lanser's case, the comparatist who crosses time to examine early sapphic modernity – might also be understood as being partially constituted through comparison and the resulting denaturalization. This power of comparison to generate queer subjectivities is just beginning to be theorized.

Higonnet, Spurlin, and I thought that, by queering the discipline of comparative studies, we could make our own contribution to the history of sexuality by challenging a certain model of writing lesbian and gay history, a challenge in which pre- and early modern studies as well as postcolonial studies have a stake, even if their stakes are slightly different. In one model, lesbian and gay history looks a lot like a narrative of progress, in which the rise of "homosexuality as we know it today," as the cliché goes, is structured much like a coming-out story. As we argued, this story – a colonial narrative of development – associates cultural others with a primitive past (see Fabian): "By coming out, the contemporary [lesbian or gay] subject leaves the dark continent of her past behind; by becoming homosexuality, same-sex desire does the same" (Hayes, Higonnet, and Spurlin 16). Comparison across time, we argued, transforming queer historiography into a comparative practice, could be therefore thought of as paralleling comparisons that have occurred across cultures as part of the multicultural movement as well as postcolonial studies, especially as these have now intersected with queer studies. In addition, a significant body of recent work grouped under the rubric of "queer temporalities" has taught us that sequence, linear narrative, narratives of progress or development – that is, the conventional if not dominant modes of history writing as well as the gay-history-as-coming-out-narrative model – have a certain sexuality, one that is hetero- and repronormative.

Regarding a potential *erotics* of comparison, we looked to Carolyn Dinshaw's theorization of an erotics of cruising the past, which she articulated in *Getting Medieval* (whose title is taken from an expression for sadistic sodomy in the film *Pulp Fiction*). This erotics even allowed her to bring essentialist John Boswell and constructionist Michel Foucault into a surprising embrace. Dinshaw also turned to postcolonial theory in general and, more specifically, Homi K. Bhabha for queer models of embracing the past. It is the potential, and potentially dangerous, desire on the part of the comparatist for her object of comparison that I would especially like to push further in my intervention here.

As I look back on my first book-length project, I can now see that as a younger scholar I was much more preoccupied with the *danger* of crossing cultures. When I was a graduate student, some compared my initial inquiries into a queer

Maghreb with the sexual tourism of European and American gay men who had "visited" North Africa before me. My first impulse was to reject this desire of "Oriental sex" and distance myself from what I then considered to be the predominant paradigm by which gay Westerners approached the Maghreb. So in the first chapter of my first book, *Queer Nations: Marginal Sexualities in the Maghreb*, entitled "Reading and Tourism: Sexual Approaches to the Maghreb," I aligned myself with a certain critique of sexual tourism while challenging the abjection of homosexuality and homoeroticism that one often finds in such critiques.

Yet even in that first chapter, I began to notice other ways of reading some gay men's attraction to the Maghreb. Think, for example, of Jean Genet, who offered the impetus for the following remarks by Kobena Mercer in his 1994 *Welcome to the Jungle: New Positions in Black Cultural Studies*:

> Under what conditions does eroticism mingle with political solidarity? When does it produce an effect of empowerment? And when does it produce an effect of disempowerment? When does identification imply objectification and when does it imply equality? . . . Genet's affective participation in the political construction of imagined communities suggests that the struggle for democratic agency always entails the negotiation of ambivalence subjectively.
> (219)

Around the same time, the very author of *Orientalism*, Edward W. Said himself, published his own reading of Genet's *Screens* and *Prisoner of Love*:

> Genet was no ordinary visitor, no simple observer or Western traveler in search of exotic peoples and places to write up in some future book . . . In the context of a dominant Orientalism that commanded, codified, articulated virtually all Western knowledge and experience of the Arab/Islamic world, there is something quietly but heroically subversive about Genet's extraordinary relationship with the Arabs.
> ("On Jean Genet" 232, 235)

While I might not be as generous as Said – I hope that it is obvious that I am not advocating a "return" to sexual tourism – I think that embracing rather than eschewing the dangers of an erotics of comparison might produce hitherto unacknowledged possibilities for a comparative queer studies.

Many Maghrebian writers, for their part, would find in certain Orientalist narratives an allegory of the very critique Said articulated. Rachid Boudjedra's *Les 1001 années de la nostalgie* (1001 Years of Nostalgia; 1979) and Leïla Sebbar's *Shérazade: 17 ans, brune, frisée, les yeux verts* (1982; translated as *Sherazade*, 2014), as well as her *Le pédophile et la maman (L'amour des enfants)* (Mommy and the Pedophile: Loving Children, 1980), first come to mind. Boudjedra's novel is about an American film crew that comes to a North African village to adapt the *Arabian Nights* for cinema. Their Orientalizing take literally becomes a form of colonization as they expropriate local goods and labor to make their film and even kill locals to use as corpses. The indigenous governor Bender Chah becomes their accomplice in this endeavor. Yet this enterprise is ultimately met with an anticolonial – in this case, also anti-Orientalist – revolt. In *Shérazade*, the eponymous character is the object of a number of Orientalist gazes. Her boyfriend Julien is literally an Orientalist, a student of Orientalist paintings and obsessed with photographing Shérazade. Shérazade opposes his gaze by destroying all his photos of her in his apartment except one, which she allows him to keep along with those he has not yet put up. Yet this anti-Orientalist resistance seems measured compared to her literal destruction of the means of production of Orientalist discourse when she destroys the camera of a photographer taking her picture at a party and ransacks the studio of a quasi-pornographic photographer with her friends.

Sexuality plays a crucial role in these anti-Orientalist double crossings. In Boudjedra's novel, Bender Chah's wife betrays her husband (and, allegorically, the institution of marriage) by reappropriating one of the giant fans used to propel magic carpets in the film in order to castrate the filmmakers. She thereby lays siege to a phallocratic colonialism and a phallocentric collaboration with the colonizer on the part of any indigenous elite. The eponymous pedophile in Sebbar's *Le pédophile et la maman* is a critic of sexual tourism, and its second-wave feminists are vociferous critics of pedophilia.

Yet the resistance of Sebbar's protagonists to Orientalism is not absolute; Shérazade's rejection of the Orientalist gaze does not lead her to break up with Julien. The very same feminists in *Le pédophile et la maman* have homoerotic relationships with their daughters, and Sebbar's eponymous mother identifies with the critique of the heteronormative family articulated by the radical pedophile movement in France. Her eponymous Mommy and Pedophile thus turn out to have something in common: loving children. In a sort of follow-up to *Le pédophile et la maman*, Sebbar published an essay entitled "Toute femme est une pédophile et une maman" (Every Woman Is a Pedophile and a Mommy). This is dangerous territory indeed. She even offers photographs of her own sons to accompany it. Boudjedra relies on the same Orientalist clichés and *idées reçues* as the American filmmakers to write his story of anti-Orientalist revolt. And Shérazade, at the end of Sebbar's novel, buys up all the postcard reproductions of Matisse's *Odalisque à la culotte rouge* to place into circulation from various points along the route of the anti-racist Beur March, which she follows along her way to a return to the Algeria of her ancestors. Implicitly acknowledging that, when it comes to Orientalist representation, there is no original reproduced on the postcards – all Orientalist representations are copies of some prior copy – she writes her own text on and over Matisse, thereby transforming his images to her own ends.

Such texts complicate Said's *Orientalism* by indulging in the pleasures of self-exoticization to turn Orientalist desire back against the colonizer. The empire does indeed write back in Sebbar and Boudjedra (see Ashcroft et al.), and it does so with a vengeance. Against the grain of colonialist texts, the protagonists, unable to return to a time prior to colonialism, fashion their selves in the fissures of discourses that justified and accompanied it. Othered by Orientalist texts, yet seeking out a possible subject position therein, writers like Sebbar and Boudjedra become both the subject and object of comparison in a splitting of the kind theorized by Bhabha, into more than one but not quite two. The relation between the Maghrebian writer and Orientalism is thus doubly comparative. Orientalism was already a comparatist act – although not one that we would usually want to embrace uncritically – in that it always compares the Orient to the West. But when writers like Sebbar and Boudjedra situate themselves as both "Orientals" and Orientalists, they transform the comparatist, usually the apogee of subjectivity, into an object of comparison as well. So in both Boudjedra's and Sebbar's cases, double-crossing Orientalist discourse splits the colonial subject into one that is simultaneously Orientalizing and Orientalized, a comparatist subject that is also an object of comparison.

Higonnet, Spurlin, and I sought to make such a splitting of the comparatist central to the field of comparative studies. When the Western comparatist becomes an object of comparison as well, the object of comparison becomes susceptible to a denaturalization that destabilizes the Eurocentrism that has traditionally defined the field. And it is precisely this kind of denaturalization that is central to queering as a critical move, so we sought to explore connections and establish parallels between geo-cultural, historical, and sexual denaturalizations as one possible way of queering the comparatist, and not just comparative studies as a field. This queering of the comparatist through comparison, then, might be thought of as a first step in a queer approach to the field that also queers it.

An expansion of what counts as comparison is also key to our understanding of what queer comparative studies might entail. Obviously, questioning the comparatist subject is part of this expansion. Comparative studies, of course, also crosses national borders, but one of the dimensions of comparative studies we sought to highlight and challenge in *Comparatively Queer* was the "national literatures" that have conventionally served as the objects of comparative literature, whose borders are often reinforced, not challenged, through comparison. When I interviewed at the MLA convention for a split appointment between comparative literature and French with a newly minted PhD in French, a prominent comparatist patiently explained to me that comparatists were expected to work in at least three national traditions. Misremembering the languages I had listed in my CV, he asked what my three were. Even then, I knew what *not* to say – Algeria, Morocco, and Tunisia – even though these were the "national" traditions of my dissertation.

A challenge to such Eurocentric notions of "national traditions" has been an underlying current of the decennial reports since the 1995 Bernheimer Report (see also Saussy). It continues in the current discussion, particularly in David Damrosch's contribution, "World Literature as Figure and as Ground" (this volume), which defines the concept of world literature not only interculturally but also intraculturally – for example, as the challenge to national literatures that minor literatures à la Deleuze and Guattari can carry out from within. I would align our desire for inversion in making the subject of comparison its object with

Damrosch's notion of intracultural comparison. For this is where the double crossings I have described take on their full potential as a betrayal of comparative literature's national interests, following the example of Jean Genet, who cast his betrayal of Frenchness as a queer form of revolt.

So the crossing of borders in both directions becomes a double-crossing in the sense of a treason that goes both ways in the literal and figurative senses of the expression, the latter referring to bisexuality. So whereas the colloquial expression "comparatively queer" can mean queerer than some, but nonetheless not too queer, we proceeded as if there could be no such as thing as too queer. *Comparatively Queer* thus became for us a way of naming our project of queering comparative studies and making comparatist strategies central to queer studies. This particular example of going both ways was inseparable in our minds from inverting the subject of comparison to its object. Paradoxically, this becoming-object double-crosses his (and I chose this word carefully) objectivity. Comparatively queer studies should, again, queer the comparatist as well.

In *Death of a Discipline*, Gayatri Chakravorty Spivak calls for "a new Comparative Literature . . . supplemented by Area Studies" (68, 72): "The new step that I am proposing would . . . work to make the traditional linguistic sophistication of Comparative Literature supplement Area Studies (and history, anthropology, political theory, and sociology) by approaching the language of the other not only as a 'field' language" (9). In spite of her characterization of these comments as "the last gasp of a dying discipline" (xii), she does not actually kill off the field as much as reimagine it. A comparatively queer studies, then, can further reimagine this betrayal, this death as what the French call "la petite mort," the sweet and painful ecstasy of orgasm.

Works cited

Ashcroft, Bill, Gareth Griffiths, and Helen Tiffin. *The Empire Writes Back: Theory and Practice in Post-Colonial Literatures*. London: Routledge, 1989. Print.

Bernheimer, Charles, ed. *Comparative Literature in the Age of Multiculturalism*. Baltimore: Johns Hopkins UP, 1995. Print.

Boudjedra, Rachid. *Les 1001 années de la nostalgie*. Paris: Gallimard, 1979. Print.

Deleuze, Gilles, and Félix Guattari. 1975. *Kafka: Notes Toward a Minor Literature*. Trans. Dana Polan. Minneapolis: U of Minnesota P, 1986. Print.

Dinshaw, Carolyn. *Getting Medieval: Sexualities and Communities, Pre- and Postmodern*. Durham: Duke UP, 1999. Print.

Duberman, Martin Bauml, Martha Vicinus, and George Chauncey, Jr., eds. *Hidden from History: Reclaiming the Gay and Lesbian Past*. New York: New American Library, 1989. Print.

Fabian, Johannes. *Time and the Other: How Anthropology Makes Its Object*. New York: Columbia UP, 1983. Print.

Foucault, Michel. *The History of Sexuality*. Vol. 1. 1976. Trans. Robert Hurley. New York: Random House, 1978. Print.

Halperin, David M. *How to Do the History of Homosexuality*. Chicago: U of Chicago P, 2002. Print.

Hayes, Jarrod. *Queer Nations: Marginal Sexualities in the Maghreb.* Chicago: U of Chicago P, 2000. Print.

Hayes, Jarrod, Margaret R. Higonnet, and William J. Spurlin. "Introduction." *Comparatively Queer: Interrogating Identities across Time and Cultures.* Ed. Hayes, Higonnet, and Spurlin. New York: Palgrave Macmillan, 2010. 1–19. Print.

Higonnet, Margaret R., ed. *Borderwork: Feminist Engagements with Comparative Literature.* Ithaca: Cornell UP, 1994. Print.

Lanser, Susan S. "Comparatively Lesbian: Queer Feminist Theory and the Sexuality of History." *ACL(x): Otherwise.* Columbia: U of South Carolina. 6 Feb. 2015. Presentation.

———. "Mapping Sapphic Modernity." *Comparatively Queer: Interrogating Identities across Time and Cultures.* Ed. Jarrod Hayes, Margaret R. Higonnet, and William J. Spurlin. New York: Palgrave Macmillan, 2010. 69–89. Print.

———. "The Sexuality of History." *Symposium on Lesbian and Queer Historiography.* Ann Arbor, U of Michigan. 4 Feb. 2011. Presentation.

———. *The Sexuality of History: Modernity and the Sapphic, 1565–1830.* Chicago: U of Chicago P, 2014. Print.

Mercer, Kobena. *Welcome to the Jungle: New Positions in Black Cultural Studies.* New York: Routledge, 1994. Print.

Said, Edward W. "On Jean Genet's Late Works." *Imperialism and Theatre: Essays on World Theatre, Drama and Performance.* Ed. J. Ellen Gainor. London: Routledge, 1995. 230–42. Print.

Saussy, Haun, ed. *Comparative Literature in an Age of Globalization.* Baltimore: Johns Hopkins UP, 2006. Print.

Sebbar, Leïla. *Le pédophile et la maman (L'amour des enfants).* Paris: Stock, 1980. Print.

———. *Shérazade: 17 ans, brune, frisée, les yeux verts.* Paris: Stock, 1982. Print.

———. "Toute femme est une pédophile et une maman." *Sorcières* 23 (1981): 32–5. Print.

Spivak, Gayatri Chakravorty. *Death of a Discipline.* New York: Columbia UP, 2003. Print.

Trans

Jessica Berman

Over the past decade, comparative literature has become animated by what I call "trans" critical perspectives. The rubric "trans" has affinities with the kind of "transdisciplinary" work that has always characterized comparative literature and that has motivated many of the prizewinning books of the past decade. But it also draws from "transnational," "transmedial," and "transgender" critical practice. For me, "trans" does not function best attached to a noun but rather understood as an "orientation" of critical approaches, perspectives, attitudes, and habits of reading or experiencing (Berman). A "trans" approach is mobilized between and across disciplinary or conceptual categories and might be deployed in relation to several areas of critical concern at once, thereby challenging definitional assumptions that push toward separation. In this way a trans perspective helps us theorize the comparative scholarly gesture as potentially disruptive, destabilizing, and transgressive as well as grounded in comparison.

A "trans" orientation might show how transdisciplinary scholarship can become importantly transnational by examining texts outside of national or imperial circuits of travel, nonprivileged migrations of people and texts, or trajectories outside of the usual metro-centric routes of travel. Or it might intersect with the work being done in transgender, queer, and disability studies, where researchers such as Judith Halberstam and Susan Stryker have theorized the "trans-" as a challenge to normative habits of identity and the power dynamics surrounding them. Trans approaches to comparative literature informed by this theory carry an oppositional valence derived from the prefix in the word "transgress," seeking out transgressive relationships, affiliations, or interconnections among literary texts and their circuits of travel.

Several other contemporary approaches to comparative literature might be understood to deploy "trans" in this oppositional manner. In José Saldívar's concept of "trans-Americanity," trans becomes a critical attitude or approach illuminating oppositional routes of travel or transgressive relationships. Saldívar argues for trans-American approaches to literature that allow a shift in "acting and thinking from the nation-state level to a thinking and acting at the planetary and world-systems level" (xvii). The philosopher Enrique Dussel deploys the term "transmodernidad" (from Rosa María Rodríguez Magda) in a similarly "transgressive" or "transformative" way to discuss how modernity might be reconceived from the perspective of Latin America. As he puts it, "the . . . trans-modern attempts to indicate the radical novelty of the irruption . . . [of] those . . . cultures in the process of development which assume the challenges of Modernity . . . but which respond from another place, another location" (18). Recent scholarship in media studies understands work that moves from big screen to small or that plays out across several media as potentially "transmedial." Henry Jenkins also claims that "transmedia storytelling is the art of world making" (21), challenging scholars of comparative literature to recognize its power to shift the relationship between world and text.

Most significant, though, is the explosion of transgender theory in the past decade. Halberstam, Stryker, Stephen Whittle, and others have described trans theory as "anything that disrupts, denaturalizes, rearticulates and makes visible: the links we assume to exist between a sexual body and the social roles it is expected to play" (Stryker and Whittle 3). A transgender critical perspective invites us to recognize the deep connection between transgender phenomena and the discourses of power in which they are inscribed, to challenge their normativity, and to recognize the ethically and politically productive dimension of that challenge. A trans critical optic, practice, or way of practicing comparative literature can, therefore, provide a lens to see the many spheres of operation of texts and the challenges they can pose to normative regimes of embodiment and subjectivity globally. Jay Proesser has claimed that "resexing . . . is made possible by narrativization" and that "transsexuality is always narrative work" (4), pointing out the intimate connection between trans attitudes and literary study. Howard Chiang's collection *Transgender China* marks the important convergence of transgender, transnational, and transdisciplinary critical attitudes in comparative literature. All these perspectives show the power of a trans approach not only to "disrupt" and "denaturalize" but also to help us rearticulate comparative literature now.

Works cited

Berman, Jessica. "Is the Trans in Transnational the Trans in Transgender?" *Modernism/modernity* 24.2 (April 2017).

Chiang, Howard, ed. *Transgender China*. New York: Palgrave, 2012. Print.

Dussel, Enrique. "Transmodernity and Interculturality: An Interpretation from the Perspective of Philosophy of Liberation." Web. 10 Dec. 2013.

Halberstam, Judith. *In a Queer Time and Place: Transgender Bodies, Subcultural Lives*. New York: New York UP, 2005. Print.

Jenkins, Henry. *Convergence Culture: Where Old and New Media Collide*. New York: New York UP, 2006. Print.

Proesser, Jay. *Second Skins: The Bodily Narratives of Transsexuality*. New York: Columbia UP, 1998. Print.

Rodríguez Magda, Rosa María. *Transmodernidad*. Barcelona: Anthropos, 2004. Print.

Saldívar, José. *Trans-Americanity*. Durham, NC: Duke UP, 2012. Print.

Stryker, Susan, and Stephen Whittle. *Transgender Studies Reader*. New York: Routledge, 2006. Print.

Future reading

Rebecca L. Walkowitz

How will we read literary works in the future? And how does thinking about the future of literary works change the way we read?

Answer #1: *Future reading will require foreign reading.* Works of literature increasingly enter the world in several languages, originals and translations appearing at the same time or following each other closely. This is especially true for works that begin in dominant languages, such as English, French, German, Russian, Italian, and Spanish (yes, Spanish follows Italian),[1] which sometimes appear in translated editions even before they appear in what we have come to call original ones (Walkowitz, "Comparison Literature"; "Close Reading in an Age of Global Writing"; and *Born Translated*). Reading a work in its first or original edition, if we mean the edition that has appeared in the world before all others, may no longer automatically mean reading a work in the language in which it was composed. What used to be the work's future or "afterlife," as the English translation of Benjamin famously puts it (71), may now be its present or even its past. In the future, the future is now.

Therefore, we will have to approach literary works as if they exist in several languages, media, and formats and as if they are written, from the get-go, for many audiences. Conceptually, this will be true even for works that do not travel because even untranslated works are read by divergent audiences and may at some later point enter new languages and contexts. Future reading is foreign reading because it implies something about the people who encounter texts: they are not a predictable group, and they are not contained by one territory or ethnos. Future reading also implies something about the nature of the reader's encounter: it is not unique, and it can't be understood as "native" or natural.

Foreign reading, as I am calling it, differs from the kind of reading most of us do now because we generally assume, first, that literary texts belong to one language; second, that we can tell from the publication history or the author's biography what that language is; and, third, that there are readers who were born knowing that language from the start (see Yildiz). However, languages are not one, as scholars who work on Anglophone, Francophone, and Sinophone literary studies have been telling us for some time.[2] And people do not begin their lives as competent or fluent readers of any language. Reading is an acquired skill, easily accessible to some and secured with great difficulty by others. Some people read several languages well. Some have partial access to a language or to a version of that language: consider all of the English-language readers in the world, their various locations and proficiencies, including third- and fourth-language users, and also the many regional versions of English in which literary works are published. Some people do not read at all. The concept of foreign reading alters our approach to the location of texts, which now potentially belong to several places or territories. It also alters our approach to readers, whose access depends on degrees of expertise or experience rather than intrinsic knowledge. From the perspective of foreign reading, a book does not have native readers, only readers.

Answer #2: *Foreign reading, recognizing the foreignness of literary texts, animates collectivities that are both smaller and larger than the nation, and that operate both within and across languages.* Foreign reading does not create these collectivities so much as it creates the disciplinary space and nomenclature that allow us to see them. Foreign reading decouples literature from language, allowing us to consider how works appear in more than one language, how they are read and used differently across literary and nonliterary cultures, and how they enter, alter, mix, and depart languages. Like the Sinophone or Anglophone, foreign reading registers and loosens what Yucong Hao calls "the customary disciplinary divides and national literary histories" that have organized our work. In the future, we will need to acknowledge that we study literature *in a language* – "literature in English," for example – rather than a language's literature. This is because the texts we hold in our hands or read on our screens do not belong, intrinsically or permanently, to any language in particular. This does not mean that we do not study those works in languages. Indeed, we do and must. But it does mean that we avoid treating texts as if they are possessed by a language, as if they should be analyzed exclusively in that language, and as if they are intended above all for – and in the service of producing – monolingual readers (Yildiz).

The framework of literature *in languages* emphasizes system as well as series, and this is important.[3] It reminds us that languages exist in relation to other languages and that works of literature are produced within that relation, whether in a language of many readers, such as English, or in a language of fewer readers, such as Portuguese, Zulu, Japanese, or Turkish. This is especially important for languages that function in many places throughout the world. "Literature in English" intimates languages beyond English while registering that English is, in fact, a language. Pascale Casanova has noted that the dominant language is the one you don't think about; it is the language whose histories and debts can be forgotten. *We need to find strategies of unforgetting.*

From the perspective of the future, the literary work is open-ended and ongoing. Insofar as the literature of the future will be written *for* translation, calculating its presence in many languages, and *from* translation, incorporating the trace, the influence, and the needs of other readers, future reading may have to be different reading, both technically and philosophically. That will mean paying attention to elements of the text that operate across languages as well as elements that do not move languages easily: typography as well as idiom, plot as well as pun. Of course, there is no need to choose among these concerns, yet future reading, because it includes works read in translation or read in languages we know only a little, as well as works in languages we know well, will involve both partial reading (reading only some of the work; or some versions of the work) and collaborative reading (we read some parts; our colleagues and other audiences read other parts). Production may recapitulate circulation: today's literary works written for global audiences find ways to incorporate the paths of translation into the forms of composition. It seems likely that they will do this all the more inventively in the future, thus calling for reading that registers new features of literary creativity and can place those features within the institutional and technical history of literary innovation.

Answer #3: *In the future, we will need to read comparatively, by which I mean reading across editions and formats and also recognizing that any one edition and format contributes to the work rather than exhausts it. This changes reading, philosophically as well as technically, because it defines the work by its appearance in the world rather than by its inherent or original characteristics.* Approaching the language of a work as one among many, even for works that begin in that language, has the salutary effect of making languages less neutral. You may think it would be the other way around, since specifying and even celebrating the linguistic nature of a text are usually historicizing gestures. And neutrality has seemed like the ideal, as we have worked to subtract the ideological and cultural privilege attached to the languages of imperial, economic, and intellectual dominance. But in fact we engage with a work's history better the more we acknowledge its possible future as a text in other languages, other media, and other works. A literary work's past becomes simply one of its possible histories and need not precondition its lasting appearance or impact. There is nothing neutral about the history of languages. Understanding languages mechanically rather than sentimentally can help us see that.

Answer #4: *Instead of asking where or in what language a work of literature belongs, we need to ask how it belongs.* How does it get to that language, and where does it go – or not go? What are the pathways and impediments to belonging? Because we want to know, in the fullest sense, how language matters to a literary work, we will need to read more versions of works, whether editions, translations, adaptations, or rewritings. And we will need to evaluate reception at local, regional, and transnational scales. This will involve analytic strategies that complement reading and that may involve counting; and it will also involve asking how geopolitical histories have shaped what texts mean, where they appear, and who can encounter them.[4] We can begin by simply acknowledging that there are (only) readers and that what they encounter are versions of literary works. By demoting national literatures to literatures in languages, we take the first step. That's how we read – and become readers – in the future.

Notes

1 These are the top six, according to the UNESCO's *Index Translationum.*
2 One of the most recent and powerful exhortations of this argument is Simon Gikandi's editor's column, "Provicializing English." I have in mind too Shu-Mei

Shih's crucial articulation of the "Sinophone" in "The Concept of the Sinophone," and Brian Bernards's argument about how the creolization of the Sinophone "de-ethnicizes and de-territorializes" Chineseness in "Beyond Diaspora" (325). See also Yucong Hao's excellent discussion of the Sinophone and its relationship to Francophone and Anglophone literary studies in this volume.
3 I am indebted for this formulation to Barbara Cassin, who calls for analyzing "philosophy within languages" (xvii).
4 For an excellent example of how "counting" can refine the history of "reading," see Goldstone and Underwood. Goldstone takes up the relationship between reception and reading in "Hatterr Abroad."

Works cited

Benjamin, Walter. "The Task of the Translator." *Illuminations: Essays and Reflections.* Trans. Harry Zohn. New York: Schocken, 1969. 69–82. Print.

Bernards, Brian C. "Beyond Diaspora and Multiculturalism: Recuperating Creolization in Postcolonial Sinophone Malaysian Literature." *Postcolonial Studies* 15 (2012): 311–29. Web. 4 Dec. 2015.

Casanova, Pascale. "What Is a Dominant Language? Giacomo Leopardi: Theoretician of Linguistic Inequality." Trans. Marlon Jones. *New Literary History* 44 (2013): 379–99. Web. 4 Dec. 2015.

Cassin, Barbara. "Introduction." Trans. Michael Wood. *Dictionary of Untranslatables: A Philosophical Lexicon.* Ed. Barbara Cassin. Princeton: Princeton UP, 2013. xvii–xx. Print.

Gikandi, Simon. "Editor's Column: Provincializing English." *PMLA* 129 (2014): 7–17. Web. 4 Dec. 2015.

Goldstone, Andrew. "Hatterr Abroad: G.V. Desani on the Stage of World Literature." *Contemporary Literature* 55 (2014): 466–500. Web. 4 Dec. 2015.

Goldstone, Andrew, and Ted Underwood. "The Quiet Transformations of Literary Studies: What Thirteen Thousand Scholars Could Tell Us." *New Literary History* 45 (2014): 359–84. Web. 4 Dec. 2015.

Hao, Yucong. "The Sinophone." *Futures of Comparative Literature.* Ed. Ursula Heise. London: Routledge, 2017. 228–9. Print.

Shih, Shu-Mei. "The Concept of the Sinophone." *PMLA* 126 (2011): 709–18. Web. 4 Dec. 2015.

UNESCO. *Index Translationum.* Web. 14 Jan. 2015.

Walkowitz, Rebecca L. *Born Translated: The Contemporary Novel in an Age of World Literature.* New York: Columbia University Press, 2015. Print.

———. "Close Reading in an Age of Global Writing." *Modern Language Quarterly* 74 (2013): 171–95. Web. 4 Dec. 2015.

———. "Comparison Literature." *New Literary History* 40 (2009): 567–82. Web. 4 Dec. 2015.

Yildiz, Yasmin. *Beyond the Mother Tongue: The Postmonolingual Condition.* New York: Fordham UP, 2012. Print.

Close reading and the global university (notes on localism)

Rey Chow

In the early twenty-first century, the campaigns to globalize the American university are often accompanied by a narrative that reverses the US-centric approach to higher education of the postwar years.[1] During the Cold War decades, the United States attracted large numbers of foreign students to its campuses and put them through sufficient training before sending them home to their own countries to disseminate American ways. These days, the pedagogical model seems to be different. A new emphasis on the local, on how US institutions must learn from diverse cultures, their histories, and their languages, and bring all that learning back to the United States so that its institutions can improve themselves with reference to these exotic others, is much more characteristic of current higher-education administrative rhetoric. How might this turn to the local as a nexus of global agency (i.e., a connection from which meaningful, because other-centered, transactions are deemed to arise) be seen as coeval, if not codeterminant, with another dimension of higher learning today – namely, the push for a return, in the aftermath of the "high theory" decades, to the study of literature? What might close reading – the literary method associated with critics such as I. A. Richards and his contemporaries and followers, such as Allen Tate, J. C. Ransom, M. Beardsley, W. K. Wimsatt, William Empson, T. S. Eliot, and Cleanth Brooks, and strategic to the consolidation of English as a historically recent field of study – have to tell us about the shifting academic institutional relations around 2015?

In raising this question, I am, of course, thinking about close reading in a rather different manner from either its supporters or detractors. Indeed, the juxtaposition of close reading and the global university may seem at first to be a juxtaposition of incommensurates. What would the aggressively futuristic, revenue-oriented placement of US campuses in distant locales, such as Abu Dhabi, Singapore, and China, have in common with a practice by Anglo-American literature specialists, or for that matter have anything to do with them?

To begin to answer this question, it is necessary to think of the controversy over close reading, beginning with its early promoters, such as Richards, as itself symptomatic of the apparent decline of a certain kind of knowledge production, traceable to the European Romantic tradition and its cultivation of an aesthetic education in Friedrich Schiller's terms. (One of the words Richards often uses, for instance, is "feelings": the sentiments are very much at stake here.) This decline is usually perceived in relation to the type of labor that is language – specifically, to language's loss of power and impotence to change or *affect* the world.

In response to the putative decline of language, humanities scholars have to this day tended to reinvest in language's relevance by emphasizing the antagonism and incompatibility between humanistic learning, on the one hand, and science and technology, on the other. Martin Heidegger is an outstanding example of a philosopher who tries to reanimate language from this perspective. For Heidegger, language not only is the dwelling of Being but also is equipped with the mystical power to interpellate, to call and bid things to come forth (see in particular 189–210). Similarly turning to poetic language as a way to reclaim the universal significance of humanistic learning, the Anglo-American New Critics exemplify the appreciation of a poem taken in isolation, whose reality they consider independent of historical happenings and authorial intention. "A poem should not mean/But be": in this well-known announcement from Archibald MacLeish's "Ars Poetica" (127), one detects a desire for the work of art to be (understood as) ontologically self-sufficient, as though any swerve into meaning would amount to a compromise. For its New Critical advocates, thus, close reading as a theory of literary labor seems, even in its nascent stages, a *redemptive* undertaking, designed to restore something that is threatened from all sides – by modernization, urbanization, science, technology, mass culture, and consumerism. A text read by itself is believed to yield truths of a kind that, notwithstanding their commonsense, are unique to the act of poetic articulation.

In ethnographic terms, what is sometimes invoked in derogation as "textualism" in this context may in fact be seen as a practice of localism, whereby the text is treated as a kind of native informant, one that can speak for itself while its interlocutors, its readers, painstakingly engage such speech and take note. This intense, meticulous attentiveness to the words on the page is, however, only part of a more basic belief in an organic whole that unifies disparate meanings. Richards, for his part, readily identifies the arts, and in particular poetry, as a type of activity that, albeit not necessarily different from other mundane activities, offers the quintessential access to such an emotionally integrated experience. Close reading, he writes, is instrumental in bringing about this access:

> All will agree that while delicate intellectual operations are in progress brass bands should be silent. But the band more often than not is an essential part of the poetry. It can, however, be silenced, if we wish, while we disentangle and master the sense, and afterwards its co-operation will no longer confuse us. A practical "moral" emerges from this which deserves more prominence than it usually receives. It is that *most poetry needs several readings – in which its varied factors may fit themselves together – before it can be grasped.* Readers who claim to dispense with this preliminary study, who think that all good poetry should come home to them in entirety at a first reading, hardly realize how clever they must be.
>
> (*Principles* 190; my emphasis)

With a vocabulary consisting of words such as "wholeness," "unity," "integration," "connection" (of things which are otherwise disparate), and "ordering" (of experience into a single response), Richards alludes to a certain presence, one that endows what exists at the verbal level with the import of a profound emotional *fit* or coherence. If "a poem should not mean/But be," it is less because a poem is complete in and of itself than because some larger condition of possibility – a certain ground if you will – enables it to speak. The poem's autonomy, in other words, is pre-articulated by a larger if intangible Being (to borrow from Heidegger) whose essence or power is exactly one of *holding things together*. One can interpret this integrative relation with a larger Being in religious or secular terms, by way of the existence of divinity or something like a social contract. Whether it is God or the social collective will, the pre-articulation suggests that a bigger force is there to mediate, regulate, and indeed govern the production of meanings through the poetic text.

In revisiting the New Critical tradition, subsequent generations of literary critics, notably Paul de Man, have targeted precisely this implicit organicism as a nonviable point of departure for literary criticism. "Richards postulates a perfect continuity between the sign and the thing signified," de Man writes ("Dead-End" 232; see also "Form and Intent"). In the wake of poststructuralist theory, the New Critical project's epistemic and moral premise for close reading – the groundedness of what some might call a metaphysics of wholeness – is fundamentally disrupted. To this end, Richards's discussion of "pseudostatements" interestingly foreshadows Jean-François Lyotard's discussion of the postmodern condition (Richards, "Pseudo-Statements"; Lyotard). Like the metanarratives that, according to Lyotard, have lost their exclusive claims to truth in the postmodern era, pseudostatements for Richards are the kinds of assertions that, even though not scientifically verifiable, have lent emotional equilibrium to the ordinary person's sense of the everyday world. As it is increasingly difficult to believe in pseudostatements, as aspirations become increasingly conflictual without shared bases, Richards writes, "Our attitudes and impulses are being compelled to become *self-supporting*" ("Pseudo-Statements" 25; my emphasis): self-supporting, that is, in a world in which different claims to truth, all contending for legitimacy, are becoming ever more incompatible and irreconcilable with one another. What, then, is close reading in this desolate condition of modernity and postmodernity? What may the literary labor of close reading accomplish?

Deconstruction has provided one kind of answer: the text may be regarded as a material phenomenon that keeps doubling on itself, referring to itself, in a potentially endless series of reflexive moves that reveal language's alterity (or perpetual self-alienation) as its ultimate purpose. In pursuing the text in this manner that some term "regressive," deconstruction brings into the open a question that is implicitly foreclosed in New Criticism: what is meant by "close" in close reading? Is close reading simply a matter of reading repeatedly, as Richards's phrase "several readings" suggests, or is it a matter of reading symptomatically, approximately, or seamlessly, without gaps? Is close reading a quest for some ultimate oneness? Unlike for the New Critics, close textual reading for de Man, Derrida, and their followers is not a means of inferring a transcendent unity somewhere. Rather, it is an intimate engagement with the text that is, nonetheless, *forever unmet* by a definitively reciprocating or holding ground. However precise and penetrating, this close textual reading is now readily sliding off – and horizontally displaced onto other words in play, in the literal sense of allegory ("other speak"), *ad infinitum*.

In this shift to reading as an allegorical mode of operation in the deconstructive sense, it is details, what often turn out to be unfitting or ill-fitting *parts*, that acquire a new conceptual significance: details detached from a presumed final cause, such as social or communal connections; details that are eccentric or singular; details that multiply by self-generation. Close textual readings after poststructuralism may be said to be engagements with linguistic details or parts of this kind, leading much less to a restoration of any deeper connectedness than to a series of ongoing allegorical performances. No longer rooted in an organic whole, a textual detail can acquire an existence of its own, in the sense that any part or bit of information – verbal, visual, sonic, narrative, numerical, and otherwise – is now potentially an allegory ready to take off in the performative mode.

Although we are a long way from the lone poem that should not mean but be, the New Critics seem, in hindsight, to have helped pave the way for this ascendency of the allegorical-as-performative in our time. For, grounded or not, once ontological self-sufficiency has been given the status of a moral virtue, it inevitably becomes an ideal to which everyone aspires. Our postmodern trends in proliferating narratives, in particular narratives about the self, may in this light be seen as a continuation of the revitalization of poetic language as native informant or as *native performant*.[2] The "postmodern condition" is one in which everyone feels entitled to such poetic rejuvenation: however trivial or odd, any human being's life story deserves to be received as an organically whole work with its self-originating, self-validating, and, as Richards writes, "self-supporting" value. To this extent, the US academy's celebration of multicultural identities, multiethnic literatures, and exotic local cultures around the world – in so many varieties of "Let X speak!" – may be seen, historically speaking, as a logical extension of the unfinished New Critical project on a transnational scale.

Returning to the questions I asked at the beginning, let me propose that the valency of allegorical parts becoming generative native performants underscores the epistemic affinities between what at first appear to be incommensurate realities – the secluded and arcane practice of close reading, based on literary texts, behind the walls of academe, on one hand; and the financially ambitious, jet-setting business dealings of the global university, on the other. On the world map – a very large text – "local" places, such as Abu Dhabi, Singapore, and cities in China, are the hitherto unconnected parts that Western institutions of higher learning are eager to close read – to hover over, to scrutinize, to mine, to bore into, to open up – in a word, to perform and let perform. Once these institutions close in upon these other places and spaces, however, what becomes inevitably clear is the necessity for a different order of reading – namely, translation, interpretation, and historicization – as people realize that nothing, not even ordinary, everyday communication, is straightforward or can be taken for granted.

Are performances of the global text in the guise of valorizing the local redemptive, restorative exercises, then, as the New Critics and their followers imagine close reading to be, or are they exercises in groundless allegorical proliferation, as suggested by poststructuralist theory's reading of New Criticism? On these large and abstract questions hangs the balance of the mindboggling ramifications of the global university that implicate all academic workers today.

Notes

1 A version of this short essay was presented on the panel "I. A. Richards Now" at the MLA Annual Convention in Vancouver, January 2015. My sincere thanks to Bill Brown, Ming-bao Yue, and the audience for their responsive questions and comments.
2 I am indebted to Zak Sitter for this perceptive term.

Works cited

De Man, Paul. "The Dead-End of Formalist Criticism." *Blindness and Insight: Essays in the Rhetoric of Contemporary Criticism.* 2nd ed. Minneapolis: U of Minnesota P, 1983. 229–45. Print.

———. "Form and Intent in the American New Criticism." *Blindness and Insight: Essays in the Rhetoric of Contemporary Criticism.* 2nd ed. Minneapolis: U of Minnesota P, 1983. 20–35. Print.

Heidegger, Martin. *Poetry, Language, Thought.* Trans. Albert Hofstadter. New York: Harper Colophon, 1971. Print.

Lyotard, Jean-François. *The Postmodern Condition: A Report on Knowledge.* Trans. Geoff Bennington and Brian Massumi. Minneapolis: U of Minnesota P, 1984. Print.

MacLeish, Archibald. "Ars Poetica." *Poetry* 28.3 (1926): 126–7. Print.

Richards, I. A. *Principles of Literary Criticism.* New York: Harcourt Brace, 1925. Print.

——— "Pseudo-Statements." *Twentieth Century Criticism: The Major Statements.* Ed. William J. Handy and Max Westbrook. New York: Free Press, 1974. 22–7. Print.

Sitter, Zak. "The Native Performant: Linguistic Authority in the Text of Romantic Orientalism." *Differences: A Journal of Feminist Cultural Studies* 21.2 (2010): 109–41. Print.

Worlds

World famous, locally
Insights from the study of international canonization

Mads Rosendahl Thomsen

The two previous ACLA reports on the state of the discipline both felt confident enough to sum up the age in one word in their titles: "multiculturalism" in the 1995 Bernheimer Report and "globalization" in the 2006 Saussy Report. Both volumes dealt with the changing status and configuration of nation-states, but it is striking that the dominant accompanying term in Saussy's report, "world literature," was nowhere to be found just a decade earlier. The shift toward world literature was and is meaningful, emphasizing the cosmopolitan desire to read across languages and calling for new ways of thinking about comparison in a way that is less dependent on national frameworks. As if to strengthen this point, the past decade has been marked by the success of migrant and bicultural writers. This complicates the idea of comparing literatures, as Rebecca Walkowitz among others has shown, but it also emphasizes the complexity of contemporary identity formation (Walkowitz 527–29).

The relative success of world literature as a new agenda has provided a welcome critique or supplement to the practices of comparative literature, which in many ways lacked the essential curiosity for all kinds of literature and excused itself for not living up to the global aspirations of the discipline with references to linguistic barriers and institutional divisions. At the same time, it is a good thing that the discourse of world literature has not become too dominant or generally agreed upon. The local and the national are as important as they were in the times of Johann Wolfgang von Goethe, Georg Brandes, and Erich Auerbach, to mention three proponents of world literature who did not promote what Kwame Anthony Appiah has called "ruthless cosmopolitanism" (220–1). World literature is always seen from somewhere, and even if there is a unified system of literature, as Franco Moretti has pointed out ("Conjectures" 55–6), there is not one agreed-upon world literature. Yet, there are many ways to put the differences to work. Beyond the entangled definitions of the object of comparative literature, there is also a divide between qualitative and quantitative approaches, which will become more important in the future.

A starting point for exploring such divisions between the qualitative and the quantitative could be the significant, but understudied, difference between national canons and the international influences of works. "Canonization" is in this respect neither the use of power to determine curricula nor an idiosyncratic scholar's projection of his or her own preferences onto a general idea of what literary history should be. Canonization should instead be seen as the complex social mechanism through which numerous agents – readers, critics, teachers, publishers – take part in a continuing conversation about what has value as literature. Some agents are more powerful than others, but one can look at literature as a vast system of communication about what interests people, and how we respond to texts by strangers and integrate new perspectives on the world. Canons are not static, but they do offer ample resistance to idiosyncratic statements such as "Forget Shakespeare, focus on Jonson," or "No one should bother to read Gilgamesh." As such, canonization can be an important starting point for exploring the structures of literary cultures and cross-cultural influences, and, as I shall argue at the end of this chapter, digitization and access to data have opened up new ways to study them.

Local and global canonization

Several benefits come from putting the difference between local or national and international canonization to more serious use. The growing interest in world literature has been accompanied by a more nuanced perspective on translations and their vital role in enabling a cosmopolitan literary community beyond that of experts, whose expertise would in any case be too limited to talk of "the world." But even if it has been recognized that translations are also a particular footprint of interest – a window of insight with a distinctive shape – which may be a distortion of the original literature, much more work could be done to explore that difference.

Long-term influences often tell a story of strange attractors, winners that take all the attention in the long run and make the range of literatures read in the international circuits appear narrow compared to the complexity of the local traditions and historical memory. The idealist vision of world literature as the canon of the best works and those that enlighten readers most about other cultures (which is not always the same) is often countered by the harsh reality of the works that actually get translated, republished, anthologized, and taught. Still, I believe that it is comparative scholars' task to highlight the difference between specialists' valuation of particular works and the cultural transfers that actually take place so as to uncover different kinds of reception and circulation. The difference between a text's potential for influence and its actual adoption by other literary cultures becomes even more interesting in literatures that share the ability to produce what I have termed "lonely canonicals," writers who are far more circulated and recognized internationally than their contemporary compatriots and whose works are very different in kind from the mainstreams of their local literary culture (Thomsen 44–49).

Translations remain the most reliable source of describing the international influence of literature (Moretti, *Atlas*; Sapiro). Even if people around the world read more and more in English, vernaculars still dominate local markets, and the circulation of world literature is still very much dependent on patterns of translation. But rather than stopping at the sociological facts of cultural exchange, the discipline should use the streams of translations to reflect upon the different value systems and preferences for genres, styles, and themes that give shape to the world's literary communities. A more nuanced approach to the difference between local and international canonization would also help the collaboration between specialists and generalists that is a precondition for working with world literature (Damrosch 287–8).

There is also an important, if not always fortunate or flattering, side to the difference between local and international canonization – namely, the way it risks misrepresenting literary cultures and cultures at large: no, Denmark is not exactly like a Hans Christian Andersen fairy tale or the world of Søren Kierkegaard, and more importantly, these authors are not quite representative of the Danish literature of their time. The magical realism that works so effectively not only in the Latin American fiction of the Boom but also in authors such as Haruki Murakami and Salman Rushdie is not necessarily representative of Latin American, Japanese, or Indian culture. The partial misrepresentations of cultures through their international canonization can be captured through a better description of the international republic of letters and its seemingly autonomous existence beyond national preferences, as Pascale Casanova, for example, has shown. On the other hand, one should also be skeptical of the misrepresentations and ask if enchantment, authenticity, and magic cast large shadows over the international representations of a literature.

For these reasons, the critic, teacher, or scholar will have to balance the roles of the disinterested analyst of canonization and the activist who points out overlooked treasures that deserve as much attention in world literature as those works that have established themselves. In this way, the critic becomes an envoi by analyzing international circulation with the hope to bring a work to world attention.

The digital moment

Is there a proper tag or label for the present moment of literary scholarship? The process of globalization has by no means come to an end, and the continued influence of migrant writers is evident in numerous studies, recently and very impressively summed up in Sigrid Löffler's survey *Die neue Weltliteratur und ihre grossen Erzähler*. In many ways the lack of a "next big thing" may not be the worst that could happen. Pluralism and respect for the complexity of literature are welcome sentiments that go against the lure of narrow theories, whether they promise to alter our relations to texts or to society at large.

However, there are trends changing all disciplines in the humanities at present which could make it the moment of digitization and big data. Even though developments in scanning, stylometrics, and data visualization, for example, are not completely new, the availability of tools and the sheer mass of digitally accessible works and material make a difference. It probably leaves most comparatists a bit weary and nervous of losing the close relation with the text. Comparative literature, more than any other discipline, treats texts not just as sources or means to explain something else, but invests them with aesthetic value in and of themselves. As seductive as a Google Ngram can be, it can never replace the words themselves.

That does not mean that comparative literature should refrain from taking on the challenges of large data, in particular when it comes to the study of cultural influences. A number of sources are available today in a completely different form than just a decade ago: publication records, world library holdings, coverage of literature in news media, and even approximate sales figures and sales ranks. In online communities, in addition, the large number of readers' comments has turned them into a serious analytical tool, and methods for analyzing large bodies of texts are developing rapidly. The crucial task is not to let the technology determine the questions we want to ask, but to investigate more boldly how and why a work of literature matters in culture, and how technological tools might help to answer these questions. Rather than abandoning the central questions of comparative literature, we should seek to answer them with the new approaches to studying texts.

In the perspective I have presented here, the digital humanities are opening new doors for the study of both canonization and the large number of books that may not be read anymore by anyone, but which are part of the history of literature (Moretti, "Slaughterhouse" 225–7). The digital humanities can help to establish a more nuanced perspective on canonization, to dig deeper into the preferences of academics, critics, and lay readers in terms of devices, styles, and themes of texts, and to see new patterns in literary history. They will also give a much more solid foundation to some claims that used to be only approximate, such as "Herman Melville and Emily Dickinson did not get real attention until the 1920s" (see Figure 1). And they will help to ask new questions about the relation between literature and culture at large, when unlikely canonized works demand explanation. Qualitative and quantitative approaches will need to be balanced so that the aesthetics of a text will not be drowned out by numbers. Quantitative methods allow us to address questions that have been asked before, but answered less clearly than one might have hoped. In the continuing process of globalization, providing more and better knowledge of intercultural influences is both an interesting and a worthwhile challenge for the discipline.

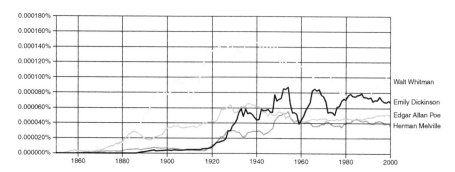

Figure 1 A Google Books Ngram Viewer search. The y-axis shows frequency of the search term among the bi- and tri-grams of each year during 1850–2000.

Works cited

Appiah, Kwame Anthony. *The Ethics of Identity*. Princeton: Princeton UP, 2004. Print.

Auerbach, Erich. "The Philology of World Literature." *World Literature: A Reader*. Ed. Theo D'haen, César Domínguez and Mads Rosendahl Thomsen. London: Routledge, 2012. 65–73. Print.

Bernheimer, Charles, ed. *Comparative Literature in the Age of Multiculturalism*. Baltimore: Johns Hopkins UP, 1995. Print.

Brandes, Georg. "World Literature." *World Literature: A Reader*. Ed. Theo D'haen, César Domínguez, and Mads Rosendahl Thomsen. London: Routledge, 2012. 23–7. Print.

Casanova, Pascale. *La république mondiale des lettres*. Paris: Seuil, 1999. Print.

Damrosch, David. *What Is World Literature?* Princeton: Princeton UP, 2003. Print.

Löffler, Sigrid. *Die neue Weltliteratur und ihre grossen Erzähler*. Munich: Beck, 2013. Print.

Moretti, Franco. *Atlas of the European Novel, 1800–1900*. London: Verso, 1998. Print.

———. "Conjectures on World Literature." *New Left Review* 1 (2000): 54–69. Print.

———. "The Slaughterhouse of Literature." *Modern Language Quarterly* 61.1 (2000): 207–27. Print.

Sapiro, Gisèle, ed. *Translatio: Le marché de la traduction en France à l'heure de la mondialisation*. Paris: CNRS, 2008. Print.

Saussy, Haun, ed. *Comparative Literature in an Age of Globalization*. Baltimore: Johns Hopkins UP, 2006. Print.

Thomsen, Mads Rosendahl. *Mapping World Literature: International Canonization and Transnational Literatures*. London: Continuum, 2008. Print.

Underwood, Ted. *Why Literary Periods Mattered: Historical Contrast and the Prestige of English Studies*. Stanford: Stanford UP, 2013. Print.

Walkowitz, Rebecca L. "The Location of Literature: The Transnational Book and the Migrant Writer." *Contemporary Literature* 47 (2006): 527–45. Print.

"World," "Globe," "Planet"

Comparative literature, planetary studies, and cultural debt after the global turn

Christian Moraru

Critical vocabulary, epistemology, and the worlds of scholarship

Taking our cue from Oedipa Maas's famous question "Shall I project a world?" in Thomas Pynchon's *The Crying of Lot 49*, we might ask: what kind of world are we projecting as comparatists after the "global turn"? How do we map it? What and how do we "know" about this world of ours, which has been coming together – has been worlding, to recall Martin Heidegger – faster and faster after 1989? A perennial attribute of Heideggerian Da-sein, being in the world with others, has been heightened of late by the accelerated "de-distancing" of the world's places, actors, and sociocultural practices (Heidegger 97). As previously disconnected or loosely connected regions have brought modernity's world *en miettes* closer together, the spatiality tied into Being has now become worlded spatiality in which presence plays out as copresence. So characteristic of our age, this onto-topological world condition of vicinity marks the unprecedented, ever-expanding contiguity and codependency of agents, discourses, and settings formerly imagined to be autonomous. What "worlds" (*weltet*, in Heidegger) this world, and what "welds" its independent clauses into a worldly syntax of subordinating, coordinating, juxtaposing geo-ontology, is a world picture (*Weltbild*) that must be grasped both objectively, as what is, and subjectively, as what it appears to us and what it should eventually become.

Comparatism and, in it, the world on which it rests conceptually are not extraneous to this becoming. These comparative sites and protocols in and through which we "compare" the world's artifacts by "placing them together" (see Lat. *comparō*) are homologous to the world itself, to the juxtapositions (*comparationes*) its worlding sets off. So it is also important to ask: what does it mean to know our world and lay out this knowledge in our research? And, still in the Heideggerian spirit: if we, humans, have a world, and an increasingly "comparative" one to boot, then is that world the same as that on which we rely as twenty-first-century comparatists, epistemologically speaking? The usual answers go round the old chestnut of globalization. What is not so clear is to what degree the hegemonic rhetoric of "globe" and "globalism," irrespective of its pro- or antineoliberal inflections, already construes the world's worlding processes in a certain fashion, thus ending up, ironically enough, further homogenizing the world, making it into a conquerable and commodifiable place rather than remaking it anew. In this rhetoric, globalization is routinely dealt with – approvingly or not – as the only fashion in which a worlding scenario has unfolded or as the only sort of globalization possible. "Globe" is neither the "world" (Moraru, *Reading for the Planet* 28–31; Cheah 30) nor all the world can be, but the mainstream discourse of globalization often gives the ideological illusion of this equivalence. It is helpful, then, to think of this discourse as a Nietzschean "army of tropes" not only because of its tendency to naturalize itself as the default modality and thus "globalize" itself across and at the expense of other kinds of talking about and behaving in our world, but also because, more basically, "world," "globe," "planet," "earth," and the like are not synonymous and therefore should not be used interchangeably. But, since globalization discourse has played up one way of looking at our world and at the relation between culture and this world, seeing the latter's face in literary-cultural artifacts has reached an impasse. To get out of it, lexical rigor is required, for the distinctions it affords provide the stepping stone for critical action about and in the world.

It is noteworthy, to begin with, that, following Heidegger, thinkers and critics across disciplines have tackled "worlding" as the world's *fuite en avant* toward worldedness, as its innate tendency to agglutinate its pieces and thus morph into a worlded ontosyntax. Of course, this need not be the monolithic macroentity implied by even ethically minded "one-world" descriptions. This worlded setup has a worlding history in which the Cold War marks an earlier stage. The decades coming immediately after World War II were, comparatively speaking, poorly worlded. In some situations, the Cold War standoff made writers world-hungry, but, overall, it put a check on the world's relationality and could not but dampen the connective impetus of the world's literary and cultural imaginary. This poverty, this limitedness, this censorship even did not stimulate artists' endeavors to "make out" the world-as-world. For aesthetic, political-economic, and technological reasons, relational wordings of the world – world pictures keen on the world's worldedness, on the world-as-world – did not supply, regardless of their orientation and despite the inevitable exceptions, the "cultural dominant" of the years right after World War II. Neither would they become fully defining with late modernism and modernism's successor, postmodernism, which, of late, has been insistently approached as a Cold War phenomenon.

They would, however, after 1989. The fall of the Berlin Wall and of the world-system leaning on it was a tipping point in world history. A new world worlded into being around this event, into a new system all of a sudden notably more integrated than ever. I call this system the earth's *netosphere*, with a wink at the "net" of "network," "Internet," Manuel Castells's "network society," and even Teilhard de Chardin's earlier "nöosphere." This increasingly world-systemic assemblage weaves together the economic-communicational sites, forms, channels, links, and technologies of data storage of the hyperwebbed era. This geosystemic novelty was so sharply felt throughout the world that many concluded that, to deal with this new reality, a new interpretive apparatus and a new vocabulary were called for. Before long, the top if highly controversial contender proved to be "global" along with "globalization," "globalism," "global age," and the rest of the "globe" family. The discourse coalescing around them sent shock waves across the human sciences, which underwent a turn comparable to the linguistic, postmodern, and cultural turns of decades past. As most globalization critics would quickly point out, the process can be summed up as totalization. A rhetorically "perfect word" for the ideological purposes of globalization, "globe" and "global" suggest a "frictionless," complete, and perfect world (Chandra 4). The large-scale multiplication and strengthening of relatedness – ties, connections, and barterings among individuals, communities, and cultures – reinscribe the world as globe by "rounding off" its body, fashioning the polymorphic world into a sphere-like totality whose "smooth surface allow[s] the unimpeded flow of capital, information[,] and language" (Apter 78). As the "globe" in most accounts of globalization, "world" is neither an open biocultural system, nor our natural environment or ground (the "earth"), nor our cosmic address ("Earth"), but a mundane whole that flaunts its totality. The global world purports to be a well-rounded, existentially integrated, and politically definitive closed system, a teleology enforced from a center of power by feedback loops, symmetries, parallels, and exchange procedures across a web of links progressively overlapping with the world itself. The world worlds into globe, goes global, once the infinite and multitudinous potentiality of worldly ontology has been repurposed materially and conceptually as domains of the one, the homogeneous, the circular, the repetitive, and the selfsame.

Topologically, both the empirical world and the globe are measurable, even though the world remains a resilient trope and space of the variegated, mysterious, and illimitable, and thus considerably more complex as structure than the globe. The difference between them does not lie in volume, scope, or geometry but in ontology, culture, and politics. Redolent of the "centering" and "smoothing" technology of control, command, and monitoring that went into its making, the globe is a controlled system and a containment fantasy, a disciplined panopticon and a limit. It is a terminus to what the world and those in it can be. The globe is or rather becomes, through the very rhetoric presuming to critique it, a multitude, a multiplicity, and a potentiality shrunk down to the measurable and the measured. The world and the globe are both immensities. Both boggle the mind quantitatively. But, unlike the world and insofar as it results from relationally totalizing reinscriptions of the world, the globe is no longer an open-ended boundlessness, a project. Once it has been brought under the regime of rational calculability as globe, largely on economic, administrative, and technological grounds – whether through worldly developments such as neoimperial geopolitics and unification of financial markets or through rhetorical overadjudication – it is reduced ontologically and does not function as an endless space of qualitative leaps, as a playground of being anymore. This ontological reduction has left its imprint on the entire paradigm of globality.

Supplying an alternative to this paradigm, "planet" is the terminological hub of the alternate model of planetarity. Lying behind the latest epoch-making turn, this model is central to recent scholars' efforts to project a world increasingly at odds with the mainstream definitions of the "globe" (Elias and Moraru; Moraru, *Reading for the Planet*). Granted, there are many overlaps between the two. In some ways, "planet" is a subset of "global," and, if there is something like planetary studies these days, it would not have been possible without the rise of global studies in the early 1990s. And yet the world in "planet" wants to be a different kettle of fish. The planet is not an accomplished oneness, a structured, coherently administered, and measured geopolitical expanse but a relational world-system at once "calculable and beyond reckoning" (Rapaport 221). Therefore, this system is characterized, both geoculturally and epistemologically, by multiplicity, open-endedness, and sociocultural and political potentialities. The planet is not a "closed system" properly speaking. Its spatial, shareable finitude only begins to reveal itself gradually to humans, from space or on the ground, in the second half of the twentieth century (221–2). This system is mutating, and its architecture and meaning do remain exceptionally complex, topoculturally shifty, and thus "necessarily . . . difficult to define" (Emery 49). Neither an attained finitude nor a teleology, the planet is a soft system: young, evolving, and expanding, a world but not *the* world, a "webbed interrelatedness" covering most of the world but not coterminous with it (49).

If it is a world-system, the planet is so under the aegis of the toposystemic "relativity" Immanuel Wallerstein foregrounds when he draws attention to the spelling of his celebrated catchphrase. "Putting in the hyphen was intended," he says, "to underline that we are talking not about systems, economies, empires of the (whole) world, but about systems, economies, empires that are a world (but quite possibly, and indeed usually, not encompassing the entire globe)" (16–17). The planet is not a globality. Therefore, it cannot be a totality, at least in a monistic sense. Ontologically and philosophically, it is not coextensive with our existential and cognitional gamut as humans, with all we can be and envisage. We are and dream of being and doing things, as thinkers from Heidegger and Maurice Merleau-Ponty to Gilles Deleuze and Félix Guattari keep repeating, always within a world's "with" and "and" relational ambiance. Nor does the planet span the entire world understood, in a more Wallersteinean way, as geophysical earth, which is only the planet's cosmic background, physical foundation, and natural stage. As a world-system, the planet looks like a "spatial/temporal zone which cuts across many political and cultural units" (Wallerstein 17). The planetary system is, then, "relative" – that is to say, approximate, partially systematic in its extensity and loosely systematic in its intensity or functioning. Because it is not a totalist whole, the planet geomodel can be, geographically, culturally, and philosophically, many worlds or parts of worlds, "nested" inside each other at once rather than hierarchically ("vertically") organized, and it can be so in one place no matter how small. This spatial deployment of the planetary entails a geometry quite different from the global. Correspondingly, the individual committed to a planetary *Weltanschauung* may see himself or herself, not unlike the Greek and Roman Stoics, as participating in a number of worlds and world orders while physically located in a particular *polis*. The planet functions as a geodiscursive projection across, astride, and sometimes against the one fixed on modern world maps by the spatiality of the nation-state and the global. In fact, spearheading as it does a cultural-imaginary remapping of the empirical world, the planetary messes deliberately with official cartography by rearranging the topographic and geopolitical distribution of space on our road atlases, maps, and GPSs so as to challenge the worldviews of such neatly delineated spatial encodings.

In his 2001 article "Turn to the Planet: Literature, Diversity, and Totality," Masao Miyoshi was probably the first to point to a manifestly planetary, epistemological change. As Neil Turnbull would venture a bit later, this change had "heighten[ed] the conceptual importance of the earth" (133) across all forms of material and cultural practice. "The world," he clarifies, "has moved back to [the] centre of political consciousness, not in the traditional sense of the 'earth as Garden,' but as new technologically worlded and neo-stoic cosmopolitical percept of the 'earth-as-planet'" (128). This shift, usually referred to as globalization, is "exclusionist," as Miyoshi holds, insofar as it is underpinned by global economics. In his opinion, to be genuinely global is to be inclusive. The global world is indeed global – shared in, lucrative, accessible, enjoyable – but only for those whom relatedness benefits. Thus, the globalized world is not, nor is it likely to beget, a "true totality that includes everyone," and neither is "the return to the nation-state." "There is," however, says Miyoshi, "one such core site for organizing such an inclusiveness, though entirely negative at present: the future of the global environment. For the first time in human history, one single commonality involves all those living on the planet: environmental deterioration" (295). Acknowledging this "total commonality" as the premise for "map[ping] out our world and [for] engag[ing] in research and scholarship" leads to the recognition that

> literature and literary studies now have one basis and goal: to nurture our common bonds to the planet – to replace the imaginaries of exclusionary familialism, communitarianism, nationhood, ethnic culture, regionalism, 'globalization,' or even humanism, with the ideal of planetarianism. Once we accept this planet-based totality, we might for once agree in humility to devise a way to share with all the rest our only true public space and resources.
>
> (295–6)

Planetarity, indebtedness, and comparative analysis

Two years before Miyoshi's article, Gayatri Spivak had already acknowledged her uneasiness with the world-leveling, universalist legacy of Western rationalism, whether in economic globalism or in cultural analysis. Thus, she proposed "us[ing] the planetary – if such a thing can be used! – to control globalization interruptively, to locate the imperative in the indefinite radical alterity of the other space of planet to deflect the rational imperative of capitalist globalization"

(*Aesthetic Education* 348). In her view, life on the planet must be "lived as the call of the wholly other." This emphasis on ethics will remain crucial to the planetarity paradigm. The "imperative to re-imagine the planet" is profoundly ethical (Spivak 1999) – and, I might add, inevitably ethical, insofar as the reimagination engages the problematic of otherness. The Spivakian "imperative" is not totalizing because the ontologized relatedness built into it largely reaffirms a Levinasian, nonrationalizing ethics of alterity. In warranting descriptions of relational arrangements, planetary ontology calls, by the same token, for humility, sharing, and other ways of owning up to the otherness that made relationality possible in the first place. Spivak's landmark contribution to planetary studies, *Death of a Discipline* (2003), takes the next step by offering up the "planetary" as a remedy to the protracted crisis in comparative literature and cultural studies generally.

Since then, the planet, planetary, and their lexical-methodological cognates have made inroads into disciplines and debates old and new: world-systems analysis; globalization studies with various foci and political-theoretical leanings from neoliberalism to antiglobalization and altermondialité; trans- and postnationalism in the "hemispheric" and "oceanic" context (Ralph Bauer, Robert Levine, Hester Blum, Yunte Hwang, Paul Jay, Paul Giles); ecocriticism, (neo)cosmopolitanism (Amanda Anderson, Bruce Robbins, Anthony K. Appiah, Rebecca Walkowitz, Jessica Berman, Seyla Benhabib), and their "eco-cosmopolitan" cross (Ursula K. Heise); "world risk society sociology" (Ulrich Beck) and "network society" economics and communication theory (Castells, Steven Shaviro, Eugene Thacker, Alexander R. Galloway); human rights, ethics, and world governance; the "empire"/"new commons" critique of Deleuze-Guattarian persuasion in the Michael Hardt and Antonio Negri vein; studies of (post)ethnicity and "voluntary affiliation" à la David Hollinger; some approaches within postcolonialism, drawn by the challenge a planetary angle of vision might pose to the old colony/metropolis binary (Paul Gilroy); new comparatism, world literature (David Damrosch, Pascale Casanova, Emily Apter, Eric Hayot), "planetary literary history" (Frances Ferguson), and studies of genre as world-system (Franco Moretti, Wai Chee Dimock), as well as new modernist studies (Susan Stanford Friedman) and "global modernism(s)" (Mark Wollaeger and Matt Eatough). The rise of larger topo-interpretive units, fields, and concerns in comparative cultural studies and, chiefly with Bertrand Westphal, the advent of geocriticism also speak directly to the growing role played by the planetary as an analytical metaphor. Historically co-articulated with the global lexicon and concerns as it has been, the planet model may be at this point well positioned to fulfill Spivak's dream of "interrupting" or "overwriting the globe." Ideally, such a critical operation would supplant globalization and globality by planetarization and planetarity; the global world-system by the planet's own system ("which we inhabit . . . on loan," as Spivak underscores); "global agents" by "planetary subjects;" and globalism's rationality by planetary relationality or "planet-thought" (Spivak, *Death* 73).

This is fine but a little vague for my money. I would like to propose that, to renegotiate its ties with the discourse of globalization, and possibly usher in a planetary, "postglobal age" in literary-cultural analysis, the planetary paradigm must be sufficiently emancipated rhetorically and theoretically from the global. To the extent that it also rests on the relational, the planetary both critiques and gives the global, or at least a part of it, a new lease on life. As Mary Lou Emery recognizes, the "planetary" is "neither equivalent to the global nor opposed to it" (49). If the global-planetary connection is symbiotic, the whole point is to remake it into a truly critical symbiosis. I suggest that, to accomplish this, "planet-thought" or "planetarism" needs to rethink the world planetarily. If living culture is what we are talking about, then another relational concept is required, one that would reworld the world into planet by resetting the netosphere ethically rather than by discarding it. What makes this venture possible at this point, I maintain, is a planetary counterdiscourse that rethinks the rationalization of relationality comparatively. Wherever and whatever the planet is ontologically, in the world – for it is neither the globe's nor the world's synonym – it exists "in the species of alterity" (Spivak, *Death* 72) – that is, underpinned by an ethical infrastructure. Ontologically, as already existing reality, the planet is partially already in place and can be described as such. In its projects and world-projections, planetarism augments this presence aesthetically and critically, as subject to an "aspirational" planetary imaginary that tries out various possibilities of fully and ethically world-ing the world into planet.

What makes this planetary ensemble ethical is the fundamental credit-debt nexus subtending it. Planetarily minded cultural analysis is a "thick description" of the indebtedness that goes into the ecumenical manufacturing of original-ity. One thing the planetarity model of analysis should attempt is a revaluation of indebtedness, a reaccreditation of the discredited notions of credit and debt. Remember the "greed is good" line? I do not know about greed in the Wall Street sense, but I do know, I think, about debt, and what I would like to pro-pose is that debt, in an important sense, *is* good, all the more so in today's world. Debt, the thing that we lack and need, has constitutive force. What we call "sub-ject formation" is nothing less than going into debt, to others. We would not be if it were not for that originating and originality-spawning deficit. This shortage is ontological. More accurately, it has ontological potential: we can be or become, make the "most of ourselves" if we live up to it. Otherwise, as Emmanuel Levinas insists, its nature is ethical: what that absence carves out inside ourselves is a space of otherness, and the debt accrues a duty, a responsibility in and to the world. In this light, it is important to realize that this debt is originary rather than sup-plemental to being. We do live on borrowed time *ab origine*. We do not incur debt after we have somehow made and spent our fortune or have blown away our "inheritance." It is already in there before we set about being and expressing our-selves. Our "credentials" are predicated on this credit. As humans and humanists, we "rise up" to our potential from that abyss of alterity. This debt is, indeed, a precondition to being human, as Giorgio Agamben explains in *The Coming Com-munity* (43–4), let alone being an author. As Jean-Michel Rabaté insists in one of his Joyce books, no authority is self-begotten. Unable to authorize itself, it must be accredited. Thus, it presupposes a credit – in other words, indeed, a credit in, or of, others' words, texts, and representations, which authorities and authors like Joyce do credit, so much so that their oeuvres turn on this admission of debt. We come into our own through references to others and not before we find our "balance," a way of owning up to what we owe them. The puns may be over the top, but they help stress how embedded in language, and with it in culture, in our humanity, is this seldom acknowledged indebtedness.

In his 1996 article "Global Debt and Parallel Universe," Jean Baudrillard zeroes in on a different kind of incommensurable debt: the financial sublime of the global age. It is world debt that further globalizes the world. Increasingly shared one way or the other by the planet's population – although by some more than others – this debt is practically infinite because impossible to pay off while still mounting *ad infinitum*, beyond measuring and representation. This is why, Baudrillard claims, it is financially meaningless. Its only value is symbolic because this debt speaks to a "symbolic credit system whereby people, corporations, nations are attached to one another by default" (38–40). But, I would contend, world insolvency points, in an admittedly twisted way, to the very meaning of symbolic values in general at the dawn of the new millennium, to the concrete "attachments," circuitries, and exchanges underlying them – in brief, to the global formation and reach of a cultural capital that grows as it finances narratives, trends, and values across traditional lines of influence, taxation, and jurisdiction. Nonreferential as it may be, unevenly distributed as it certainly is, global monetary debt nonetheless supplies a serviceable model for coming to terms with the worldwide circulation of symbolic capital and the swelling planetary indebtedness derived from it.

Cultural indebtedness – the indebtedness comparative analysis with a planetary bent focuses on – is neither sinful nor virtual. Setting aside for now financial debt's history and the banking and political practices behind it, one must come to terms with its reality: its "credit lines" tie us together in real or quasi-real time and space; it "worlds" us, sets us side by side, "pairs" us up, "com-pares" us as we are credited so that, in turn, we can also "compare" the world, acquire it (another meaning of *comparō*), get a purchase on it aesthetically, as representation. Most notably, in this material landscape, cultural interconnectedness expands and becomes more visible. Here, money, a signifier of value, supplies a homology to a worthier axiology, and accordingly, debt is the other name of all-pervasive influence and the cultural *métissage* coming on its heels. Here, self and other farm their discourse out to one another frenetically, so we are all becoming more indebted to others elsewhere than we have ever been. These others and their locations hold liens on our times and spaces. And vice versa: we ourselves are jump-off points, investments, "seed money" for joint cultural ventures that come to fruition somewhere else, now more than at any other point in history. In the "compressed" space and time of interweaving world cultures, authority is increasingly "on loan," authenticity and originality intertextual affairs, and "individual talent" and "personal tone" often echo from afar, ventriloquisms. In this cultural credit/debit arena a new physical and nonphysical proximity arises, a culturally woven immediacy with my culture and yours intermingling and fostering new assemblages. It is within this exchange horizon that what I call the outsourcing of identity takes place and planetary studies stakes out its territory. Here, the familiar is less and less a function of the familial. As a result, the economy of my being – mine, ours, everyone else's – is hardly self-sufficient, depending as it does on others for "loans" and "parts" – myths, fantasies, stories, and the like, and this calls for a comparative approach, specifically, for a de- or, better still, transterritorialization of literary histories. As appendices to various national histories still indebted to a nineteenth-century mind-set, these histories have been territorialized – defined and confined in terms of coverage – on the model of the nation-state. While national borders and jurisdiction continue to exist, the way planetary scholars map developments across the arts overlaps less and less with the nation. Pre-, sub-, and transnational scales of aggregation challenge the classical paradigm of national territoriality. Thus, where US literature "is," where it "comes from," and where it occurs may differ from the geographic location of the nation. What this new, cross-territorial, cross-cultural, and cross-linguistic scalarity helps us visualize cartographically and appreciate critically is how much national cultures have borrowed from world cultures and, accordingly, how much of the nation's cultural fabric consists of credit lines from elsewhere. It is our job as comparatists to take comparative literature into the planetary era and read, accordingly, between and across these lines so as to assess both the investments and their returns.

Works cited

Agamben, Giorgio. *The Coming Community*. Trans. Michael Hardt. Minneapolis: U of Minnesota P, 2009. Print.

Apter, Emily. *Against World Literature: On the Politics of Untranslatability*. London: Verso, 2013. Print.

Baudrillard, Jean. "Global Debt and Parallel Universe." *Digital Delirium*. Ed. Arthur and Marilouise Kroker. New York: St. Martin's, 1997. 38–40. Print.

Chandra, Sarika. *Dislocalism: The Crisis of Globalization and the Remobilizing of Americanism*. Columbus: Ohio State UP, 2011. Print.

Cheah, Pheng. "What Is a World? On World Literature as World-Making Activity." *Daedalus* 137.3 (2008): 26–38. Print.

Elias, Amy J., and Christian Moraru, eds. *The Planetary Turn: Relationality and Geoaesthetics in the Twenty-First Century*. Evanston, IL: Northwestern UP, 2015. Print.

Emery, Mary Lou. "Caribbean Modernism: Plantation to Planetary." *The Oxford Handbook of Global Modernisms*. Ed. Mark Wollaeger and Matt Eatough. New York: Oxford UP, 2012. 48–77. Print.

Heidegger, Martin. *Being and Time: A Translation of Sein und Zeit*. Trans. Joan Stambaugh. Albany: SUNY P, 1996. Print.

Miyoshi, Masao. "Turn to the Planet: Literature, Diversity, and Totality." *Comparative Literature* 53.4 (2001): 283–97. Print.

Moraru, Christian. *Reading for the Planet: Toward a Geomethodology*. Ann Arbor: U of Michigan P, 2015. Print.

Nietzsche, Friedrich. *On the Genealogy of Morals: A Polemic*. Trans. Douglas Smith. New York: Oxford UP, 1996. Print.

Rapaport, Herman. *The Literary Theory Toolkit: A Compendium of Concepts and Methods*. Malden: Wiley-Blackwell, 2011. Print.

Spivak, Gayatri Chakravorty. *An Aesthetic Education in the Era of Globalization*. Cambridge, MA: Harvard UP, 2011. Print.

———. *Death of a Discipline*. New York: Columbia UP, 2003. Print.

Turnbull, Neil. "The Ontological Consequences of Copernicus: Global Being in the Planetary World." *Theory, Culture & Society* 23.1 (2006): 125–39. Print.

Wallerstein, Immanuel. *World-Systems Analysis: An Introduction*. Durham, NC: Duke UP, 2004. Print.

World literature as figure and as ground

David Damrosch

World literature has become a subject of lively – sometimes heated – debate in recent years, both as a body of texts and as "a problem," as Franco Moretti remarked in his influential pair of articles, "Conjectures on World Literature" (2000) and "More Conjectures" (2003). Much of the discussion since then has focused on issues of scale and the challenges of incorporating a meaningful range of the world's literatures into our work, whether in teaching a sophomore-level survey course or in mapping the global spread of the novel. The perspective on world literature as a vast landscape stretching out into the far distance has been widely shared both by those who praise the expansion to a planetary scale as offering a way to move beyond Eurocentrism and all sorts of regional paro-chialism, and by those who criticize literary globalists (planiterati?) for cultural imperialism or for sacrificing the linguistic rigor and cultural depth traditionally emphasized by more circumscribed comparative literary studies.

Certainly there have been good reasons for the global approaches to world literature pursued by a growing number of people during the past decade, as well as principled grounds for disputing those approaches. But world literature is almost always experienced by readers within the national context in which they live, and more particularly within the national markets in which books are published, reviewed, and assigned in classes. In a kind of figure/ground reversal, it is the nation that frames most experiences of world literature, at least as much as it is world literature that frames any national canon. My personal hope for the coming decade is that we will look more deeply into the presence of the world within the nation, even as we continue to develop further our exploration of national traditions in the wider world.

An emphasis on national markets doesn't mean returning to the crypto-nationalism of much nineteenth-century comparative literature, and not only because literary markets have a significantly international dimension. The national literary traditions themselves were never as self-contained, after all, as nationalistic literary histories have often supposed. Yet even our comparative literature departments often carry on the Herderian assumptions deeply engrained in many national literature departments: that the essence of a nation is carried by its national language, embodied in its highest form by the masterpieces of its national literature. The presence of minority or foreign languages within almost all national cultures has often been studied only minimally, if at all. Until recently, American poets who wrote in Spanish were rarely included in survey courses or anthologies of American literature. In England, Irish and Welsh were similarly neglected by scholars of English literature, and for many years were actually suppressed in schools. Countercanonical and contestatory works are increasingly welcome in literary studies, but rarely in ways that disturb the paradigm of the national language, at most allowing for a very limited subset of national languages. Spanish is now in play in American studies, but it is a rare Americanist who learns Navajo or Yiddish. Few scholars of Israeli literature learn Arabic, and few students of Indian literature go beyond Bengali, English, and Hindi to work in Gujarati or Malayalam unless they have a heritage connection to one of those languages.

Bilingual writers are often seen primarily through their work in whichever language is dominant in a particular setting. Even in the case of a major canonical writer such as Milton, only his English-language works are commonly studied: no survey anthology of English literature that I know of includes any of Milton's Latin poetry. Milton was fluent in Latin and proud of his poetic ability in the language of his epic forebear Virgil, but we take it for granted that his Latin poems aren't worth our while. This is a judgment that most of us have made without ever having read any of them. Similarly, in India the great nineteenth-century poet Mirza Ghalib is beloved as a writer of Urdu ghazals and ignored as a Persian poet – even though Ghalib himself preferred his Persian ghazals to his Urdu ones. In Iran, conversely, he is honored purely as a Persian poet.

Along with understanding the importance of alternatives to the "national language," we need to give greater weight to translated works, not only as foreign influences from which we can plot the distinctiveness of our great national writers, but also in many cases as works that become integral parts of the literary culture into which they are translated. For present purposes, a short story by Julio Cortázar can provide a case in point. Latin Americanists rightly consider him one of the great modern Argentine writers, and on a broad transnational scale he can be studied as a leading exemplar of global postmodernism. Here, though, I'd like to consider how these two aspects come together in a very particular time and place: Paris in the early 1950s. And more specifically: in the 5ème Arrondissement, in the spring of 1951, in an exhibition hall of the Jardin des Plantes. This was the time and place in which Cortázar conceived one of his breakthrough fictions, the enigmatic short story "Axolotl." What I hope to show is that a great deal of the world is present within the few pages of this story, and that both Cortázar's Argentine identity and his worldliness can best be understood by close attention to the presence of the wider world within a small aquarium in a Parisian exhibit hall.

To locate "Axolotl" squarely in the time and place of its composition doesn't at all mean reducing Cortázar to a merely French writer, much less an *almost* French writer – a grateful immigrant from a peripheral region far from the hexagon whose chief value is his testimony to the glory of the *ville lumière*. This is the impression given in *Le Monde* in 2013, in a blog entry written by the journalist Paulo Paranagua for the fiftieth anniversary of Cortázar's masterpiece, *Rayuela*

(*Hopscotch*). Paranagua praises the novel as "sans doute l'un des plus beaux hommages rendus par un Argentin à la capitale française" (certainly one of the most beautiful homages ever made by an Argentine to the French capital), and then regrets that the ungrateful city hasn't properly returned the sentiment:

> Inutile néanmoins de chercher une plaque de rue à son nom – excepté une à l'un de ses domiciles et l'autre sur sa tombe au cimetière du Montparnasse. La Mairie de Paris semble ignorer combien de lecteurs de *Rayuela* sillonnent la ville avec en tête une carte du tendre faite des itinéraires parcourus par ses personnages. [Yet it would be pointless to go looking for a street sign bearing his name, apart from one on one of his residences and another on his tomb in the Montparnasse cemetery. City Hall seems unaware of how many readers of *Rayuela* crisscross the city carrying in their heads a mental map made of the itineraries taken by its characters.]

The plaque at Cortázar's former residence underscores the French pride of ownership in this important Argentine – or formerly Argentine – writer:

ICI VÉCUT
JULIO CORTÁZAR
1914–1984
ÉCRIVAIN ARGENTIN
NATURALISÉ FRANÇAIS
AUTEUR DE "MARELLE"

And it isn't only the *écrivain* who has been *naturalisé*: *Rayuela* here appears under its French title.

We may wonder just how many tourists really come to Paris, like belated Hispanic Emma Bovarys, seeking to realize the literary map in their heads, and here we may note that it's a specifically French source that Paranagua is evoking: the "carte du Tendre" is the map of the imaginary land of love created by Madeleine de Scudéry in her 1654 novel *Clélie*. Nor is it so clear that *Rayuela*'s motley crew of bohemians necessarily offers such a *bel hommage* to their adoptive city. Yet though Paris is only one of the transatlantic poles of Cortázar's hopscotching narrative, the Parisian setting is central to "Axolotl." Not a tourist but a resident of Paris, the narrator loves to bike over to the Jardin des Plantes to commune with the lions and panthers kept at the garden's menageries. The setting is hardly random: like its counterparts in such imperial capitals as London and Madrid, the Jardin des Plantes is a testimony to the metropole's acquisitive passion for exotica, often including artifacts of "primitive" societies as well as plants and animals brought from distant lands. Here, the Cortázar-like narrator finds one day that the lions are gloomy and his favorite panther is asleep. On a whim, he heads into the aquarium building, where he becomes transfixed by the unwavering gaze of a tiny axolotl, a Mexican species of salamander. Returning repeatedly to commune with the "Aztec" axolotl, by the story's end the narrator has become one with the little creature, trapped within the aquarium. In the story's final lines, either the narrator or the axolotl consoles himself that "he" who is now outside may one day write "all this about axolotls" (8; "todo esto sobre los axolotl" [168]).

"Axolotl" is undoubtedly a work of Argentine literature: Cortázar published it in 1952 in the new journal *Buenos Aires Literaria*, of whose editorial board he was a member. Yet it is equally a regional work of Latin American literature, as Cortázar chooses a Mexican creature as his narrator's silent interlocutor and shadow self. In this respect, his experience can be compared to that of James Baldwin during the same period. As Baldwin recounts in his 1950 essay "Encounter on the Seine: Black Meets Brown," he had fled America for Paris, disgusted with American racism and homophobia, and in Paris he encountered actual Africans for the first time. He discovered that they didn't see him as their soul mate but as an American, and he began to realize just how American he was. So too, Cortázar's narrative stand-in discovers his Latin American identity while in Paris.

He also partakes directly in European world literature. "Axolotl" resonates with Ovid's *Metamorphoses* and Kafka's *Die Verwandlung*, and also with Dante: the axolotls float in "ese infierno líquido" (Cortázar 167). The most direct intertext, though, is Rilke's great poem "Der Panther," subtitled "Im Jardin des Plantes, Paris." Already in Rilke's poem, it is the caged animal's gaze that transfixes the poet-viewer:

> Sein Blick ist vom Vorübergehn der Stäbe
> so müd geworden, daß er nichts mehr hält.
> Ihm ist, als ob es tausend Stäbe gäbe
> und hinter tausend Stäben keine Welt. (68)
> [His gaze has been so worn by the procession
> Of bars that it no longer makes a bond.
> Around, a thousand bars seem to be flashing,
> And in their flashing show no world beyond. (69)]

In Rilke's brilliant image, so great is the spiritual power of the restlessly pacing panther that it seems to be the bars that move back and forth; the viewer is held in the panther's steady gaze. In the poem's third and final quatrain, the panther becomes an image of the modern poet, with his gaze now theatricalized through raising the curtain of his eyes:

> Nur manchmal schiebt der Vorhang der Pupille
> sich lautlos auf –. Dann geht ein Bild hinein,
> geht durch der Glieder angespannte Stille –
> und hört im Herzen auf zu sein. (68)
> [Only from time to time the pupil's shutter
> Will draw apart: an image enters then,
> To travel through the tautened body's utter
> Stillness – and in the heart to end. (69)]

Cortázar's axolotl represents a severely ironized reworking of Rilke, whose majestic panther is no longer available to writers in a postmodern age: pointedly, the narrator falls back on visiting the axolotl because "mi pantera dormía" (161). The axolotl is less majestic than Rilke's panther, but also more uncanny, and the narrator is mesmerized: "Usted se los come con los ojos," as the guard in the aquarium remarks (165; "You eat them alive with your eyes, hey" [6]). There's no escape from the axolotl's cannibalistic gaze: its eyes are lidless, and instead of being consumed, it's the axolotl that consumes his viewer. In describing the axolotl's triumph as "canibalismo," Cortázar underscores the deep identity of these seemingly opposite beings. Has the writer from the periphery been consumed by the greater force of European world literature? Such an understanding of the narrator's metamorphosis, the narrator suggests, would be too easy: "Parecía fácil, casi obvio, caer en la mitología. Empecé viendo en los axolotl una metamorfosis que no conseguía anular una misteriosa humanidad" (165; "It would seem easy, almost obvious, to fall into mythology. I began seeing in the axolotls a metamorphosis which did not succeed in revoking a mysterious humanity" [6]).

If it would be too easy to be consumed by Ovid and Rilke, or conversely to absorb and merely rewrite their works, in the mode of Oswald de Andrade's 1928 "Manifesto Antropófago," who might be a worthier secret sharer for Cortázar's narrator? The question of a too easy rewriting of a European predecessor is the central issue of another breakthrough Argentine story, published a dozen years before "Axolotl": Jorge Luis Borges's "Pierre Menard, autor del Quijote," the first of Borges's great *ficciones*. In seeking to rewrite Cervantes for his own era, Menard famously begins with a method described as "relativamente sencillo": to convert to Catholicism, fight the Moors, become fluent in sixteenth-century Castilian, forget the intervening centuries of European history, and in short, "ser Miguel de Cervantes" – to "*be* Miguel de Cervantes" (44 [91 in the English translation]). He discards this plan, however, as too easy ("pero lo descartó por fácil"), opting instead for the more challenging attempt to rewrite the *Quixote* while remaining himself. So too Cortázar forgets neither himself nor the history of European literature that he inscribes within his text. Instead of simply trying to rewrite Rilke, he mobilizes the European tradition in service of the struggle to free himself from the patron to whom he owed the greatest artistic and practical debts: Borges himself.

As the story proceeds, the enigmatic axolotls start to sound notably Borgesian: "Oscuramente me pareció comprender su voluntad secreta, abolir el espacio y el tiempo con una inmovilidad indiferente" (163–4; "Obscurely I seemed to understand their secret will, to abolish space and time with an indifferent immobility" [5]). The axolotls transfix him with a gaze strikingly described as blind: "Sus ojos, sobre todo, me obsesionaban . . . Su mirada ciega, el diminuto disco de oro inexpresivo y sin embargo terriblemente lúcido, me penetraba como un mensaje" (164–5; "Above all else, their eyes obsessed me . . . Their blind gaze, the diminutive gold disc without expression and nonetheless terribly shining, went through me like a message" [5–6]).

Cortázar wrote "Axolotl" in 1951, shortly after exiling himself from Perón's Argentina and settling in Paris. In 1949, after years of writing without publishing, not wanting to appear before the public until he had found his own voice, he had finally had his first mature work published: a closet drama entitled *Los Reyes*, a meditation on the character of the Minotaur in the labyrinth of Crete. The mentor who had given this work to the world was none other than Borges, who published it in a Buenos Aires journal. In the same year, Borges also published his collection *El Aleph*, which included his own meditation on the Minotaur's labyrinth, "La casa de Asterión," first published in magazine form in 1947.

The recently emigrated Cortázar, at once losing and finding himself in Paris and in the wider world, gradually made a path of his own through the Borgesian labyrinth. At the end of "Axolotl," the narrator declares, "Ahora soy definitiva-mente un axolotl . . . Y en esta soledad final, a la que él ya no vuelve, me consuela pensar que acaso va a escribir sobre nosotros, creyendo imaginar un cuento va a escribir todo esto sobre los axolotl" (167–8; "I am an axolotl for good now . . . And in this final solitude to which he no longer comes, I console myself by thinking that perhaps he is going to write a story about us, that, believing he's making up a story, he's going to write all this about axolotls" [8]). These words can be compared to Borges's famous short parable "Borges y yo," written four years later: "Al otro, a Borges, es a quien le ocurren las cosas . . . No sé cuál de los dos escribe esta página" (65–6; "It's Borges, the other one, that things happen to . . . I am not sure which of us it is that's writing this page" ["Borges and I" 324]). Speaking most directly about his own authorial identity, Borges may also be expressing an ambivalent awareness of his growing influence on younger writers whose *beaux hommages* were threatening to upstage him by 1955, the year in which his blindness became complete. Which of the two writers is rewriting which? Perhaps both fictions could be given a common title: "Axolotl y yo."

Taken together, the multiplying reversals between consumer and consumed – Borges and Cortázar, narrator and axolotl, Kafka and Rilke, Paris and Buenos Aires – play out the shifting figure/ground reversals of the world and the nation that we can explore through the study of world literature in its local metamorphoses. Far from having to choose between the nation and the world, or between close and distant reading, comparatists have the opportunity today to look freshly at the intimate interanimation of these seemingly opposed terms. The world in a grain of sand; or in an aquarium, in the Jardin des Plantes, in the spring of 1951.

Works cited

Baldwin, James. "Encounter on the Seine: Black Meets Brown." *Collected Essays*. New York: Library of America, 1998. 85–90. Print.

Borges, Jorge Luis. "Borges and I." *Collected Fictions*. Trans. Andrew Hurley. New York: Viking, 1998. 324. Print.

———. "Borges y yo." *El hacedor*. New York: Vintage Español, 2013. 65–6. Print.

———. "Pierre Menard, Author of the *Quixote*." *Collected Fictions*. Trans. Andrew Hurley. New York: Viking, 1998. 88–95. Print.

————. "Pierre Menard, autor del *Quijote*." *Ficciones*. Barcelona: Ediciones Destino, 2004. 37–51. Print.

Cortázar, Julio. "Axolotl." *Final del juego*. Mexico City: Punto de Lectura, 2008. 161–8. Print.

————. "Axolotl." Trans. Paul Blackburn. *Blow-up and Other Stories*. New York: Collier, 1968. 3–8. Print.

Moretti, Franco. "Conjectures on World Literature." *New Left Review* 1 (2000): 54–69. Rpt. in *Distant Reading*. London: Verso, 2013. 43–62. Print.

————. "More Conjectures." *New Left Review* 20 (2003): 73–81. Rpt. in *Distant Reading*. London: Verso, 2013. 107–20. Print.

Paranagua, Paulo A. "Les cinquante ans de "Marelle", livre culte de l'Argentin Julio Cortázar." *América latina (VO): Acutalités, idées, sociétés*. *Le Monde*, 10 May 2013. Web. 18 Mar. 2014. http://america-latina.blog.lemonde.fr/2013/05/10/les-cinquante-ans-de-marelle-livre-culte-de-largentin-julio-cortazar/

Rilke, Rainer Maria. "Der Panther: Im Jardin des Plantes, Paris." *The Best of Rilke: 72 Form-True Verse Translations with Facing Originals, Commentary, and Compact Biography*. Trans. Walter Arndt. Hanover: UP of New England, 1989. 68. Print.

————. "The Panther: Jardin des Plantes, Paris." Trans. Walter Arndt. *The Best of Rilke: 72 Form-True Verse Translations with Facing Originals, Commentary, and Compact Biography*. Hanover: UP of New England, 1989. 69. Print.

Baku, literary common

Nergis Ertürk

I know of only three rivals to Stalin's telegenic body: the bodies of Nasser, Mao Tse-tung, and Khomeini. A rigorous comparative analysis would be necessary here. But I now know less than ever if the concept of "comparatism" can sustain the necessity and the dimensions of such a task.
– Jacques Derrida, "Back from Moscow, in the USSR"

"The Communist International wants to unite under its banners speakers of all the languages of the world," Grigorii Zinov'ev observed in his introductory remarks to the First Congress of the Peoples of the East, convened in the Azerbaijani city of Baku from 1–8 September 1920 (see Ertürk 183–5). This was the first mass meeting of representatives of West European, US, and Russian Communist parties with communist and nonparty delegates of countries ranging from Azerbaijan, Armenia, and Georgia to Afghanistan, India, and China. Described by H. G. Wells as "a quite wonderful accumulation of white, black, brown, and yellow people, Asiatic costumes and astonishing weapons," the Congress is considered an important moment in the history of anticolonialism (Wells 96). Gathering close to two thousand delegates who spoke languages including Russian, German, English, French, Bulgarian, Persian, Turkish, Azerbaijani, Kumyk, Uzbek, Chechen, and Kabardian, the 1920 Congress is equally interesting for what it tells us about the double bind of communist translation and plurilingualism.[1]

Despite Zinov'ev's intentions and his rhetoric, the Congress records show that by its fourth session, a frustrated presiding committee decided to limit the number of translations to three "official" languages (Russian, Azerbaijani Turkic, and Persian) and requested that each translation be abridged so as to "proceed economically." This reduction of linguistic multiplicity marked the necessity of translation to establish shared channels of communication, but the extensive quarreling over accuracy also foregrounded the impossibility of translation as a task. In their introduction to the English translation of the Congress proceedings, entitled *To See the Dawn: Baku, 1920 – First Congress of the Peoples of the East*, John Riddell and Ma'mud Shirvani remind us (via the US communist John Reed) that the British delegate Thomas Quelch's "timid and hesitant remarks were translated [into Russian] by Peter Petrov with such enthusiasm and such a spirit of invention that the hall soon erupted with cheers and shouts of 'Down with British imperialism!' as swords and rifles were brandished in the air." The "dismayed British delegate" objected, "I'm sure I never said anything like that; I demand a proper translation" (Riddell 27). Another noteworthy disruption occurred during the translation of the Azerbaijani delegate Dadash Buniatzade's speech into Russian: discovering that the translator Musazade had omitted portions critical of Ottoman and German imperialism in Transcaucasia, other delegates protested, demanding a complete translation.

Regarding the linguistic confusion imagined in the biblical story of Babel, Jacques Derrida has observed that "[i]f there is a transparency that Babel has not impaired, this is surely it, the experience of the multiplicity of tongues and the 'proper' sense of the word 'translation' " (199). My goal in reminding us of these nonbiblical episodes, and their illustration of the double bind of communist translation and plurilingualism, is to suggest that we might reclaim the history of the First Congress of the Peoples of East as another genealogy for the discipline of comparative literature – and to experiment with allowing it to displace our other founding stories: Goethe's invention of *Weltliteratur* in conversation with Eckermann, and Leo Spitzer and Erich Auerbach's missed encounter with an Orientalized Istanbul.

In suggesting that we look to the unfulfilled promise of the First Congress of the Peoples of the East for another genealogy of comparative literature, I do not mean to overlook the real limits of that promise. Certainly the organizers of the Congress, who included such prominent "Eastern" revolutionaries as the Azeri playwright and novelist Nariman Narimanov and the former theater actor Buniatzade, did their part in constructing an uncritically Orientalist "gray-haired East" destined to be awakened and led by a fraternal proletarian West. And the Congress paved the way for the new institutions of Soviet Orientology, including the All-Union Scientific Association of Oriental Studies (VNAV, Vsesoiuznaia Nauchnaia Assotsiatsiia Vostokovedeniia), established in Moscow in 1921, whose legacy we cannot accept uncritically. Directed by the chairman of the Baku Congress's Council for Propaganda and Action, Michael P. Pavlovich, VNAV played a key role in the linguistic engineering of Turkic languages in the 1920s (see Kemper).

The historical circumstances of the First Congress of the Peoples of the East are in some ways unique: it took place in a translation zone overdetermined by both external and internal imperialism. But understood as a linguistic event, the Congress might be imagined as a rewriting of the biblical story of Babel, offering in place of a transcendent God an immanent, heterogeneous commons in alterity. As such, it reminds us of the deepest ethico-political stakes of the translingual inquiry we pursue in comparative literature. The comparative literature of the past decade has neglected this history, and the comparative literature of the next decade might do better.

Important new work by Katerina Clark, Maria Khomitsky, and Susanna Witt, among others, suggests a way forward. Khomitsky's study of the World Literature Publishing House (Izdatel'stva "Vsemirnaia literatura"), established in Petrograd in 1918 under Maxim Gorky's supervision, suggests the broader significance of a neglected episode in early twentieth-century Soviet history. Clark describes an interval in the "latinate" *longue durée* of comparative literary history as interwar Stalinist Moscow was rebuilt as a secular, transnational imperial center – "a fourth Rome" – of world culture through the "Great Appropriation" of the European Enlightenment. And Witt, suggesting an opportunity for both Soviet studies and translation studies, has observed that "[l]iterary translation in the Soviet Union may well be the largest more or less coherent project of translation the world has seen to date" (Witt 149).

The comparative literature of the next decade might let such work guide it toward the imagination of a literary and linguistic common, and a literary and linguistic communism, marked by the linguistic multiplicity of the First Congress of the Peoples of the East. To be sure, such work will need to account for the violence of, and develop an alternative to, the particular form of the romantically aestheticized literary common imagined by Pavlovich:

> Let popular education spread in the republic of soviets, including the open-
> ing of thousands and thousands of schools, evening courses, academies . . .
> All the separate streams, tributaries, rivulets and great rivers will intermingle
> in a fantastic and harmonious way, merging and feeding with their living
> waters one common international ocean of the poetry and learning of toiling
> humanity, freed for the first time from national and class oppression. This
> will shine with such unprecedented, incomparable beauty as neither classical
> Greece, with all its amazing works of art, nor the civilization of the medieval
> and capitalist epochs, with all their blazing galaxy of immortal poets, artists,
> thinkers and scholars, could give the world.
>
> (Riddell 161–2)

Following the consolidation of the USSR in 1922 as a federation with national-territorial autonomy, the Soviet Union embraced what Yuri Slezkine has called a program of "compensatory nation-building" in the modernization and nation-alization of "culturally backward" nations (414), following an evolutionary Marxist timeline leading "to the lightening of labour, to democracy, to social-ism," in Lenin's phrase. At the cultural level, such compensatory nation-building involved the development of selected local vernaculars into national languages, at the expense of others that were suppressed. If this communist common can be understood merely as an amalgamation of self-enclosed, autonomous, national linguistic and literary units, then a comparative literature for the next decade, working from and across the languages of the former Soviet Union and the Third International, might revive the Congress's more radical and unrealized promise of a heteronomous, nonproprietary comparative common.

Note

1 African languages were not represented at the Congress, but were invoked by
  Zinov'ev, who imagined a transcontinental alliance between peoples of Asia and
  Africa (see Riddell 85).

Works cited

Clark, Katerina. *Moscow, the Fourth Rome: Stalinism, Cosmopolitanism, and the Evolution of Soviet Culture, 1931–1941.* Cambridge, MA: Harvard UP, 2011. Print.

Derrida, Jacques. "Des Tours de Babel." *Psyche: Inventions of the Other.* Vol. 1. Ed. Peggy Kamuf and Elizabeth Rottenberg. Stanford: Stanford UP, 2007. 191–225. Print.

Ertürk, Nergis. "Toward a Literary Communism: The 1926 Baku Turcological Congress." *boundary 2* 40.2 (2013): 183–213. Print.

Kemper, Michael. "Red Orientalism: Mikhail Pavlovich and Marxist Oriental Studies in Early Soviet Russia." *Die Welt des Islams* 50 (2010): 452–58. Print.

Khomitsky, Maria. "World Literature, Soviet Style: A Forgotten Episode in the History of the Idea." *Ab Imperio* 3 (2013): 119–54. Print.

Riddell, John, ed. *To See the Dawn: Baku, 1920—First Congress of the Peoples of the East.* New York: Pathfinder, 2010. Print.

Slezkine, Yuri. "The USSR as a Communal Apartment, or How a Socialist State Promoted Ethnic Particularism." *Slavic Review* 53 (1994): 414–52. Print.

Wells, H. G. *Russia in the Shadows.* New York: George H. Doran, 1921. Print.

Witt, Susanna. "Between the Lines: Totalitarianism and Translation in the USSR." *Contexts, Subtexts and Pretexts: Literary Translation in Eastern Europe and Russia.* Ed. Brian James Baer. Philadelphia: John Benjamins, 2011. 149–70. Print.

Aesthetic humanity and the great world community
Kant and Kang Youwei

Ban Wang

Thinking beyond nation and geography

Comparative literature straddles a fault line between the focus on national literature and a quest for a normative superstructure above relations among different
cultures. To study Kantian aesthetics, one must trace the genealogy of thought
in the Enlightenment of eighteenth-century Europe and attend to the particular Prussian context. To discuss the Chinese thinker Kang Youwei (1858–1927),
known for his vision of world community, one must consider his innovations
within Confucianism in response to China's encounter with the modern world.
The basic unit of the modern world is the nation-state, which shapes our ideas
of identity, politics, and culture. Yet Kant and Kang Youwei pit a cosmopolitan
vision against the nation-state. Writing from a prenational context, Kant advanced
a cosmopolitan ethic to criticize the self-interested and absolutist state in the Westphalian system. Drawing on the idea of all under heaven (*tianxia*), Kang Youwei
envisaged a world of common humanity that transcends the boundaries of nation-
states, class, gender, and territory. A comparative study of both thinkers may reveal
a ceaseless dialectic between national particularities and universal aspirations.

Together with his student Liang Qichao, Kang was one of the first literati
reformers who attempted to transform the imperial Qing monarchy into a modern
nation-state. Confronted with the crisis, Kang and Liang rallied over 1,300 exami-
nees of the imperial civic examination in 1895 to launch a campaign, endorsed by
Emperor Guangxu, to modernize China's political, social, and economic system.
Engaging with and critical of the international system, Kang Youwei, in his best-
known work, 大同書 (*Datong shu*; The Great World Community), envisioned
a cosmopolitan world of harmony and sociality beyond the narrow confine of
nation-states. The Chinese thinker's cosmopolitan vision compels us to explore
affinities between two thinkers who are geographically and historically far apart.

In the current talk of a world-literary republic, cultural difference is to be
superseded by an overview that transcends national and historical distinctions.
I beg to differ. Although the aspiration to a world culture may go beyond the
boundaries of a national tradition, the quest for the universal has to work through
the particularity of a culture in order to access a common ground. While access
to the common world seems more dream than reality, the road to the commons

must begin from home: it has to engage one's native culture reflectively and creatively. Far from an inward turn toward an authentic, entrenched essence, the dialectic looks out and in to ascertain how a particular culture grows by engaging and recreating universal values without and within.

This quest for the universal through the particular or the growth of the particular via the universal is especially poignant in Chinese writers who thought about China's place in the world. Speaking about Kang Youwei's notion of world community, Hsiao Kung-chuan identified three ways in which Chinese thinkers approached the West. The first was outright dismissal of the need for "learning from the barbarians" in a conservative insistence that China, boasting five thousand years of civilization, already knows best. The second view claimed that China was ill-equipped for modernity, and that a partial or even total embrace of Western civilization was the way to move forward. But Kang Youwei followed a third, more synthetic path: like many Chinese thinkers who considered human knowledge a common property for all under heaven, Kang assumed that "differences between East and West were more nominal than basic" (Hsiao 413). To transform "China's outmoded political, economical, and educational systems was not Westernization but in reality universalization – bringing Chinese culture up to that stage of civilization to which all mankind should do well to attain" (413). Deeply embedded in the Confucian tradition, this normative claim evolved as a prominent doctrine in the Song dynasty. Its motto is that "the truth permeates all under Heaven" and that the same principle holds good for all.

Kang Youwei addressed China's past and new crises by engaging universal values sharable by different national traditions. When new forms of knowledge or insights arise, they not only stem from the appeal to a deep-seated logic dubbed "Confucian" or "Chinese" but also derive primarily from the common concerns of humanity. Only on the basis of sharable and mutually intelligible values can a Chinese writer speak beyond China and catch the ear of the world public, thus transcending the parochial traditions and taking on the universal significance of all under heaven.

Joseph Levenson raised the similar prospect of bringing Chinese history into world history through a hermeneutical exercise that is at once immanent and transcendent. World history is not something given and fixed, but an open-ended, ongoing conversation aimed at mutual reading and interpretation among individual nations and interlocutors. Rather than a grand narrative of Western modernity, a triumphant story of capitalist globalization peopled by rootless individuals, world history is a discursive process of reading in sympathy, imagination, and understanding. Eschewing ahistorical images, Levenson opted for a way of understanding China and the West in the spirit of rooted cosmopolitanism, projecting a worldly China as firmly grounded in its own history yet eminently conversant with the world:

> An historian, bringing China into a universal world of discourse, helps to unify the world on more than a technological level . . . I saw a world made when an understanding of Chinese history, without violence to its integrity

and individuality, and an understanding of western history reinforced each other. The two histories belong together . . . because minds of observers can transpose the problems (not, transplant the problems) of one into the other . . . And Chinese history, then, should be studied because . . . it can be seen to make sense in the same world of discourse in which we try to make sense of the West. If we can make this kind of sense, perhaps we help to make this kind of world.

(xxviii)

Crucial to this vision of world history are culture, ideas, and imagination. I suggest that the discourse of the aesthetic contributes to this transposing, cross-fertilizing process, and is capable of projecting a vision of an international society composed of civilized humans.

The aesthetic as the way of the world

The "aesthetic" opens up the inquiry to diverse qualities and connections, including artistic design, subjective impressions, sensuous, emotional life, personal taste, artistic style, forms of everyday life, and cultural patterns. In the West and in China, the aesthetic has been granted an important role in sociopolitical formations: it bears the burden of activating rituals and maintaining values, shoring up the polity, sustaining social cohesion, and legitimizing the ideological apparatus. All these are supposed to happen by way of ritualistic, experiential immersion in emotion, corporeality, pleasure, intersubjective relations, images, and arts. From Plato and Aristotle through Kant, Hegel, Schiller, and Burke to Marx, the aesthetic is a branch of philosophy not separate from ethical and political concerns. More than an analysis of sense and sensibility, of art, poetry, or music, the aesthetic is the vital lifeline of social cohesion, character formation, and political legitimacy.

In the Chinese tradition, the aesthetic, understood as ceremony and ritual, poetics, and the arts, is meant to maintain social and political order. Poetry, music, and song, for example, are the affair of the state in regulating moral profiles, ideology, family values, and communal cohesion. The aesthetic experience is integral to the development of a virtuous personality. Studying classics, playing instruments, and ritual participation map out a trajectory of self-cultivation and socialization akin to *Bildung* in German Romanticism. In this process, the individual builds up his character and attains the status of civilized social member committed to the common good and devoted to a shared morality.

A legacy of the Enlightenment, aesthetic thinking goes beyond civil society to take on a language of humanism and cosmopolitanism, invoking presumptions of rights of man and the possibility of a world community. In Kant, the aesthetic may be read as a cultural venue whereby cosmopolitan thinkers envisage a community of feeling subjects in hopes of harmonizing antagonistic states. In the classical Chinese way, Kang Youwei also made an aesthetic and ethical case for a vision of world order. From Confucian classics Kang reinvented a language of

Heaven as endowed with universal reason and as the highest moral authority. For both Kant and Kang, this vision arose in response to a world torn asunder by geopolitical forces, colonialism, and competitive nation-states. In what follows, I discuss Kant's aesthetic notion of *sensus communis* in relation to Kang Youwei's vision of world community.

Aesthetic community of sense and sensibility

One historical context for the rise of the aesthetic is the disintegration of a religious, unitary world order. From the ruins of the theocratic ancient regime emerged the market and civil society in Europe, but modern society was constantly torn asunder by rival interests. The divided feelings and conflicted sentiments were rampant among individuals and states. Kant diagnosed this fragmentation and disharmony with a blanket term, "unsocial sociability" (*Political Writings* 44). By this he meant the paradoxical tendency of individuals to associate with others socially while simultaneously competing with them in the pursuit of private interest. Social members were "bound together with mutual oppositions that threaten to break up the society," and each individual pursues private agendas detrimental to others (*Political Writings* 44). In his cosmopolitan essay, "Idea for a Universal History with a Cosmopolitan Purpose," Kant extends this antagonism from domestic society to the international arena of mutually opposed, self-serving states. Although in Kant's day increasing global commerce and transportation facilitated interaction among peoples worldwide and a sense of interdependence was in the air, interstate relations were conflicted because of the parochial agendas of each state.

In the face of this antagonism, the aesthetic, which envisaged a shared plane of sense and sensibility over and above geopolitical conflict, offered an attractive solution to bridge the constant schisms. Aesthetic experience in culture and the arts may gesture toward a vision of rationally conceived society, where intersubjective feelings resonate and a picture of harmonious community seems tantalizingly close. Kant writes,

> Beautiful arts and sciences, which by means of a universally communicable pleasure and an elegance and refinement make human beings, if not morally better, at least better mannered for society, very much reduce the tyranny of sensible tendencies, and prepare humans for a sovereignty in which reason alone shall have Power.
>
> (*Critique* 301)

The aesthetic is a gateway of sense and sensibility leading to reason and understanding. Humans, sunk in their private spheres and sensuous needs ("the tyranny of sensible tendencies"), and engrossed in material gains and survival, are bound to antagonize each other in the struggle for self-preservation like barbarians. The aesthetic elevates humans to a higher level of culture and morality.

Aesthetic judgments point to a common ground of social interactivity over conflict, a platform captured by the idea of *sensus communis*. Rather than crudely sensuous life and instinctive drives, the notion of *sensus communis* claims the achievable ability to transcend one's private sphere, a capacity of putting oneself "into the position of everyone else, merely by abstracting from the limitations that contingently attach to our judging" (*Critique* 173). The outreaching sense and sensibility require a broad-minded subject able to set "himself apart from the subjective private conditions of the judgment, within which so many others are as if bracketed" and to reflect on his own judgment "from a universal standpoint" (*Critique* 175) by putting himself into the vantage point of others. The individual of enlarged mind will suspend his own narrow-mindedness and rise above his subjective conditions.

In aesthetic judgments, sensuous experience contains pleasure common and sharable with all humans. Aesthetic experience has the power to forge sensuous, affective, and imaginary bonds conducive to reciprocity and sociality. It works in a social setting where interaction and mutual sympathy take place. Aesthetic taste fosters the capacity to behave in refined but sociable ways. Rather than fraught with rivalry and conflict, civil society is now reimagined as a public space for experiencing sharable pleasure in arts and refined ritualistic activities. A human being with aesthetic taste is sociable rather than self-indulgent, outgoing rather than inner-directed: such a subject is inclined to communicate his pleasure to others and derives little pleasure from an object until he is able to feel his satisfaction in unison with others.

Thus, the public sphere is pitted against the private sphere, social against asocial behavior, broad-mindedness against the egotism of "asocial sociability." Underlying the notion of *sensus communis* is an idea of human beings as cultural agents. The cultural agent wields aesthetic power and practically remakes the existing world in pursuit of political freedom. The figure refers to the aesthetic capacity of humans to inscribe the world with human values and transform man's natural drives and external objects, thus humanizing the world with aesthetic forms (Muthu 144). The humanized world, rising above creaturely needs and material wants, in its turn conditions and appeals to humans' aesthetic sensibility. The cultural agent is a far cry from the familiar essentialist view in that it bridges the universal and the particular. The idea that all humans are equally endowed with the ability to reflect on and beautify their own inherited situation honors their commonality, whereas their specific trajectories show the influence of circumstances, customs, and regions. Although actors of diverse histories cannot choose where they are born, they can choose to reflect upon and try to transform the world they are born into – therein lies agential aesthetic humanity.

Cosmopolitanism, aesthetics, and all under heaven

If Kantian aesthetics is founded on universal reason, Kang Youwei resorts to a Confucian language of Heaven and nature to assert the universal basis for aesthetic communication. Kang Youwei's thinking arose in a traumatic confrontation with the modern world system of nation-states. The modern world eroded and broke up the Chinese worldview embodied by *tianxia*. Literarily meaning "all under heaven," *tianxia* refers to a moral and political order sustained not by a legal system and coercion but by ritual, music, moral values, tributary networks, administrative hierarchy, and reciprocity among East Asian regions. The concept denotes a sphere of culture and values to be internalized by all individuals and groups. In radical opposition to the interstate conflict characteristic of the Warring States in early dynastic history and more recently to the Westphalian system of nation-states, *tianxia* has been invoked in recent decades as a radically different vision of world order (see Wang). Deeply entrenched in Confucian political culture and collective consciousness, *tianxia*, according to Levenson, describes a world "whose values were Value, whose civilization was Civilization, a transnational antithesis to barbarism" (20).

But confronted with modern crises, Kang realized that the ancient *tianxia* order was in shambles as China was dragged into the forest of nations. As he notes in *Datong shu*, now that "the globe is completely known, what was called the central empire (*zhongguo*) and adjacent territories are but one corner of Asia and one-eighteenth of the world" (*Ta T'ung Shu* 54; English translation, with my modifications, from page 80 of the same volume). Against the slaughter-bench landscape of interstate conflict, Kang raised the question of how the sensibility of one person can and must connect and resonate with another in a world divided, and how a far-reaching moral sensibility can be articulated. How can moral sensibility enable one individual to empathize with another? What forms of aesthetic culture might foster this far-reaching sensibility? In Kang, the aesthetic lies in learning from and immersing oneself in diverse cultures in a way that involves all senses and the soul. Learning allows us to have intimate access to others and fosters sympathy and shared appreciation of pluralistic cultural forms. The way to a unitary world is through aesthetic enjoyment and circulation of cultural traditions across national boundaries:

> I have drunk deeply of the intellectual heritage of ancient India, Greece, Persia, and Rome, and of modern England, France, Germany, and America. I have pillowed my head upon them, and my soul in dreams has fathomed them. With the wise old men, noted scholars, famous figures, and beautiful women of all countries I have likewise often joined hands, we have sat on mats side by side, sleeves touching, sharing our meal, and I have grown to love them. Each day I have been offered and have made use of the dwellings, clothing, food, boats, vehicles, utensils, government, education, arts, and music of a myriad of countries, and these have stimulated my mind and enriched my spirit. Do they progress? Then we all progress with them. Are they happy? Then we are happy with them. Do they suffer? Then we suffer with them. It is as if we were all parts of an electrical force, which interconnects all things, or partook of the pure essence that encompasses all things.
>
> (*Ta T'ung Shu* 3–4; this translation is from Spence 66)

This passage presents a vignette of long-distance learning and interaction by way of far-reaching sense and sensibility. The "I" as an aesthetic subject is broad-minded and sensitive, intellectually embracing several civilizational heritages across the globe. The approach to foreign cultures is sensuous and embodied but also intellectual. The lessons and wisdom to be had are highly revered – the best that has been written and thought in a tradition and preserved by "old men, noted scholars, famous figures, and beautiful women." The parallel progress and shared happiness imply a common, world-historical path, a universal measure of civilizational advancement. The "I" projects a normative standard to be derived from as well as to measure the specific value of each heritage and envisages a narrative of human progress as an educational project akin to the aesthetic *Bildung* in German Romanticism. While *Bildung* seeks to build up through aesthetic cultivation a character of civic virtue purged of "unsocial sociability," Kang's moral progress aims at the cultivation of noble virtue of intercultural proportions.

This cross-cultural reciprocity stems from the Confucian idea of *qi*, the "electric force" in the quoted passage. Running through all boundaries of race, states, and regions, *qi* is an embracing process and cosmic substance, at once physical, biological, spiritual, and moral. It permeates heaven and earth, flows and circulates through humans, animals, and plants. Similar to the Western concept of ether, *qi* drives and facilitates our perception and sympathy with everything and everybody outside of us, fostering knowledge about them. Kang writes, "I have a body, then I share with coexisting bodies that which permeates the air of Heaven, permeates the matter of Earth, permeates the breath of Man" (*Ta T'ung Shu* 2–3; translation 64). The body is but a link in the all-flowing stream of *qi*. Rather than a socially and historically conditioned body, the *qi*-filled body is endowed by heaven under the cosmic rubric of *tian-ren* (天人) and is equivalent to any other body, be it man or woman, high class or low. In *Datong shu*, this heavenly endowed body functions as an equalizing principle and a source of critique against all divisions of gender, class, ethnicity, and nation-states.

Qi-based perception is driven by the moral principles drawn from the Confucian classics. Envisioning a moral republic, Kang goes beyond Kant's political view to rethink the ethico-political doctrine of benevolent governance. Linking aesthetic perception to the Confucian notion of *ren*, Kang extends this connection to relationships with other cultures and nations in search of a vision of humane political community. More than an experience of intersubjective resonance, benevolence is institutionalized in the Confucian vision of the Kingly Way – benevolent governance. Based on a capacious sensitivity to people's pain and suffering, the Kingly Way operates on the Mencian principle of commiseration captured by the motto "All men have a mind which cannot bear [to see the sufferings of] others" (人皆有不忍之心).

As we saw in Kant, aesthetic experience may facilitate social cohesion and sustain political order. In Kang, benevolent government is based on ritualistic, aesthetic bodily experience, sensitivity, and compassion. Benevolent governance is embodied in all its creaturely, sensuous, and emotional attributes – the fulcrum of political culture. As Terry Eagleton observes, the aesthetic concerns

> nothing less than the whole of our sensate life together – the business of affections and aversions, of how the world strikes the body on its sensory surfaces, of that which takes root in the gaze and the guts and all that arises from our most banal, biological insertion into the world.
>
> (13)

Benevolent government does not simply take care of the well-being of the population. Its aesthetic aspect lies in the efforts to promote shared pleasure and seal the bonds of emotional solidarity. Kang resorts to Mencius's notion of shared aesthetic experience as the basis for the Kingly Way, which is well illustrated by a scenario in *The Works of Mencius*. Worried about his indulgence in the excessive pleasure of music, King Lianghui of the state of Qi expresses his concern to Mencius and receives a reassuring answer. Mencius advises, "if the king's love of music were very great, the kingdom of Qi would be close to a state of good government." But it makes a huge difference whether the king indulged in music on his own or with a select few, or shared music with the majority of people. In the former case people would complain that the king, absorbed in self-pleasures or confined to a small circle, ignored their distress, needs, and families. Similar aesthetic privileges, like the beauty of the king's plumes, horses, and entourage, would be greeted with frowns and grievances from the disadvantaged strata of the population. But if the king shared music with his people, and if the high and the low collectively enjoyed music in concert, people would have a chance to enjoy it as much as the king. The people would then rejoice in looking at the majestic beauty of the king's carriages and pleasures (Mencius, Book II, Chapter 1).

This ethical sensibility informs an unbroken chain of being extending from person to family to community and government, all the way to humanity as a whole. Kang depicts a rising scale of obligations from the narrower human unit to the broadest one:

> Master Kang says, being that I am a man, I would be uncompassionate to flee from men, and not to share their grief and miseries. And being that I was born into a family, and [by virtue of] receiving the nurture of others was able to have this life, I then have the responsibilities of a family member. Should I flee from this [responsibility], my behavior would be false . . . And why would it not be the same with the public debt we owe to one country and the world? Being that we are born into one country, have received the civilization of one country, and thereby have its knowledge, then we have the responsibilities of a citizen. If we flee from this [responsibility] and abandon this country, this country will perish and its people will be annihilated, and then civilization will be destroyed.
>
> (*Ta T'ung Shu* 48; translation 65)

By this widening gyre of sympathy, imagination, and obligation, Kang claims that the member of a local community could become a citizen of the world. Increasing allegiance to higher and higher political units broadens the mind and virtue of the citizen, taking him out of unsocial sociability, competitive society, and interstate conflict.

World literature and aesthetic bonding

Ever since Herder, literature has sunk its roots in national traditions and languages marked by distinctive traits. But the aesthetic *sensus communis* suggests that world literature is possible between different national traditions. Rather than a consecrated structure that transcends national boundaries, world literature can be conceived as a space of mutual reading and shared sensibility between one national context and another. As Fredric Jameson notes, the nation-state persists in globalization, and world literature cannot bypass national boundaries. Rather, the vision of world literature offers a space of communication and resonance between national situations. An aesthetic hermeneutics allows the concern of one national situation to "achieve contact with the text of another nation by way of mediation of the relationship between two national situations" (Jameson 5–6). Literary affinities may arise between nations and peoples trying to stand on their own on the world stage.

In the light of aesthetic humanity enacted by the cultural agent, this nation-based worldview is not a defense of the nation-state. The challenge is to work through and to go beyond it. Given the current world of nation-states, culture needs a national polity to survive, grow, and flourish. On the other hand, mutual respect and learning across cultures rest not on the hegemonic power of the nation-state but on the self-determination, autonomy, and creativity of cultural agents. The figure of the cultural agent not only describes members of respectable cultures nestled in an instituted framework of nation-states but also bridges groups and peoples without nation-state forms.

Rather than the denationalized capital of hegemonic powers, world literature stems from multiple origins among different but autonomous, self-creating peoples, be they national communities or subnational groups. Different nations and groups may make common cause in the shared drive to claim equal rights to world literary space. The authentic voice, the deep-seated tradition, and the cultural roots of a people may become intelligible and translatable to others. Rather than barriers, a national or local heritage may be a source of inspiration for another nation or people, inviting learning, sympathy, and admiration and engendering solidarity. During the European Enlightenment, the German Romantics identified with English culture and Shakespeare, and deployed other nations' literature as useful sources to affirm Germany's independence. On the other hand, "the critical assessment of Shakespeare by the German Romantics was used by the English to claim him as the chief repository of their national literary wealth" (Casanova 79).

A cosmopolitan politics is at work here. The concept of the cultural agent entails the collective quality of freedom, which for Hannah Arendt is "actually the reason why men live together in political organization at all" (146). In Kant and Kang Youwei, "political organization" is on a world scale and is to be forged via aesthetic sympathy and understanding. Finding a similar aesthetic empathy at the heart of the political, Terry Eagleton writes, "At the very root of social relations lies the aesthetic, source of all human bonding" (24). Kantian aesthetic disinterestedness does not mean self-centeredness and lack of interest in morality and politics. Aesthetic detachment means indifference, it is true, yet indifference not to others' interest but to one's own. The aesthetic subject is detached from his own narrow sphere and self-absorption, from unsocial sociability. Eagleton speaks of the aesthetic implications of Rousseauian civic virtue in a way that resonates with Kang's ideas about sympathy, benevolence, and governance. Civic virtue is a "passionate affection for his fellow citizens and for shared conditions of their common life" (Eagleton 24). The aesthetic sensibility stems from the pity we feel for each other in the state of nature and is based on the empathetic imagination. This empathetic imagination makes us capable of

> transporting ourselves outside ourselves, and identifying ourselves with the suffering animal, leaving our being, so to speak, in order to take his . . . Thus no one becomes sensitive except when his imagination is animated and begins to transport himself outside himself.
>
> (Eagleton 24)

Civic virtue, in connection with aesthetic sensitivity, resonates with Kang's version of Confucian benevolence. Mediated by far-reaching sympathy and understanding, the aesthetic can foster a civic, public virtue compatible with the cosmopolitanism of a global civic society. The aesthetic enhances the possibility of globally imagined and shared sentiments among different peoples. In the age of digital information, rather than functioning as a mere ideological apparatus, the incessant production of images, emotions, and ideas has the potential to become dissociated from economic utility and authoritarian control, forging ahead as a force at once aesthetic, social, and political (Hardt and Negri 66). Aesthetic production is nothing less than making change with a vision of a more just, livable, and socially connected world as envisioned by Kant and Kang. The individual can feel global by cultivating imagination and sensibility, by learning about different cultures, and by nurturing a sensitivity to commiserate with all those suffering in the world.

Works cited

Arendt, Hannah. *Between Past and Future*. New York: Penguin, 1968. Print.
Casanova, Pascale. *The World Republic of Letters*. Trans. M. B. DeBevoise. Cambridge, MA: Harvard UP, 2004. Print.
Eagleton, Terry. *The Ideology of the Aesthetic*. New York: Blackwell, 1990. Print.

Hardt, Michael, and Antonio Negri. *Multitude: War and Democracy in the Age of Empire*. New York: Penguin, 2004. Print.

Hsiao, Kung-chuan. *A Modern China and a New World: K'ang Yu-Wei, Reformer and Utopian, 1858–1927*. Seattle: U of Washington P, 1975. Print.

Jameson, Fredric. "Whether World Literature Has a Foreign Policy?" Holberg International Memorial Prize Lecture. Duke University, Durham, NC. 10 Nov. 2008. Lecture transcript.

Kang, Youwei. *Datong shu*. Shanghai: Guji Chubanshe, 2005. Print.

———. *Ta T'ung Shu: The One-World Philosophy of K'ang Yu-wei*. Trans. Laurence Thompson. London: Routledge, 2011. Print.

Kant, Immanuel. *Critique of the Power of Judgment*. Trans. Paul Guyer and Eric Mathews. New York: Cambridge UP, 2000. Print.

———. *Political Writings*. Trans. H. B. Nisbet. Cambridge: Cambridge UP, 1991. Print.

Levenson, Joseph. *Revolution and Cosmopolitanism: The Western Stage and the Chinese Stages*. Berkeley: U of California P, 1971. Print.

Mencius. *The Works of Mencius*. Ed. and Trans. James Legge. New York: Dover, 1970. Print.

Muthu, Sankar. *Enlightenment against Empire*. Princeton: Princeton UP, 2003. Print.

Spence, Jonathan. *The Gate of Heavenly Peace: The Chinese and Their Revolution*. New York: Penguin, 1981. Print.

Wang, Ban, ed. *Chinese Visions of World Order: Tianxia, Culture, and World Politics*. Durham: Duke UP, 2017. Print.

Comparative literature, world literature, and Asia

Karen Thornber

For most of its history the field of comparative literature, as practiced in much of the world, has focused largely on certain privileged European literatures. In recent years, there has been a blossoming of interest in Western-language writings not only from previously marginalized European literatures but also from former European colonies in Africa, the Americas, the Middle East, Oceania, and South and Southeast Asia. Yet even today, scholars working on non-Western-language literatures – the creative texts of billions of people with thousands of years of literary heritage – remain a disproportionate minority in most comparative literature departments.[1] Most notably, although Asian peoples make up more than half of the world's population, departments of comparative literature generally have no more than one or two members with expertise in East or South Asian languages; very few departments include anyone with even a basic understanding of a Central or Southeast Asian language, despite the fact that Central and Southeast Asia together have nearly the population of Europe.[2]

Moreover, intra-European comparative scholarship, indeed even intra–Western European comparative scholarship, is rarely if ever thought of as "area studies." In contrast, despite the fact that East and South Asia both have twice the population of Europe and longer and more diverse cultural histories, intra–East Asian and intra–South Asian, even *intra-Asian* scholarship is sometimes dismissed as "area studies." The same holds true for scholarship on Central and Southeast Asian literatures, notwithstanding the plethora of languages involved. In addition, when they have been studied in a comparative context, non-Western-language literatures, as well as Western-language literatures from outside Western power centers, have mainly been examined in terms of their connections with literatures from Western power centers, either as inspirations and appropriations or as exhibiting similarities and differences. And often, Europe remains the standard for comparison. But Europe is as much an "area" as other sections of the Eurasian landmass; it makes as much sense to call Europe a separate continent as to call the Indian peninsula one continent, with the remainder of Eurasia – from Korea to Portugal – another (Lewis and Wigen 36).[3]

As its name suggests, world literature – a branch of comparative literature once associated primarily with an established canon of mostly Western classical masterpieces – has embraced literatures written in non-Western languages more readily than the broader field of comparative literature. In "What Is World-Literature?" (1886), the opening section of his discussion of world literature, the early Irish comparatist Hutcheson Macaulay Posnett demonstrates real openness to a broad spectrum of the world's literatures (50). More than a century after Posnett, David Damrosch, in his own *What Is World Literature?*, expresses similar flexibility:

> I take world literature to encompass all literary works that circulate beyond their culture of origin either in translation or in their original language . . . a work only has an *effective* life as world literature whenever, and wherever, it is actively present within a literary system beyond that of its original culture.
>
> (4)

In theory, Posnett's and Damrosch's responses to the question "What is world literature?" include not only texts that circulate among European and North American nations or between these and other cultures but also those texts inaccessible to readers unfamiliar with non-Western languages.

Yet in practice, literary networks within and among non-Western regions, especially contacts of the last few centuries, receive much less notice than those where Europe and North America figure prominently, most frequently as a source (e.g., Chinese engaging with European aesthetics), but also as a destination (e.g., Europeans engaging with Chinese aesthetics). As Kan Wang has observed, "[Because] the hierarchy privileging Western language literature has become increasingly solidified . . . [Chinese and other non-Western writers] cannot enter into the ranks of 'universal writers' without recognition from the West" (571). Similarly, Stephen Owen observes, "For a young Korean poet to be translated into Tagalog and acclaimed in Manila is, no doubt, a matter of satisfaction; but it has less cachet than to be translated into English or French and invited to New York or Paris. It is unfair but it is a fact" (533). Likewise, although an Asian-language text that has been translated into other Asian languages but not into any Western languages would generally not be spoken of as world literature, a European-language text that has circulated widely in Europe but not been translated into a non-European language would even today likely be regarded as world literature. As Owen asserts, these are facts. Yet we must be careful to use them to expose rather than to perpetuate inequities.

By working more assiduously to unearth the multiple, multidirectional, forever mutable, and frequently precarious textual pathways that have crisscrossed the globe across time, the field of comparative literature will be able not only to deconstruct cultural assumptions and hierarchies, including the absolute authority and precedence of conventional European and North American power centers, but also to create more pluralistic understandings of literatures, cultures, nations, regions, and even continents. Moving more closely to region neutrality, where cultural contacts among Western spaces or between Western and non-Western sites are no longer privileged above those that involve Western power centers only secondarily if at all, will provide clearer perceptions of interactions among peoples and cultures the world over – whether those involve shunning, embracing, or, far more frequently, rigorously negotiating with one another in their attempt to make better sense of human experience.

Focus on relationships among peoples and cultural spaces within the so-called global South has uncovered many pathways of knowing and relating among Africa, Latin America, the Middle East, parts of Oceania, and much of Asia, as well as marginalized Western communities; Western power centers are not disregarded, but neither are they necessarily prioritized.[4] Instead, this field of inquiry brings to light the complex, multitextured, and ambiguous connections among peoples and cultures globally, revealing Europe in many cases as one space among many. Yet to date, most academic writing on literature and the global South has highlighted relationships among Western-language creative productions.[5] Although such scholarship – which reads creative work within, across, and against formal, national, regional, and continental boundaries (Ramazani 304) – aptly dismantles many conventional groupings, it remains relatively confined linguistically and paradoxically has the potential to duplicate some lacunae of more conventional comparative scholarship.

Closely related to transnational studies of the global South, scholarship on circulation of texts in local, national, and for the most part non-Western languages within and among non-Western regions, including East, Central, South, and Southeast Asia, breaks linguistic barriers more radically and illuminates a number of heretofore excluded cultural contact spaces. Intra-Asian comparative work dispels common and primarily Western misperceptions of the Asian continent as either a space of excess, extravagance, and near-chaos, one where commonalities are so general as to be insignificant, or as a space of near unchanging uniformity, an undifferentiated, even exotic immobile other (see Wigen 37).[6] Even more importantly, intra-Asian comparative scholarship pushes comparative literature closer to region neutrality and provides greater impetus to radically restructure the field. It also offers new understandings of the dynamics of literary networks themselves, including those that have accompanied major cultural shifts in world history (e.g., the spread of Islam to South and Southeast Asia), as well as those whose attributes create or reinforce, diverge from or even clash with official discourse and power imbalances, such as significant economic, political, military, and social hierarchies (e.g., transculturation in early twentieth-century East Asia between imperial Japan, semicolonial China, and colonial Korea and Taiwan: see Ricci; Thornber, *Empire*). To go one step further, focusing on the relationship between networks of Asian literatures and such regional and global challenges as atrocity, disease, environmental degradation, poverty, and war not only deepens understandings of globally renowned Asian writers but also brings to light many texts, writers, and literary dynamics that have been relatively overlooked by Western power centers. Additionally, it gives new perspectives on transnational issues, contributes significantly to the medical and environmental humanities, and guides the humanities writ large to engage more directly with a broader array of global concerns.

Extant comparative and world literature scholarship, as well as that on national literatures, provides important foundations for these types of studies. So too do secondary sources in a number of other fields, particularly world and global history, with their attention to empire, trade, demography, economics, religion, cultural production, disease and health, slavery, and environmental degradation among cultures and geographic regions. But as might be expected, intra-Asian comparative scholarship as well as research on other understudied literary networks relies heavily on intensive scrutiny of primary sources and vernacular archives in multiple sites. Hardly neutral ground, and often incomplete, archives nevertheless offer some of the field's best hopes of unearthing the many creative trajectories that have been buried over the decades, allowing comparative literature to diverge significantly from conventional pathways. The digital humanities are certain to help with this endeavor as they excavate materials that have not traveled and elucidate barriers to motion. Just as important to recognizing what has circulated and examining how and why particular texts crisscross nations, regions, and the globe is knowing what has not, and understanding, at least in part, why this has been the case.

An illustrative example is the Korean writer Yi Ch'ŏngjun's novel *Your Paradise* (Tangsindŭl ŭi ch'ŏnguk, 당신들의 천국, 1976) on the Sorokdo (Korea) leprosarium, one of many East Asian texts that have circulated in the region and beyond; the novel has been translated into English, French, Japanese, Spanish, and Urdu. Although it focuses in large part on the abuse and absolute segregation of Hansen's disease patients, *Your Paradise* concludes with the marriage of an individual with Hansen's disease to one without, an event celebrated as bringing together the island's two communities. As a former director of Sorokdo declares, "This longstanding embankment road [둑길] now is connected and the road [길] has opened up. And your neighbors will unite their strength [힘을 합하다] and will protect/keep watch over [지키다] and broaden this road" (438; translation mine). The English translation additionally has the neighbors "traveling freely" across the newly opened road as well as "buttressing" it, describing more explicitly precisely how this space will be both used and safeguarded (511; see Thornber, "World Literature"). The same can perhaps be said of scholarship, the concluding lines of *Your Paradise* helping us to reimagine the potentials of comparative literature.

Broadening and creating pathways among what often have been taken as relatively discreet linguistic and cultural entities, comparative literature scholarship – particularly when it goes global, in every sense of the word – can give us a much better sense of how diverse societies both within Asia and around the world have interacted with one another and with pressing global concerns. This understanding is crucial if we are to address these problems more effectively. The "buttressing" to which the former director of Sorokdo refers at the conclusion of *Your Paradise* is anything but ossifying. Pathways are safeguarded not against change

– not against more deeply interconnecting people, places, and cultural products –
but instead to facilitate motion and thereby to decrease response time not only to
difficulties in particular disciplines, including the alleged crisis in the humanities,
but also to those facing humanity as well as the nonhuman world more broadly.

Notes

1 To be sure, a number of European languages are not well represented in departments of comparative literature either, but the training of most scholars in these
literatures overlaps significantly with that of scholars of the more dominant West
European literatures. Bringing on board scholars with expertise in Dutch, Swed-
ish, or Ukrainian, for example, is important, but far less urgent than including
those with expertise in non-European languages – for example, Arabic, Sanskrit,
Chinese, and Swahili – whose training has given them access to a vastly different
canon.
2 Europe's population is approximately 740 million (about half that of China),
compared with Southeast Asia's 610 million and Central Asia's 48 million.
3 Martin Lewis and Kären Wigen also argue that viewing Europe and Asia as
belonging to a single continent would be more accurate geographically, but
would undermine European claims of distinctiveness and ultimately superiority.
4 Asian nations belonging not to the global South but instead to the so-called global
North are Japan, South Korea, and Taiwan from East Asia; and Singapore from
Southeast Asia. Israel is the one Middle Eastern nation not included as part of
the global South, although a number of other countries in the Middle East enjoy
great wealth. Australia and New Zealand are part of the global North. Also generally excluded from the global South are China's Special Administrative Regions
of Hong Kong and Macau. Mainland China's own position between South and
North varies.
5 There are exceptions. See, for instance, Tiwari's "Comparative Literature," which
examines interconnections among Hindi, Bengali, and Hispanophone Latin
American literatures. But the far more dominant trend, as embodied in such active
fields as Anglophone, Francophone, Lusophone, Hispanophone, and Sinophone
studies (see Hao, this volume), is to focus on the literatures of a single language
as manifested globally.
6 March elaborates on this paradox. Europe is far from a homogeneous entity, but
differences among European cultures have tended to be less significant than those
among their Asian counterparts: the major Asian languages are not nearly as cognate as the Romance and Germanic languages of Europe; the spoken languages
of China alone are more diverse than the spoken Latinate languages of Europe.
Moreover, with their multiplicity of cultural systems (including religions), many
regions of Asia, not to mention the continent itself, have nothing like the commonality of their European counterparts. It goes without saying that removing
misconceptions of Asia helps scholars reconceptualize the European engagement
with the continent.

Works cited

Lewis, Martin W. and Kären Wigen. *The Myth of Continents: A Critique of Metageog-
raphy.* Berkeley: U of California P, 1997. Print.
March, Andrew. *The Idea of China.* New York: Praeger, 1974. Print.

Owen, Stephen. "Stepping Forward and Back: Issues and Possibilities for 'World' Poetry." *Modern Philology* 100.4 (2003): 532–48. Print.

Ramazani, Jahan. "Poetry, Modernity, and Globalization." *The Oxford Handbook of Literary Modernisms*. Ed. Mark Wollaeger and Matt Eatough. New York: Oxford UP, 2012. 288–309. Print.

Ricci, Ronit. *Islam Translated: Literature, Conversion, and the Arabic Cosmopolis of South and Southeast Asia*. Chicago: U of Chicago P, 2011. Print.

Thornber, Karen Laura. *Empire of Texts in Motion: Chinese, Korean, and Taiwanese Transculturations of Japanese Literature*. Cambridge: Harvard UP, 2009. Print.

———. "World Literature and the Health Humanities – Translingual Encounters with Brain Disorders." *Geographic Imaginaries for the Twenty-First Century*. Ed. Diana Sorensen. Durham: Duke UP, forthcoming in 2017.

Tiwari, Bhavya. "Comparative Literature: Three Case Studies from the Global South." Diss. U of Texas at Austin, 2013. Print.

Wang, Kan. "North America, English Translation, and Contemporary Chinese Literature." *Frontiers of Literary Studies in China* 6 (2012): 570–81. Print.

Yi Ch'ongjŭn. *Tangsindŭl ŭi ch'ŏn'guk*. Seoul: Munhak kwa Chisŏngsa, 2012.

———. *Your Paradise*. Trans. Jennifer M. Lee and Timothy R. Tangherlini. Los Angeles: Green Integer, 2005. Print.

Neoliberalism

Snehal Shingavi

In *A Brief History of Neoliberalism*, David Harvey lays out the two primary ways that neoliberalism has been understood in the academic and popular press:

> either as a utopian project to realize a theoretical design for the reorganization of international capitalism or as a political project to re-establish the conditions for capital accumulation and to restore the power of economic elites . . . The evidence suggests, moreover, that when neoliberal principles clash with the need to restore or sustain elite power, then the principles are either abandoned or become so twisted as to be unrecognizable.
>
> (19)

Harvey's suggestion that idealized versions of neoliberalism (a suite of libertarian principles articulated by Friedrich Hayek, Ludwig von Mises, Milton Friedman, and the Mont Pelerin Society) have stood in for differentiated state policies explains the unevenness of neoliberalism throughout the globe, why neoliberals do not demand the elimination of all state intervention in the economy everywhere, and why some neoliberals have also been proponents of authoritarianism and antidemocratic principles. Some state intervention has been necessary to maintain markets and property rights, foundations for capitalist expansion. Neoliberalism might also be understood as an umbrella term that captures different responses to crises of profitability that occurred globally during the 1970s in various post–World War II regimes of state-backed capitalism and large welfare provisions ("embedded liberalism"): the failure of Keynesianism (USA); the stagnation of social democracy (Germany, UK); the crisis of postcolonial autarky (India, South Africa, Egypt); the limits to state-led planning (China, USSR); the balance of payments crisis in the Third World (Mexico); and the paradoxical success of developmental states which produced a stronger capitalist class now attempting to undo the fetters of developmentalism (Korea, Taiwan).

The policies that were implemented between the 1970s and 1990s in response to the long crisis in profitability necessarily took different shapes in different national economies: monetarism and an attack on the welfare state (Anglo-American economies); IMF-enforced structural adjustment (Latin American and African economies); state-manipulated market economics (China); newly formed capitalist class networks (East Asian economies); protracted attacks on labor unions (formal social democracies); and shock therapy (former Soviet economies). There was a convergence around a set of policies, such as the move toward greater liberalization of financial markets; privatization of national industry; elimination of regulation while guaranteeing property rights; deindustrialization and relocation of important manufacturing; flexibilization of labor through casualization and just-in-time production; evisceration of the state-sponsored social provision; and attacks on labor unions. All of these were necessary parts of the restructuring of capitalism to attempt to recover profitability, primarily by weakening the bargaining power of labor and unions, or in the classical Marxist terms, the rise in the "organic composition of capital." Regrettably, most academics conclude that this signals the working class has lost its world-historical role, even though labor has renewed its militancy in a number of neoliberal zones, such as India, China, Egypt, Greece, Brazil, and Argentina.

Concepts crucial to literary studies also tend to converge and become reorganized in their historical connectedness to shifts in the economic structure of global capitalism. Postcolonialism now appears as attempts by the indigenous capitalist class to gain a greater share of the national profits as much as a hangover from colonial organizations of the economy. Postmodernism appears as a result of a specific logic of "late capitalism" which prioritized the individual over other forms of solidarity. Transnationalism tends to be understood less as voluntary flows of cosmopolitan peoples than the ruthless battering of national boundaries by global capitalism. And the "politics of identity" seem to appear as a residue of a more robust international solidarity.

Bibliography of relevant works

Bardhan, Pranab. *Awakening Giants, Feet of Clay: Assessing the Economic Rise of China and India*. Princeton: Princeton UP, 2010. Print.

Breman, Jan. *Outcast Labour in India: Circulation and Informalization of the Workforce at the Bottom of the Economy*. New Delhi: Oxford UP, 2010. Print.

Chandra, Pratyush, ed. *Neoliberalism, Primitive Accumulation and Politics in India*. Delhi: Radical Notes, 2011. Print.

Chibber, Vivek. *Postcolonial Theory and the Specter of Capital*. London: Verso, 2013.

Davis, Mike. *Planet of Slums*. London: Verso, 2006. Print.

Freeman, Samuel. "Illiberal Libertarians: Why Libertarianism Is Not a Liberal View." *Philosophy and Public Affairs* 30.2 (2009): 105–51. Print.

Harvey, David. *A Brief History of Neoliberalism*. New York: Oxford UP, 2005. Print.

———. *Spaces of Global Capitalism: Towards a Theory of Uneven Geographical Development*. London: Verso, 2006.

Hensman, Rohini. *Workers, Unions, and Global Capitalism: Lessons from India*. New York: Columbia UP, 2011. Print.

Lazarus, Neil. "The Global Dispensation since 1945." *The Cambridge Companion to Postcolonial Literary Studies*. Ed. Neil Lazarus. Cambridge: Cambridge UP, 2004. 19–40. Print.

McNally, David. *Global Slump: The Economics and Politics of Crisis and Resistance*. Oakland: PM Press, 2011. Print.

Nanda, Meera. *The God Market: How Globalization Is Making India More Hindu.* New York: Monthly Review Press, 2011. Print.

Nigam, Aditya. *Desire Named Development.* New Delhi: Penguin, 2011. Print.

O'Flynn, Michael. *Profitable Ideas: The Ideology of the Individual in Capitalist Development.* Chicago: Haymarket Books, 2012. Print.

Oza, Rupal. *The Making of Neoliberal India: Nationalism, Gender, and the Paradoxes of Globalization.* London: Routledge, 2006. Print.

Parry, Benita. *Postcolonial Studies: A Materialist Critique.* London: Verso, 2004. Print.

Counterinsurgency

Joseph R. Slaughter

> Some of the best weapons for counterinsurgents do not shoot.
> —Headquarters Department of the Army

Comparative literature has mostly disregarded the weaponization of culture under the counterinsurgency doctrine (COIN) crafted for US military operations in Iraq and Afghanistan, released as Army Field Manual (FM) 3–24 and published simultaneously by the University of Chicago Press (Headquarters Department of the Army; United States Department of the Army). However, COIN has not ignored comparative literature. During the "counterinsurgency decade," as General David Petraeus called it, comparative literature was, like everything else, entangled in the contest between insurgency and counterinsurgency.

Although Petraeus and his COIN coauthors may be unlikely theorists of comparative literature, comparatists are unlikely to dismiss basic premises of counterinsurgency: "The central mechanism through which ideologies are expressed and absorbed is the narrative . . . Narratives are central to representing identity, particularly . . . collective identity . . . Stories . . . provide models of how actions and consequences are linked" (FM 3–24, 1–76). We might not be so empiricist as to believe that a "culture's belief systems can be decoded by observing and analyzing its cultural forms" (3–49), but we often defend comparative literature in similar Herderian terms. Moreover, we produce knowledge about "secondary cultures" for the counterinsurgency (3–21), "open-source intelligence" that includes "books, magazines, encyclopedias, . . . journal articles and university professors" (3–11).

Perhaps "counterinsurgency" seems retrograde, recalling earlier "small wars" in Algeria and Indochina, Northern Ireland, and Central America. But the revival of once dubious concepts seems to characterize the neoliberal ethos of the early 2000s, in comparative literature as in geopolitics. Under the name of world literature, especially after Pascale Casanova and Franco Moretti, we reactivate center-periphery models of cultural dependency largely discredited by economists and postcolonial theorists in the 1980s, and an emerging global modernist studies "discovers" for itself world texts that were already well read in their original domestic contexts and internationally during the Cold War. Such projects seem to be mainstreaming postcolonial, ethnic, and Third World literatures and ideas from another time under new institutional names. Likewise, COIN revives theoretical paradigms refined in the jungles of El Salvador during the Reagan years.

Today, we might describe the 1980s culture wars as a clash of anticanonical insurgencies and canonical counterinsurgency, when it seemed ethically and institutionally responsible to side with the insurgency – with insurrectionary *testimonios* like Rigoberta Menchú's or with women's and gender studies, African American and Latino/a studies, postcolonial studies, and queer studies. Now it often seems as difficult to resist affiliation with the counterinsurgency as it appears unreasonable not to want world literature, or global modernism, or any Atlantean project carrying the name of world or globe. But comparative literature, like counterinsurgency, can be messy business. Through soft power, COIN sought to "reconcile with as many insurgents as was possible, seeking to maximize the number of reconcilables" through cultural or narrative conversion; "irreconcilables" were to be eliminated by other means (Manea). Counterinsurgents must know (just) enough about local narratives and societies to reconcile them to global counterinsurgency culture.

There are numerous other reasons why comparative literature should take note of counterinsurgency. Chief among them is that COIN has taken careful note of developments in comparative literature and related disciplines; or, rather, it took notes without making note of what it took. The parts of FM 3–24 I've quoted were all plagiarized from well-known critical theorists: Paul Ricoeur, Hayden White, Pierre Bourdieu, William Labov, and Donald Polkinghorne (see David Price's "Faking Scholarship"). Along with work by sociologists and anthropologists, the writings of narrative theorists have already been enlisted to weaponize comparative literature and cultural studies.

The forces of insurgency and counterinsurgency constitute some of the factors and conditions under which contemporary literature is produced and circulated – and practiced – in the world today. Disentangled from counterinsurgency, comparative literature would be the name of a resistant discipline whose practices and goals are not directed to maximizing the number of reconcilables or eliminating irreconcilability in the world.

Works cited

Headquarters Department of the Army. *Counterinsurgency* (FM 3–24). Washington, DC: 2006. Print.

Manea, Octavian. "Reflections on the 'Counterinsurgency Decade': Small Wars Journal Interview with General David H. Petraeus." *Small Wars Journal* 1 September 2013. Web. 29 May 2015.

Price, David. "Faking Scholarship." *The Counter-Counterinsurgency Manual*. Ed. Network of Concerned Anthropologists. Chicago: Prickly Paradigm Press, 2009. 59–76. Print.

United States Department of the Army. *Counterinsurgency Field Manual*. Chicago: U of Chicago P, 2007. Print.

Human rights

Sophia A. McClennen

One keyword summarizing a critical trend in the field of comparative literature today may well be that of human rights. Regardless of period or region, one would be hard pressed to find a field of comparative literary research that has not been touched by "the human rights turn." If the cultural turn signaled the critical response to post-1960s politics, and the 1990s were marked by the postcolonial turn, then perhaps the human rights turn best characterizes the period following the attacks of 9/11/2001.

Rights became the primary critical lens to make sense of post-9/11 geopolitics for two main reasons. First, for critics in the United States, rights became a safe way to interrogate the abuses of power that immediately followed the attacks. Approaches to the new iterations of empire, millennial biopolitics, and neoliberal social structures were commonly framed in rights theories that asked how we come to value human life, how it is represented, and how it is destroyed. Such a logic allowed critics working under the spotlight of the US Patriot Act to claim the cover of defending rights while investigating the sinister new forms of governmentality, disaster capitalism, and militarization that were becoming the dominant political mode.

Second, the rights turn put pressure on some of the slippery ways in which poststructuralist critique often seemed to retreat from offering concrete ways to think about how to value and defend life. Through the prism of rights one can critique the legacies of the Enlightenment, the master narratives of empire, and the self-righteousness of liberal humanism while retaining the goal of a utopian critical outcome. While no scholar working on rights could remain immune to how the idea of rights has repeatedly been used with the sole intent of violating them, the grounding of human rights allows for the recovery of much-needed utopian yearnings within a framework that is anything but naïve. Or at least that was the idea.

In the first decade of rights work, a number of key texts and special journal issues charted new directions for the fields of postcolonial studies, identity-based studies, trauma theory, and translation studies, among others. What is perhaps of even greater interest, though, is what will become of the human rights turn in its second decade. The rush to rights-related work was inspired, at least in part, by a desire to make comparative literature socially relevant, politically engaged, and academically meaningful. But as scholars dig more deeply into the nuances of the human rights story and its multiple representations, it is no longer possible simply to point to a given text as representing humanity's salvation – or its downfall. Such readings may have been common in the first decade after 9/11, but they are rare now. In the next decade, comparative work will increasingly have to go beyond the notion that literary texts offer specific aesthetic connections to human rights and develop instead truly comparative frameworks for the very idea of rights as well as a greater interest in moving beyond the Anthropocene as the limit of rights. As the human rights turn enters its second decade, it is necessarily challenged to make the sort of critical interventions that will help the field of comparative literature remain not just relevant but indispensable.

Bibliography of relevant works

Agosín, Marjorie. *Women, Gender, and Human Rights: A Global Perspective*. New Brunswick, NJ: Rutgers UP, 2001. Print.

Anker, Elizabeth S. *Fictions of Dignity: Embodying Human Rights in World Literature*. Ithaca: Cornell UP, 2012. Print.

Balfour, Ian, and Eduardo Cadava, eds. *The Claims of Human Rights*. Spec. issue of South *Atlantic Quarterly* 103.2–3 (2004): 277–588. Web. 3 May 2014.

Butler, Judith, and Domna Stanton, eds. *The Humanities in Human Rights: Critique, Language, Politics*. Spec. issue of *PMLA* 121.5 (2006) 1518–661. Web. 3 May 2014.

Cubilié, Anne. *Women Witnessing Terror: Testimony and the Cultural Politics of Human Rights*. New York: Fordham UP, 2005. Print.

Douzinas, Costas. *Human Rights and Empire: The Political Philosophy of Cosmopolitanism*. London: Routledge-Cavendish, 2007. Print.

Goldberg, Elizabeth S. and Alexandra S. Moore. *Theoretical Perspectives on Human Rights and Literature*. New York: Routledge, 2012. Print.

McClennen, Sophia A. and Henry J. Morello. *Representing Humanity in an Age of Terror*. West Lafayette, IN: Purdue UP, 2010. Print.

McClennen, Sophia A., and Joseph R. Slaughter, eds. *Human Rights and Literary Form*. Spec. issue of *Comparative Literature Studies* 46.1 (2009): 1–212. Print.

Slaughter, Joseph R. *Human Rights, Inc: The World Novel, Narrative Form, and International Law*. New York: Fordham UP, 2007. Print.

Wenzel, Jennifer. *Bulletproof: Afterlives of Anticolonial Prophecy in South Africa and Beyond*. Chicago: U of Chicago P, 2009. Print.

Areas and regions

Areas
Bigger than the nation, smaller than the world

Christopher Bush

Surely I was not the only one surprised by Gayatri Spivak's having become, over the last decade, a kind of defender of a kind of area studies. As one of the definitive critics of colonialisms past and present, a tireless advocate for the value of close reading, and an outspoken opponent of "world literature" (Damrosch and Spivak), Spivak seemed an unlikely proponent of this largely social-scientific group of disciplines whose ideological underpinnings have so often been vilified by literary scholars and many historians (Anderson). Yet not only did her 2003 *Death of a Discipline* suggest that comparative literature might save itself from the fate of becoming a monolingual discipline of world literature by borrowing certain key features of area studies, but also *Other Asias* (2007) called for strategic essentialism on a continental scale, making a "claim to the word 'Asia,' however historically unjustified" (213). Neither, of course, an appeal to a necessary, original identity – racial, religious, cultural, or other – nor a straightforward embrace of the legacies of Euro-American geographies, *Other Asias* attempted to provoke a "critical regionalism" that might superficially resemble area studies or the pan-movements of a century ago, but without their underlying essentialism. While the term "critical regionalism" does not yet seem to have been widely adopted as a name for this kind of critical agenda, I would argue that it is in fact indicative of a general trend in literary scholarship over the past decade: the pursuit of new (or renewed) geographies that go beyond the nation but resist the centrifugal pull, the temptation, of "the world."

   One of the virtues of these areas, as I will call them, is that they make it easier to avoid some of the false dichotomies that have come to structure debates about "world literature." The justifications for these areas have been, among other things, oceanic, as in the transatlantic (Mejías-Lopez; Infante), the Black Atlantic (Gilroy; Edwards), various framings of the Pacific (Gillies et al.), and most recently the Indian Ocean (Bose); continental (the Americas, Europe, Asia); imperial (Ottoman, Mongol, post-Soviet, Qing; see Doyle); linguistic, such as the Sinophone (Shih et al.) or the Sanskrit cosmopolis (Pollock); and commercial (the Silk Road; the Mediterranean). These areas are heterogeneous and, unlike the areas of area studies, by no means mutually exclusive. We might think, for example, of all the different ways in which Latin American literary studies has engaged in alternative geographies: the "literatures of the Americas";

Hispanophone and/or Lusophone versions of "the Atlantic" in which Spain and Portugal gain renewed importance; a more regular and more vigorous inclusion of Brazil in the study of "Latin America" as a region. "Asia," perhaps most obviously, has been transformed from a vaguely Orientalist conceptual relic to a stage on which to act out diverse arguments about alternative modernities: Spivak's critical regionalism; revisionist global economic histories of the time before European hegemony (Pomeranz); scholarly gambits (the founding of the journal *Verge: Studies in Global Asias*; various "Asian Humanities" initiatives); and diasporic identity politics, from below and above (Asian American; Singapore). This has also included a renewed interest in major figures of historical pan-Asianism who had for some time been considered reactionary, such as Okakura Kakuzo and Takeuchi Yoshimi (Calichman; Chen). While many of these areas have long histories in other disciplines or even in literary studies, it is only in the recent past that we have witnessed both their quantitative increase in literary studies and a qualitative transformation of their meaning in relation to the idea of world literature.

To the factual claim that areas have been a trend in recent literary studies, I wish to add the value claim that this has been a good thing, and that there ought to be more of it. At a time when monolingual, nation-based departments and disciplines seemed to many hopelessly out of touch with contemporary realities, "world literature" emerged as the ultimate challenge to parochialism, even the enhanced parochialism of Eurocentric comparative literature. In many respects world literature can be said to have won that battle, but I would argue that this very victory has revealed "world literature" to be not one thing but rather a name for a variety of disparate and even mutually contradictory possibilities for what might come after nation-based literary studies. Supernational but subglobal areas are one such possibility. Areas represent not just a quantitative compromise between nation and world but also a variety of specific, qualitative responses to the challenge of thinking literary studies beyond the nation. They break open the limits of the national while retaining enough specificity to allow for in-depth research and knowledge of the relevant languages, for example. (I opt for "area" precisely because it foregrounds the equation of places in the world and fields of academic expertise, but others might prefer "region," "zone," or some other terms with a different set of pros and cons.)

If areas are less sublime than the world, they should prove sufficiently challenging to most of us. The fact that areas have been and could continue to be good things for literary studies does not mean they are free of methodological headaches: they challenge national and linguistic borders in very productive ways, but they also violently yoke together disparate worlds and exclude others with equal violence. The same is true, however, of every nation, language, and world. Neither the nation, nor the area, nor the world is inherently a good or evil, progressive or reactionary concept. Each does different kinds of work in different contexts, as the dramatically shifting meanings of "nationalism" have famously made clear. A newly self-conscious embrace of the area – a "critical regionalism" – would represent not so much a critique of "world literature" as a way of more effectively putting it into practice, following the ambition of the latter's spirit even if more modest in name. The area might, just temporarily, relieve us of the burden of "the world."

Works cited

Anderson, Benedict. *The Specter of Comparisons: Nationalism, Southeast Asia and the World*. London: Verso, 1998. Print.

Bose, Sugata. *A Hundred Horizons: The Indian Ocean in the Age of Global Empire*. Cambridge, MA: Harvard UP, 2009. Print.

Calichman, Richard, ed. *Takeuchi Yoshimi: What Is Modernity?* New York: Columbia UP, 2005. Print.

Chen, Kuan-Hsing. "Tekeuchi Yoshimi's 1960 'Asia as Method' Lecture." *Inter-Asia Cultural Studies* 13:2 (2012): 317–24. Print.

Damrosch, David, and Gayatri Spivak. "Comparative Literature/World Literature: A Discussion with David Damrosch and Gayatri Spivak." *Comparative Literary Studies* 48.4 (2011): 455–85. Print.

Doyle, Laura. "Inter-Imperiality: Dialectics in Postcolonial World History." *Interventions* 16.2 (2014): 159–96. Print.

Edwards, Brent. *The Practice of Diaspora: Literature, Translation, and the Rise of Black Internationalism*. Cambridge, MA: Harvard UP, 2003.

Gillies, Mary Ann, Helen Sword and Steven Yao, eds. *Pacific Rim Modernisms*. Toronto: U of Toronto P, 2009. Print.

Gilroy, Paul. *The Black Atlantic*. Cambridge, MA: Harvard UP, 1993. Print.

Infante, Ignacio. *After Translation: The Transfer and Circulation of Modern Poetics across the Atlantic*. New York: Fordham UP, 2013. Print.

Mejías-Lopez, Alejandro. *The Inverted Conquest: The Myth of Modernity and the Transatlantic Onset of Modernism*. Nashville: Vanderbilt UP, 2009. Print.

Okakura, Kakuzo. *Ideals of the East*. 1904. Mineola, NY: Dover, 2005. Print.

Pollock, Sheldon. *The Language of the Gods in the World of Men: Sanskrit, Culture, and Power in Premodern India*. Berkeley: U of California P, 2009. Print.

Pomeranz, Kenneth. *The Great Divergence: China, Europe, and the Making of the Modern World Economy*. Princeton: Princeton UP, 2000. Print.

Shih, Shu-mei, Chien-hsin Tsai and Brian Bernards, eds. *Sinophone Reader*. New York: Columbia UP, 2013. Print.

Spivak, Gayatri. *Death of a Discipline*. New York: Columbia UP, 2003. Print.

———. *Other Asias*. New York: Wiley-Blackwell, 2007. Print.

Comparative literature and Latin American literary studies

A conversation with José Quiroga, Wander Melo Miranda, Erin Graff Zivin, Francine Masiello, Sarah Ann Wells, Ivonne del Valle, and Mariano Siskind

Guillermina De Ferrari

In the summer of 2015, Guillermina De Ferrari asked seven experts in Latin American literary studies for brief responses to the following three questions:

- Assuming that there is a field called "Latin American comparative literature," what are its critical and theoretical concerns?
- What is the contribution of comparative literature to the field of Latin American literary studies?
- What is the contribution of Latin American literature and criticism either to new critical and theoretical paradigms or to the formation of new corpora?

Their responses are gathered in what follows.

QUIROGA: I am not sure that there is a field called "Latin American comparative literature." If this refers to a comparative framework between different national literatures within Latin America, then I think a big part of the field has always been "comparatist." At least from the point of view of Caribbean studies, C.L.R. James, Roberto Fernández Retamar, Nicolas Guillén, Alejo Carpentier, Langston Hughes, and Luis Palés Matos have all benefitted from comparatist frameworks that shed light on different aspects of their work. But I think the question points in a different direction – to a shift away from, or out of, an initial focus on authorship, national literatures, or genre, toward what we may call a "poetics" of the literary text. In this sense, we can definitely point to a Latin American comparative literature whose beginnings we can see in the work of Emir Rodríguez Monegal and Roberto González Echevarría at Yale in the late 1970s and early 1980s.

Rodríguez Monegal's work as editor of *Mundo Nuevo* (1966–1971) in Paris reconfigured a notion of cultural exchange that was important for writers as dissimilar from each other as Octavio Paz, Jorge Luis Borges, and Juan Carlos Onetti, as well as for those who would be later called part of the

Latin American "Boom." Suffice it to say that it was in *Mundo Nuevo* where Gabriel García Márquez published for the first time the second chapter of what would become *One Hundred Years of Solitude*, and Octavio Paz his critique of the work of Claude Lévi-Strauss. Monegal's work paid particular attention to Brazil, thus creating a bridge between literary traditions that still, regrettably, remain somewhat disconnected from each other.

If Monegal's work was, let's say, "old-school comparatist," González Echevarría's was already attuned to the structuralist and poststructuralist tsunami that entered the United States via Johns Hopkins and then centered at Yale, where it also reconfigured what we now know as comparative literature. González Echevarría's work on the picaresque as a genre rooted in sixteenth-century Spain that then migrated, ran undercover, resurfaced, and continued to permeate Latin American and European literature up until the present allowed us to see genre as template as well as transformation, in light of structuralist poetics. The same can be said for González Echevarría's work on the Baroque and the Neo-Baroque, as well as for his seminal contributions to the field that would later become colonial studies, where the very notion of literary text would be questioned repeatedly.

Together and separately, these two very different critics took note of the fact that, while the field of Latin American literature in itself was preoccupied with questions of political and social change within national contexts, something entirely different (yet related) was happening in Latin American societies: the growing interaction between Latin American capitals among themselves and with Europe allowed us to speak of communicating networks, of differential resonances that can be felt, for example, in César Fernández Moreno's collection *América Latina en su literatura*, where, in the words of one of its contributors, Haroldo de Campos, "languages of exclusion" were replaced by a kind of "potlach" that engaged codes, paratexts, and intertexts in delirious combinations. From then on, Latin American literature would be "comparatist" in the sense that the foremost critical questions were not centered on historical resonances, but rather on what we may term the "scandal" of the literary text – not only its production and reception but also its defiant stance vis-à-vis normative authority. One of Rodríguez Monegal's later works, coauthored with the Brazilian Leila Perrone de Moises, uncovered the intertextual grammar in *Les Chants de Maldoror* by the Montevidean Lautréamont (Isidore Ducasse). From São Paulo, Jorge Schwartz then assembled his studies on the Latin American avant-garde of the early twentieth century in relation to the European and Anglo-American avant-garde.

To speak of contributions one way or another, from comparative literature to Latin American literature and vice versa, still assumes a degree of separation that is more a function of the parochialism of the US academy than anything else. Present critical and theoretical concerns in both pertain to two distinct aspects: the text as a unit of production within a shifting media landscape, and questions of race and gender as they are reflected in the text.

One of the most important critical concerns of Latin American comparative literature is the examination of the text as something other than the normative distinctions of genre that demarcate fiction from nonfiction, or prose from poetry. In contemporary terms, this translates into an understanding of the text as one element in the media landscape; in the pre-1900 period, it translates as an understanding of a textual universe that does not quite fit into our notions of literacy. As examples, I would point to the work of Walter Mignolo, Mary Louise Pratt, Mabel Moraña, Francine Masiello, and Julio Ramos.

Studies of race and gender have engaged comparatists' frameworks not only between the different societies and cultural traditions of, for example, the Caribbean, Brazil, and the United States, but also in relation to European contexts. The work of Carlos Monsivais, Sylvia Molloy, Daniel Balderston, Édouard Glissant, and Antonio Benítez Rojo has been followed by incisive analyses in later work, such as that of Yolanda Martínez-San Miguel, Jossianna Arroyo, and Rubén Ríos Avila. While monographs like Licia Fiol-Matta's *A Queer Mother for the Nation* can still produce paradigm-shifting knowledge about particular authors and texts, one of the salient characteristics of these new approaches is that they read a textual context that goes beyond what was formerly understood as the literary work of an author itself. This context includes photography, correspondence, and public and private discourses and encompasses national as well as comparative horizons that include women and gender studies, history, and political science.

MELO MIRANDA: The traffic between the various literatures within Latin America has contributed to the creation of a rich critical apparatus. Since the 1920s, Latin American thinkers have developed concepts like "antropofagia" (Oswald de Andrade), "transculturación" [transculturation] (F. Ortiz, A. Rama), "entre-lugar" [space-in-between] (Silviano Santiago), "ideas fuera de lugar" [misplaced ideas] (Roberto Schwarz), and "post-autonomía" [post-autonomy] (Josefina Ludmer).

For better or for worse, our European cultural legacy has provided the basis for the formation of a literary criticism mainly concerned with sources and influences. This approach not only is limited in scope but also has political consequences, since the inherited methods also presuppose that cultural production in Latin America is inferior to that in metropolitan centers. This perception, which corresponds to an evolutionist understanding of literary history, values universal rationalism. The result is a binary form of comparativism limited to unilateral symbolic exchanges.

The modernist project of writer Oswald de Andrade (1890–1954) approaches the subject from the prism of *antropofagia* – a Tupi ritual that consisted of devouring enemies to incorporate their valor. In his *Manifesto Antropófago* (1928), Andrade states, "I am only interested in what doesn't belong to me." On the basis of a desire for appropriation and expropriation, Andrade describes a mitigated (or masticated) dependency. Transcending its historical circumstances, the violent act of transforming a taboo into a totem has become a conceptual operator for future use. When Brazilian poet and translator Haroldo de Campos restated the need to incorporate artistic production into the international context, he proposed to build on our debt to dominant culture and pointed to "anthropophagic" practices as a way to transcend that debt.

The conceptual break with the supremacy of origins allows Silviano Santiago (1936) to formulate the concept of "entre-lugar" in the article "O entre-lugar do discurso latino-americano" (The "Space-in-Between" in Latin American Discourse; 1971). Santiago rescues the figures of contradiction and paradox, usually absent from Latin American thinking, to rethink the rigid oppositions between localism and cosmopolitanism, the particular and the universal in order to reconsider the idea of the national and the process of modernization through the import of foreign ideas. The "entre-lugar" is neither a philosophical abstraction nor a rhetorical expression to soothe the pride of the "Third World" intellectual. Rather, it is a position that sees Latin American culture as a culture between cultures, which is thus capable of producing new theoretical formulations both from fiction and from critical reflections of a variety of national origins.

Ultimately, all Latin American theories of cultural mobility and transformation follow the steps of one of the most important critical concepts of Latin America. Fernando Ortiz coined the term "transculturación" (transculturation) in his book *Contrapunteo cubano del tabaco y el azúcar* (Cuban Counterpoint: Tobacco and Sugar; 1940), a term that was further developed by authors such as Ángel Rama in "Los procesos de transculturación en la narrativa latinoamericana" (Transculturation in Latin American Narrative; 1974). "Transculturation" is both a cultural and a metacritical term. It opens up a new way of understanding cultural processes, while creating the conditions of possibility for the emergence of new critical concepts.

Because of the speed with which information circulates around the planet today, cultural isolation has been eroded to the point, in some extreme cases, of wiping out any traces of difference. Efforts to reclaim local traditions limit such processes through recuperations of memory and the revitalization of local practices. Any recuperative process must look into the way in which different traditions – popular, educated, mass culture – are constructed and deconstructed. The resulting cultural exchanges make visible the degree to which the reception of foreign models supplements local ones while encouraging the emergence of new values, which in turn help expand the range of choices and experimentation available to individuals and to communities.

Reading is always reading comparatively. We can think of Latin American literatures in terms of what Derrida calls the "supplement" to metropolitan literatures rather than an imitation of them. This would produce an important political, theoretical, and critical shift within the "Western literary field." Transcultural and transdisciplinary comparison does not simply mean switching binary terms so that Latin American becomes the central element in the comparison. Cultural difference – the Other that resists totalization – intervenes in the field, transforming the scene where knowledge is articulated. Latin American comparative literature makes sense as long as it involves unearthing the hidden aspects of cultural formations on the continent, as well as questioning the theories and interpretations that feed monopolized truths and predetermined sets of values.

GRAFF ZIVIN: If we are to assume that there is a field called "Latin American comparative literature" – and I am not sure that we should – it would have, minimally, one or more of the following defining characteristics: Latin American comparatists or comparative Latin Americanists might be those scholars working across national or linguistic borders within Latin America or between Latin America and another region, across genres, or would conduct research with reference to a conceptual frame that she brings to the foreground as an object of analysis.

More concretely, during the period 2004–2014, we could identify several clusters of scholars who could loosely be characterized as both Latin Americanists and comparatists. Each of these thematic or conceptual clusters of scholars has grown substantially in the last ten years. First, there are critics who have a strong theoretical or philosophical bent. Second, there are now well-known scholars with PhDs in comparative literature who have moved beyond the once determining national or regional borders to do comparative work between, say, Brazil and Mexico, or Brazil and Cuba; or to carry out intraregional comparisons between Cuba and the Dominican Republic, the Hispanophone and Francophone Caribbean, for example. Third, we are seeing an increasingly vibrant group of scholars working on visual culture. Finally, there are several significant recent contributions to debates on world literature and postcolonial studies – theoretical bents that decenter a more "traditional" comparatism – from a distinctly Latin Americanist perspective.

Theoretically or philosophically inflected Latin Americanism is not new. Yet while throughout the 1990s these scholars often faced resistance within the more traditional field of Latin American literary studies, still rooted in a philological approach on one hand, and identitarian politics on the other, post-9/11 Latin Americanism has been far less hostile to "theory." Examples from the last decade include Patrick Dove's *The Catastrophe of Modernity*, Kate Jenckes's *Reading Borges after Benjamin*, Bruno Bosteels's *Marx and Freud in Latin America*, Susana Draper's *Afterlives of Confinement*, Moira Fradinger's *Binding Violence*, Jon Beasley-Murray's *Posthegemony*, Guillermina De Ferrari's *Community and Culture in Post-Soviet Cuba*, Adriana Johnson's *Sentencing Canudos*, and Abraham Acosta's *Thresholds of Illiteracy*. What these books have in common, beyond their conceptual and political differences, is a readiness to engage with the *encuentros* and *desencuentros* between what we call "theory" (deconstruction, Marxism, psychoanalysis) and aesthetic production.

The group of regional comparatists has become increasingly vital as we move away from nationalist and identitarian ways of organizing and interpreting literary production, and as Brazilian and Caribbean literatures become a more central part of Latin American literary studies. Scholars such as Joshua Lund (*The Impure Imagination*), Jossianna Arroyo (*Travestismos culturales*), Justin Read (*Modern Poetics and Hemispheric American Cultural Studies*), and Rachel Price (*The Object of the Atlantic*), as well as more recent PhDs, such as Brenno Kaneyasu-Maranhão and Adam Joseph Shellhorse, have joined Idelber Avelar, who was already publishing widely on the intersection between theory and Brazilian and Spanish American literature in the 1990s. What these scholars share, beyond the transnational focus, is an emphasis on conceptual, thematic, formal, and critical-political concerns, such as mourning, subalternity, *concretude*, modernism, hybridity, race, and sexuality, even when these are called into question.

In the visual arts, Esther Gabara's *Errant Modernism*, Gabriela Nouzeilles and Eduardo Cadava's *The Itinerant Languages of Photography*, Samuel Steinberg's *Photopoetics at Tlatelolco*, and Rachel Price's *Planet/Cuba* reorient a traditionally narrative-based approach to Latin American literary studies to include photography, film, and the visual arts more broadly. This kind of comparative work, too, engages with the critical tradition(s) that have found an easier home in comparative literature than, say, in art history.

I would identify two final Latin Americanist inflections within comparative literature that are very recent. The first has to do with the world literature debates. Mariano Siskind and Héctor Hoyos, among others, have been active and important Latin Americanist voices in these discussions, and their recent books *Cosmopolitan Desires: Global Modernity and World Literature in Latin America* and *Beyond Bolaño: The Global Latin American Novel*, respectively, question and transform concepts such as "world," "globality," and "cosmopolitanism" from the peripheral literary tradition(s) of Latin America. Within postcolonial studies, one-third of the three-volume *Encyclopedia of Postcolonial Studies*, edited by Sangeeta Ray and Henry Schwarz, is dedicated to Iberian postcolonialities. This volume, coedited by Alberto Moreiras and José Luis Villacañas, makes a radical intervention into the conceptual framework of postcolonial studies, analyzing and – more significantly – deconstructing key concepts such as democracy, empire, hegemony, hybridity, literature, orality-literacy, Orientalism, populism, transculturation, and writing, from the vantage point of Latin American studies.

MASIELLO: Comparative literature has been committed to expansion and redefinition since the 1990s. The Bernheimer Report of 1993 is a useful benchmark to situate a new vision for the discipline, identifying a broader context in which to place comparative studies in the United States, and stretching the geographic focus of comparative literature beyond the usual emphasis on European literatures. This expansion carried with it a larger regard for interdisciplinary work and cultural critique, while it also embraced continental philosophy's program of decentering the standard truths; in the process, it gave rise to a cultural project that enlarged the number and kinds of objects that were brought under the critical lens.

This programmatic revision was matched by a simultaneous expansion of area studies in which scholars of Asian, African, and Latin American studies began to be heard; the cultural canon was beginning to stretch. True, a series of so-called culture wars emanated from this wider vision, and often its advocates met with stern reproach for the choice of their inclusions (how well I remember vilification of Mary Pratt in the press when she introduced the poetry of Sor Juana and the testimony of Rigoberta Menchú in a Great Books course at Stanford!).

Indeed, the new comparative literature introduced questions of multiculturalism, globalism, and identity politics. In this context, adherents of left critique encouraged scholars to pursue comparative manifestations of colonialism and resistance in culture, to study the plight of subalterns, and to track the voices of otherness emerging in literature and art. With the center/periphery divide as a guideline, comparative literature began to think of Third World cultures in light of global epistemic shifts – for example, in Walter Mignolo's work.

So how are these intellectual inquiries carried on by a new generation of scholars? For some, the landscape offers a map for reading of frontiers and borders, migrations and margins, for claiming indigeneity as the basis of cultural and historical analysis. It allows regional affirmations set against a global whole, trans-American linkages and alliance. And, of course, it permits an exposé of the kinds of physical and lettered violence that came with conquest and colonialization. For others, there is a return to the archive to see how these discourses were formed.

More recently, a Latin American comparative literature has teased out meanings from difficult texts in order to consider, for example, material culture, the evolution of the affects, the emergence of new media, and the ways in which mobility places comparative modernism in international focus. Otherness, which was so central to our debates in the 1980s and 1990s, is currently being reconsidered through a shift in the political and aesthetic lens.

I agree with David Palumbo-Liu when he writes in *The Deliverance of Others* that "otherness" is not just a phrase that we utter, but requires a study of archive and book in order to make sense of the distance that separates the observer from her object of study. Otherness has made us aware of shifts in translation, of the sights that were set by the traveler, of the ways in which memories are managed by different participants in a community or nation. Otherness leads us to think of the ways in which community is built or divided. But otherness is also part of the twists and turns of language. It emerges from the opaqueness of texts, in the blind spots of a poem. It depends on our comparative work to stretch our definitions of Latin American otherness, and not get caught in a prefabricated web that locks the term into a discourse on abjection.

Perhaps we need to follow the steps of artist Joaquín Torres García and invert the map of the Americas as well as our thinking. We need to begin our research not from the Anglo-American and European point of view but from an equal footing of nations and cultures. Of course, there is the interesting work of Latin American scholars who read the West, tracing maps of colonial and imperial distortions, but there's also the recent work of those who take the Americas in dialogue with each other, organizing new questions about the interactions among creative writers and political figures, rethinking the boundaries of nations at key moments of cultural formation, rethinking even the design and ideology of the map.

The new Latin American comparative literature is trying to deconstruct this North/South puzzle, to bring submerged alliances out of the dark and make them available for cultural critique. What's extraordinary is the return to the nineteenth century, divided either in North/South categories or in transatlantic work, the studies of gendered travel writing and trans-American pacts, and the sturdy investigations of immigration and border settlements (Raul Coronado's new book on the eighteenth- and nineteenth-century Mexican scholastic roots undergirding Chicano discourse is an excellent case in point). But then there's the new material regarding the ways in which North and South each envision ecology and landscape (Gisela Heffes, George Handley) and how, through translation studies, the reverberation of language and tones are heard (Anna Deeny, Sergio Waisman).

Much has been made of how we are stalled in a perpetual present, but the new comparative literature examines the different national dimensions of a more complicated temporal representation. Is time the same in each megalopolis? Does temporal experience find its meaning through traditional venues, such as the clock and the map, or is the temporal quality of public and private life explained through other media? Comparative studies have also addressed the way in which material culture is determined by a desire for novelty and change – for instance, in the work of Victor Goldgel, who studies how newness reaches Spanish America, or Regina Root's analysis of couture and consensus in the nineteenth century. Mayra Bottaro hones in on different temporalities as they set the clocks of Spanish America and Europe, from astrology and the almanac to the representation of time in the discourses on credit and debt found in periodical culture and serialized fictions.

The comparative lens has recently gained considerable note through the Flashpoint series at Northwestern University Press, where a crop of very talented scholars has adopted Spanish America as the main anchor through which international models are set: Mariano Siskind, for instance, presses for a style of cosmopolitanism that refutes the cultural differences separating Latin American and Europe, and Rachel Price draws on the Iberian Atlantic to explain empire and slavery in terms of the technological change.

Comparative North/South studies are also driven by an overriding interest in technology and media, on the one hand, and by a challenge to what we previously understood as regional divisions of the field, on the other. Sarah Wells argues for the interconnectedness of 1930s fiction and film, periodical literature, and factory-line assemblies to capture a sense of serial disruption not usually registered by studies of late modernism of the South. Tom

McEnaney takes on the interrelationship between sound studies and media across Cold War politics of the Americas. Running from the work of Dos Passos to Sarduy and Puig, his study focuses on the ways in which radio broadcasts and tape recordings slice through national boundaries to create new communities of listeners and alter our understanding of property and possession. Finally, the focus on postmodernity brings a host of writers and problems together, inviting upcoming scholars to deal with affects and sense theory, race and location. The trans-American moment is here as we rethink the "South" in its global dimensions.

WELLS: Assuming there is a field called "Latin American comparative literature," this field would seek to question the persistent tendency of scholars working on other literatures to regionalize and therefore marginalize Latin American literary studies. By this I mean the long-standing, persistent assumption that working on France and Italy, or Germany and England is comparative (pairs of national literatures with interconnected but clearly differentiated histories, in two different language groups), but working on Argentina and Brazil (pairs of national literatures with interconnected but clearly differentiated histories, in two different language groups) is working on a region. Different scales are implied in each configuration. Region is "less than" comparative or transnational, and both of these are "less than" global or world in terms of scale. Regionalizing Latin America means that studies that compare nation-states within the continent are almost always left out of discussions of trans-national or comparative models, which welcome Latin American literature only when a third term is introduced (traditionally, Western Europe or the United States). If we look at the works labeled "transnational," or the winners of the ACLA book prizes, we rarely find Latin Americanist texts.

On one hand, then, Latin American comparative literature would seek to produce the terms by which the diversity among national literatures in the region would be accounted for outside of the field of Latin American literature, in dialogue with other fields. On the other hand, it would also involve an internal intervention, highlighting the features that both link and fracture the continental identity. Comparative literature therefore asks, what is this object called Latin America? And why do our academic institutions (including the job market, PhD exams, and book publishing) continue to almost unanimously function on a national model?

I often revisit my decision to get a BA and PhD in comparative literature instead of Hispanic studies or Luso-Brazilian studies (where the job market is more robust, and where I held my first two tenure-track positions). I always come back to the same answer: the differences between the fields are not differences in kind but in degree. Training in comparative literature is almost always informed by an interest in literary theory and in asking "meta" questions about literature: the institution, language, how theory travels. This perspective helps to de-essentialize the regionalization of Latin American literature. It also asks scholars to think in terms of problems, rather than at times tautological identities (it is fairly common to discover that what one thought was particular to the literature one was working on has parallels with other parts of the world). Comparative literature does so both by the close attention to theory and the way in which identities are questioned and produced through difference and comparison. Being a scholar of Latin American literature does not automatically make one a comparatist; comparison requires these methodologies. I do not think that comparison is superior to just doing "plain old Latin American literary studies." It's a question of emphasis, rather than an ethical, political, or intellectual imperative. Finally, I think comparative literature has a value for Latin American literary studies because it insists on the specificity of the literary as a critical category. Comparative literature helps us question the bleed into area studies that often takes place in Spanish/Portuguese departments.

Some of the most exciting work I have been reading lately has been produced by scholars working on Latin America and other areas of the world, particularly those that are not frequent nodes of comparison: for example, Pedro Erber's *Breaching the Frame: The Rise of Contemporary Art in Brazil and Japan* (2014). Comparative work with Brazil and Spanish America is also experiencing a boom. Collaborations with scholars in other fields that work toward this deregionalization are also innovative.

I think we will also see more works that consider Latin American literature as a way of thinking institutional and theoretical paradigms – works along the lines of Natalie Melas's *All the Difference in the World: Postcoloniality and the Ends of Comparison* (2008), which employs Francophone and Anglophone Caribbean literature to offer a critique of the discipline. Mariano Siskind's recent book, *Cosmopolitan Desires: Global Modernity and World Literature in Latin America* (2014), offers such a critique with respect to the category of world literature.

Latin American literary scholars can also address the persistent problem with translation and the fact that not only academic publishing but also literary publishing is almost uniformly focused on English-language books. In this sense, it is easier to market, read, analyze, and teach books on Anglophone India or Africa than Latin America. The limitations of the publishing market in the United States mean that one or two Latin American (almost always Spanish American) authors tend to be anointed every ten years or so: Borges, García Márquez, Roberto Bolaño, and now César Aira. Scholars of Latin American literature can (and should) call attention to the political and economic imperatives undergirding what we read, and why.

Latin American literary studies have produced an extensive body of criticism dedicated to the relationship between modernism and modernization. The burgeoning field of global modernisms could learn a lot from "classic" Latin Americanist interventions, like those of Julio Ramos, Ángel Rama, Flora Süssekind, Beatriz Sarlo, Roberto Schwarz, or Néstor García-Canclini, to name a few. All of these authors were translated into English quite a few decades ago, but their contributions to global modernisms have yet to be fully recognized. My emphasis here lies less on producing new paradigms than in engaging more robustly with a tradition that has been for the most part occluded in recent calls to globalize modernist studies. I imagine that similar turns toward the archive could make for interesting rereadings of other periods and fields as well.

Calls to be transnational have increased at the same time that national literature departments – and comparative literature departments in particular – are under duress in many universities across North America. If comparison is increasingly assumed to be working outwards from the United States or England to incorporate broader swaths of the globe, Latin American literary studies, along with other non-Anglophone literary studies, offers us the chance to radiate outward from a different point of departure that has tended to be marginalized in discussions of world literature.

DEL VALLE: The colonial and early modern field is currently engaged in two far-reaching projects. The first one revisits the emergence of capitalism. The research agendas around this issue take many forms and touch upon many socioeconomic changes that made possible or accompanied the development of this economic system: the expansion of credit; the formation of powerful corporations; the "contributions" of slavery and other forms of coerced labor, and of violence in general, to the creation of wealth and the improvement of its administration.

This interest in capitalism and the cultural worlds it creates appears to be stimulated by recent crises related to the economy: growing inequality even in places previously protected from it, global warming and other ecological disasters, racial and religious strife, the elision of national boundaries or the *de facto* removal of citizenship for some people (e.g., the growing number of refugees and displaced populations). In a Foucauldian way, these overlapping crises call for an investigation into the origins of our current economic and political system.

The second general trend, closely related to the first one, focuses on questions about how the past talks to the present and informs it. Studies on the environment, technology, labor regimes, and corporations (economic, religious), as well as on comparative empires, early modern globalization, and networks, fit into this area of interest. The early modern period saw the simultaneous formation of empires, nations, and states along with the proliferation of (new) institutions – including literature. Therefore, beyond the question of the economy, Latin American comparative literature of the sixteenth to eighteenth centuries has fostered rich conversations between past and present. Trying to understand the endurance of older forms of power seen in contemporary literature, or positing similar theoretical concerns between past and present – for example, through postcolonial theory or subaltern studies – research on the sixteenth to eighteenth centuries has steadily made connections with other literatures and periods.

These concerns are not exclusive to comparative literature or to literature departments, of course. Nonetheless, what is interesting is that the very nature of these explorations calls for a comparative approach. How were

Protestant and Catholic empires organized? How were scientific endeavors carried out? How was sovereignty imagined or created in different territories? What was the relationship between sovereignty and economic pursuits? In fact, much work done on these centuries is comparative by nature: not only for the comparisons it draws between different European traditions but also vis-à-vis the literature and the religious and economic practices of the indigenous communities Spain conquered, for example. As extraneous as these concerns might seem to literature departments, drastic changes like those of the colonial and early modern period leave their imprint on literature, where some of their most intense yet subtle effects are often discernible. In this sense, without neglecting the study of literature as an aesthetic practice, literary studies have much of more general interest to contribute.

SISKIND: Comparative critical discourses have the potential to destabilize Latin Americanism, or rather to offset the Latin Americanist ideology of Latin American literary and cultural studies, to make Latin Americanism (finally!) strange to itself. Understood as the dislocation of the same in relation to itself, comparative approaches can disrupt the particularistic, static provincialism that has traditionally structured the prevailing research and pedagogical agendas of the discipline, as well as the identitarian self-reaffirmations of the fossilized cultural-political imagination that sustains them. Approaching the field with a comparatist's anxiety about its predominant foundationalist tendencies and about its fetishized notion of cultural difference should produce an object of study incommensurate with the idea of "Latin America," perhaps even with the institution of "literature." Instead, it should shed light on new and unstable cultural cartographies, both hyperlocal and global, where the Latin American predicate is dissolved in the irreducible materiality and contingent structures that ground texts and cultural objects.

   The most interesting and productive reconceptualizations of world literature, cosmopolitanism, neoliberal globalization, transnationalism, transatlantic studies, and other trans-, inter-, intra-, post-, and infracritical practices attempt to dislocate the Latin Americanism of Latin American culture from the perspective of an antifoundationalist comparatism positing new, contingent geographical montages to imagine the aesthetic and political making of literature and art. Montaged, assembled, imagined geographies – because of the lack of a foundational, transcendental principle at the center of the cultural and political void that we usually tag with Latin American signifiers – demand constant rearticulations of the structural determinations of geographical formations, and of the grounds on which these literatures are topologically imagined as a field of study. We may or may not want to call these rearticulated local and global formations "worlds," where the plural signals a break with the "world" in world literature – a figuration of the world marked by multicultural ideological fantasies of universal evenness and abstract horizontality which mirrors the regime of general equivalence that defines the circulation of capital.

These rhetorical worlds (I insist: the hyperlocal and transcultural, assembled worlds of these critical practices) underscore the situational particularity of each act of comparison and the contingency that cracks any totalizing illusion. For instance, the worlds our field has begun to articulate within and outside of Latin American culture tend to undermine more or less deliberately its particularistic determinations, regardless of whether they adopt national and regional-nuestroamericanist shapes, or any other form of identitarianism. They open up discursive spaces of contestation from where it is possible to imagine a culture without predetermined attributes that will be created and recreated outside of itself, dislocated from its cultural particularity, according to the changing political horizons and libidinal drives of comparatists across wide worlds of critical freedom and institutional boundaries.

Arabic and the paradigms of comparison

Waïl S. Hassan

To speak of the current status of Arabic in American comparative literature requires us to look back at the history of the discipline since it declared its openness to the world beyond Europe. Such a retrospective is necessary, first, because Arabic does not figure in any of the previous reports on the state of the discipline; and second, because the Arabic field is divided along historical and disciplinary lines that have distinct methodologies and institutional histories. The intersection of those histories with that of comparative literature has been fraught with problems that reveal something about the scope, horizons, and paradigms of American comparative literature at the present time.

I take my cue from the titles of the last two ACLA reports on the state of the discipline, the Bernheimer Report of 1993, which was included in a volume called *Comparative Literature in the Age of Multiculturalism* (1995), and the 2004 Saussy Report, published in *Comparative Literature in an Age of Globalization* (2006). The immediately noticeable difference between the two titles (the second obviously echoing the first) is the replacement of the definite with the indefinite article as the "age" of "multiculturalism" gave way to that of "globalization" while we crossed the threshold of the twenty-first century. Does the phrase "the Age of Multiculturalism" mean that the period in question was the first of its kind in which culture was "*multi*ple," however that may be understood, such that it deserved an "-ism" all to itself, to set it apart from other "ages" in the history of humanity? Do such ages succeed one another universally, or do multiple ages coincide in time, each pertaining to a different "culture"? If so, does the "-ism" in "Multi-cultural-ism" designate a particular formation at a particular time in a particular location – let us say, the United States, since the report in question is an official document of the American Comparative Literature Association, rather than, for instance, India or Brazil, great multicultural nations in their own right? Is it possible that other cultures were, are, or could become "multi-cultures," with or without an "-ism" of their own? If so, that was not, in any case, something with which the Bernheimer Report concerned itself, since it described the state of comparative literature in "the" – read "the one and only" – Age of Multiculturalism. Perhaps it was simply the case that "the age of multiculturalism" was the first time that the multiplicity of "culture*s*" in the United States was registered by mainstream "Culture," giving rise to a tension

between multiplicity and unity that revealed the fault lines of the so-called Culture Wars of the period. The discipline of comparative literature was sufficiently
affected by this to engage – somewhat belatedly, as the apologetic tone of the
1993 report intimated – in the kind of self-examination that led it to question its
parameters, methods, and objects of study.

Then something happened, in the prehistory of the Saussy Report, to usher
in "*an* age" (i.e., one of many) of "globalization." We can again speculate about
the multiplicity denoted by the indefinite article. There are certainly those who
argue that the world has seen other ages of globalization, that the ancient Silk
Road was a superhighway of sorts, and that Alexander's imperium was a globalizing enterprise, as were those of Islam during the so-called medieval period, and
of Europe from the Renaissance onwards. In that sense, the American version is
the latest of a number of "ages" of globalization that the world has witnessed. It
is also arguable that the particular form of globalization that has emerged since
the end of the Cold War, a hegemonic regime of American unilateralism that the
report condemns (Saussy, "Exquisite" 25–26), is not necessarily the only one
imaginable or possible. Whatever the case may be, neoconservative arguments for
globalization as Americanization that dominated political discourse during the
Bush era did not derive from a claim of first-ness, but rather from belatedness,
in an evolutionary sense, as the latest and the most pervasive global order. This
empire's confidence derives from its currency, its having succeeded or outlasted
other empires.

If American multiculturalism was a process of self-examination and reinvention of self, based on the recognition of earlier shortcomings, globalization has been a projection of a self-assured centeredness onto the rest of the
world. And while multiculturalism led literary studies to be consumed with
the critique of the canon, in *this* age of globalization, comparative literature is
preoccupied with world literature and, consequently, with translation theory.
The implicit logic of this development is this: as our country leads the world,
we teach the world. In this formulation, the world is the double object of our
teaching, in that, first, it is the literary field that we *construct*, anthologize,
and compress into our syllabi in order to make it intelligible; and second, it
is also the world that we *instruct* or train in the ways in which it should see
itself as that which we make of it, the world to which we hold up the mirror
of "world literature."

To suggest how the shift from multiculturalism to globalization has changed
the status of Arabic literature in a way that registers the pulse of the discipline
in the last quarter-century, I offer a personal anecdote. When I met my graduate advisor, Michael Palencia-Roth, for the first time in the fall of 1990 as a new
student freshly arrived from Egypt, I learned two new words. He explained to
me that American comparative literature had been "Eurocentric," but that in
recent years it had begun to "globalize." He hastened to add that, as director of
the Comparative Literature program, he had been trying for a number of years to
win college approval for a position in Arabic literature (not the Arabic language,
which was taught in another department). His efforts proved unsuccessful, and

many years later he confided that the failure to secure that position during the 1980s and 1990s had been due to concerns, as one dean reportedly put it, about potentially bringing terrorists to campus. With "the age of multiculturalism" in full swing, comparative literature, with characteristic foresight and vanguard initiative at least in some of its quarters, was already trying to globalize itself. But that effort was hampered by institutional gatekeepers who had decided that Arabic was out, not to be admitted into American "multiculture."

That was also the time when, as Edward Said remarked, Arabic literature was "embargoed" by major New York publishers who regarded Arabic as a "controversial language" (Said 278). The commercial embargo thus complemented the academic boycott of Arabic. Throughout the 1990s, as multiculturalism bequeathed cultural and postcolonial studies to comparative literature, to be a postcolonialist meant to specialize in African, Caribbean, or South Asian, but not Arabic literature – a curious thing if we consider that the founding text for postcolonial studies, Said's *Orientalism* (1978), focused mainly on the representation of the Arab Middle East. This situation did not change until the logic of "Know Your Enemy" imposed itself on the heels of the Second Intifada of September 2000 and the terrorist attacks of September 2001, both of which ushered in the first decade of the twenty-first century.

Unlike "the age of multiculturalism," this "age of globalization" has witnessed an unprecedented boom in literary translation from Arabic, with dozens of new titles appearing each year. During the same period, sessions on Arabic literature have increased at the annual meetings of the ACLA and the MLA, and in the latter organization a discussion group formed in 1999 quickly grew into a division, which in turn became two "forums" in the MLA's revamped structure. This growth has been steady, such that the 2014, 2015, and 2016 MLA conventions have each featured on their programs at least twenty sponsored, cosponsored, and special sessions focusing partly or entirely on Arabic. Volumes on Arabic literature have even begun to trickle onto lists of MLA publications. There are more modern Arabic literature scholars with comparative training now than at any time in the past, and Arabic literature is slowly making inroads into comparative literature departments, with many hiring their first Arabist during the past decade. In the year of the Saussy Report, my graduate department was finally able to hire not one but two Arabists – proof that we had, indeed and at last, globalized, as my advisor had hoped.

As encouraging as those developments may be, there is every reason to believe that they are among the incalculable, and sometimes contradictory, repercussions of conflicts in the Middle East, which can in no way be dissociated from US foreign policies there since World War II – the period in which comparative literature took hold in American universities as a direct result of that war, as the Levin Report duly acknowledged in 1965. The exclusion of Arabic up to the end of the twentieth century, then its sudden introduction into the discipline in the 2000s, is therefore part and parcel of the history of American comparative literature, which has never been independent of national or international politics. The Europe-only comparative literature of the 1950s to 1980s was very much in line with the West/East dichotomies of the Cold War, a context in which the expansion of Russian studies represented a national security imperative. The multiculturalist turn of American comparative literature in the 1990s reflected the discipline's somewhat belated acknowledgment of the oppositional politics of the civil rights, feminist, and anticolonial movements, which triggered the Culture Wars and the critique of the canon.

Finally, the end of the Cold War brought "globalization," a code word for the global dominance of the United States, which intensified after 9/11, exchanging the sanguine and celebratory airs of the Clinton era for the belligerence of the Bush Doctrine and the War on Terror. As Djelal Kadir argued in his contribution to the 2004 report, the discipline in the early 2000s could be called "Comparative Literature in the age of terrorism" (68–77). This is the context in which Arabic language instruction has expanded as never before, such that it is now taught at almost all major and many regional institutions, a boom driven by government funding and the promise, especially in a bleak job market, of employment opportunities in greatly expanded state security agencies.

Needless to say, this instrumental approach to the Arabic language is indifferent to literature, which is usually housed in two distinct institutional settings in the United States: Near East studies and comparative literature departments. Historically, Arabic is part of centuries-old European Oriental studies and their US extension, Near East studies. Within that domain, "Arabic literary studies" is divided into two fields: classical and modern. Classical literature (traditionally dated from the pre-Islamic period to roughly the twelfth century) remains largely the subject of philological and literary-historical approaches, with the annual conference of the Middle East Studies Association (MESA) as its major forum since its founding in 1966. Classical Arabic literary scholarship, in other words, squarely belongs within area studies, and its history can be written within the narrative of Middle East studies' reconstruction since Said's critique of Orientalism. Where classical Arabic literary studies brushes elbows with comparative literature is usually in medieval Iberian studies or in *Arabian Nights* scholarship; otherwise, it is not part of the training of comparatists, nor ipso facto are the majority of its specialists trained in comparative literature programs.

Scholarship on modern Arabic literature, the period from the early nineteenth century to the present, has a much more recent beginning.[1] Nevertheless, it has by now bifurcated into Near East studies and comparative literature tracks, each with a distinct institutional history. The area studies track was pioneered at Oxford in the mid-1960s by M. M. Badawi, an Egyptian professor of English literature who directed the first doctoral thesis on modern Arabic literature, defended by Roger Allen in 1968, and founded the *Journal of Arabic Literature* in 1970, which still publishes work on classical to modern literature. Until then, the consensus among Arabists in Britain and the United States had been that modern Arabic literature was not worth studying. The new interest in modern Arabic literature migrated to US Near East studies departments in the 1970s, with the arrival of scholars such as Allen, Pierre Cachia, and Trevor Le Gassick, among others. Methodologically, modern Arabic literature scholarship attempted to break free from the philological and literary-historical approaches characteristic of classical Arabic studies by borrowing some of the prevailing critical approaches of English literary criticism – namely, those of F. R. Leavis, I. A. Richards, René Wellek, and Austin Warren.[2] *Edebiyât: Journal of Near Eastern Literatures,* founded in 1976 at the University of Pennsylvania, began to publish studies of modern and classical Arabic, Persian, and Turkish literatures, although it did not promote comparative approaches per se, since precious few scholars were (or are today) qualified to work on more than one literature from the region. As such, while the Near East studies field includes several literatures, they are not studied comparatively in relation to each other but as discrete national literatures, or in the case of Arabic as a supranational but single-language tradition.[3]

Another development occurred in the 1990s, thanks largely to multiculturalism and the impact of postcolonial theory on comparative literature: Arab students, native speakers of Arabic who had majored in English or French at Arab universities, began to be admitted to comparative literature departments in the United States and turned their attention to modern Arabic literature within postcolonial or related theoretical frames. Their academic trajectories mirror that of M. M. Badawi, except that they are now enrolled in American comparative literature graduate programs, and their training includes the heavy dose of literary and cultural theory typical of comparative literature graduate programs. For these scholars, the MLA and the ACLA are regular haunts, although some also attend MESA. The current generation of Arabists working on the modern period is, therefore, the product of these two distinct academic trajectories – the area studies and the comparatist tracks. More than the classicists, they are the ones who have made an impression on American comparative literature in the last two decades by way of publishing comparative scholarship and engaging in discussions on the nature and practices of the discipline.

Paradigms of comparison that have governed American comparative literature as a whole since World War II determine the place of modern Arabic literary studies within the discipline. Those paradigms can be described in directional terms as North-North, East-West, North-South, and South-South. The North-North paradigm includes inter-European and Euro-American comparison, which German Romance philology bequeathed to American comparative literature in the mid-twentieth century, the only model of comparison at that time. In the 1980s, when interest in China among American comparatists began to develop, what was described with the now dated terminology of "East-West" comparison came into play. This terminology reproduced a discredited Orientalist dichotomy in which "East" and "West" constituted civilizational essences.[4] North-South comparison refers mainly to postcolonial studies, whose focus on colonial history opened the doors of the discipline to African and Asian literatures and their diasporic offshoots. Finally, South-South comparison, which considers relations among literatures of the global South, remains in its initial phase, a theoretical possibility with some promising manifestations, but not yet established as a trend either in the training of comparatists or in the hiring practices of comparative literature departments.

The study of modern Arabic literature within comparative literature in the "ages" of multiculturalism and globalization (the latter arguably extending into the current decade) has remained by and large confined to the North-South axis as a small subset of the postcolonial paradigm, and has focused mainly on Arabic in relation to English and French.[5] The reasons for this should be clear enough: English and French are the foreign languages most widely taught in the Arab world, a colonial legacy. Moreover, and as part of the same legacy, modern Arabic literature from the late nineteenth through at least the first half of the twentieth century looked to European literature for models, be it new genres (novel, short story, drama) or modes and movements (Romanticism, Realism, Symbolism, Modernism). These two factors normalize the North-South approach, with or without the oppositional thrust of postcolonial politics. That is to say, the North-South paradigm accommodates *both* postcolonial critique, which rejects the hierarchy of superior and inferior cultures, *and* the Eurocentric comparatism that assumes European cultural superiority and Arab backwardness and dependency, and which judges Arabic literature by European norms, only to find it wanting.[6]

Because of the backgrounds and linguistic skills of Arab graduate students and the rising enthusiasm for postcolonial studies in American comparative literature departments, reinforced by the job market, modern Arabic literature has found a place within the North-South paradigm, which does not allow it to be studied in connection with African, South Asian, Latin American, or East Asian literatures – that is, in South-South configurations. Postcolonial studies have thus had the paradoxical effect of creating a space for Arabic, African, Caribbean, and South Asian literatures by tying them to the center-periphery, or North-South paradigm. The enormously rich area of South-South comparison remains largely unexplored. Tertiary models of comparison that merge or triangulate the verticality of North-South with the horizontality of North-North and South-South – for example, Arabic literature studied in relation to Arab diasporic literatures in North and South America, which would require knowledge not only of English and French (for Arab-Québecois literature) but also of Portuguese and Spanish – are not on the agenda of comparative literature in the age of globalization and terrorism (Hassan, "Which Languages?" 8–9).

Instead, Arabic in this age has been subject to two logics, one that sees Arabic as an extension of foreign policy imperatives (an instrumental "language-plus" approach), and another one that broadens the scope of the discipline. The current boom in Arabic studies is largely driven by the instrumental imperative. Government funding is directed toward language programs because Arabic is now seen, for obvious reasons, as vital to national security (although you can still be stopped and questioned at US airports for carrying Arabic-language materials). If, following this logic, Arabic remains ancillary and tangential to the intellectual agenda of a globalized comparative literature that is content to make room for the North-South axis in the shadow of the dominant North-North, this boom may well undergo a bust similar to the one Russian and Slavic studies experienced during and after the Cold War.

But there is another historical vision that holds more promise for an enriching integration of Arabic into a discipline continually in the process of self-renewal, and that is the institutional genesis of comparative literature itself in this country following World War II. Funded at first through the National Defense Education Act, comparative literature took hold in American universities on the premise that greater cross-cultural understanding through literature would help avert another global conflict. If this belief in the humanistic mission of literary education that enabled our discipline to come into its own seven decades ago can now take us beyond the ideological and institutional constraints of multiculturalism and globalization, Arabic literature will play its part in broadening the imaginative scope of comparison.

Notes

1 The intermediary period between the conventional end of the classical and the beginning of the modern has long been considered an "age of decay" or "decadence" (*'aṣr al-inḥiṭāṭ*). The reasons for this now highly contested view are too complex to summarize here, but a certain account of Arab cultural history sees it, in a reflection of its European counterpart, as progressing from a "classical" to a "Dark" age to a "Renaissance" (the conventional translation of the "*Nahḍa*," the name of the nineteenth-century modernization movement in Egypt and the Levant). See Allen and Richards; al-Musawi.

2 In his introduction to *The Study of the Middle East* (1976), an extensive "state of the discipline" report, Leonard Binder describes the difficulty of wrenching the multidisciplinary study of the modern Middle East from the Orientalist tradition's overwhelming focus on the Arab-Islamic past – an approach that Orientalism inherited from its founding model of classical studies (Greek, Roman, and ancient Hebrew). Allen's contribution to the chapter "Literature" in that report attempts to establish criteria for bringing the study of Arabic literature up to date with that of European literatures (the chapter is coauthored with William Hanaway and Walter Andrews, who focus on Persian and Turkish literatures, respectively).

3 This is in stark contrast to, say, the German tradition of Romance philology, the parent discipline of American comparative literature, in which students were expected to acquire competency in several Romance languages. Thus, while traditional American comparative literature focused on inter-European relations, Near East studies has overlooked inter–Middle Eastern literary relations. The reasons for this presumably have to do with scholars' linguistic competencies as well as the assumption that the most important cultural contacts for Middle Eastern peoples in the modern period have been with Europe rather than with neighboring cultures.

4 I hope it is clear that I in no way mean to imply that studying Chinese or Japanese literatures in relation to European, American, or any other literatures is an outdated thing, but only that framing such work in the Orientalist dichotomy of East versus West is no longer tenable.

5 On the relationship of postcolonial theory to modern Arabic literature during the 1980s and 1990s, see Hassan, "Postcolonial Theory." On the conceptual and institutional limitations of postcolonial studies from a comparative perspective, see Hassan and Saunders.

6 Abdelfattah Kilito illustrates this sort of comparatism in the work of Charles Pellat and 'Abd al-Rahman Badawi (Kilito 10–16, 96–98).

Works cited

Allen, Roger, William Hanaway and Walter Andrews. "Literature." *The Study of the Middle East: Research and Scholarship in the Humanities and the Social Sciences*. Ed. Leonard Binder. New York: Wiley, 1976. 399–509. Print.

Allen, Roger, and D.S. Richards, eds. *Arabic Literature in the Post-Classical Period*. Cambridge: Cambridge UP, 2006. Print.

Al-Musawi, Muhsin. *The Medieval Islamic Republic of Letters: Arabic Knowledge Construction*. Notre Dame: Notre Dame UP, 2015. Print.

Bernheimer, Charles, ed. *Comparative Literature in the Age of Multiculturalism*. Baltimore: Johns Hopkins UP, 1995. Print.

Binder, Leonard, ed. *The Study of the Middle East: Research and Scholarship in the Humanities and the Social Sciences*. New York: Wiley, 1976. Print.

Hassan, Waïl S. "Postcolonial Theory and Modern Arabic Literature: Horizons of Application." *Journal of Arabic Literature* 33 (2002): 45–64. Print.

———. "Which Languages?" *Comparative Literature* 65 (2013): 5–14. Print.

Hassan, Waïl S., and Rebecca Saunders. "Introduction." *Comparative (Post)colonialisms*. Spec. issue of *Comparative Studies of South Asia, Africa, and the Middle East* 23 (2003): 18–31. Print.

Kadir, Djelal. "Comparative Literature in the Age of Terrorism." *Comparative Literature in an Age of Globalization*. Ed. Haun Saussy. Baltimore: Johns Hopkins UP, 2006. 68–77. Print.

Kilito, Abdelfattah. *Thou Shalt Not Speak My Language*. Trans. Waïl S. Hassan. Syracuse: Syracuse UP, 2008. Print.

Said, Edward W. "Embargoed Literature." *The Nation* (17 September 1990): 278–80. Print.

Saussy, Haun, ed. *Comparative Literature in an Age of Globalization*. Baltimore: Johns Hopkins UP, 2006. Print.

———. "Exquisite Cadavers Stitched from Fresh Nightmares: Of Memes, Hives, and Selfish Genes." *Comparative Literature in an Age of Globalization*. Ed. Haun Saussy. Baltimore: Johns Hopkins UP, 2006. 3–42. Print.

Postcolonial studies

Sangeeta Ray

To think about postcolonial studies is to think in terms of crisis, death, and futurity. Since its very inception, postcolonial scholars themselves have been highly critical of the term and its disciplinary force. We enjoy self-flagellation much more than our critics give us credit for. Lionnet and Shih, in fact, have argued that because of

> the difficulty of giving an account of oneself in the dominant and hegemonic language of the colonial power, [postcolonial critics'] work has tended to generate a self-perpetuating and politically unproductive anxiety that could be said to be self-absorbed . . . [and thus] fall under the rubric of reactional theorizing rather than actual theorizing, as privileged by Fanon.
>
> (20)

This criticism too hastily and harshly dismisses not just Anglophone but also much Francophone and Hispanophone postcolonial theory.

If the term "postcolonial" sometimes lacks a referent or historical specificity, this may simply reflect its multiplicity – the various postcolonialities and postcolonial temporalities. There is no single postcolonial condition. The recently published three-volume *Encyclopedia of Postcolonial Studies*, with almost five hundred entries, demonstrates this clearly. Thus, I want to indulge in the optimism that lies in the promiscuous use of the term itself. The term resides (not remains) adjacent to other categories and flourishes there. Think of the postcolonial rubbing up against other terms – the transnational, the global, the planetary, (dare I say it?) the Third World, the nation, the state, the city, the body. Promiscuity also allows the postcolonial to rear its not so accommodating head in discussions that ignore or dismiss the myriad ways in which it has shaped academic disciplines.

Comparative literature, one such discipline, needs to keep the postcolonial alive in discussions of world literature that sometimes act as though comparative postcolonial literary studies never existed. Postcolonial literature does not have to imagine itself as world literature. Its status as world literature is shaped by the calamities of colonialism, imperialism, nationalisms, capitalism, globalization, and transnationalism. If we are to truly contend with Pascale Casanova's idea of a "world literary space," we must shift our focus to the global South, whose impact on the global literary marketplace has yet to be fully understood and measured. The term "postcolonial" could allow us to critique engagements with world and global literature that privilege translation and distant reading. Many scholars who may not consider themselves to be invested in the term postcolonial foreground postcolonial studies' fundamental tenets as they take up the hegemony of English in what passes for world literature. Scholars such as Aamir Mufti, Gayatri Spivak, Toral Gajarawala, Joey Slaughter, Elliot Cola, Emily Apter, Peter Hitchcock, and Eric Hayot, among others, have clearly demonstrated the limitations of the concept of world and global literature.

Postcolonial studies are inherently comparative. The institutionalization of postcolonial studies in places like the United States, the UK, and Australia often ends up erasing postcoloniality's comparative dimensions. But a course on postcolonial literature taught in an English department can read Aimé Césaire's uncompromising theoretical and biographical engagement with colonialism and imperialism and show how Francophone postcolonial studies resonate and differ from the dominant Anglophone model in US academia influenced by Edward Said, Spivak, and Homi Bhabha. That same course could juxtapose Caribbean writers like George Lamming, Jamaica Kincaid, Andrea Levy, Simone Schwarz-Bart, Maryse Condé, Patrick Chamoiseau, and Alejo Carpentier with Édouard Glissant, Antonio Benítez Rojo, Shalini Puri, and Belinda Edmondson. Translation would come up of necessity, and one could then highlight the impossibilities of a neat and tidy comparative trafficking in ideas enabled precisely by the possibilities of translation (see Ray).

Traffic between postcolonial studies, comparative literary studies, and world literature could be invigorating. If postcolonial studies and world literature are emboldened and captivated by the availability of texts in translation, a renewed emphasis on the importance of learning languages would enable us to critically examine our relation to worlds and texts (and world-texts; text-worlds). Instead of mourning the demise of postcolonial studies, we should celebrate the possibilities opened up by promiscuous encounters. We need to share critical, theoretical, and literary beds more generously, more intimately, and perhaps even with a certain recklessness.

Works cited

Lionnet, Françoise and Shu-mei Shih. "The Creolization of Theory." *The Creolization of Theory*. Ed. Françoise Lionnet and Shu-mei Shih. Durham, NC: Duke UP, 2011. 1–33. Print.

Ray, Sangeeta. "Towards a Planetary Reading of Postcolonial and American Imaginative Eco-Graphies." *A Companion to Comparative Literature*. Ed. Ali Behdad and Dominic Thomas. Chichester: Wiley-Blackwell, 2011. 421–36. Print.

Ray, Sangeeta, Henry Schwarz, April Shemak, Alberto Moreiras, José Luis Villacanas Berlanga, and Dinaw Megestu, eds. *Encyclopedia of Postcolonial Studies*. 3 vols. Oxford: Wiley-Blackwell, 2016. Print.

Fundamentalism

Mohammad Salama

In a seminal essay, "The Religious Fanatic in the Arabic Novel," Egyptian critic Jābir 'Asfūr lamented "the failure [of Arab novelists] to keep an aesthetic distance that would allow for a calmer artistic perspective on the heated phenomenon of fundamentalism." Thirteen years later, 'Asfūr would perhaps agree that Arabic literature has achieved that Brechtian distance. In Arabic, fundamentalism derives from the root (ل ص أ), denoting origin or genesis. The root also connotes purity and unsullied sources. Any search for a cultural and linguistic origin is a futile chase after evasive signifiers, yet religious fundamentalism tends to jettison all that is "new" in its ardent pursuit of origins. The return of fundamentalism, however, further extends the work of veteran practitioners of postcolonialism. Nor should we forget the original form in which religious zealotry appeared as a subject of debate – namely, modern Arabic criticism, as in the work of Taha Husayn and the important variants introduced by his intellectual disciple, Nasr Hamid Abu Zayd, and Moroccan intellectuals Muhammad Arkoun and Muḥammad 'ābid al-Jābrī.

While the Algerian Tahar Ouettar was perhaps the first Arab author to make fundamentalism an overriding theme in a work of art (*The Quake*, 1974), contemporary Arab writers continue to explore the topic. Portrayals of the fundamentalist, mostly achieved through characters of confused young men – Ṭāhā in Alaa al-Aswany's *Yacoubian Building* (2006) or Yāsīn in Muhammad al-Ash'arī's *The Bow and the Butterfly* (2010) – still mark an ineluctable clash between the native and the foreign, the sacred and the profane, where fundamentalists believe that their pure and undefiled origins have been hijacked by the laic principles of secular modernity. But secular critique, of which the novel is a symptom, has fought its own war against fundamentalist doctrines, and has done so at a cost. If the Arabic novel now occupies a significant space in reinforcing the freedom of (artistic) expression and other individual rights, many Arab authors faced death, torture, and imprisonment for their work. In 1993, Algerian Tahar Djaout was assassinated by the Armed Islamic Group for his critique of fundamentalism. In 1994, Nobel Prize awardee Naguib Mahfouz was almost killed by two Islamists for his secularist *Awlād Ḥāritnā* (Children of the Alley). And in 1995, Egyptian critic Naṣr Ḥāmid Abū Zayd was forced to divorce his wife and leave Egypt for his critique of the country's Islamist discourse.

Although the principle of antisecularist revolt has been thematized in the con-temporary Arabic novel, the last decade has allowed for a contemptuous famili-arity with religious fanaticism. In the writings of Yūsuf Zaydān, Muḥammad al-Ashʿarī, and Huda Barakāt, for example, while fundamentalism never gets away with its crime, the punishment no longer falls upon the perpetrator alone. Instead, fundamentalism becomes a signature of institutional and educational failure, a sign of late postcolonial loss and identitarian malaise, a wildcard in the political semantics of world power, the stamp by which neocolonial imperialism distinguishes foes from allies. Nor is the fundamentalist the religious zealot on steroids or the callous-hearted and immediately disciplinable villain, but rather a complex pharmakon à la Northrop Frye, a protagonist caught in the grand sectarian confusions of postmodernity, as Barakāt reminds us in *The Kingdom of This Earth* (2012). Likewise, al-Ashʿarī's *The Bow and the Butterfly* begins, and ends, with the news that nineteen-year-old Yāsīn, studying architecture in France, has fallen prey to the siren call of jihadist "martyrdom" in Afghanistan, prompt-ing us to interrogate not only the fundamentals of fundamentalism but also the convoluted human drive that stems from self-interest, be it paradisiacal lunacy or postcapitalist monopoly.

Works cited

al-Ashʿarī, Muḥammad. *Al-Qaws wa-al-Farāshah* [The Bow and the Butterfly]. Casa-blanca: al-Markaz al-Thaqāfī al-ʿArabī, 2010. Print.

al-Aswany, Alaa. *The Yacoubian Building*. Trans. Humphrey Davies. Cairo: American U in Cairo P, 2004. Print.

ʿAsfūr, Jābir. "The Religious Fanatic in the Arabic Novel." *Al-Ahram* 23 June 2003. Web 31 July 2016. http://www.ahram.org.eg/Archive/2003/6/23/WRIT1.HTM.

Barakāt, Huda. *Malakūt hādhihi al-arḍ* [The Kingdom of this Earth]. Beirut: Dār al-ādāb, 2012. Print.

Ouettar, Tahar. *Al-Zilzāl* [The Quake]. Beirut: Dār al-ʿIlm lil-Malāyīn, 1974. Print.

Afropolitan

Aaron Bady

"Afropolitan" is not a politics, but it dresses in the commodified residue of political struggle, Fela Kuti's style stripped of its revolutionary substance. In a displacement characteristic of our neoliberal age, the flows of capital become the pathway to individual self-realization. The Afropolitan declines to be Afro-pessimistic, then, because she has the privilege of declaring victory from the dance floor in London, the art exhibition in Rome, or the runway in New York.

This, at least, is the critique. The term was first popularized by Taiye Selasi, in her 2005 essay "Bye-Bye Babar," which offered to speak for a generation of young and glamorous African cosmopolitans, to proclaim their coming of age. Africans in the West were no longer out-of-place migrants, she said, no longer caught in-between and at home nowhere.

> Most of us grew up aware of 'being from' a blighted place, of having last names from countries which are linked to lack [but] somewhere between the 1988 release of *Coming to America* and the 2001 crowning of a Nigerian Miss World, the general image of young Africans in the West transmorphed from goofy to gorgeous.
>
> (Selasi)

Critics – and the term has so many critics – will say that the Afropolitan is all empty style, a crass and shallow effort to make African identity into a fashion accessory, skin-deep at best, exoticizing at worst. If you google the term, you'll find "Exorcizing Afropolitanism," "The Afropolitan Must Go," and "Why I Am Not an Afropolitan" alongside the occasional lifestyle puff piece (e.g., CNN's "Young, Urban and Culturally Savvy, Meet the Afropolitans"). Meanwhile, academics who use the term often decline to cite Selasi at all. If you look only in peer-reviewed journals, for example, you might come to the conclusion that Achille Mbembe and Sarah Nuttall coined the term in 2008.[1] Yet as novelist Teju Cole observed, "The discourse around Afropolitanism foregrounds questions of class in ways the 'I'm not Afropolitan' crowd don't want to deal with (and in ways the 'I'm Afropolitan' crowd are often too blithe about)." Class is a problem, a term that has often been unsettling when applied to Africa, and which has historically been displaced onto race. For the literary left, Africa has long served a particular symbolic function in the West, standing in as the racial proletariat par excellence, the wretched of the Earth. For this Fanonian tradition, African literature was necessarily political, from the beginning: to speak was to curse the West, and those who did not were dismissed as the co-opted bourgeoisie, a neocolonial elite class.

Why should "African" name a politics? It is hard to see an Afropolitan through this expectation. If Fanonians expect to find revolutionary subjectivity in Africa, they will not find it in Taiye Selasi, but one cannot help but observe that such an obligation is rarely placed on the backs of White middle-class writers. Indeed, the backlash against the Afropolitan reveals a nostalgia for a time when African culture-work was thought to be, as such, a revolutionary act, when simply to exist, and to speak, was to resist imperial hegemony. But that time has surely passed, as the "Afropolitan" teaches us. And if Taiye Selasi – or Lupita Nyong'o – is admitted to be African, or even to be representative of a cultural moment, then "Africa" can no longer serve as the perfect figure for the global proletarian struggle. Africa has its West, just as the West has its Africa. Or maybe the distinctions collapse under the strain.

Note

1 Somewhere between 2004 and 2008, their *Public Culture* essay "Writing the World from an African Metropolis" absorbed the term "Afropolitanism" as it was expanded for the introduction to *Johannesburg: the Elusive Metropolis*, but they do not cite a source for the term. It was likely an adaptation of the word "Negropolitain," used by musician Manu Dibango in his autobiography *Three Kilos of Coffee*.

Works cited

Cole, Teju (tejucole). "@Keguro_ @zunguzungu The discourse around Afropolitanism foregrounds questions of class in ways the 'I'm not Afropolitan' crowd." 9 March 2014. Web. 30 Aug. 2016. Tweet.

Cole, Teju (tejucole). "@Keguro_ @zunguzungu . . . don't want to deal with. And in ways the 'I'm Afropolitan' crowd are often too blithe about." 9 March 2014. Web. 30 Aug. 2016. Tweet.

Dabiri, Emma. "Why I'm Not an Afropolitan." *Africa Is a Country.* 21 January 2014. Web. 30 Aug. 2016. africasacountry.com/2014/01/why-im-not-an-afropolitan

Dibango, Manu. *Three Kilos of Coffee.* Chicago, IL: University of Chicago Press, 1994. Print.

Mbembe, Achille, and Sarah Nuttall. "Writing the World from an African Metropolis." *Public Culture* 16 (2004): 347–72. Print.

Nuttall, Sarah, and Mbembe, Achille. *Johannesburg: The Elusive Metropolis.* Durham, NC: Duke UP, 2008. Print.

Santana, Stephanie. "Exorcizing Afropolitanism: Binyavanga Wainaina Explains Why 'I am a Pan-Africanist, not an Afropolitan' at ASAUK 2012." *Africa in Words.* 8 February. 2013. Web. 30 Aug. 2016. africainwords.com/2013/02/08/exorcizing-afropolitanism-binyavanga-wainaina-explains-why-i-am-a-pan-africanist-not-an-afropolitan-at-asauk-2012

Selasi, Taiye. "Bye-Bye Babar." *The Lip Magazine.* 3 March 2005. Web. 30 Aug. 2016. thelip.robertsharp. co.uk/?p=76

Tutton, Mark. "Young, Urban and Culturally Savvy, Meet the Afropolitans." *CNN.* 17 February 2012. Web. 30 Aug. 2016. www.cnn.com/2012/02/17/world/ africa/who-are-afropolitans

Tveit, Marta. "The Afropolitan Must Go." *Africa Is a Country.* 28 November 2013. Web. 30 Aug. 2016. africasacountry.com/2013/11/the-afropolitan-must-go

Why must African literature be defined? An interview with Aaron Bady

Barbara Harlow and Neville Hoad

Most of Aaron Bady's growing set of interviews with contemporary African writers – conducted and laboriously transcribed over the past several years – could have happened only with the assistance of Skype. While some of these cross-regional and interdisciplinary exchanges have appeared as occasional publications, they also, collectively, constitute two substantial electronic collections curated in 2014–15 by Bady himself, for Yale's *Post45* (http://post45.research.yale.edu) and *The New Inquiry* (http://thenewinquiry.com). Both collections provocatively suggest new directions in the modern currents and currencies of African writing, continental and diasporic alike, as well as the innovative challenges that emergent media impose; Bady addresses these same concerns in the remarks that follow. He engages with topics ranging from the dubious celebrity conferred by the circuit of literary prizes and competitions to the isolationist risks entailed by vernacular emphases on an authenticity that can threaten political secessionism, generational successionism, or self-defeating cultural solipsisms. Popularly blogging and tweeting under the moniker of zunguzungu, Bady, however, resists any such fragmentary abandon in his interviews, engaging instead the very dissonances and symphonic chorales that animate contemporary African writing and critical global discourse. Seeking to probe the new engagements of the interview as a genre, we have interviewed an interviewer of repute and consequence. Our hope in this undertaking is to take the pulse of the field of African literature in relation to African literary scholarship in particular and its ramifications for the discipline of comparative literature more generally.

HARLOW/HOAD: In reference to the recent discussion, "What Is African Literature?" in *The Guardian* about the 2015 Caine Prize Shortlist, you asked, "Why is this (always) THE question? Why must African literature be defined?" For whom is this always the question – the writers themselves, publishers, scholars, pundits? Is it a more significant question for African readers, African diasporic readers, readers in world literature more generally? And why does it persist as a question?

BADY: You're making me answer my own question! One reason I like to interview writers is so I can put them on the spot, instead of listening to my own opinions; I think it's good scholarly practice to see what writers have to say about the sorts of debates that literary critics usually have (about them) in our scholarly isolation. I don't think that kind of isolation is healthy, especially when we find ourselves talking about writers who are more than capable of speaking for themselves. They can and will, if you find the right way to ask them.

But to answer your question, I'm sure I was being rhetorical, complaining rather than looking for a serious answer. "What is African literature?" is a bad question, and it's the sort of question that produces bad answers. It's unavoidable, of course, because so much of the discourse about contemporary writing – and about contemporary African writers – gets produced through and in relation to intermediaries like the Caine Prize (or the media around it), which tend to insist on asking that precise question. So it's part of the atmosphere, even if many African writers have a pretty cynical relationship with it. Laila Lalami told me, for example, that what bothered her was when writers from Africa get called "African writers" (while other writers are just writers, full stop). But when the Booker Prize longlist came out, and Chigozie Obioma was described as the one "African writer" on the list, Laila was quick to observe that *she* is an African writer as well. There's a wholehearted identification with the label that's often simultaneous with a recoil from its more restrictive usage, and she has that in common with lot of other African writers.

It isn't only African writers who experience this, of course. It's a problem that many "minor" literatures have. White writers in the West can be read in terms of what they say, what they do with form, and how they reinvent their media, and so they tend to take that privilege for granted. But "subaltern" writing tends to get fixed in place by the critical insistence that *identity* be its defining framework, the doorway in. You can see this happen to women writers, Arab writers, or any other category of minority writing. It's not an "African literature" problem, just a *literature* problem, the blindness of a literary establishment that takes whiteness as the default and the universal, and which therefore sees other writers as defined by whatever it is that makes them not the default, not the universal.

HARLOW/HOAD: Is the issue, then, just who asks the question?

BADY: Yes, though it's also just about knowledge and respect. "What is African literature?" is the question you ask if you literally have nothing else to say, almost the most basic, zero-level inquiry possible. It's a step above going to a novelist and saying, "So, you write novels! What is a novel?" When moderators or interviewers haven't done their homework – when they haven't read the novel of the novelist they're interviewing, for example, or if it's the only novel by an African they've ever read – then a question like "What is African literature?" comes off as ignorant and disrespectful, because it is. But a lot of discussions of African literature – in Western media, though not only there – proceed from this place of ignorance, and from the assumption it's okay, that you don't have to respect African literature enough to actually know anything about it. African writers can get pretty tired of that, as you'd expect.

HARLOW/HOAD: Is it ever a useful question to ask? Do you still ask that question, or variations on it? Are the various writers you interview attached to it?

BADY: It's an interesting question if you're interested in the ambivalence. It just doesn't have one answer, which is what people are looking for when they ask it, sometimes – a box in which to put the writers. This is why writers can be very skeptical about the reasons the question is being asked or the assumptions behind it.

My approach is to always ask it, but very self-consciously, something like: "So, how do you answer people when they ask you the question about 'Are you an African writer?'" That gives them an opportunity to reframe the question, or ask a new one, to address the issue in the terms that feel right. And they tend to do so in useful and interesting ways. Sofia Samatar and Tope Folarin, for instance, are delighted to be considered African writers, but they were both hesitant about claiming it: they were both born in the United States, but to African parents, so for them, the issue is appropriation. But the irony is that their families have no doubts at all. "Of course you're African!" they'd say. Namwali Serpell suggested that an African writer is a person who is uncomfortable being asked if they're an African writer.

HARLOW/HOAD: You mentioned the Caine Prize. What useful work does the Caine Prize do, and what pitfalls does it open up? Are there alternatives on the continent to the kinds of prizes administered and awarded in the UK?

BADY: I think the Caine is basically a good thing; it's better that it exists than if it didn't. For all its problems over the years, it has put a lot of new Anglophone African writers on the map. That map is a neocolonialist geography centering on London, but, as Chinua Achebe once said about the English language, it's the tool he was given, so he was going to use it. It might not take apart the master's house, but maybe it can do other things that are worth doing. Literary prizes are good at laundering dirty money; people like to point out that the Nobel Prize originally came from arms-manufacturing profits, and that the Booker Prize was originally funded by money made in sugar plantations in the Caribbean. But it works the other way, too: writers who get these awards also get the freedom to do what they want with it. Even critics of the Caine Prize, like Binyavanga Wainaina, have the position of prominence that they have, in part, because of the Caine Prize and the space it has opened up and curated. I don't think this means he has to be grateful to the Caine Prize. It's the reverse: it shows that one can get the prize without being beholden to it.

There have been problems with how the Caine Prize has selected its winners, of course, though show me a prize that doesn't deserve criticism! And we could have a good conversation about what those problems are. But for me, the real problem has been that there hasn't been much of an alternative, until recently. Being the only game in town is not a good thing, but it's hardly the Caine Prize's fault that those alternatives have mostly not existed. But it makes trouble for the Caine Prize people: they get tasked with doing it all, and then they get doubly criticized when they can't, and don't. They can't, and they don't: one short story a year is never going to come close to representing the diversity of contemporary African literature, and the more it gets held up to that standard, the more glaringly it will fail.

HARLOW/HOAD: You said "until recently." Is the situation changing?

BADY: Slowly, but yes, there are starting to be some very credible alternatives. The Etisalat Prize, the Writivism Short Story Prize, and Short Story Day Africa are three that come immediately to mind, and they're all based on the continent. But they also each do something slightly different than the Caine Prize. The Etisalat is for a first *novel*, for example, which is nice because there's always been something patronizing in the idea that the "African Booker" would be given for a short story, as if Africans don't have novels (the novels that have won the Etisalat are spectacular, and the shortlists too).

Another criticism of the Caine Prize is that it replicates the biases of the publishing industry; the Booker Prize goes only to fiction published in the UK, for example, which means many of the novels on the Etisalat shortlist wouldn't be eligible for the Booker. There used to be a prize specifically for African publishing – the Noma Award for Publishing in Africa – which ran from 1980 to 2009, but the Japanese corporation that funded it stopped doing so. In any case, while the Caine Prize is certainly open to African publishing – even, recently, to works published on the Internet – it's still mainly limited to the pool of work that has already been deemed acceptable by a publishing industry that's dominated by the West. So initiatives like Writivism and Short Story Day Africa select *unpublished* stories and publish them. The quality can be a little variable; the second Writivism anthology was a lot better than the first, I thought, and Short Story Day Africa (SSDA) was completely dominated by Southern Africa at the beginning. But they're all works in progress, like "African literature" itself, and I think what they're going to do in the future is a lot more interesting than what they've already done. The Caine Prize has been around for sixteen years, after all, but none of these other prizes is more than three years old. A lot of the antagonism is unnecessary, since these new prizes are also intimately related to the Caine Prize, which has been pretty supportive, as far as I can tell. Lizzy Attree, the director of the Caine, is on Writivism's board, and there's sort of a broader prize ecology. NoViolet Bulawayo's 2011 Caine Prize–winning short story, "Hitting Budapest," for example, became the novel *We Need New Names* (2013), which won the Etisalat. And the inaugural anthology of Short Story Day Africa's competition contained two stories that ended up on the Caine shortlist, including the winner, Okwiri Oduor's "My Father's Head."

In *The Economy of Prestige: Prizes, Awards, and the Production of Cultural Value*, James English observed that cultural awards have a tendency to proliferate, and that prizes tend to spawn more prizes, and this has been the case with the Caine Prize. But there's also a stepladder hierarchy: a story might first find its way into print through Writivism, find its way to prominence with the Caine – and thus, find its way into a novel – and eventually, as a result, contend for the Etisalat or Booker. At the same time, if these prizes form an ascending ladder of prestige – if Writivism or SSDA leads to the Caine, which leads to the Booker – then it's worth pointing out that an African author's trajectory from unpublished short story to novelist traces an ascent out of Africa, along with the rising awards: $400 for Writivism, 10,000 rand for SSDA (about $800), £10,000 for the Caine Prize, and £50,000 for the Booker.

HARLOW/HOAD: Much of the liveliest discussion of this persistent definitional quandary takes place on blogs, websites, Twitter, even Facebook. How important do you think so-called digital media are or will be in the shifting formation of this object of uncertain lineaments – African literature?

BADY: One of the gadflies of the online literary scene, a Nigerian named Ikhide Ikheloa (affectionately called Pa Ikhide), likes to insist that the best African literature is being produced on Facebook. I don't think "best" is the right word for it, and I'm not even sure about the word "literature." But it's certainly true that Africans are writing for Africans online, and especially on social media, *far* more than they are in conventional print publication. For all their limitations, the penetration and spread of digital media into and across Africa have been enormous, and the kinds of reading communities that are being formed by these media tend to be off the radar of literary scholars. We tend to be very comfortable talking about the relationship between print circulation and imagined communities and nation-states; arguments like Benedict Anderson's about the rise of the novel and the rise of the nation-state are almost cliché. But we've been comparatively slow to take seriously the kinds of *African* imagined communities that the Internet has made possible: Kenya and Nigeria can seem very close to each other on Facebook and Twitter. Or at least Lagos and Nairobi. And if there's one place where non-European African languages are being written and read, it's social media; Facebook threads are often bilingual or trilingual, and there are flourishing branches of Twitter in a variety of languages. It's not particularly visible in Anglophone print publication, though, and I suspect that most academic readers of Ngũgĩ's *Decolonising the Mind* would not suspect it.

To answer your question in a more "literary" vein, some of the most important and promising new journals and publications on the continent are online. *Saraba* in Nigeria and *Jalada* in Kenya are two that come to mind, though both of them are explicitly pan-African, and a kind of pan-Africanism that the Internet enables: these literary networks can network with the other literary networks online. Lagos gets connected to Nairobi. But the work of connecting to writers who aren't so close to broadband connections is sometimes much more difficult; the *Jalada* editors have found it really difficult to connect to Tanzanian writers, for example, despite how geographically close they are to Tanzania. So the next issue of *Jalada* is going to be a language issue, and they're making a real effort to move past the limitations of Anglophone Africa.

As a scholar, I'll say this: without the Internet, almost none of my work would be possible. I skype with writers, make contacts on Facebook, and got invited to the Writivism festival a few months ago only because my online writing was noticed by the African organizers. If I wrote exclusively for print journals, I don't think that would have happened.

HARLOW/HOAD: If venues like the Caine Prize and the public discussions that congregate around such events don't address literatures in African vernaculars, where are the discussions of African vernacular literatures happening? And do these discussions look very different from the ones one might find on the pages of *The Guardian* and other Euro-American publications?

BADY: It's hard to comment on what's being said in different spaces than the one you're speaking in. And while I'm *aware* that it's a thing – simply because it's visible online, and I'm online a lot – I don't speak Yoruba or Chichewa or isiZulu, so I can't really comment on *what's* being said. Which is the perennial problem: Anglophone discussions of the African language problem tend to occur in English, and only English, the language *Decolonising the Mind* is written in. That said, writing in non-European African languages is a problem that a lot of writers are still trying to solve, but it's less of an existential political problem than it was for the Ngũgĩ generation. It's just an issue of how to do it.

Of course, what often gets lost when we divide Africa between its colonial languages and its "local" languages are nations where a non-European language is also the state language, or where it has a substantial literate population. Ngũgĩ staged the debate between colonizer and colonized, between English and Gikuyu. But what about Kiswahili, the language both of colonial administration in Tanzania and of the postcolonial state? Or Ethiopia, which was not formally colonized during the scramble? Literary spaces like Ethiopia or Tanzania have been totally absent from these discussions, but Ethiopia is Africa's second-largest nation by population, with a classical literary tradition going back millennia. If English literature likes to look back to the Dantes, Bedes, and Chaucers that precede the Shakespeares and Miltons, it's curious that discussions of African literature never talk about, for example, Ge'ez works like the fourteenth-century *Kebra Nagast* or the fifteenth-century *Ta'amra Maryam*. But along with the long history, there's the short one: the Amharic writer Afawark Gabra Iyasus wrote *Libb-waled tarik* in 1908 and *Haddis alem* in 1924, but even these "modern" works never figure in stories about the "rise" of the African novel, nor does a novel like Shabaan Robert's 1951 *Kusadikiki* or the many Tanzanian novels in Kiswahili that followed it (nor the thousand years of popular poetry that preceded it on the East African coast). Kiswahili writers in Tanzania remain outside of "African literature" for most who opine about it, in the same way that Ethiopian Amharic writers do. And that's to say nothing of how writers in Ethiopia's *other* languages are little known and politically volatile, even in Ethiopia itself.

My stab at a description of what conversations about vernacular languages and literatures tend to be like, actually, would be that they express the discontents internal to the nation-state, the way Oromo speakers often feel more colonized by Amharic speakers than by English speakers, or the way the Somali language expresses a sense of pan-Somali nationality. In Kenya and Nigeria, too, languages like Gikuyu and Igbo are not always innocent expressions of anticolonialism; they've been enmeshed in decades of ethnic strife and even civil war. But one can't really generalize.

HARLOW/HOAD: Questions of cultural brokerage, cultural capital, and career can cluster in interesting ways at all these sites. Your interviews with the writers themselves are exemplary of expanding opportunities for critical exchange and inquiry. Do you think the genre of the interview with the writer offers new, timely insights into the state of African literature now? What might be its limits?

BADY: It's important to me that my interviews defetishize literature. I mean that in a very literal, Marxian sense: by turning the labor of writers into a *commodity*, the literary marketplace tears works out of their interpretive contexts and political spaces, and makes them into something other than human labor. Talking to writers helps bring the human being – and the human labor – back into focus in a way that I think is really important. We can still be critical of the writers themselves, and we should be; sometimes it's easy to become totally sympathetic to the writers, and lose that critical distance. But the other trap is more common: to imagine that the author is dead the same way the labor behind any commodity disappears once it appears on the shelf. For critics schooled in the literature of literally dead authors, the authorial fallacy makes a lot more sense than it does for critics of living literatures, whose authors not only are around but also sometimes read the criticism and have smart things to say about it.

Interviews don't aspire to conclude the discussion, so they can seem like something other than scholarly work. For me, that's the best part of it: I value the way the interviews force me to learn something new, to respond to answers that I wouldn't have expected from the question, and the way they don't close down what comes next. Interviews will never get treated as peer-reviewed scholarship, but I think that talking with writers about writing produces texts which, because they are very obstinately provisional, are also generative and forward-looking.

HARLOW/HOAD: How have individual writers responded differently to the challenges of the interview? How has your own process as an interviewer evolved since, let's say, the early Chimamanda Adichie interview?

BADY: For most writers, I think, it's a very familiar ritual. They're usually happy that I actually know their work, and have things to say to them about it, and even challenge them. By and large, they enjoy talking to someone who has enough respect for their work to engage seriously with it. Some of them even read my previous interviews and comment on them; discussions with one writer can continue with another.

As for me, I have a much better sense of the discourse than I first did, and of how to finesse it. Interviews are so often conducted in the language of publicity, the conventions of book tours and readings, because that's how writers often find themselves discussing their work. That means there are a host of prepared answers that most writers have found themselves coming back to, as they get asked the same questions over and over. I want to either sidestep those questions or find ways to come at them aslant. And I think the best parts of my interviews come from asking follow-up questions to questions they've already been asked a million times, pushing them to take them in a new direction or interrogate the premise of their standard answer. A lot of interviews are question, answer, question, answer, question, answer; I try to make mine more question, answer, follow-up, and then follow-up again. The most interesting ones are almost dialectical, in that they go somewhere different than where you started. I know the interview is going well when I'm able to ditch my prepared questions.

HARLOW/HOAD: Thinking about prizes as modes of publicity, orchestrating events, occasions for dispute as well as assessment, the 2015 Man Booker Prize had African writers as its finalists – five of the ten and none of them writing in English. African literature was once part of a scholarly project called postcolonial literature, then less confidently – with the exception of a few mostly South African celebrity authors – part of a formation called world literature: how can we think more cogently about the places of African literature – however we define it – in an interdisciplinary formation of much longer duration: comparative literature?

BADY: Well, it was actually the Man Booker *International* Prize, which was started in 2005 (after the Man Group began to sponsor the Booker); it's a totally separate prize from the original Booker. And it was only four African writers: Mia Couto (who writes in Portuguese), Marlene Van Niekerk (Afrikaans), Alain Mabanckou (French), and Ibrahim al-Koni (Arabic). When the "regular" Man Booker longlist was announced, in fact, a few weeks ago, it had only two Africans among the thirteen finalists, and both of them write in English: Laila Lalami and Chigozie Obioma. But it speaks to the way these prizes fetishize literature: the longlists seem to come out of nowhere, obscuring the conditions of their production. But if you know the structure of the prize competition, it's actually a very predictable result: the Man Booker Prize is a glorified Commonwealth prize – which now includes and is dominated by Americans – while the international prize is "everything else."

To be completely crass and reductionist, the two African writers on the Booker longlist both live in the United States – as does Marlon James, the Jamaican writer – and it's a very Anglo-American list in general (four American-born writers, three British writers, one Irish writer, and one from New Zealand). Anuradha Roy was born in India and lives in New Delhi, but the list otherwise reflects the provincial Anglophone world of British publishing. The international prize tries to account for everything else by including works published in Britain in translation, and so it comes pretty close to what you'd get if you had an official quota. There is precisely one writer from each of these categories: Lusophone Africa, Afrikaans Africa, North Africa, Francophone Africa, the Francophone Caribbean, Latin America, the Middle East, South Asia, the former Soviet bloc, and the United States. I'm not saying the judges had an actual list of boxes to tick, but if they had, they ticked them precisely (though they missed East Asia).

If you put the two lists together, I'd be hesitant to say that very much is changing in how the world of literature is construed. The original Booker Prize was an astoundingly colonial artifact: it was originally funded by the royalties from the rights to the James Bond novels, believe it or not, which the Booker people bought using the profits from a century of Guyanese sugar plantations. Today, it's sponsored by the Man Group, an international financial services firm, and so the Commonwealth-oriented "regular" Booker Prize has been supplemented by an *international* prize, which very precisely includes writers from outside the Commonwealth.

In a way, I'm an unreconstructed postcolonialist, because I'm totally skeptical about terms like "world" or "comparative" literature: both can be traced back to a figure like Goethe (through entirely Eurocentric genealogies), and both seem to find ways to place Western Europe at the center, while pretending not to. The value of "postcolonial" as a frame of reference, then, is that we admit that Europe is still at the center, and that we wish it were otherwise. But institutions don't change unless you change them. The Booker is a colonial artifact, and that logic still defines the picture of world literature that it produces.

Hemispheric American literature

Antonio Barrenechea

In July 1980, Earl E. Fitz, a professor of Spanish, Portuguese, and comparative literature at Penn State University, predicted that

> inter-American literary studies, naturally of a comparative nature, will prove themselves to be a major trend of the near future, one which will eventually establish itself as a permanent and vital part of every comparative literature department and program in the country.
>
> (10)

Over thirty years later, comparatists know that Fitz was only half right. While inter-Americanism has resurfaced in the 2000s as a key idea, the majority of teaching posts, fellowships, and seminars designated as "Literature of the Americas," "Transnational," or "Hemispheric American Literature" are housed in English departments, where Anglophone literature holds precedence. This historically anachronous approach places British before indigenous, Spanish, French, and Portuguese American cultures. The institutional frame subsumes the hemisphere under the United States, rather than the United States under the hemisphere.

Caroline F. Levander and Robert S. Levine's 2008 collection *Hemispheric American Studies* is a torchbearer for a recent resurgence of academic inter-Americanism. The book, Levander and Levine say, aims "to serve as a sort of handbook (or guidebook) to a burgeoning field" that would "chart the interdependencies between nations and communities throughout the Americas" and "enlarge the critical frame of Americanist debate by moving beyond traditional area studies paradigms through analyses of the multiple geopolitical terrains encompassed by the hemisphere" (3, 6). Most notably, the editors affirm their commitment to "doing literary and cultural history from the perspective of a polycentric American hemisphere with no dominant center" (7). The volume thus explores the promises and perils of hemispheric approaches to, among others, early American, African American, Asian American, and Southern US literatures and cultures. But, as this list suggests, the volume is resolutely US-centric, and remains limited by a conception of the hemispheric that means little more than an expanded US national terrain.

As presently constituted, then, hemispheric American studies uneasily reflects the uneven political relations that govern the hemisphere, as well as the dominance of a nation-centered model as the ground or source for innovative scholarship in the Americas. The field that "burgeons" under such constraints awaits, still, the fulfillment of Fitz's decades-old vision.

This is, in some sense, the most obvious critique one could make of the field, one Levander and Levine address in their introduction: "How can one de-center the United States in American Studies, and how can American Studies become transnational without bringing about what George Handley has called 'a neoimperial expansion into the field of Latin American studies'?" (9). The answer may be as simple as: *comparative literature*. For American literature is comparative literature, de facto, once one recognizes the hemisphere as its ground, as the site and source of a multiplicity of languages, cultures, and modes of power. Books written by comparatists during an earlier wave of inter-Americanism know this (see Fitz; Kutzinski; Pérez Firmat; Zamora). To engage the hemisphere without starting from the United States, American literature will have to be multinational, plurilingual, allowing for multiple points of entry between and among major and minor traditions. In order to avoid both US-led hemispherism and hemispheric isolationism, scholars will need to address, within transatlantic and transpacific contexts, the sociopolitical specificities that make identity in the Americas plural and often contradictory, and that nonetheless can, considered together, generate a meaningful sense of the hemisphere as a historically active social and cultural space. Reactivated as a comparative object of study, American literature can form a hemispheric macro-terrain within the grander scales encompassed by world literature.

Works cited

Fitz, Earl E. "Old World Roots/New World Realities: A Comparatist Looks at the Growth of Literature in North and South America." *Council on National Literatures/Quarterly World Report* 3.3 (1980): 8–11. Print.

———. *Rediscovering the New World: Inter-American Literature in a Comparative Context*. Iowa City: U of Iowa P, 1991. Print.

Kutzinski, Vera M. *Against the American Grain: Myth and History in William Carlos Williams, Jay Wright, and Nicolás Guillén*. Baltimore: Johns Hopkins UP, 1987. Print.

Levander, Caroline F. and Robert S. Levine, eds. *Hemispheric American Studies*. New Brunswick, NJ: Rutgers UP, 2008. Print.

Pérez Firmat, Gustavo. *Do the Americas Have a Common Literature?* Durham, NC: Duke UP, 1990. Print.

Zamora, Lois Parkinson. *Writing the Apocalypse: Historical Vision in Contemporary US and Latin American Fiction*. Cambridge: Cambridge UP, 1993. Print.

Languages, vernaculars, translations

Reading and speaking for translation

De-institutionalizing the institutions of literary study

Lucas Klein

Institution

Does the future of "comparative literature" mean anything independent of departments of comparative literature? I cannot see how it does, though I'm sure I'm afforded such a perspective by virtue of the fact that I neither teach in nor have any degrees from a comparative literature department. And yet my work, which engages with different formations and interactions between the notions "translation" and "Chinese literature," is comparative enough that I have often suspected I must suffer from a kind of "comparative literature envy," writing and thinking as if I were part of the institution and discussion of comparative literature.

The institutional pull of comparative literature is great indeed. One reason literary theory has the cachet that it has had for so long, for instance, derives from comparative literature's institutionality: without a common language such as those assumed for "national literature" departments, comparatists have had to search for new groundwork upon which to base their comparisons. This has in turn made previously underdiscussed literary (or even nonliterary) works and texts available for discussion within comparative literature, and these new texts have provided their own groundwork for changing the theoretical common language. Premodern Chinese poetry, for instance, was brought into comparative literature by James Liu under the common language of New Criticism and by François Cheng under the common language of structuralism. Once established as part of the conversation, it could then be used to support or rebuff other attempts at theoretical common language, with scholars such as Stephen Owen, Pauline Yu, Zhang Longxi, Haun Saussy, and others putting Chinese poetry in dialogue with New Historicism, deconstruction, postcolonialism, and other theoretical paradigms. Who knows what languages we'll be speaking by 2025? While in some ways the institutional need for a common language or reference points keeps us talking about what we already know, it also institutionalizes the ability to add to the conversation.[1]

Of course, the institution of comparative literature has been fraught with an anxiety about its own institutionality that can be traced through much of the discipline's history, and which informs the impulse, in the United States, to report on its state every ten years. But these institutional reports have also been influential outside the discipline of comparative literature. In large part because of literary theory, members of departments of English, French, German, film studies, cultural studies, anthropology (on a good day), philosophy (on a bad day), and Chinese are all likely to pay attention to the decennial report on the state of comparative literature.

The question beneath the state of comparative literature is, I think, the state of literary studies. If I further assert that the particular future of "comparative literature" fades in relevance compared to discussions of *literature*, I am not making a statement on the future of departments of comparative literature: I believe neither that literature exists as a self-evident, transhistorical category nor that all departments of literary studies, national and transnational, should necessarily merge. While not all work in comparative literature strictly "compares," many of the trends and topics that have first shown up in comparative literature deserve better dissemination in all departments of literary studies in the future, especially world literature. I'll focus here on the relationship between translation and national literatures.

Translation studies

Over twenty years ago, Susan Bassnett wrote that comparative literature "should look upon translation studies as the principal discipline from now on, with comparative literature as a valued but subsidiary subject area" (*Comparative Literature* 161). Though she later described both translation and comparison as "ways of reading that are mutually beneficial" ("Reflections" 6), I would like to echo her earlier call for more attention to translation.

Translation has long proven embarrassing for ideas of comparative literature, and perhaps even more so for ideas of national literature. In 1963, René Wellek disparaged translation by lumping it with "externals," such as "second-rate writers . . . travelbooks, [and] 'intermediaries,'" too much study of which would turn his beloved field into "a mere subdiscipline investigating data about the foreign sources and reputations of writers" (284). Later generations of Marxist and Marxian comparatists have based their superstructural analyses on what Wellek called "the foreign trade" of literatures, but suspicion of translation has remained. If we talk more about the problems of translation than about their solutions, though, or if we make the critique of translation more important than its promotion, we end up encouraging a world of *more* pressures to learn English and *fewer* reasons to study other languages and the understandings such learning brings. Certainly not every translation demonstrates good ethics or aesthetics, but even the most high-minded critiques of an industry that can claim less than three percent of all books published in English – including cookbooks, travel guides, children's literature, politicians' memoirs, economics blockbusters, and *manga* – represent us neither at our boldest nor most valiant.[2]

Understanding translation, and institutionalizing our understanding of translation, will require an adjustment of how we read. This should even manifest itself in our vocabulary: epistemologically, the denigration of translation relies on a privileging of the "original" as read in the language of its composition. The reason we in translation studies use the terms "source" and "target texts" is to keep from reiterating the trope of translation as secondary to or derivative from the original. Calling a source text an "original" not only implies an ideological faith in the sanctity of the text, and by extension the authenticity of its culture, but also exalts the interpreter sanctioned by access to said authenticity.

I am not suggesting, of course, that we stop reading or studying texts in the language in which they were first written. We do, however, need to master the art of reading translations. While experts in language and literature who research the interplay, manipulation, reflection, and refraction of power and ideology exhibited in instances of language and literature might seem to be good candidates for knowing and teaching how to read translations, we need more direct practice. This practice entails understanding, appreciating, and valuing translations not only as reproductions of texts over which we assert expertise, whose success or failure then depends on the extent to which it agrees with our presumably preformed interpretations (and which must be "checked" the way we check our students' exams). Rather, it implies approaching translations as their own elucidations, representations, and performances of texts of which our expertise constitutes only one competing or complementary understanding. In other words, we must begin to understand translations as works of literary scholarship equivalent to our own articles and monographs. This is not to overlook the necessary nonscholarly artistry of the act of translation, but rather to say that without appreciating both the art and scholarship of translations, translations are bound to seem secondary, and we are bound to make ideological statements about the "untranslatability" of terms and genres (see Tageldin, this volume).

National literatures

One of the terms and genres we too often see as taking place beyond translation is that of national literature. While translation is too often proposed as a problem rather than as a solution, though, it is indeed a problem for concepts such as that of the nation. David Damrosch explains that what I referred to earlier as the common language for national literature departments leads too easily to deeply engrained "Herderian assumptions": "that the essence of a nation is carried by its national language, embodied in its highest form by the masterpieces of its national literature" (this volume; see also Saussy). Yet many of the paradigmatic forms of national literatures were in fact developed out of translations: blank verse was invented for the translation of the *Aeneid* by Henry Howard, Earl of Surrey (c. 1516–1547), who also created the English sonnet by dividing the Italian sonnet into rhymed, metered quatrains (Ridley 32). Does the conceit of Elizabeth Barrett Browning's *Sonnets from the Portuguese* represent the form's residual foreignness? The stakes I see in paying more attention to translation are not, then, limited to comparatists but extend also to people who think in and about and from institutions of national literature.

The idea of "cultural translation" has a long history, but putting it to such concrete use will realize Bassnett's vision of translation as a basis for comparison, as well as Emily Apter's imagination of translation studies as "a field in which philology is linked to globalization" (11). By "globalization" I mean any interconnectedness between peoples around the world as far back as we dare consider, such as what brought people and their cultures up against each other across the Silk Road, the Champagne Fairs, or the Triangle Trade. I have had these kinds of heuristics in mind in my research on how the echoes of Indic poetics in Tang dynasty regulated verse compel a reconfiguration of our ideas of world literature and the disparagement of translation beneath those ideas (Klein). Apter's coupling of "globalization" with "philology" makes possible what Sheldon Pollock proposed as a way for comparative literary studies to move past not only its Eurocentric bias but also its modernity bias.[3]

Comparative approaches to national literary histories can help correct such biases. The past, or so L. P. Hartley tells us, is a foreign country, and they do things differently there (1). Certainly the cross-historical comparative approach will be easier for languages like Chinese than for those with shorter histories, but if we bring time into our consideration of translation – say from Sanskrit, Arabic, classical Greek, and Latin – we will be able to understand the discontinuities beneath the continuities upon which national traditions assert themselves (see Beecroft; Tian).[4] Applying what we learn of translation and the assertions and desertions of meaning it entails to translations of the literary past into the present, we may be able to work against the hold that the institution of the nation has over our study of literature.

Translation

Extrapolating from translation studies a point of view that can dismantle the lock nations have on our study of literature is, of course, implicitly political, but none of these implicit antinationalist politics will mean much or, I think, come to fruition in the absence of a more explicit politics. Translation studies applied to national literatures will do and mean little if we do not base such application on a demonstrated respect for the act of translation; learning to read translations also means we need to know how to *speak* for translation. As a way of proving our respect, then, we as scholars of literature must promote translation at every level, including in particular the academic credit for published translations in tenure and promotion procedures. If we want to teach any iteration of international or world literature, I believe we will find teaching without translations even more difficult than teaching literature with no available secondary scholarship – and rather than translation as a form of scholarship, for instance, we may begin to consider scholarship as a form of translation, as Brigitte Rath's concept of "pseudotranslation" suggests (this volume). Insofar as a translation is an interpretation of a text and its culture, it presents an argument with which we can agree or contend in our written work as well. Translation deserves our endorsement and active support, because translation's work makes our work work.

Notes

1 See Karen Thornber's essay in this volume on the need to "expose rather than to perpetuate inequities." For instance, she points out that "an Asian-language text that has been translated into other Asian languages but not into any Western languages would generally not be spoken of as world literature."

2 Some of us like to talk about big data and how it will change our field, but consider this bit of small data: 2013 was the first year ever in which more than five hundred new translations of poetry and fiction saw publication in the United States (Post). We know very little about what is and has been going on in world literature, however defined.

3 Haun Saussy refers to Pollock's plenary address as "a scolding": "Although we claim to be limited only by the dialectical conditions of possibility and to welcome works from every imaginable language, time and tradition," Saussy writes, "Pollock showed, numbers in hand, that the great majority of the doctoral dissertations written in the field and a similar share of the articles in our main journals deal with English, French and German literature between 1800 and 1960."

4 Tian holds medieval China and early Chinese modernity up against each other not only for mutual illumination but also to highlight China's intercultural absorptions. Beecroft takes a similar approach that is not limited to China.

Works cited

Apter, Emily S. *The Translation Zone: A New Comparative Literature*. Princeton: Princeton UP, 2006. Print.

Bassnett, Susan. *Comparative Literature: A Critical Introduction*. West Sussex: Wiley-Blackwell, 1993. Print.

———. "Reflections on Comparative Literature in the Twenty-First Century." *Comparative Critical Studies* 3 (2006): 3–11. Print.

Beecroft, Alexander. *An Ecology of World Literature: From Antiquity to the Present Day*. London: Verso, 2015. Print.

Hartley, L. P. *The Go-Between*. London: Hamish Hamilton, 1953. Print.

Klein, Lucas. "Indic Echoes: Form, Content, and World Literature in Tang Dynasty Regulated Verse." *Chinese Literature: Essays, Articles, Reviews* 35 (2013): 59–96. Print.

Pollock, Sheldon. "Cosmopolitan Comparison." *American Comparative Literature Association Convention*. New Orleans: 2010. Presentation.

Post, Chad. "Updated 2013 Translation Database: The First Year to Break 500!" *Three Percent* 24 January 2014. Web. 16 May 2014.

Ridley, Florence H. "Introduction." *The Aeneid of Henry Howard, Earl of Surrey*. Ed. Florence H. Ridley. Berkeley: U of California P, 1963. 1–46. Print.

Saussy, Haun. "Cosmopolitanism." *ACLA Report on the State of the Discipline*. 3 Mar. 2014. Web. 29 December 2015.

Tian, Xiaofei. *Visionary Journeys: Travel Writings from Early Medieval and Nineteenth-Century China*. Cambridge, MA: Harvard University Asia Center, 2012. Print.

Wellek, René. "The Crisis of Comparative Literature." *Concepts of Criticism*. Ed. Stephen Nichols. New Haven: Yale UP, 1963. 282–95. Print.

The end of languages?

Gayatri Chakravorty Spivak

I think the emphasis on languages is getting less and less important as the corporatized university goes toward globalized uniformity. Perhaps the only exception is Chinese, and Chinese language acquisition is not often in the service of comparative literature. There is a good deal of seeming comparativism when hyphenated Americans declare their mother tongue as a foreign language; but the comparativist impulse is ill-served by this. We also have not yet escaped the national language and literature impulse. In a dwindling job market, there is an understandable competition between the language departments and comparative literature. The enrichment of comparative literary studies with social science methodologies (and vice versa) that we had hoped for a decade ago seems to have dissipated into various fundable directions, courting international civil society imperatives rather than research methods. Language learning has also become instrumental to human rights work. In this way, the focused discipline of comparative literature has undergone transformations that may not be always to the good.

At this point, I do not see ways of combating these tendencies. In the context of multilingual postcolonial nations, I have suggested that they might take the study of the imperial language and literature as an "extramoral" borderlessness imposed by colonialism and develop comparative literatures of the languages native to the country by this means. This would be competitive with the tendency toward a canonical "world literature" – often practically in translation – that is being propagated, generally from the old metropole. My own university has no campuses abroad, but it does have global centers. We are engaged in working with these centers in the interest of epistemological change in teachers and learners that might feed the comparativist impulse. I have no experience of how we could use the campuses abroad for such an effort. My hunch is that the student body at these campuses would be less susceptible to comparativism, but I would gladly be proven wrong.

This is by no means as negative a picture of the discipline as it might superficially appear. I think we should publish a small volume through the Modern Language Association to show how many career choices can be strongly supported by undergraduate and graduate degrees in comparative literature, including the development of comparative literature in lesser-known languages. The use of migrant women for primary language learning seems too close to the coding activities of the first explorers and therefore I am hesitant to support it, although it has been suggested here and there as a politically useful direction, especially to give a sense of self-value to a gendered community often considered a burden these days.

The vernacular

S. Shankar

Where I come from, you did not want to be "vernac." To be vernac was to be backward, gauche, naïve. It was the epithet with which, during my teen years in Bombay and Madras, you dismissed the kid from a distant village who, knowing no better, slicked his hair down with coconut oil, tucked in his T-shirt, and spoke English with the wrong accent (all our postcolonial accents were wrong, but some were wronger than others). Never mind that he read and wrote in three languages to your one English, or that he had made it to college against odds that you couldn't even contemplate. All you needed to know to dismiss him was that he was "vernac."

Despite the testimony of my teen years, the vernacular is an ambiguous term. On the one hand, it is easy to understand the dismissal the vernacular routinely invites – after all, the term has always had the taint of the subordinate(d) (cf. the etymology in "Vernacular"). On the other hand, there also exist neutral and even positive usages of the term, as in "vernacular architecture." It is in this context of ambiguity that "vernacular" has in the last decade or so begun to do some heavy lifting as a critical term. An early example is Henry Louis Gates's *The Signifying Monkey*, where Gates develops for his critical purpose already prevalent usages within African American intellectual traditions. In Gates, "vernacular" appears, among other things, as a marked sign of difference from a Eurocentric standard (e.g., xix–xxii). The last decade or so has seen the fitful pursuit of similar work in a wider variety of cultural contexts as evident in Pascale Casanova, Sheldon Pollock, and Emmanuel Eze, to name three examples. Contemporary usages are diverse in motivation and in how they understand the vernacular, but they share at a minimum a sense of the term as oppositional to the transnational, the national, and the standard.

I do not always agree with contemporary usages. Sometimes they cast the vernacular as simply the inauthentic or the indefensible mark of the provincial (echoes of my teenage encounters). For me the vernacular is one point of vantage from which to resist *conceptually*, which is rather different than saying *ethically*, the overwhelming force of the national and transnational. Scholars situated in the North American academy routinely overestimate the material and affective force of the national and the transnational. Recourse to the vernacular as a critical term is a way to temper the force of this overestimation.

For comparative literature, the vernacular is still a horizon of possibility – still the difference by which to (dis)orient the work of comparison. Learning from architecture, comparative literature under the banner of the vernacular might begin the painstaking work of understanding literary texts in terms of locality. "Vernacular literature" might be explored as a notion indicating not simply works in languages regularly characterized as vernacular (e.g., Tamil) but rather – more expansively and perhaps idiosyncratically – works expressing a vernacular sensibility. Understood appropriately, such a notion could disturb the headlong pursuit of a world literature canon in ways that might lead to a richer understanding of diverse literary practices: "literatures of the world" rather than world literature, as I have suggested in a recent book (see especially 124–37). Vernacular knowledges can also be goads to alternative theory-making. All this and more: the work of critically engaging the vernacular, begun in a somewhat fragmentary way in the decade gone by, promises much if taken up more concertedly in the decade to come.

Works cited

Casanova, Pascale. *The World Republic of Letters.* Trans. M. B. DeBevoise. Cambridge, MA: Harvard UP, 2004. Print.

Eze, Emmanuel Chukwudi. *On Reason: Rationality in a World of Cultural Conflict and Racism.* Durham: Duke UP, 2008. Print.

Gates, Henry Louis. *The Signifying Monkey: A Theory of African-American Literary Criticism.* New York: Oxford UP, 1988. Print.

Pollock, Sheldon. "Cosmopolitan and Vernacular in History." *Cosmopolitanism.* Ed. Dipesh Chakrabarty, Homi K. Bhabha, Sheldon Pollock, and Carol A. Breckenridge. Durham, NC: Duke UP, 2002. 15–53. Print.

Shankar, S. *Flesh and Fish Blood: Postcolonialism, Translation, and the Vernacular.* Berkeley: U of California P, 2012.

"Vernacular." *Oxford English Dictionary.* Web. 12 Mar. 2014.

African languages, writ small

Jeanne-Marie Jackson

I am employed as a specialist in world Anglophone literature, and my research focuses in large part on sub-Saharan Africa. It shouldn't be that surprising, then, that I would want to study two southern African languages spoken by ten million people each. And yet Africanists pursuing this dimension of their training often find themselves forced to seek out language opportunities "on the side": 1970s textbooks, amateur YouTube videos, and long-retired Foreign Service training recordings are just some of the materials through which I've cobbled a pedagogy together over the past year. Comparatists, on the whole, come of age with a sense that pastures are greener in English departments down the hall. With that feeling lurking behind our attempts to find market appeal, it's clear why learning a language that no one funds, no one knows, and no one associates with field-changing questions might feel a little quixotic.

In the past few years, though, there has been cause to think that this may be changing, with universities wising up to the problematic trade-offs between globalist scholarship in its English department versions and work by comparatists in the literatures of the global South. There has been a flurry of conversation in generalist venues like *The Chronicle of Higher Education* about the "rise" of African writing – a debate that often seems, in its stock tones of accusation and naïveté, like a distraction from more interesting questions (see Dimock; Bady). English departments at elite universities, including, recently, Yale, have hired faculty with regional credibility instead of the pick-a-country, pick-a-book, cross-a-border projects that still dominate the field as a whole. Perhaps most influential of all, Simon Gikandi, whose early work put Ngũgĩ wa Thiong'o's Englishness in conversation with his Gikuyu roots, is now at the helm of *PMLA* (see Gikandi).

Still, it is one thing to *say* that studying African languages is a good thing, and another to imagine how this might play out at both the institutional and intellectual levels. There is no easy transposition between the Eurocentric comparative literature of old (French, German, Russian if you're lucky) and the "Africa Rising" narrative of today. There are just too many African languages, spread across too much territory, to make Europe a viable model. Nor is there a clear analogy with fields like Arabic or East Asian studies, in which single languages – admittedly across wide-ranging dialects – cover large geographical swathes. To study southern Africa alone, as a comparatist, will cost you years of toil for relatively little payoff in terms of territorial gain: after a PhD and three years of employment, I work in just *two* regional languages in addition to English. (I am both embarrassed by and smug about this, which should say a lot.) If you want to write the big, prizewinning book on the continent writ large – a book that gets read by people without any regional investment – you're likely to be stuck with the mercifully more manageable model of the Anglophone world.

In terms of Christopher Bush's piece in this volume, "Areas: Bigger than the nation, smaller than the world," the opening-up of the African literary field (as far as American scholars are concerned, at least) means thinking smaller, rather than bigger. Claiming far-reaching knowledge of African writing, when you think like a comparatist, is inevitably doomed. You will *always* be faced with another tradition you cannot access, balancing depth and breadth in a balance beam routine that leaves you heaving with envy of your colleagues whose work on "global" modernism might include a single well-known writer from a non-Western canon. This is also why it is doubtful whether the future of African language study, which could and *should* transform world Anglophone literature, can rely on a resurgence of support from large-scale initiatives, like the now-defunct Summer Cooperative African Language Institute (SCALI). Nor is a revitalized African studies, with its downside of methodological and intellectual provincialism, the best answer going forward. As the contributors to *Africa and the Disciplines* noted in 1993, Africa has never been on its own (Bates et al.).

There are just too many African languages and traditions – too many tongues that crucially *influence* books that travel, but do not travel themselves – to make suggestions like hiring more Africanists or funding more language courses feasible for the humanities in most places or on a broad scale. If an economic interest in Nigeria leads to increased enrollment in Yoruba courses, this is the exception rather than the rule. The challenge is to think about African language study in more oblique but essential relation to our intellectual work, rather than only as a subject of inquiry in its own right. A quick example of this, on account of its easy recognition, is the relationship between J. M. Coetzee and Afrikaans. Does one need to know Afrikaans to read Coetzee? Obviously not. Does having a sense of what Afrikaans is, what it means to South African intellectual culture, help one understand him more profoundly? I would argue yes. In fact, I'd even say it's indispensable, in the way that being a specialist on Nabokov's books in English seems to demand that one dip at least a big toe into his Russian background. Too often, less-studied languages from Africa and elsewhere make their way into major intellectual movements only as disciplinary polemics. But learning African languages does not need to mean doing work that is *about* why we should look to African languages, any more than scholars who work on Goethe feel the need to constantly signal that they write about German.

The best solution, I think, is to reimagine world Anglophone literature, at least in its African variants, along the lines of the immersion paradigm that no comparatist can avoid. This tradition – the time spent "in the field," taking language pledges and living with host families, that is an integral part of undergraduate French, German, Spanish, or Russian majors – admittedly has its own perils.

(There is the risk, I'm told, of failing to maintain a clear sense of one's empowered positionality vis-à-vis the host culture, but that hardly seems more harmful than not knowing what the host culture is.) If scholars with an interest in African literature see language study as a necessary box to check in even beginning to form an intellectual project, then intra-African comparison becomes essential to studying the African writers who *do* write in English. Rather than choose from a bifurcated supply of Africanist scholars studying vernacular print cultures, on the one hand, and "global" scholars with book chapters on Chimamanda Ngozi Adichie, on the other, we might envision someone at least able to grapple with how Igbo and Yoruba traditions *inflect* Nigerian writing in English. This is not a new idea in itself: scholars like Gikandi, as well as younger colleagues like Wendy Belcher or Olakunle George, have been doing this for some time (see Belcher; George). There are still steep challenges, however, for getting "regional" work published in generalist journals or by academic presses without regional lists.

Going forward, we would be better served to imagine and even encourage smaller, more idiosyncratic pockets of scholars with African language training across the larger discipline. I used to joke with a graduate school colleague that were I ever to get rich (which seems unlikely, at this point), I would endow a "Language Maintenance Grant" at my home institution for which comparatists would be eligible with no questions asked. The usual funding rationales – archival work, human-subject research, and, on occasion, a formal language course – overvalue Africanist scholarship with immediate payoffs, and undervalue the deeper commitment to "*getting*" a place that I remember from my better-funded years learning Russian. Until we have an institutionalized expectation that language immersion is part of an organic coming-to-terms with a literary tradition, rather than *only* a tool to ferret out archival minutiae, the unspoken schism between "conceptual work" and "regional work" will remain. A designated immersion grant of even $1,000 would help young scholars immensely in getting to a place that requires a $1,500 flight. It would also acknowledge, implicitly, that practical matters like distance, transportation, and a dearth of organized language programs that are preapproved for funding by US institutions are often the biggest hindrances to opening up new linguistic vistas.

Because the fact is, African languages are not often accessible through organized group courses at well-known universities. A range of inexpensive and individualized programs that encourage students and young scholars to self-design their learning is far more in tune with Africanists' needs than is plugging for scarce tenure-track lines in dozens of languages, with just a few students each. Rather than fight a losing battle for faculty lines in individual languages aside from the most-spoken ones (typically resulting in adjunct hires, a problem in its own right), we should cultivate umbrella organizations, with one or two permanent positions, that are oriented specifically to helping get people abroad and access the resources available there. Yale has a program called Directed Independent Language Study that works to this end, in which graduate students, pending a convincing application, are provided with paid native-speaking tutors (often local residents), access to language lab resources, guidance in choosing textbooks and media materials, and examination by a qualified expert at the end of each semester. At Johns Hopkins University this term, we've discussed partnering with the historically Black public university up the road to build language options into African humanities courses across the curriculum, offering, perhaps, an extra credit to students who are capable or so inclined.

The onus is on us, and on English departments, especially, to both demand and support a higher and, yet, less operational standard of Africanist credibility. This means hiring and peer review practices that are attentive to what you can and cannot get away with as a comparatist, versus as a global Anglophone scholar, in terms of the sheer amount of territory covered. It means questioning the degree of hypocrisy in terms of what's assumed in European critical traditions, versus what's even *allowed* for in "global" ones. And it means, finally, thinking in focused and sustainable ways about how to embed African languages in our critical practices, rather than see them as exotic and logistically unfeasible ends in themselves. Then, and only then, will Africa "rise" in American scholarship to the level at which it's always already been.

Works cited

Bady, Aaron. "Academe's Willful Ignorance of African Literature." *The Chronicle of Higher Education* 4 March 2015. Web. 30 Dec. 2015.

Bates, Robert H., V. Y. Mudimbe and Jean F. O'Barr, eds. *Africa and the Disciplines.* Chicago: U of Chicago P, 1993. Print.

Belcher, Wendy. *Abyssinia's Samuel Johnson: Ethiopian Thought in the Making of an English Author.* New York: Oxford UP, 2012. Print.

Dimock, Wai Chee. "A Literary Scramble for Africa." *The Chronicle of Higher Education* 17 February 2015. Web. 30 Dec. 2015.

George, Olakunle. *Relocating Agency: Modernity and African Letters.* Albany: SUNY Press, 2003. Print.

Gikandi, Simon. "Traveling Theory: Ngugi's Return to English." *Research in African Literatures* 31 (2000): 194–209. Print.

The Sinophone

Yucong Hao

Sinophone literature, a term coined by Shu-mei Shih in 2004, refers to Sinitic-language literature written "on the margins of China and Chineseness" (Shih 33). As an emerging field of inquiry, the Sinophone provides a conceptual alternative to the paradigm of China-based national literary studies; as an organizing category, the Sinophone evinces the plurality of cultural identities, linguistic practices, and ethnicities of Sinitic-language communities around the world. It also crystallizes discussions – the destabilization of Chineseness in the era of transnationalization and reflections on the hegemony of China and Sinocentric discourses – that have penetrated the field of Chinese studies since the 1990s.

The affinity between the Sinophone and ideas of Francophone or Anglophone studies is immediately obvious: all of them, theoretically indebted to postcolonialism, propose a reconceptualization of center and periphery, empire and colony, imperialism and the colonial language. Yet the Sinophone is not simply derived from the Francophone or the Anglophone, but highlights a more intriguing dynamic between geographical entities and linguistic practices that may complicate and complement the existing postcolonial articulations. Drawing from recent historiography on Qing China (1644–1911), Shu-mei Shih identifies Qing China as an empire – not the mere victim of Western imperialism – that manifests distinctive forms of colonialism: continental, internal, and settler colonialisms. However, it remains much disputed whether the modern empire-colony relationship would be an effective explanatory model for the complex historical interactions between China and Sinophone locales since the premodern age and whether Chinese would qualify as a colonial language, since the decision to preserve Sinitic languages as well as Chinese literary traditions in overseas communities is often made by choice rather than by force.

As the concept of the Sinophone rejects a monolithic representation of Chineseness, it similarly defies a uniform definition. Different formulations that are constantly emerging demonstrate contending ideologies and politics of culture and identity that construct, deconstruct, or reconstruct Chineseness at a time when China stages itself as a world power. For Shu-mei Shih, the imperative is to confront the hegemony and homogeneity of Chineseness and the marginalization of cultural productions outside China. Resisting constant calls to return to the ancestral land and claims of China-centrism, Shih focuses on local identities, urging the Sinophone population to live "as a political subject within a particular geopolitical place in a specific time with deep local commitments" (38). Shih strategically excludes Chinese literature produced in China from the world map of the Sinophone, demonstrating that the center is always already a margin.

A more inclusive definition of the Sinophone as "Sinitic-language speaking" would include literary productions from China and thus piece together a global picture of the Sinophone. Despite the differences, both the inclusive and the exclusive perspectives subvert "the hegemonic focus of a 'national' Chinese literature" (Tsu and Wang 6) but aspire to a reconfiguration of it. For David Wang and Jing Tsu, the Sinophone is less about choosing local commitments over China-centrism than about removing disciplinary and geographical boundaries, which enables Sinophone studies to engage in interdisciplinary and transnational dialogues:

> Looking at Sinophone writing as an interaction between the production of literatures and moving agents, one might subject the narrative of customary disciplinary divides and national literary histories to similar shifts. More important than the coinage of new terms is the creation of new dialogues among the fields of area studies, Asian American studies, and ethnic studies.
>
> (Tsu and Wang 3)

Works cited

Shih, Shu-mei. "Against Diaspora." *Sinophone Studies: A Critical Reader.* Ed. Shu-mei Shih, Chien-hsin Tsai and Brian Bernards. New York: Columbia UP, 2013. 25–42. Print.

Tsu, Jing, and David Der-wei Wang. "Introduction: Global Chinese Literature." *Global Chinese Literature: Critical Essays.* Ed. Jing Tsu and David Der-wei Wang. Leiden: Brill, 2010. 1–13. Print.

Pseudotranslation

Brigitte Rath

In 1721, Montesquieu published, anonymously, his *Persian Letters*. In the preface, he claimed that two Persians had lodged with him, and that he had translated into French the letters they wrote to and received from Persia. The dates of the letters retain Persian names for the months, and the "translator" provides some footnotes with explanations on Persian customs. The text invites readers to imagine a preceding, original, authentic text in Persian, and to picture the first audience for these letters, one that would not need the additional information provided in the footnotes, because they would belong to what was, for French readers, a markedly unknown culture. Even as it marks the foreign as opaque, Montesquieu's text makes it readable; it plays with the readers' voyeuristic desire to gain access to the inaccessible: private letters written in a foreign language, and an alien perspective on the readers' familiar world.

The translation studies scholar Gideon Toury defines pseudotranslations as "texts which have been presented as translations with no corresponding source texts in other languages ever having existed" (40). In Toury's view, pseudotranslation is a property of texts; because there was no Persian original, the *Persian Letters* are a pseudotranslation, regardless of whether the reader is aware of this. Beyond this text-centered model, I propose thinking of pseudotranslation as a mode of reading that oscillates between seeing the text as an original and as a translation pointing toward an imagined original, produced in a different language and culture for a different audience.

The idea of pseudotranslation sharpens some central concepts of comparative literature. "World literature," according to David Damrosch, is "always as much about the host culture's values and needs as it is about a work's source culture" (283). Foregrounding a text's imaginary origin in a different culture reads this "double refraction" as already built into a text. It thus stresses the conjecture and transnational imagination that are always involved in reading a text as world literature. Pseudotranslation as a mode of reading has also much to contribute to questions of translatability, representation, voice, authorship, authenticity, and multilingualism.

Pseudotranslation opens up a new approach to literary texts spanning languages and periods, among them Cervantes's *Don Quixote* (1605/15), MacPherson's

Ossian (1761), Markoe's *Algerine Spy in Pennsylvania* (1787), Mérimée's *Guzla* (1827), Holz/Schlaf's *Papa Hamlet* (1889), Raja Rao's *Kanthapura* (1938), Lem's *Głos Pana* [His Master's Voice] (1968), Makine's *Fille d'un héros de l'Union soviétique* (1990), and Bitov's *Преподаватель симметрии* [The Symmetry Teacher] (2008). This apparent ubiquity of original texts that invite their audience to read them as if they were translations merits more attention. It further strengthens, for instance, arguments for a transnational history of literature and genres since, as Aravamudan, Ballaster, and Lombaz (among others) have shown, pseudotranslation shapes the development of the novel and the prose poem (see also McMurran; Monte; Vincent-Munnia; and Marmarelli).

Pseudotranslation is an idea of the (past) decade. Of the 154 sources that use the term "pseudotranslation," roughly two-thirds were published in the last decade (Figure 2), and more deal with the same phenomenon under different names, such as "fictitious translation," "assumed translation," "supposed translation," or "original translation" (e.g., see Lombez).

The overabundance of terms coincides with a scarcity of cross-references between the individual contributions, which often show little awareness of the developing field. This seems about to change: two recent conferences focused exclusively on pseudotranslation, some articles frame their case studies more broadly, and the first edited volumes and books dedicated to the topic have appeared; the new field has reached a tipping point (see, e.g., Apter; Martens; Santoyo; Martens and Vanacker; Beebee; and Jenn). Reading texts like Montesquieu's *Lettres persanes*

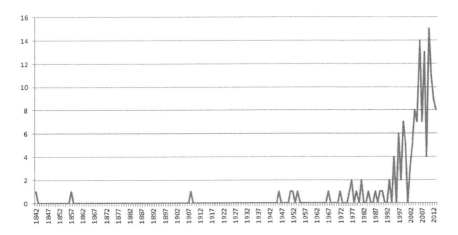

Figure 2 154 reviews, articles, chapters, and books use the term "pseudotranslation" or "pseudo-traduction," "Pseudoübersetzung," "seudotraducción"; 104 of them in the decade 2003–2013.

Source: Brigitte Rath.

as original and as translation of an imagined original challenges us to engage with the preconceptions and projections involved when comparing texts across languages and cultures.

Works cited

Apter, Emily. "Translation with No Original: Scandals of Textual Reproduction." *Nation, Language, and the Ethics of Translation*. Ed. Sandra Bermann and Michael Wood. Princeton: Princeton UP, 2005. 159–74. Print.

Aravamudan, Srinivas. *Enlightenment Orientalism: Resisting the Rise of the Novel*. Chicago: U of Chicago P, 2012. Print.

———. "Fiction/Translation/Transnation: The Secret History of the Eighteenth-Century Novel." *A Companion to the Eighteenth-Century English Novel and Culture*. Ed. Paula Backscheider and Catherine Ingrassia. Chichester: Wiley-Blackwell, 2005. 48–74. Print.

Ballaster, Ros. "Narrative Transmigrations: The Oriental Tale and the Novel in Eighteenth-Century Britain." *A Companion to the Eighteenth-Century English Novel and Culture*. Ed. Paula Backscheider and Catherine Ingrassia. Chichester: Wiley-Blackwell, 2005. 75–96. Print.

Beebee, Thomas O. *Transmesis: Inside Translation's Black Box*. New York: Palgrave Macmillan, 2012. Print.

Damrosch, David. *What Is World Literature?* Princeton: Princeton UP, 2003. Print.

Jenn, Ronald. *La pseudo-traduction, de Cervantes à Mark Twain*. Leuven: Peeters, 2013. Print.

Lombez, Christine. "La 'traduction supposée' ou: De la place des pseudotraductions poétiques en France." *Fictionalising Translation and Multilingualism*. Ed. Dirk Delabastita and Rainier Grutman. Antwerpen: Hogeschool Antwerpen Hoger Inst. voor Vertalers en Tolken, 2005. 107–21. Print.

Marmarelli, Trina. "Other Voices: Strategies of Spatial, Temporal, and Psychological Distancing in the Early French Prose Poem." *Pacific Coast Philology* 40.1 (2005): 57–76. Print.

Martens, David. "De la mystification à la fiction: La poétique suicidaire de la fausse traduction." *Translatio in fabula: Enjeux d'une rencontre entre fictions et traductions*. Ed. Sophie Klimis. Brussels: Facultés universitaires Saint-Louis, 2010. 63–81. Print.

Martens, David, and Beatrijs Vanacker, eds. *Scénographies de la pseudo-traduction*. Spec. issue of *Les lettres romanes* 67.3–4 (2013). Print.

McMurran, Mary Helen. *The Spread of Novels: Translation and Prose Fiction in the Eighteenth Century*. Princeton: Princeton UP, 2010. Print.

Monte, Steven. *Invisible Fences: Prose Poetry as a Genre in French and American Literature*. Lincoln: U of Nebraska P, 2000. Print.

Montesquieu. *Lettres persanes*. Amsterdam: P. Brunel, 1721. Gallica. Web. 28 Aug. 2016.

Santoyo, Julio-César. "Seudotraducciones: Pre-textos & pretextos de la falsificación." *Mundus vult decipi: Estudios interdisciplinares sobre falsificación textual y literaria.* Ed. Javier Martínez García. Madrid: Ediciones Clásicas, 2012. 355–66. Print.

Toury, Gideon. *Descriptive Translation Studies and Beyond.* Amsterdam: John Benjamins, 1995. Print.

Vincent-Munnia, Nathalie, S. Bernard-Griffiths and Robert Pickering, eds. *Aux origines du poème en prose français (1750–1850).* Paris: Champion, 2003. Print.

Untranslatability

Shaden M. Tageldin

Impasse and imposture – if not sheer impossibility – haunt the dream of translatability. If translatability has underpinned "efforts to revive World Literature" within and against the discipline of comparative literature over the last decade, as Emily Apter has argued in *Against World Literature* (3), surely its obverse – *untranslatability* – is a ghostwritten word of that decade and a watchword of the next.

Like Gayatri Chakravorty Spivak, whose *Death of a Discipline* (2003) and later writings critique the world literature paradigms of Franco Moretti and David Damrosch for sparing Anglophone students in the United States the trouble of learning other languages and greeting other literatures in their potential difference, Apter sees in untranslatability an antidote to the anodyne globalism of world literature. Under the guise of "worldliness," she suggests, world literature homogenizes the world itself, imposing Eurocentric taxonomies on literature and literary history. Both Spivak and Apter oppose comparative literature to world literature, and both make untranslatability a hallmark of comparative method, which negotiates linguistic difference and views the comparability of the world's literatures as made, not given.

Why does untranslatability compel us now? I would suggest that untranslatability fascinates comparatists today because the idea teeters on the threshold between the imagined absolutism of the theological and the imagined relativism of the worldly, cross-contaminating both.

Take the case of Arabic, an avatar of untranslatability in US comparative literary studies of late, thanks in part to Apter's interest in the work of Moroccan theorist Abdelfattah Kilito in *Lan Tatakallam Lughati* (2002; *Thou Shalt Not Speak My Language*, 2008). Apter ties untranslatability to the theological – to the insistence that a sacred text *not* be, even *cannot* be, translated – and takes seriously its sacred dimension. She hints that sacrality clings with particular force to (Qur'anic) Arabic. Yet the "untranslatability" of Arabic unfurls, for Kilito, along a Möbius strip that ever twists it toward translatability. Disarticulating medieval Arab refusals to translate Greek poetry from Islamocentric hubris, Kilito cites the ninth-century polymath al-Jahiz, who deemed Greek poetry untranslatable for the very reason that *Arabic* poetry is untranslatable: the particularism of poetic language. Indeed, the untranslatability of Greek, Kilito slyly suggests, *translated into* the untranslatability of Arabic. Giving "bad" Arabic "equivalents" for Greek tragedy and comedy, Matta ibn Yunus's tenth-century Arabic translation of Aristotle's *Poetics* allowed the Arabs to indulge the singularity of Arabic, to "go on believing their poetry is the poetry and their language the language" (98). Contorting the tautology of translatability/untranslatability, which Lydia Liu critiques in *The Clash of Empires* (2004) and elsewhere, Kilito exposes the work of translation at the heart of Arabic's "untranslatability." He upends the association of untranslatability with theology and of translatability with worldliness. Worldly interdictions too can pronounce taboos on translation. And such taboos make both (pagan) Greek and (Qur'anic) Arabic sacred in their earthly particularism, inimitable in their contingency. "Untranslatable" language is at once relative and absolute, human and divine.

After untranslatability, what? I turn to an essay by Chinese intellectual Lu Xun, " 'Hard Translation' and the 'Class Character of Literature' " (1930). Dismissing the argument that Chinese is "unlike other languages" (recall Arabic) and thus unreceptive to foreign ideas (80), Lu Xun fights untranslatability with *hard translation*, confronting the materiality of the foreign language and its resistance to his own. "I stole fire from abroad," he declares of his forays into modern Western thought, "to cook my own flesh" (92). Hard translation – the strike of matter on matter – ignites the fire that at once immolates and recreates the native tongue. The foreign language fuels; the native changes form. Comparative literature in the next decade might abandon untranslatability for "hard translation" and its nonreciprocal combustions.

Works cited

Apter, Emily. *Against World Literature: On the Politics of Untranslatability*. New York: Verso, 2013. Print.

Kilito, Abdelfattah. *Thou Shalt Not Speak My Language*. Trans. Waïl S. Hassan. Syracuse: Syracuse UP, 2008. Print.

Liu, Lydia H. *The Clash of Empires: The Invention of China in Modern World Making*. Cambridge: Harvard UP, 2004. Print.

Lu Xun. " 'Hard Translation' and the 'Class Character of Literature.' " Trans. Yang Xianyi and Gladys Yang. *Lu Xun: Selected Works*. 3rd ed. Vol. 3. Beijing: Foreign Languages Press, 1980. 75–96. Print.

Spivak, Gayatri Chakravorty. *Death of a Discipline*. New York: Columbia UP, 2003. Print.

Media

Archive of the now

Jacob Edmond

Early in 2014, the *Archive of the Now* was removed from the Internet. In a statement claiming responsibility for the action, the hacktivist group Anonymous said that Queen Mary College, University of London, where the archive was hosted, and "other universities should be much more interested in protecting their own data . . . than in analyzing the data of others" (qtd. in Afifi-Sabet). Founded and run by scholar and poet Andrea Brady, the *Archive of the Now* is a collection of free downloadable audio and video recordings of contemporary poets. It appears to have been collateral damage in an action intended to target Internet research at the university funded by the UK Ministry of Defense, such as a project on "cross-cultural attitudes and the shaping of online behaviour in crisis situations." The blurring of the lines between comparative cultural studies, military analysis, and contemporary poetry (see Slaughter, this volume) highlights broader questions that attend attempts to construct an archive of the now, to historicize the present or very recent past, as in this report on the futures of comparative literature. Who owns, controls, and uses the archive? What economic and geopolitical realities does it reflect and maintain? What practices does it enable or inhibit?

The practice of comparative literature today is increasingly shaped by the contested archive of the now that is the Internet. Websites such as Brady's have allowed me to write from New Zealand about contemporary poetry in China, Russia, the United States, the United Kingdom, and elsewhere in ways that would have been impossible before the development of the World Wide Web.[1] Contemporary works of poetry increasingly assume that web searching is a precondition of reading (Reed 757). Though massive and massively larger than a decade ago, the Internet is a highly skewed and partial archive, subject to corporate and state control, as Anonymous's hacktivist actions and Edward Snowden's revelations about the National Security Agency remind us. The NSA and its partners, including those in New Zealand, from where I write, are also busy compiling an archive of the now, one that would have been the envy of twentieth-century totalitarian states such as the Soviet Union, and which at the same time may well be the most extensive archive ever compiled for the comparative study of everyday life. To speak, then, of the archive of the now is also to acknowledge the now of the archive: the pervasiveness of archiving in our present moment, including in the theory and practice of comparative literature.

I want here to connect these various archives of the now by using contemporary literature to explore the historical contingency of recent comparative literary practices, methodologies, and theories. Current theories and practices of comparative literature are shaped by our historical moment, but this historical contingency is rarely acknowledged sufficiently in our discipline. We forget at our peril that the archive is "always finite and therefore selective, interpretative, filtering, and filtered, censuring, and repressive"; it "always figures a place and an instance of power" (Derrida 100). We can guard against approaches that continually place "us" at the center of things and that offer "[g]lobalization stories as the new form of modernization narratives" by interrogating and so questioning how the present technological, economic, and geopolitical environment shapes comparative literature (Saussy, this volume).

Over the past two decades, the link-node hypertext structure of the Internet and the increasing mobility of goods and global elites have encouraged a comparative practice that "sees, instead of discrete national literatures, all literatures as participating in a network of power-inflected relations" (Shih 84). This sense of global connectivity is even more pervasive now than a decade ago, when the last report on the discipline already noted that "the current 'space of comparison,' rather than requiring that different works or traditions be deliberately wired up to communicate, sees them as always already connected" (Saussy, "Exquisite Cadavers" 31). Susan Stanford Friedman recently wrote of "circulation" and "world-system" theories as the main competing paradigms for comparative literature, world literature, and global modernism ("World Modernisms" 501). Whereas world-systems theorists draw on the work of Immanuel Wallerstein to emphasize the unequal relations between core and peripheral economies in a global system, the circulation model of comparison envisages network-like structures that "avoid the categorical violence of comparison within the framework of dominance" through translation, transculturation, "juxtapositional comparison," or "incommensurable relationality" (Friedman, "Why Not Compare?" 40–1; Melas 36). Yet even as they divide over the relative weight given to the network's nonhierarchical possibilities and its "power-inflected relations," both circulation and world-systems theorists share a view of the world in which everything is connected. In each case, the sense of global connectivity is reinforced by the archive of the now that is the Internet. Read in this way, what was once a particular strength of our discipline – to make unexpected connections, to cross national boundaries – now becomes the normative practice of the Internet age.

In the mid-1990s, some pioneers of digital literature, such as the poet-programmer John Cayley, were already criticizing hypertext's restrictive ontology of nodal entity and fixed relations (168). Cayley's reservations parallel recent criticisms of David Damrosch's influential account of world literature, both for its assumption that literary works have a single place of origin and for its restriction of the term "world literature" to those works that cross national or linguistic boundaries (Walkowitz 171–2; Shih 83). When Cayley proposed a "holographic" poetics in which texts, like light waves, would continuously diffract and change each other and themselves, he was seeking an alternative to the regimented mode of thinking proposed by nodes and links (172). Cayley's collaboration with poet

Yang Lian 杨炼 on a bilingual HyperCard performance piece, *Dahai tingzhi zhi chu* 大海停止之处/*Where the Sea Stands Still* (1997), for example, allows for different parts of the text to appear on four screens simultaneously in sometimes reinforcing and sometimes contrasting ways. The work reminds us that things repeated are never quite the same, just as "now" is never the same now – "now is furthest away" (现在是最遥远的) in the words of Yang's poem. Cayley and Yang's use of repetition and interference suggests an alternative, diffractive way of imagining world literature in which nodal entities and relational links are themselves in continuous flux.

Comparative literature has also responded to rapid increases in the quantity and availability of information, to what was termed in the online version of this report "the wave of big data flooding all subjects" (Thomsen). Just as the development of the Internet was driven by and drove the use of enormous datasets in fields such as genetics and astrophysics, the great upsurge in digital information and its near-instantaneous communication around the globe find an analogue in comparative literature's turn to very large scales, including – in addition to world literature – Gayatri Spivak's "planetarity" (71–102), Wai Chee Dimock's "deep time," Laura Doyle's "interimperiality," Franco Moretti's "distant reading," and the even vaster geological scale suggested by the Anthropocene (e.g., Wenzel, this volume).

Many contemporary works of art and literature also address big data and the global scale. These works extend a tradition of art and poetry "informed by data excess" that "has been with us at least since the emergence of modernism" (Whitelaw; Stephens 2). Artistic responses to information overload remind us that *"Raw Data" Is an Oxymoron*, as Lisa Gitelman has stressed in her book of that title. Digital data are never separable from their material context of instantiation, never "transcendental," despite our tendency – encouraged by the template structure of increasing numbers of webpages – to imagine "data pours" as the seamless transference of data from one form or container to another (Liu 211–36).

Kenneth Goldsmith's *Printing Out the Internet* (2013), for instance, is a crowd-sourced installation and performance piece in which people from around the world were invited to print off a part of the Internet and send it to the Labor Gallery in Mexico City. The impossible task of printing the entire Internet was not achieved, of course, though mountains of printouts were accumulated. Goldsmith thereby highlighted the size of the Internet and the difference between its digital, ink-and-paper, and oral materializations, as his statement accompanying the work emphasizes: "IF YOU PRINTED THE INTERNET, READING IT WOULD TAKE 57,000 YEARS, 24 HOURS A DAY, 7 DAYS A WEEK NON-STOP AND IF YOU READ IT FOR 10 MINUTES A NIGHT BEFORE BED, IT WOULD TAKE 8,219,088 YEARS" ("Marathon Group Reading"). Goldsmith here echoes the postscript to a much earlier work, *Soliloquy*, which contains a transcription of every word he spoke in one week in 1996:

IF EVERY WORD SPOKEN IN NEW YORK CITY DAILY
WERE SOMEHOW TO MATERIALIZE AS A SNOWFLAKE,
EACH DAY THERE WOULD BE A BLIZZARD. (489)

Elsewhere, he extends the metaphor: "Perhaps the materialized language would be taken to digital encoding centers, where it would be loaded onto high density CDs and stored as a record of our thought" ("I Look to Theory"). Goldsmith's vision of language transformed into data echoes the popular idea that "all words ever spoken by human beings" could be contained in five exabytes of data, an idea apparently first put forward by CalTech physicist and computer and information scientist Roy Williams in 1995, not long before Goldsmith made his *Soliloquy* recording.[2] Such imagined archives of speech have to some extent been realized in the NSA's project to record every single phone call made in selected countries (Gellman and Soltani). But whether in the fantasies of the NSA or of students of world literature, stores of language frozen as data project positivist visions of totality that increasingly inflect understandings of language, literature, and culture, even as contemporary works like Goldsmith's highlight the impossibility of collecting all the world's words.

Goldsmith's treatment of language as vast quantities of data to be stored, sculpted, and mined finds an obvious analogue in the work of Franco Moretti and the Stanford Literary Lab's vision of data-driven studies of world literature. But references to data size are to be found across a wider range of contemporary approaches to comparison. In opposition to the treatment of literature as data, Haun Saussy, in his contribution to the last state of the discipline report, *Comparative Literature in an Age of Globalization*, noted the smallness in bytes of such a large and complex work of literature as Tolstoy's *War and Peace*, which can be contained within a text file of 1.15 megabytes (Saussy, "Exquisite Cadavers" 32). Anxieties about the relative smallness of literature (or even of all language) compared to the Internet and scientific data are reflected in the continuous upping of the scale of comparative literature – from world to global to planetary to even (though tongue-in-cheek) "interplanetary literature" (Saussy, "Interplanetary Literature"). Contemporary poetry likewise responds to big data by, among other things, upping the stakes through the potential literature pioneered by the Oulipo writers. Raymond Queneau produced a sonnet with one hundred trillion permutations. Similarly, Simon and Christine Morris initiated a vast potential project when they used a computer program to generate and print reorderings of all 223,704 words in Freud's *Interpretation of Dreams* (Morris and Morris). Tolstoy insisted that the only way to explain *Anna Karenina* was to repeat all its words in exactly the same order (292). Combining the Morrises' and Tolstoy's insights and Saussy's 1.15 megabyte file, we could imagine all the possible combinations and permutations of the words contained in *War and Peace* as a potential text so large that the entire Internet would appear vanishingly small beside it.[3] Just as physicists suggest dark energy and matter constitute most of our universe, so potential literature dwarfs even the mightiest database.

Such absurd imaginings seem a long way from the everyday tasks of comparative literature and recall instead the 'pataphysics or "la science des solutions imaginaires" of Alfred Jarry, whose influence is acknowledged by Goldsmith in the name of what is arguably his greatest work, the online archive of avant-garde poetry and film *UbuWeb*. Like works of potential literature, however, comparison in literary and cultural studies highlights the myriad possibilities of textual permutation, which only increase in the Internet age. While a decade ago Saussy bemoaned the flatness of the Internet, web pages are in fact rich reminders of historical depth. Because they are frequently updated and often, like the *Archive of the Now*, disappear entirely, web pages accentuate the complexities of the historical record and of our "textual condition" (Gitelman, *Always Already New* 123–50; McGann). The web shows us what comparatists already know: texts live multiple and changeable lives across space and time. An oft-repeated way of describing large amounts of data is to speak in terms of multiples of all the books held in the Library of Congress. Yet as students of literature understand, the meaningfulness and interpretative history of the books in a library's collection far exceed their word count. Even the vast digitizing project Google Books reveals markers of materiality that defy quantitative summation. *The Art of Google Books*, a collaborative Tumblr site edited by new media artist Krissy Wilson, contains thousands of images highlighting the original print and paper materiality (foxed pages, library stamps, marginalia, and the like) of scanned books and the process of their digitization (scanned hands turning pages, neon moiré on images, and so on).

Like *The Art of Google Books*, Dmitri Prigov's installation *Videnie Kasparu Davidu Fridrikhu russkogo Tibeta* (*Caspar David Friedrich's Vision of Russia's Tibet*, 2004; Figure 3) explores databasing and global connectivity not as the opposite of literature but as a material, affective, and aesthetic condition of

Figure 3 Dmitri Prigov, *Videnie Kasparu Davidu Fridrikhu russkogo Tibeta* (*Caspar David Friedrich's Vision of Russia's Tibet*) as exhibited in the group show "En un desordre absolut: Art contemporani rus," Centre d'Art Santa Mònica, Barcelona, 2012. The installation was originally exhibited in a different form at the State Tretyakov Gallery in Moscow in 2004. Photograph by Costanza Baldini. Reproduced courtesy of the Estate of Dmitri Prigov and Costanza Baldini.

contemporaneity. In the last decade, some of the best work on the contemporary – such as Lauren Berlant on "cruel optimism" and Sianne Ngai on the "stuplime" and the "interesting" – explores the structures of feeling underlying how, say, a work of conceptual art or a John Ashbery poem generates a sense of "impasse," a low-affect, minor, or cool resistance to the "free-floating and impersonal" post-modern sublime of global networks and information overload (Ngai, *Ugly Feelings* 248–97; Ngai, *Our Aesthetic Categories* 147–73; Berlant 23–7; Jameson 16). Prigov's installation, in particular, exemplifies Ngai's account of how modernist and contemporary works of "stuplimity" draw on but revise the romantic sublime by replacing shock in the face of the infinite with shock and boredom in a continuous encounter with the iterations of "finite bits and scraps of material in repetition" (Ngai, *Ugly Feelings* 271). As in Friedrich's *Der Wanderer über dem Nebelmeer* (*The Wanderer above the Sea of Fog*, 1818), Prigov presents an over-whelming vision. Yet instead of marking the encounter with an unrepeatable, inexpressive, and infinite nature, Prigov confronts us with the mass-produced and finite but extremely numerous products of newsprint – snowdrifts of paper that recall similar accumulations in the work of writers like Cage, Beckett, Ashbery, and Goldsmith.

Situated in Russian as well as Western conceptual and contemporary art tra-ditions, however, Prigov's work cautions that data overload and postindustrial affect can generate quite different aesthetic and emotional categories depending on the "us" in question. Prigov's *Vision* superficially resembles, but differs from, the "cool" or "merely interesting" aesthetic on display in Goldsmith's adapta-tion of conceptual art to literature (Ngai, *Our Aesthetic Categories* 146). If "stu-plimity drags us downward into the realm of words rather than transporting us upward toward an unrepresentable divine" (Ngai, *Ugly Feelings* 273), Prigov's work keeps both options in play, inviting the viewer to attend to the close-up, exhaustive task of reading the newspapers, and to survey them from a distance, to look beyond the fog of paper to the returning gaze of the monstrous or divine eye. On the one hand, Prigov stresses the messy materiality and fragility of the archive of the now through the medium of print newspapers: impermanent mark-ers of the daily that are under threat from the rise of digital technologies and, in the Russian context, increasing government monopolization and control of the press. On the other, in decanting newspapers into the given form of Friedrich's painting and its many subsequent iterations, Prigov presents a materialization of the transcendent digital "data pour" that at the same time invokes the heights of German Romanticism and Russian nationalism through the towering Altai peaks known as "Russia's Tibet." While, like Goldsmith, Prigov confronts today's vast snowdrifts of information, his work's emotional register is at odds both with the cool immateriality of the postmodern and data sublime, and with the aesthetics of minor affective resistances. By fusing the transcendental data pour with resistant materiality and romantic nationalism with the geographical expanses of global feeling, Prigov's work suggests the need to question the oppositions between network and node, data and materiality, totality and locality, stuplimity and sub-limity on which "our" comparative forms and contemporary aesthetics are built.

To archive the now is also to write it. Data do not speak for themselves, just as speech is not just a certain quantity of data. As the production and availability of literature have increased exponentially over the past few decades, gatekeepers and filterers of information – the archivists – have become increasingly important (Dworkin 21). Yes, in their role as archivists, comparatists should expand the field and seek to escape their various provincialities. But forms of expansion or relation are not in themselves enough. To assume otherwise is to fall prey to the romance of technology – to think that we can overcome the historical blind spots and inequities of our discipline merely by increasing the size of the data set or by adding further links to the network. Comparatists need also to attend to the historical, cultural, and technological contingency of such conceptual assumptions. Here our discipline can learn from those arts of the present that explore the assumptions and structures of feeling that attend the archive of the now.

Notes

1 Websites that have proved rich sources for my writing about contemporary poetry include *Vavilon* (http://www.vavilon.ru), *Novaia literaturnaia karta Rossii* (http://www.litkarta.ru), *Shi shenghuo* 诗生活 (http://www.poemlife.com), *Electronic Poetry Center* (http://epc.buffalo.edu), *UbuWeb* (http://www.ubu web.com), and *PennSound* (http://writing.upenn.edu/pennsound).

2 The webpage where Williams equates all words ever spoken to five exabytes of data is no longer online. According to a 2002 version of the page archived at *The Way Back Machine*, the page was created in 1995. A Czech translation confirms that the page and this phrase were online prior to January 1996 (Kohoutková).

3 If we assume a vocabulary of, say, ten thousand words, and employ Zipf's law to estimate word distribution, then for a book with five hundred thousand words (roughly the length of *War and Peace*), there would be 10 to the power of 1,425,020 unique permutations – that is, a one followed by 1,425,020 zeros, with each permutation being about one million bytes in size. The amount of digital data worldwide is currently estimated in zettabytes, a measure of bytes with a one followed by twenty-one zeros.

Works cited

Afifi-Sabet, Keumars. "Anonymous Hacks Queen Mary University for Its Role in MoD-Funded Research." *Independent* 27 Jan. 2014. Web. 15 Dec. 2015.

Berlant, Lauren. "Cruel Optimism." *Differences* 17.3 (2006): 20–36. Print.

Cayley, John. "Beyond Codexspace: Potentialities of Literary Cybertext." *Visible Language* 30.2 (1996): 164–83. Print.

Cayley, John, and Yang Lian. *Dahai tingzhi zhi chu* 大海停止之处/ *Where the Sea Stands Still*. Institute of Contemporary Arts, London. 27 May 1997. Performance.

———. *Dahai tingzhi zhi chu* 大海停止之处/ *Where the Sea Stands Still*. ICA Archive, 1997. Videocassette.

Derrida, Jacques. *Without Alibi*. Ed. and Trans. Peggy Kamuf. Stanford: Stanford UP, 2002. Print.

Dimock, Wai Chee. *Through Other Continents: American Literature across Deep Time*. Princeton: Princeton UP, 2006. Print.

Doyle, Laura. "Modernist Studies and Inter-Imperiality in the Longue Durée." *The Oxford Handbook of Global Modernisms*. Ed. Mark Wollaeger and Matt Eatough. New York: Oxford UP, 2012. 669–96. Print.

Dworkin, Craig. "Seja Marginal." *Consequences of Innovation: 21st-Century Poetics*. Ed. Craig Dworkin. New York: Roof, 2008. 7–24. Print.

Friedman, Susan Stanford. "Why Not Compare?" *Comparison: Theories, Approaches, Uses*. Ed. Rita Felski and Susan Stanford Friedman. Baltimore: Johns Hopkins UP, 2013. 34–45. Print.

———. "World Modernisms, World Literature, and Comparativity." *The Oxford Handbook of Global Modernisms*. Ed. Mark Wollaeger and Matt Eatough. New York: Oxford UP, 2012. 499–525. Print.

Gellman, Barton, and Ashkan Soltani. "NSA Surveillance Program Reaches 'into the Past' to Retrieve, Replay Phone Calls." *Washington Post* 19 Mar. 2014. Web. 15 Dec. 2015.

Gitelman, Lisa. *Always Already New: Media, History and the Data of Culture*. Cambridge, MA: MIT, 2006. Print.

———, ed. *"Raw Data" Is an Oxymoron*. Cambridge, MA: MIT, 2013. Print.

Goldsmith, Kenneth. "I Look to Theory Only When I Realize That Somebody Has Dedicated Their Entire Life to a Question I Have Only Fleetingly Considered (A Work in Progress)." *Electronic Poetry Center*. Web. 15 Dec. 2015.

———. "Marathon Group Reading of the Entire Internet." *Printing Out the Internet*. 14 July 2013. Web. 15 Dec. 2015.

———. *Soliloquy*. New York: Granary, 2001. Print.

Jameson, Fredric. *Postmodernism; or, the Cultural Logic of Late Capitalism*. London: Verso, 1991. Print.

Kohoutková, J. "Data v mocninách deseti." *Zpravodaj ÚVT MU* 6.4 (1996). Web. 15 Dec. 2015.

Liu, Alan. *Local Transcendence: Essays on Postmodern Historicism and the Database*. Chicago: U of Chicago P, 2008. Print.

McGann, Jerome. *The Textual Condition*. Princeton: Princeton UP, 1991. Print.

Melas, Natalie. *All the Difference in the World: Postcoloniality and the Ends of Comparison*. Stanford: Stanford UP, 2007. Print.

Moretti, Franco. *Distant Reading*. London: Verso, 2013. Print.

Morris, Simon, and Christine Morris (Christine Farion). *Re-writing Freud*. 2005. Wall mounted touch screen kiosk, computer program, printer. First exhibited in *Un art de lecteurs*. Galerie Art & Essai. Université de Rennes 2. 16 Mar.–15 Apr. 2005.

Ngai, Sianne. *Our Aesthetic Categories: Zany, Cute, Interesting*. Cambridge, MA: Harvard UP, 2012. Print.

———. *Ugly Feelings*. Cambridge, MA: Harvard UP, 2005. Print.

Queneau, Raymond. *Cent mille milliards de poèmes*. Paris: Gallimard, 1961. Print.

Reed, Brian M. "In Other Words: Postmillennial Poetry and Redirected Language." *Contemporary Literature* 52.4 (2011): 756–90. Print.

Saussy, Haun. "Exquisite Cadavers Stitched from Fresh Nightmares: Of Memes, Hives, and Selfish Genes." *Comparative Literature in an Age of Globalization*. Ed. Haun Saussy. Baltimore: Johns Hopkins UP, 2006. 3–42. Print.

———. "Interplanetary Literature." *Comparative Literature* 63.4 (2011): 438–47. Print.

Shih, Shu-mei. "Comparison as Relation." *Comparison: Theories, Approaches, Uses.* Ed. Rita Felski and Susan Stanford Friedman. Baltimore: Johns Hopkins UP, 2013. 79–98. Print.

Spivak, Gayatri Chakravorty. *Death of a Discipline.* New York: Columbia UP, 2003. Print.

Stephens, Paul. *The Poetics of Information Overload: From Gertrude Stein to Conceptual Writing.* Minneapolis: U of Minnesota P, 2015. Print.

Thomsen, Mads Rosendahl. "World Famous, Locally: Insights from the Study of International Canonization." State of the Discipline Report, American Comparative Literature I Association. 6 March 2014. Web. 1 December 2016. https://stateofthe discipline.acla.org/entry/world-famous-locally-insights-study-international-canonization

Tolstoy, Lev. Letter to N.N. Strakhov, 23 Apr. 1876. *Tolstoy: The Critical Heritage.* Ed. A.V. Knowles. London: Routledge, 1978. 292–3. Print.

Walkowitz, Rebecca. "Close Reading in an Age of Global Writing." *Modern Language Quarterly* 74.2 (2013): 171–95. Print.

Whitelaw, Mitchell. "Art against Information: Case Studies in Data Practice." *Fibreculture Journal* 11 (2008). Web. 15 Dec. 2015.

Williams, Roy. "Data Powers of Ten." California Institute of Technology. Archive of the page at 2 Aug. 2002. *The Way Back Machine.* Web. 15 Dec. 2015.

Wilson, Krissy, ed. *The Art of Google Books. Tumblr.* Web. 22 Dec. 2015.

Electronic literature as comparative literature

Jessica Pressman

Electronic literature is comparative literature. It operates across machine and human languages, requiring translation of these languages before it even reaches the human reader. It is born digital – meaning that it is procedural and computational, processed across multiple platforms, protocols, and technologies in real time and in accordance with the very real constraints and technical specificities of the hardware, software, and network configuration of the reader's computer. What is presented onscreen – the artwork and poetic – is multimedia and multimodal. Combining text, image, sound, movement, interactivity, and design, such works challenge traditional disciplinary boundaries (is a Flash animation a film, literature, a hybrid, or something else entirely?) as well as genre categories (is this narrative, poetry, or performance?). For these reasons and more, electronic literature requires its reader to read and think comparatively.

Electronic literature demands that readers compare not only language and text but also the media formats and ecologies that support them. Examining the medial contexts and networked configurations that support digital literature exposes the inextricable connections between the technological, linguistic, cultural, and political. We are compelled to recognize that there is never text without media and mediation; moreover, that literary studies *is*, at least in part, media studies.

In my scholarly work, I have tried to show the benefits of approaching electronic literature comparatively, comparing it to earlier literary traditions and to other textual media platforms. In this essay I suggest that reading electronic literature can support a paradigmatic shift *within* the discipline of comparative literature – a medial turn that can facilitate understanding not only specific art objects but also the larger paradigms, practices, and ideologies involved in such study.

Electronic literature

In the last few decades, electronic literature has emerged as a robust field across diverse genres, languages, readerships, and nations. Such work invites comparative reading practices that combine analysis of different languages and media forms. Let's take a look at a few examples of how digital works present onscreen poetics that promote comparative literary reading approaches.

First and foremost, Young-hae Chang Heavy Industries: these digital artists – one American, one Korean – challenge simple designations of nationality, genre, and language. In *Nippon* (2002) and other works, Young-hae Chang Heavy Industries present a choreographed conversation between Western and Eastern languages that flashes upon a horizontally divided screen (Figure 4). The visual design invites translation and comparison but the speed at which the languages flash dispels comprehensive conclusions. The work promotes comparative reading ambitions and expectations but also awareness of how media challenge such traditional practices (see Pressman, "Reading").

William Poundstone similarly uses Flash to present a one-word-at-a-time aesthetic that also invites comparative literary analysis. In *Project for Tachisto-scope {Bottomless Pit}* (2005), text and icons are embedded as image-texts (see Mitchell, *Picture Theory*). Their appearance onscreen is cued to ambient sounds, heightened speeds, and subliminal messages (Figures 5 and 6). Semiotics is here

Figure 4 Screenshot from Young-hae Chang Heavy Industries.
Source: *Nippon* (2002). Reproduced by permission.

Figures 5 and 6 Nonconsecutive screenshots from William Poundstone.
Source: *Project for Tachistoscope {Bottomless Pit}* (2005). Reproduced by permission.

not limited to the visual or linguistic, and literary interpretation requires attention to the temporal, multimodal, and computational. Reading such a work makes explicitly and affectively clear that digital literature is not just about text but also about interface, interactive design, and programming code.

Other works of electronic literature promote comparative linguistic analysis by presenting different versions of the same work in different languages. For example, David Jhave Johnston's "Sooth" (2005) prompts readers to choose the language in which to read the work and thereby invites comparison between the different language-based versions. In addition to promoting comparison across languages, electronic literature can also invite consideration of the relationship between human and machinic languages. An early genre of electronic literature called "codework" did this by placing linguistic language and programming code side by side, interspersing digital text into readable text, to create poetic neologisms that N. Katherine Hayles calls "creole" ("Print" 80) and which compel recognition of the computational languages working to produce digital text onscreen. Codework by such writers as Talan Memmott and Mez defamiliarizes language and the traditional practices of comparative literary studies by making visible and aesthetic the fact that programming code is a type of language that not only operates to produce the onscreen text but also itself can be read (see Marino).

Electronic literature invites comparison between languages and opportunities to compare how meaning operates across multiple medial and sensorial modes. Erik Loyer's *Chroma* (2001), for example, presents its reader with two ways of engaging its science-fiction narrative: viewing the novel as a visual animation with a voice-over narrative in "Perform Text" or reading the narrative as scrollable text with no animation and voice-over in "View Text" (Figures 7 and 8). The

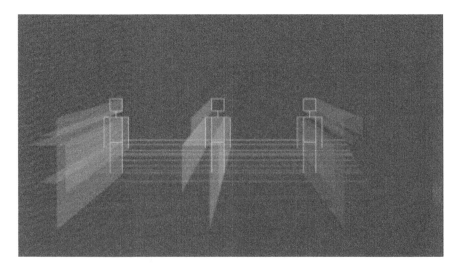

Figures 7 and 8 Screenshots from "Perform Text" and "View Text" of "Prologue" in Erik Loyer's *Chroma*.

Source. Loyer, 2001. Reproduced by permission.

PROLOGUE: AN INTRODUCTION TO HARROW
DR. IAN ANDERS
WEDNESDAY, MARCH 4, 1858

Human beings have always been digital.
The name we give to things that are perfect,
that do not decay,
that can be duplicated without end,
that are abstract
but somehow also tangible.

Some part of us has always lived in 'cyberspace,'
imagining grand structures given form by logic alone,
then ordering our physical bodies
to build their imperfect shadows.

A torturous existence,
and one we've grown accustomed to
over the millennia.

It was not always like this.

Eons ago, all human beings had the ability to enter 'mnemonos,'

Figures 7 and 8 (Continued)

reader must choose between the modes and cannot open both windows at once (see Pressman, *Digital Modernism* Ch. 5). The choice compels reflection on the actions that go into the process of performing a comparative analysis. In "Why Compare?," R. Radhakrishnan argues that comparison always involves choices, and these choices (particularly those made unintentionally) have implications for the resulting comparison. He writes that "comparisons are never neutral: they are inevitably tendentious, didactic, competitive, and prescriptive. Behind the seeming generosity of comparison, there always lurks the aggression of a thesis" (454). Loyer's *Chroma* illustrates this point. Choosing "View Text" instead of "Perform Text" suggests an understanding that one reads a novel by viewing text. But "View Text" is not the default mode of experiencing *Chroma*. Chapters open in "Perform Text" unless the reader takes action to view the text in order to, presumably, read it. This little programmatic detail is significant for understanding the comparative work that *Chroma* performs and promotes. *Chroma*'s episodic narrative about the ideological pitfalls of imagining cyberspace as a utopian Eden is predicated upon the reader making choices to access the narrative – choices that compel consideration of the actions that go into reading and comparing. Both Loyer and Radhakrishnan push us to recognize that the work of translation and comparison often happens within contexts of asymmetries in power relations – among populations, languages, and nations – which are frequently overlooked in the effort to focus on text or media.

The field of electronic literature is full of artists exploring the actions, intentions, and purposes of comparative reading. In response to their works, and indeed to the evolution of electronic literature more generally, literary critics are developing a diverse set of analytical approaches so as to read electronic literature comparatively, critically, and closely. From critically examining the programming languages that produce a literary work onscreen (as in critical code studies) and comparing the various technologies involved in producing the configuration of the digital performance (as in platform studies and media archaeology) to using data analytics software to pursue pattern recognition as an entrypoint for interpretation (as in cultural analytics), scholars are finding new ways to pursue comparativist approaches with and through electronic literature (see Marino; Bogost and Monfort; Huhtamo and Parikka; Manovich). Such approaches invite reflective consideration about the scholarly discipline of comparative literature, prompting critical questions about how this professional field must evolve along with new literature.

John Zuern argues that disciplines of comparative literature and media studies are "two ongoing initiatives in literary studies, proceeding in parallel time but rarely intersecting, [that] have something to learn from each other." Zuern identifies an opportunity to pursue comparison between these scholarly fields as a way of addressing the challenges each faces. He suggests an analogy between the confusion in digital studies over the distinction between "literary and artifactual properties" of an electronic work and the challenge in comparative literature to distinguish between "the specific 'literariness' of a text . . . and the text's presumed linguistic, cultural, and national-political specificities." Zuern cautions critics of electronic literature not to examine media at the expense of the literary, and this warning has a reverse implication: traditional comparative literary readings should also avoid the myopia of focusing solely on text and language. Bringing the practice of comparative literature to bear on electronic literature allows for readings that move beyond examinations of media formats and literary poetics to careful critiques of the cultural contexts and political practices that enable the very processes of computing and comparing. Electronic literature needs comparative literature.

But comparative literature also needs electronic literature. Rebecca Walkowitz introduces the term "comparison literature" to describe literature that "experiments with comparative structures" and therefore demands comparative reading of its content and medial format. Walkowitz uses the term as part of a larger argument that in the global networks of "world literature," critics need to read comparatively across texts, translations, and media platforms, even while reading a single literary work ("Comparison Literature" 567).[1] In an essay on Younghae Chang Heavy Industries, she claims that digitally created literature is "born-translated" because such works "not only appear in translation but are written for translation from the start" ("Close Reading" 173). Such literature, Walkowitz argues, is reflexively engaged with the network of production and distribution that enables its global poetics and thus requires readers to be attentive to the influence of translation in the digital network and the digital literature circulating on it.

"Comparison literature" might be considered a version of what N. Katherine Hayles earlier called a "technotext," a work that reflexively draws attention to its materiality and technologies of meaning-making (*Writing Machines* 25). However, instead of describing a literary practice or poetic effect in a particular work, the term "comparison literature" addresses comparative literature and literary studies more broadly. Comparison literature, Walkowitz writes, "asks us to imagine new geographies of literary production and requires methodologies that understand the history of a book to include its many editions and translations" ("Comparison Literature" 568). This is where comparative literature meets media studies. Yet, while Walkowitz's formulation of "comparison literature" supports a critical shift from focusing on text to considering materiality, it still locates that material textuality in the print-based realm: the history of the book. Here is where a focus on electronic literature can support a paradigm shift in the field of comparative literature. The works I discuss in this essay show that electronic literature pushes comparative analysis from text to process, from translation to series of translation acts, from work to network. Comparative literature must follow.

Certain genres of contemporary web-based electronic literature depend upon the Internet's technological structure for their literary effects. For these works, "comparison literature" and global literature have little to do with the history of the book and much to do with the history of the Internet. Works like the data-mined streaming poetry of "Twistori" and the Twitter-based Netprov piece "I Work for the Web" use algorithms to cull data from social networking sites and then use that content to constitute the "literary" product (Figures 9 and 10).[2] Other types of text-based, site-specific performances or public installations that include SMS messages from readers or participants bring to light new questions and concerns for critics. Rita Raley examines this type of text-as-networked-performance and explains, "What was at stake was less the physical parts of the work than a negotiation of control over property, technological systems, and public speech" (6).[3] This kind of public, site-specific performance of electronic literature, Raley writes, "allows us to think across media, platforms, and genres

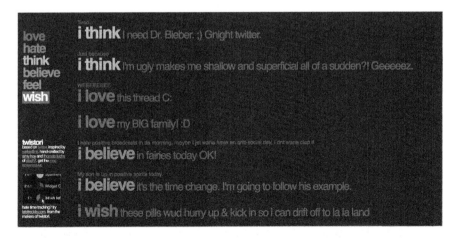

Figure 9 Screenshot from Amy Hoy and Thomas Fusch's "Twistori" (taken January 30, 2016).

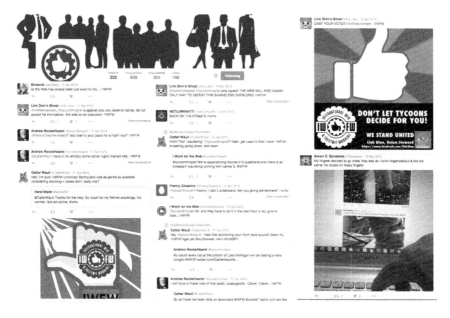

Figure 10 Composite of screenshots from Mark C. Marino and Rob Wittig's "I Work for the Web" (2015).

Source: Marino and Wittig, 2015. Reproduced by permission.

and to articulate a discourse on textual practices that are sited, social, and live" (8). Digital literature of this sort reshapes what and how comparatists compare. We can no longer just compare texts. We must now compare textual media.

Comparative textual media

Comparing media in the service of literary criticism can be transformative, both for understanding literature and for reconsidering the disciplinary fields and practices devoted to it. Hayles and I make this argument in *Comparative Textual Media: Transforming the Humanities in the Postprint Era*, a collection that proposes a paradigm shift by claiming that textual studies *is* media studies.

> [P]rint is itself a medium, an obvious fact that tends to be obscured by its long dominance within Western culture. As the era of print is passing, it is possible once again to see print in a comparative context with other textual media, including the scroll, the manuscript codex, the early print codex, the variations of book forms produced by changes from letterpress to offset to digital publishing machines, and born-digital forms such as electronic literature and computer games.

(vii)

The book collects essays on different textual media – from ancient Greek scrolls to digital literature, medieval manuscripts to paper letterhead and video games – in order to present a collective argument that reading across and between different textual formats exposes how text is always dependent upon the particularities of media. Media, of course, are dependent upon the particularities of cultural, political, and economic contexts for their development and use; a comparative focus on textual media thus compels literary scholars to reframe what we do and how we do it. Including comparative textual studies as part of comparative literary studies opens interdisciplinary channels for communication, collaboration, and, yes, comparison.

Comparative media studies have obvious relevance in our digital moment. When pundits claim the death of books – the media form most associated with literature – and question the relevance of the humanities more generally, a comparative perspective provides context. A comparative media perspective has been part of modern literary criticism since 1924, when I. A. Richards introduced his foundational *Principles of Literary Criticism* by laying out "the questions which the critic seeks to answer," such as "What gives the experience of reading a certain poem its value? How is this experience better than another? Why prefer this picture to that?" (2). He concludes: "These are the fundamental questions which criticism is required to answer, together with such preliminary questions – What *is* a picture, a poem, a piece of music? How can experiences be compared?" (2; original emphasis). Seen in this historical context, literary criticism has always been conjoined to comparative media studies. But in the age of digital media and global networks, this intersection is even more vital. As Hayles and I argue in the introduction to *Comparative Textual Media*, "A focus on media promotes awareness that national, linguistic, and genre categories (typical classifications for text-based disciplines) are always already embedded in particular material and technological practices with broad cultural and social implications" (x). This is particularly true in the age of new media and networked culture because text that circulates online is inseparable from its distributed medial instantiations.

Electronic literature supports metacritical awareness because it challenges us to identify what constitutes the literary "text" and also, of course, how to analyze it. Since electronic literature is procedural, critics can and should focus not only on onscreen poetics but also on the networked practices of production, circulation, and archiving of these products. Electronic literature thus promotes a shift of focus from objects – work, text, narrative – to processes, institutions, protocols, and relationships. How can onscreen poetics be separated from programming codes or the specificities of software versions and hardware configurations? How can we consider national, linguistic, and genre questions without considering how corporate and technological factors enable (or disable) literary aesthetics? When reading electronic literature, especially a work created in Flash and presented on an Apple product that blocks Adobe software, we cannot take for granted that the answers to such questions are purely aesthetic. Analysis of literature in the digital age, and certainly analysis of electronic literature, must include examination not only of specific delivery technologies but also of institutional and infrastructural technologies that support the production, dissemination, and reception of literature.

Comparative literary critics are trained to read across and between, to seek out and explore the connections that configure meaning. These skills are ever more important in our networked age, when we need to harness the power of comparative approaches to examine the specificities of medial ecologies – the technological configurations, governmental policies, programming protocols, corporate confederations, and cultural norms – that support the production and dissemination of literary texts. We just have to learn to shift our comparative gaze to consider text as media. A focus on electronic literature supports this perspectival and paradigmatic shift. Digital literature is comparison literature that compels comparative literature to reconsider what counts as comparison and translation – indeed, what counts as literature and literary criticism in a digital age.

Notes

1 Walkowitz describes Coetzee's novel *Diary of a Bad Year* (2007) as comparison literature: "It fits this rubric because of its circulation, to be sure, but also because of its production: formally, the text experiments with comparative structures such as lists and catalogues; typographically, it invokes historical practices of translation that emphasize comparison between source and target; and thematically, it reflects on gestures of ethical, national, and generic comparison" (567).

2 "I Work for the Web" was a Netprov performance that played out over Twitter in April 2015. It was created by Mark C. Marino and Rob Wittig and is archived at <http://robwit.net/iwfw/>. "Twistori," an experiment by Amy Hoy and Thomas Fuchs, is available at <http://twistori.com/>.

3 The "public art installations" that Raley addresses "are *interactive* (remote and on-site participants are invited to contribute an SMS message of their own to the data feed); *sited* (they cannot but engage the specificities of each place and, by extension, prompt a consideration of what is 'public' and what is 'private'); and *social* (participants are continually negotiating their relationship to the audience, crowd, and readerly communities that are themselves continually mutating)" (6).

Works cited

Bogost, Ian, and Nick Monfort, eds. *Platform Studies* series. Cambridge, MA: MIT Press. Web. 21 Jan. 2016. http://platformstudies.com.

Hayles, N. Katherine. "Print Is Flat, Code Is Deep: The Importance of Media-Specific Analysis." *Poetics Today* 25 (2004): 67–90. Print.

———. *Writing Machines*. Cambridge, MA: MIT Press, 2002. Print.

Hayles, N. Katherine, and Jessica Pressman. "Making, Critique: A Media Framework." *Comparative Textual Media: Transforming the Humanities in the Postprint Era*. Ed. N. Katherine Hayles and Jessica Pressman. Minneapolis: U of Minnesota P, 2013. vii–xxxiii. Print.

Hoy, Amy, and Thomas Fuchs. "Twistori." 2008. Web. 10 June 2014. http://twistori.com/

Huhtamo, Erkki, and Jussi Parikka, eds. *Media Archaeology: Approaches, Applications, and Implications.* Berkeley: U of California P, 2011. Print.

Johnston, Jhave David. "Sooth." 2005. Web. 30 Jan. 2016. http://collection.elitera ture.org/2/works/johnston_sooth.html.

Loyer, Erik. *Chroma.* 2001. Web. 30 Jan. 2016. http://collection.eliterature.org/2/works/loyer_chroma.html

Manovich, Lev. "Cultural Analytics." *Software Studies Initiative.* Web. 10 June 2014. http://lab.softwarestudies.com/p/cultural-analytics.html

Marino, Mark C. "Critical Code Studies." *Electronic Book Review* 4 Dec. 2006. Web. 10 June 2014.

Marino, Mark C., and Rob Wittig. "I Work for the Web." April 2015. Web. 5 Feb. 2016. http://robwit.net/iwfw/

Mitchell, W.J.T. *Picture Theory: Essays on Verbal and Visual Representation.* Chicago: U of Chicago P, 1994. Print.

Poundstone, William. *Project for Tachistoscope [Bottomless Pit].* 2005. Web. 30 Jan. 2016. http://collection.eliterature.org/1/works/poundstone__project_for_tachisto scope_bottomless_pit.html

Pressman, Jessica. *Digital Modernism: Making It New in New Media.* New York: Oxford UP, 2014. Print.

———. "Reading the Code between the Words." *Dichtung-Digital* 37 (2007). Web. 10 June 2014.

Radhakrishnan, R. "Why Compare?" *New Literary History* 40 (2009): 453–71. Print.

Raley, Rita. "TXTual Practice." *Comparative Textual Media: Transforming the Humanities in the Postprint Era.* Ed. N. Katherine Hayles and Jessica Pressman. Minneapolis: U of Minnesota P, 2013. 5–32. Print.

Richards, I.A. 1924. *Principles of Literary Criticism.* New York: Routledge, 2001. Print.

Walkowitz, Rebecca. "Close Reading in the Age of Global Writing." *Modern Language Quarterly* 74 (2013): 171–95. Print.

———. "Comparison Literature." *New Literary History* 40 (2009): 567–82. Print.

Young-hae Chang Heavy Industries. *Nippon.* 2002. Web. 30 Jan. 2016. http://www.yhchang.com/NIPPON.html

Zuern, John. "Figures in the Interface: Comparative Methods in the Study of Digital Literature." *Dichtung-Digital.* Web. 10 June 2014.

Visual-quantitative approaches to the intellectual history of the field

A close reading

Dennis Tenen

In the Hebrew Bible, an angel of the Lord appeared to Gideon, who was thresh-ing wheat, to enlist the young man into service delivering Israel from Midianite bondage. Gideon proved to be a reluctant warrior. "How can I save Israel?" he asked; "my clan is weakest in Manasseh, and I am the least in my father's house" (Judges 6:11). Gideon wanted to believe, but he needed to see a tangible sign. The angel lit his offering of meat and bread on fire in evidence of his powers. The miracle convinced Gideon to start the subversive work of destroying the altars of Baal, though his people did not yet believe.

The problem of belief is a persistent thread in the Pentateuch, whose characters must, on several occasions, distinguish between true miracles and mere trickery. The pharaoh, for example, was not impressed with Arron's show of divine favor when the latter turned his rod into a serpent. Pharaoh's own magicians worked similar miracles without divine intervention, by sleight of hand (Exodus 7:8). Gideon's fire could have been faked as well. On the evening of the battle with the Midianites, Gideon therefore asked for another miracle. "I shall put a fleece of wool on the threshing floor," he said. If, by morning, the dew collects on the fleece only and "it is dry on all the ground, then I shall know that You will save Israel by my hand, as You have said" (Judges 6:37). By morning the dew collected on the fleece alone, just as he had asked. One would think this would conclude the ordeal, yet Gideon needed more evidence. "Let not thy anger burn against me," he spoke. "Let me make this trial only this once with the fleece; pray, let it be dry only on the fleece, and on all the ground let there be dew" (Judges 6:33). His request was fulfilled again; Gideon's men went on to scatter the Midianite armies.

Why weren't Gideon and his people satisfied with the first miracle of the fleece? Once, in a conversation about game theory and market design, Alvin E. Roth, the Nobel laureate economist from Harvard Business School, suggested that this was the birth of the experimental method. For all Gideon knew, the dew *always* collected on the fleece. A point of comparison was needed to spot the difference between fraud and miracle. The move to repeat an experiment in order to isolate meaningful results from natural contingencies lies at the roots of the scientific method and also at the roots of the comparative method in literary studies. To paraphrase Saussure after Derrida: meaning makes sense only in difference. Rep-etition is needed to make difference visible.

Digital displacement

I came to comparative literature and to "theory" during my undergraduate years in the 1990s, fleeing the arid quantitative analytics of political science, my home department at the time. There was something joyful and subversive in discovering the work of Gayatri Spivak and Edward Said, in reading Fanon, Bataille, Benjamin, Bakhtin, Cixous, de Beauvoir, Sontag, Zizek, and many others, all spoken of in hushed tones among coconspirators. This was a discipline for refugees, displaced geographically and in thought, theorizing displacement. Years later, around the time of the last ACLA report, Terry Eagleton could meaningfully write about the time "after theory," what Richard Rorty would call "the ebbing tide," and Spivak, simply, "the death of the discipline" (Eagleton; Rorty; Spivak). The end made sense, for the displaced cannot long stay domesticated. To retain their identity, they must by definition abandon their cozy mental abodes, even those of their own making. We could name this necessity to move on "negation" along with Sartre, or call it "the poetics of estrangement" along with Svetlana Boym and Victor Shklovsky (Boym). That move sideways (again Boym), into the continuing retreat from "positivist" structures of knowledge formation, defines the methodological dynamics of the discipline. The retreat is both cause and effect of a perpetual crisis affecting literary studies broadly, felt more acutely at its intellectual origins in comparative literature.

The trajectory of the digital humanities becomes more meaningful in the context of these broader dynamics. Stylistically, the digital humanities can be understood as a response to some of the earlier excesses of high theory (Brooks; Radhakrishnan). The field therefore appeals to earlier, more empirically minded traditions of literary study, like formalism, structuralism, sociology of literature, and textual criticism. The rich variety of practices embodied in the digital humanities cannot be reduced to mere quantification. They are above all a pragmatic and materialist response to the perceived idealism of a speculative disciple. Neither "digital" nor "humanities" does justice to the transformative program of the project. The dialectical pendulum swings from thinking to doing and from theory to method – and not at all from analog to digital, as the label would suggest. It makes sense, then, to observe the concomitantly emerging emphasis on the material contexts of knowledge production more generally: on labs and maker spaces; on the history and future of the book; on artifactual knowledge and knowledge design; on microanalysis, forensic reading, and the reverse engineering of literary devices; on the global inequities of access to information; on free and open culture; on the praxes of sharing and trans-mediation; and on the labor conditions at the base of our intellectual life. Viewed in this light, the digital humanities are more than digital: they entail a robust engagement with the material world, supplementing thinking with doing. The field is evolutionary rather than revolutionary, in that it draws on extant practices long part of the humanities – among them critical edition making, museum conservation, librarianship, graphic design, creative computing, experimental art and philosophy, exploratory data analysis, and historical reconstruction.

Signs of the fleece

What defines an intellectual field? In Gideon's experiment, it was the fleece that made observation possible. The ground appeared undifferentiated otherwise. By unfurling the fleece on the ground, Gideon delimited a domain of topographic exclusion where purposeful activity could become extinct from natural forces. The dew had to collect here and not there – inside and not outside of the skin boundary. The second exclusion is temporal. Divine intervention was not at all necessary on that first night. Gideon merely needed to make a "reading" – any reading – against which subsequent observations could become meaningful.

For the purpose of this essay, I represent the field of comparative literature narrowly, as a list of citations extracted from a complete corpus of 8,614 articles in *Comparative Literature* between 2004 and 2014. Using Python and Sci2, I normalized the citations to unique author names and article titles in order to produce a table of relationships representing the citation network (Sci2 Team). Formally, the network is composed of "nodes" and "edges." A node represents a single text that either appears in the corpus directly (published in *Comparative Literature*) or is merely referenced in the journal (published elsewhere). An edge represents a connection between two texts through citation. Consider the case of a hypothetical article X on Shakespeare's *Hamlet* citing the play itself and other relevant scholarship (let's say by Harold Bloom and Stephen Greenblatt) that was not published in *Comparative Literature*. In this example, three edges would be drawn to connect the original article X and *Hamlet*, X and Greenblatt's paper, and X and Bloom's. Since we include only the bibliographic data culled from *Comparative Literature*, sources "secondary" to the original article can connect to each other only through other articles native to the corpus. We cannot tell, for example, whether Greenblatt cites Bloom by looking at this network, because neither text was published in the journal. Through this procedure, native sources appear as constellations of references. Frequently cited sources appear larger and darker on the resulting map (Figure 11).

Despite the apparent quantification, network analysis is more of an art than a science. Initially, the network loads as an undifferentiated mass of nodes and edges (Figure 12). In subsequent processing, I differentiate the topography using several layout algorithms. To derive Figure 11 from Figure 12 I used Force Atlas 2, which is a physics-based layout, particularly suited to exploratory data analysis (Tukey; Mathieu). Force Atlas treats nodes as particles that repel each other, where edges act as springs that bring their nodes closer together. In a sense, we are "laying bare" the device implicit in the "field" metaphor, by treating each text as an object in space. The text-objects influence each other through physical force. Influence, in this sense, is defined by having many connections or edges, each pulling a popular text closer to other texts in the cluster. In this way, influential texts usually settle in the center of the field. They are "central to the field" by the virtue of being cited often. Papers that do not cite other materials in the corpus and those papers that are not themselves well cited "float" toward the

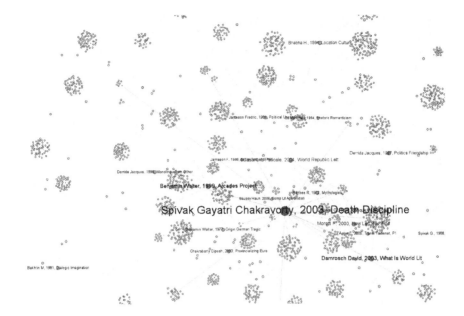

Figure 11 Citation network detail, *Comparative Literature* 2004–2014.
https://stateofthediscipline.acla.org/sites/default/files/images/figure1.jpg

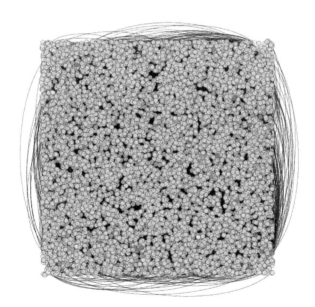

Figure 12 Citation network before clustering. *Comparative Literature* 2004–2014.

periphery. The model mimics some of the intuitions that accompany our understanding of field formation.

There are a few caveats, however. The algorithm strives toward stability in a
stochastic way. That means no two visualizations of the same network will ever
be the same. Each time I run the algorithm, Spivak's *Death of a Discipline* ends
up in a slightly different location, although similarly central. The X and Y axes
are, in other words, meaningless. The network model creates a descriptive but
arbitrary topography. Moreover, Gephi, the software used to produce these lay-
outs, exposes a number of interfaces through which I am able to "fine-tune" the
physical properties of that universe (Bastian, Heymann, and Jacomy). This has
the potential to suggest wildly differing interpretations from the same data set.
I could, for example, increase the attractive force exerted by the edges through
citation to create tighter groupings, or increase the repelling force between nodes
to make the peripheral texts float farther from the center. The visualization belies
a mathematical model, a metaphor, which should not be confused for the thing
it is meant to represent. The graphic is subject to the usual pitfalls of interpretation: it is at once overdetermined and necessarily reductive; it leads to an excess
of signification.

The reader must be particularly careful in extending the initial metaphor (fields,
constellations, peripheries) uncritically. We began with just a few simple building
blocks: nodes and edges. The complexity of the results compels us to make infer-
ences not supported by our original assumptions. For example, it is tempting
to say that the physical distance between any two nodes in our graph represents
some notion of "intellectual affinity." Yet, distance between nodes in these dia-
grams is both nondeterministic and arbitrary. A different clustering algorithm
could be used to bring any two given nodes closer together or farther apart, if
only in appearance. Much more work, quantitative and qualitative, would need
to be done to formalize and to interpret our preliminary intuitions about "intellectual affinity."

Clusters emerge as the system begins to stabilize during layout. The combined forces of attraction pull the strongly connected, frequently cited papers
toward the center of the map. Weakly connected, rarely cited papers appear
at the edges of the graphic (Figure 13). In exploring the resulting maps,
I assume, uncritically for now, that it is good to be cited. The discipline is, in
many ways, defined by a shared archive of texts and references. Authors likely
want to find themselves at the center of this graph. From these initial remarks
I intuit that connectivity in general is a common good. It is hard to imagine
an intellectual field of isolates. For example, the sparsest network would consist of papers collected at random from disparate disciplines. What are these
isolates, then, toward the edge of the graph? They could be papers on new or
esoteric themes, just entering or on the way out of the field. Alternatively, the
isolates could represent papers written by guest authors from other fields, or
just papers that, for some reason, do not share any common references with
the rest of the network. To evaluate these conjectures, we would need to contextualize isolates on a case-by-case basis, moving from distant to close reading
levels of analysis.

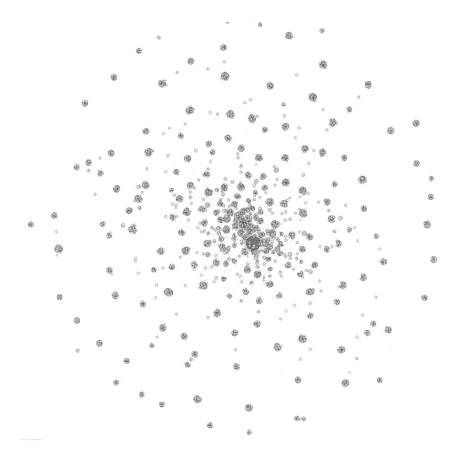

Figure 13 Center-periphery relations within the network, *Comparative Literature* 2004–2014.

https://stateofthediscipline.acla.org/sites/default/files/images/figure3.jpg

What holds a field together? Another exploratory observation confirms that, in this domain, sources rarely connect to each other directly. Rather, source articles are held together by what I would like to call the *connective tissue* of "tertiary" nodes, which, in effect, make up the shared disciplinary canon. A tertiary node bridges two documents that would otherwise drift apart under the physical conditions of our model. Reducing the map to document titles only, while bringing the most connected nodes to the front, helps us isolate the results (Figure 14). The reader will no doubt recognize Benjamin's *Arcades Project*, Derrida's "Politics of Friendship," David Damrosch's *What Is World Literature?*, Pascale Casanova's *World Republic of Letters*, Franco Moretti's *Graphs, Maps, and Trees*, and Gayatri Spivak's *Death of a Discipline* among the titles.

In Figure 15, drawn from papers appearing in the first ten years of the journal's history (1975 to 1985), the situation differs dramatically. The connective tissue

Figure 14 Network map, isolating the connective tissue, *Comparative Literature* 2004–2014.

https://stateofthediscipline.acla.org/sites/default/files/images/figure4.jpg

Figure 15 Tertiary nodes, *Comparative Literature* 1975–1985.

https://stateofthediscipline.acla.org/sites/default/files/images/figure5.jpg

reflects a domain held together by primary materials: works like Aristotle's *Poetics*, Homer's *Iliad*, Milton's *Paradise Lost*, Vergil's *Aeneid* and *Georgics*, Augustine's *Confessions*, and Ovid's *Metamorphosis*. In the intervening forty years of the journal's existence, the shared literary canon has undergone a substantive change of shared reference frameworks from "great books" to theory and related meta-discourse reflecting on the state of the discipline. As a whole, the earlier network is also more weakly connected. In traversing the nodes, we encounter more isolates, papers that do not share sources with any other documents in the corpus.

Despite the increase in connectivity over time, my initial findings suggest that the domain of comparative literature is connected (internally) more weakly and perhaps in fundamentally different ways than other fields, such as sociology, anthropology, history, or economics. Unlike many of the journals examined in my forthcoming study on the growth and decay of shared knowledge, *Comparative Literature* exhibits monolithic clustering around a single set of common texts, while in other disciplines we often observe multiple well-defined clusters. For example, the domain of economics bifurcates neatly into micro and macro camps (Figure 16). What do these findings mean normatively? Should we strive for more connectivity and for more pronounced, diverse clusters? Should we rely less on a narrow canon of theoretical texts? It seems reasonable to suggest that connectivity is a common good, that researchers should read and quote each other, and that they should, even in disagreement, share a set of theoretical or methodological assumptions. These postulates are open to further contention, particularly as our object of study, literature, expands globally, growing more decentralized in the process (Apter; Brouillette; Damrosch and Spivak; Mignolo).

The principles of knowledge domain analysis encourage us to place quantitative insights in their social, historical, and economic contexts (Birger and Albrechtsen). Citation networks form on the surface of a deeper culture. They are symptoms of the ways we teach, train, and communicate in our universities, departments, and professional societies. The way of comparative literature, like Gideon's early experimentalism, has always been to advance by the axes of contrast and correlation,

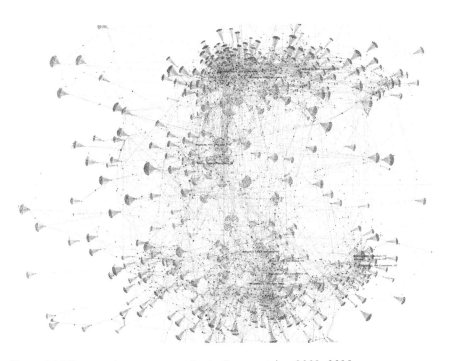

Figure 16 Micro- and macroeconomics in *Econometrica*, 2001–2011.

period and geography. The digital humanities offer yet another axis that bisects familiar concepts – in the case of this essay, ideas of canonization, center-periphery relationship, marginality, and reading – along a methodological divide. At their worst, visual-quantitative methodologies devolve into shallow futurism and blunt instrumental reasoning. At its best, the digital humanities are a force of iconoclasm, used to question and to refine the prevailing orthodoxy.

Works cited

Apter, Emily S. *Against World Literature: On the Politics of Untranslatability.* London: Verso, 2013. Print.

Bastian M., S. Heymann, and M. Jacomy. "Gephi: An Open Source Software for Exploring and Manipulating Networks." International AAAI Conference on Weblogs and Social Media, 2009. Presentation.

Boym, Svetlana. "Poetics and Politics of Estrangement: Victor Shklovsky and Hannah Arendt." *Poetics Today* 26.4 (2005): 581–611. Print.

Brooks, Peter. "Aesthetics and Ideology: What Happened to Poetics?" *Critical Inquiry* 20.3 (1994): 509–23. Print.

Brouillette, Sarah. *Postcolonial Writers in the Global Literary Marketplace.* New York: Palgrave Macmillan, 2007. Print.

Coogan, Michael David. *The Old Testament: A Historical and Literary Introduction to the Hebrew Scriptures.* New York: Oxford University Press, 2006: 217–18. Print.

Damrosch, David, and Gayatri Chakravorty Spivak. "Comparative Literature/World Literature: A Discussion with Gayatri Chakravorty Spivak and David Damrosch." *Comparative Literature Studies* 48.4 (2011): 455–85. JSTOR. Web. 9 Aug. 2014.

Eagleton, Terry. *After Theory.* New York: Basic Books, 2003. Print.

Hjørland, Birger, and Hanne Albrechtsen. "Toward a New Horizon in Information Science: Domain-Analysis." *Journal of the American Society for Information Science* 46 (1995): 400–25. Print.

Mignolo, Walter D. "Canons a(nd)Cross-Cultural Boundaries (Or, Whose Canon Are We Talking About?)." *Poetics Today* 12.1 (1991): 1–28. JSTOR. Web. 9 Aug. 2014.

Radhakrishnan, R. *Theory in an Uneven World.* Malden, MA: Blackwell, 2003. Print.

Rorty, Richard. "Looking Back at 'Literary Theory.'" *Comparative Literature in an Age of Globalization.* Ed. Haun Saussy. Baltimore: Johns Hopkins UP, 2006: 63–7. Print.

Sci2 Team. *Science of Science (Sci2) Tool.* Bloomington: Indiana University and SciTech Strategies, 2009. Web. 9 Aug. 2014.

Spivak, Gayatri Chakravorty. *Death of a Discipline.* New York: Columbia UP, 2003. Print.

Tukey, John W. *Exploratory Data Analysis.* Reading, MA: Addison-Wesley, 1977. Print.

Big data

Jonathan E. Abel

Some concepts are bigger than a single historical moment, returning cyclically with renewed force. One such idea has resurfaced at several points in modern world history with renewed urgency each time it appears, usually under different names. This concept rose to importance in the 1830s in Ghent, returned in the 1900s in Berlin, in the 1930s at the University of Vienna, again in the 1940s in Brooklyn, and then in the 1970s in Tokyo.[1] Whether under the guise of social physics, anthropometry, knowledge economy, information revolution, or biometrics, each time the quantification of the human has appeared, it has been rebranded as new; each time it purported to make predictions about the future based on analysis of present data; and each time it spoke more about the recent past than the future. Reappearing in the digital world of the 2000s, the concept, now coded as "big data," is associated with broader, deeper, and faster computer-aided information collection and analysis; the contemporary, trendy academic corollary of the industrial and political use of mass databases goes under the name "digital humanities."

Two books that are part of this history of interest in quantification and prediction may help us to contextualize and understand our current fetishes for big data and the digital humanities (without making any suggestions that we can extrapolate where they may lead in the future).

The first is a book of what I will call speculative fiction, though it is more usually classified as social science. Published in Japanese as *Jōhō kezaigaku* (literally "Information Economics," though translated as *The Information Society*) in 1976 by Masuda Yoneji, the book is neither simple economic analysis of a current social phenomenon nor a specific proposal for near-future policies reacting to the contemporary socioeconomic distribution of information. Rather, it ventures into the world of long-term sociological prediction and, therefore, into the realm of science fiction. Despite all the book turns out to have predicted correctly (e.g., computer penetration into private homes and violations of privacy), to truly understand this work of near future fiction pitched as social science, I think it helps to consider it along with some truths from a work about social science which was sold as science fiction – and here, I refer to an earlier book, Isaac Asimov's *Foundation*.

Published beginning in May 1942, the stories of Asimov's *Foundation* series are based on the premise that future history is predictable through a new science called "psychohistory" developed by the Shaman-trickster, mathematical genius Hari Seldon. The depiction of Seldon's successful predictions based on massive data sets is an allegory for prevalent utopian attitudes toward big data today. But we might also learn a lesson from psychohistory about our future "deep time" from Seldon's inversion in the character of Salvor Hardin, the shrewd, manipulating neocon who, though knowing quite well the power and truth of Seldon's science, also understands how part of its power lies in glossing it as religion for the masses who will never understand it. Hardin teaches the reader that mysticism, fictionality, and the malleability of future history through the minor and unpredictable actions of individuals are integral to the proper functioning of the larger scientific, predictable grand system.

We might read both of these books as warnings about our contemporary interest in big data. Our fetish too often denies the importance of individual or random possibilities in favor of tendencies. When we consider recent big-data processing mistakes, the risks of this approach (ignoring the individual, the outlier, or the random) appear today everywhere from 1990s banking decisions about bundling risk to the Japanese government and industry's decisions, in the 1960s, to build nuclear plants in historical tsunami paths. From health care to border security, risk management structures continually gamble our rights to privacy and individuality on probabilistic logic without regard for the disasters that lie waiting in the random or "statistically insignificant" probabilities. These are the probabilities for which the humanities were developed. Without ever forgetting the positive importance of counting, we need also to remain vigilant about our pursuits of the uncountable, unpredictable, immeasurable, sublime, and unaccountable. What this means for comparative literature is that the digital humanities may offer useful tools or means (on the same order as such traditional humanist tools as bookmarks, indexes, footnotes, underlinings, notecards) but will never rise to the point of becoming the only means – or, worse yet, the ends – of our inquiries. The recent flurry and fetish for digital humanities are but part of a long history of quantitative, positivistic humanist inquiry which supplements, but cannot supplant, the quests for information, knowledge, and truth which have formed and will continue to form the humanities.

Note

1 For Ghent, see Quetelet. For Berlin, see the historical legacy of Heinrich Braun's journal *Archiv für soziale Gesetzgebung und Statistik*. For the University of Vienna, see Machlup, *Börsenkredit*, *The Stock Market*, and *The Production and Distribution of Knowledge*. For Brooklyn, see Asimov, "Foundation" and *Foundation*. For Tokyo, see Masuda, *Jōhōka shakai no yukue*; *Jōhō-keizaigaku*; and *The Information Society*.

Works cited

Asimov, Isaac. "Foundation." *Astounding Science-Fiction* 29.3 (May 1942). 38–52. Print.

————. *Foundation.* New York: Gnome Press, 1951. Print.

Machlup, Fritz. *Börsenkredit, Industriekredit und Kapitalbildung: Beiträge zur Konjunkturforschung.* Ed. Österreichisches Institut für Konjunkturforschung. Vienna: Springer, 1931. Print.

————. *The Production and Distribution of Knowledge in the United States.* Princeton: Princeton UP, 1962. Print.

————. *The Stock Market, Credit and Capital Formation.* Trans. Vera C. Smith. London: Hodge, 1940. Print.

Masuda, Yoneji, Seiichiro Yahagi, and Shirō Shimaya. *The Information Society: As Post-Industrial Society.* Tokyo: Institute for the Information Society, 1980. Print.

————. *Jōhōka shakai no yukue: Sore wa nani o motarasu ka?* Tokyo: Nihon Keizai Shinbunsha, 1972. Print.

————. *Jōhō-keizaigaku.* Tokyo: Sangyō Nōritsu Tankidaigaku Shuppan-bu, 1976. Print.

Quetelet, Adolphe. *Sur l'homme et le développement de ses facultés, ou, Essai de physique sociale.* Brussels: Hauman, 1836. Print.

————. *A Treatise on Man and the Development of His Faculties.* Edinburgh: W. and R. Chambers, 1842. Print.

Next

The new orality

Charlotte Eubanks

Rather than discuss one of the big ideas of the last ten years, I would like to discuss what I hope will be one of the big ideas of the next ten: something we might call a "new orality."

First, a dirge for the old orality, itself a big idea of the 1980s (Ong; Goody), which erected a barrier between the spoken and the written by asserting that they belonged to separate ontologies, exclusive methodologies, and different disciplines. The introduction of writing, in this perspective, enforced global, fundamental cognitive changes to human society. That idea has exhausted itself. As Erik Mueggler notes, "the category of writing tends to dissolve internally when specific graphic practices are examined in their social context," and as a result, the scholarly conversation has "moved away from looking for cognitive implications for literacy in general to understanding how particular practices of writing and reading are implicated in social relations, especially relations of power" (20). While the notion of orality as a separate world from literacy has run its course, the structural legacies of that discourse remain in effect, so that orality typically finds its institutional home in the social sciences as traditions threatened by globalization (World Oral Literature Project), in history and communications as the underside of book history (SHARP), or in performance studies as an embodied practice enabling memory and identity production (HEMI).

But what I want to see is an investment in orality as a literary territory: researchers in departments of literature formally and concertedly grappling with those aspects and instances of the textual which are not (or not only, or not primarily) based on writing (in the restricted sense of orthographical marks on paper). Let's free ourselves of the etymological constraint that limits "literature" to the "letter," and embrace a fuller sense of textuality or "writing" (if we still want to call it that) as any act "that encodes information in order to stimulate the memory to store or retrieve information" (Carruthers 8). Let's decouple "literature" broadly conceived from a narrow conception of "literacy" which presumes modes of production based on writing-as-marks-on-paper and modes of consumption based on reading.

A new orality would overlap with current notions of "everyday literature" that are concerned largely with digital production (Tweets, YouTube threads, and so on) and would interrogate genres often judged liminal or orthogonal to literature proper: song lyrics, for instance, slam poetry (Nuyorican Poets Café), court testimony, witnessing, group recitation of religious texts (Rasmussen), extemporized taunts and traded insults, or political speechmaking. But rather than theorize the grain of voice in lapsarian terms as "secondary orality" and digital mediation, the new orality would highlight the deep history of the musical lyrics of song and of slam, acknowledging the forgotten musicality of core literary forms like the epic, the classical lyric, the waka, the fu, the saj', the praise song. Applying insights from postcolonial critique, new orality research would investigate the potentials of cyberature as a bridge between literature and orature (Ngũgĩ).

Theories of new orality would investigate the interstices of literature and sound (Kivy), not only obvious genres, such as opera or griot performance, but also the hidden musicality that permeates the literary: a vigorous return to, and rigorous theorization of, classical notions of text as woven from sound and gesture as much as from the visual "marks" of writing narrowly conceived (see, e.g., Rambelli's discussion of the philosophy of the eighth-century monk Kūkai). Bringing phonotextual elements to the fore (Stewart) provides one method of exploring the melismatic complexity of recitation, whether it be the contemporary poetry of Mahmoud Darwish or the prosody of the Qur'an (Ware). Attending closely to musical terms also promises to shed new light on translation studies, opening a window, for instance, onto techniques for moving Buddhist texts between Asian languages (Markham).

Finally, the new orality of the next decade would build on the energies of material textual studies, which have come to take a deep interest in the grain of the paper, the set of the type, the layout of the page. But it would also recognize another material matrix, the human form, investigating the ways in which oral literature is written in and by the body. In attending to both the bodies and the pages of literature, the new orality will ask us to articulate a pedagogical challenge to colonial legacies, in which institutional attempts to conquer illiteracy are often attacks on orality and on modes of oral fluency.

Works cited

Carruthers, Mary. *The Book of Memory: A Study of Memory in Medieval Culture*. Cambridge: Cambridge UP, 1990. Print.

Goody, Jack. *The Interface between the Written and the Oral*. New York: Cambridge UP, 1987. Print.

———. *The Logic of Writing and the Organization of Society*. New York: Cambridge UP, 1986. Print.

HEMI: Hemispheric Institute for Performance and Politics. Web. 21 May 2014. http://hemisphericinstitute.org/hemi/

Kivy, Peter. *The Performance of Reading: An Essay in the Philosophy of Literature*. Oxford: Wiley-Blackwell, 2009. Print.

Markham, Elizabeth. "Medieval Chinese Hymns in Japanese Buddhist Liturgy: Structure and Ornament." *Medieval Sacred Chant: From Japan to Portugal/Canto sacro medieval: do Japão a Portugal*. Ed. Manuel P. Ferreira. Lisbon: Edições Colibri, 2008. 11–44. Print.

Mueggler, Erik. "Corpse, Stone, Door, Text." *Journal of Asian Studies* 73 (2014): 17–41. Print.

Ngũgĩ wa Thiong'o. *Globalectics: Theory and the Politics of Knowing.* New York: U of Columbia P, 2012. Print.

Nuyorican Poets Café. Web. 5 Sep. 2014. http://www.nuyorican.org

Ong, Walter. *Orality and Literacy: The Technologizing of the Word.* London: Methuen, 1982. Print.

Rambelli, Fabio. *Buddhist Materiality: A Cultural History of Objects in Japanese Buddhism.* Stanford: Stanford UP, 2007. Print.

Rasmussen, Anne. *Women, the Recited Qur'an and Islamic Music in Indonesia.* Berkeley: U of California P, 2010. Print.

SHARP: The Society for the History of Authorship, Reading and Publishing. Web. 21 May 2014. http://www.sharpweb.org/

Stewart, Garrett. *Reading Voices: Literature and the Phonotext.* Berkeley: U of California P, 1990. Print.

Ware III, Rudolph T. *The Walking Qur'an: Islamic Education, Embodied Knowledge, and History in West Africa.* Chapel Hill, NC: The U of North Carolina P, 2014. Print.

World Oral Literature Project. Web. 21 May 2014. http://www.oralliterature.org/

Comparative literature and computational criticism
A conversation with Franco Moretti

Ursula K. Heise

Digital humanities

HEISE: Comparative literature is a field that is enormously diverse but also sometimes hard to pin down in its core concerns. In thinking about the last ten
years, what to you have been crucial developments and new paradigms that
have emerged in literary studies?

MORETTI: This is biographical, to a large extent: the last ten years for me have
been dominated intellectually by my involvement in digital environments,
computational criticism – call it as you wish: big digital databases and not
only quantitative but also algorithmic ways of dealing with them. Now, since
I've been one of the people who have pushed in this direction, it's not for me
to say whether it's an interesting direction or not. It has had, in my opinion,
an enormous and unfortunate consequence for comparative literature, which
is that digital humanities has basically developed within literary studies focusing almost exclusively on English corpora, English in America.

So you have the completely paradoxical coexistence of a very new – some
people might even say revolutionary – tool, and an enormous provincialism
in its field of application. Not because people involved in the field want it to
be this way, but because most problems need a consistent language to be able
to do text-lining, parsing, and so on (leaving aside the fact that the construction of digital libraries proceeds unevenly in various countries). To me, this
has been a very strange development. I would not claim that digital humanities is a conceptual breakthrough. I think it's basically more of a development in terms of the archive and the tools than the concepts. It's very strong
in its archive and very strong on tools. Conceptually, it's a different story: if
anything, it's undertheorized.

But anyway, it is a major new development that has gone hand in hand
with a noncomparative corpus.

HEISE: What's the reason for that? Is it that if you want to do, say, topic modeling, it's just too tricky to rely on translations of Balzac or Stendhal?

MORETTI: No. You can rely on translation, and that's what we've done, in a
couple of cases. But the problem is when you start to zoom in. We've done
a study that's never been published, in which we looked at plays and found

what were the most distinctive words for the chorus and the messenger in Greek plays, two very distinct entities. And we came up with words but, of course, in English. Then you go to the Greek text, and you realize that English at times has a single word when Greek uses two or three different ones. And at that point, you have to ask, what is the solidity of these findings?

HEISE: It seems perfectly conceivable that you could carry out a particular kind of study with computational tools on a body of English texts, do a parallel study on Spanish texts, and then put the results together. But that doesn't seem to have happened. Is that because the archive of literary texts in Spanish that have been digitized is smaller, or because people in Spanish literature have not had an equal amount of interest in computational criticism? Or is it actually something that's currently being done?

MORETTI: I'm about to start a joint project with people in France that will include two parallel lines of digital research. The construction of each of the digital corpora happens in the country where the language is spoken. This poses problems of coordination of a higher nature, because this also means that usually it's different teams with different intellectual backgrounds.

HEISE: Concepts of translation studies and translation theory might then come back in new ways, once you start to compare the findings of studies that have been done on corpora in two different languages. That could potentially be really interesting, and it could give a new twist to an old field within comparative literature, translation studies.

So I'm a little surprised that you see computational criticism as unfortunate for comparative literature. Starting from "Conjectures on World Literature," one of the interesting things that keeps coming up in your work on the history of the novel *is* a comparatist payoff: the European case turns out to be less normative when you look at it in a world literature context. So one result of looking at the novel in terms of distant reading and computational criticism has been enormously important for comparative literature. In Dipesh Chakrabarty's words, it's "provincializing Europe" – Europe is historically the first case, but it's not the typical case for the genre, right?

MORETTI: Yes, it's true. But still, you now have this new field of digital humanities in the United States, and within literature, I would say 95 percent of the work on digital humanities is on English and American things. It may be "provincialized" – but it's all that there is! I think it's a paradox. It's as if this new tool has given a lot of new energy to the field of national literatures: English here in the United States, French in France, Italian in Italy, and so on, which from the viewpoint of comparative literature is unfortunate. It would be interesting for the future to focus on this: How can comparative literature modify the state of the digital humanities? How can the digital humanities modify the state of comparative literature?

HEISE: In my own field of ecocriticism and environmental humanities, we've had a similar challenge. In ecocriticism, too, comparative literature was a latecomer – the field developed British and American approaches first and the global perspective later.

MORETTI: I assume that one of the things that has made possible the shift in the environmental humanities to this more global perspective is a focus on contemporary developments, both material and intellectual. In that respect, there's another problem that the digital humanities encounter, which is copyright. The construction of large corpora hits the resistance of copyright – seventy-five years after the death of the author, in the United States. People are finding ways to deal with this, but the political-economic constraint adds another very significant complication.

That's one reason for the extraordinary role that nineteenth-century literature has played in the digital humanities: simply because it's out of copyright and the print is usually in good enough condition for digital recognition, whereas eigtheenth-century texts are already more complicated (the long "s" that looks like an "f," all that stuff). But constraints can be interesting because they force you to think differently. On the other hand, they're constraints.

HEISE: But that might actually be a welcome counterweight to the pervasive presentism that you see in comparative literature. In some sense, digital humanities might actually be a good balance to the overwhelming focus on the twentieth century that defines some of the other new areas.

MORETTI: I completely agree with you. That's one of the main problems, I think. In order to reconceptualize comparative literature, every generation has to reimagine the relationship with the past because, in the end, the vast majority of forms and themes belongs to the past. Reflection on this has been scant, I think. I read the pilot essay by Beecroft on periods of world literature – that is the type of direction that I think should be taken. It's not the only direction, but that's clearly where too little work has been done.

Looking at the past also would mean measuring oneself against a great tradition of comparative scholarship, especially German – Auerbach, Curtius, Spitzer, and company. You can measure the new concepts and methods against them by engaging them on the field they dealt with, which was mostly European. Obviously, new approaches should not be as European-focused as they were, but they should find ways of coming to terms with that tradition.

HEISE: Do you think that work in computational criticism in the end leads to a different periodization than we usually use in literary studies?

MORETTI: Digital humanities has been a funny enterprise in that respect. I started working in it with the conviction that it would, indeed, change our historical knowledge. I think in terms of historical results, the gathering has been very poor so far, very slim. What digital humanities has done is rather that it's forced us, certainly me, to rethink some concepts of literary theory. You would have expected results in the field of history.

HEISE: What kinds of results did you expect?

MORETTI: At bottom, the paradigm behind digital humanities is the turn toward quantitative history in France in the 1940s. These historians were also the first ones to use computers in the humanities – the primitive kind, but nonetheless. In fact, I think Braudel, in his 1958 essay on the *longue durée*, says the historian of the future will be a programmer or nothing else, which is stunning.

The *Annales* work of Braudel and others, like Chaunu and Le Goff, immediately changed the historical landscape. It did so not just because it was quantitative history but also because it dealt with new types of historical objects: no longer legislation, political cabinets, and military campaigns, but the price of bread and demographic trends, and so forth. So it was the change of object combined with quantification that created the breakthrough, whereas in our case, there isn't really a change of object. We now can study, say, two hundred thousand novels instead of two hundred, but they're all novels (yes, in principle, we can also study newspapers and conversations overheard on the phone). But that was the naïve hope I had, that digital humanities would bring into the history of literature a change comparable to that of the *Annales*. That hasn't happened, but when you quantify, you have to define very precisely the entity you want to quantify, and that has forced us, sometimes at least, to look at the concepts we use with greater skepticism.

HEISE: But potentially, you could look at other objects like the lending libraries of the nineteenth century, at who borrowed what, as different kinds of data about literary history, right?

MORETTI: Who borrowed what – it's unfortunately very much a black hole in book history, but you could do that.

HEISE: Japanologists have done that. They have pretty good records for nineteenth-century borrowing from Japanese libraries.

MORETTI: Yes, Jonathan Zwicker's work. In principle, you can do it. But just as digital humanities has encouraged reprovincialization, so to speak, of literary study, it has also encouraged a "reliterarization." It's the euphoria of suddenly having thousands of texts – since you have such an expanded *literary* archive, the temptation to focus only on that is much stronger, at least in an initial period.

HEISE: Yes, but there is the other branch of digital humanities, which is not at all about literature, but is bringing methods of literary study to bear on digital objects. It's the mirror, I imagine, or the inverse of computational criticism – not bringing computational tools to literature but using methods of literary analysis for digital objects. I think in terms of its methods, it's not as new as computational criticism.

MORETTI: But in terms of its objects, it's much newer.

HEISE: You were saying earlier that you didn't think that the concepts that computational criticism is using are really new. You don't think that *scale* actually is a concept that people are thinking about in new and different ways?

MORETTI: Well, clearly, it's a concept that has come to the fore. I'm not sure that it is the practitioners of digital humanities who have brought this concept to the fore, necessarily. Scale: It can be temporal scale; it can be scale in the archive; it can also be the scale of the text. With sonnets, the problem doesn't really arise, but when you analyze a novel, exactly what are you analyzing? A few chosen sentences, a few chosen pages, the plot lines? There are different scales there that interplay. So it's a very important concept – or perhaps concepts – that occupies different territories.

Readers

HEISE: Do you think that question of scale could then also be extended to questions of readers? How do we actually do literary history not so much from the viewpoint of production, but of reception?

MORETTI: Maybe not yet right now, but in the future, the study of readers and literature, of readers and anything, will have to go through the neurosciences. There is this historical argument on reading, which was advanced by Rolf Engelsing, a German historian, on the shift at the close of the eighteenth century from what he called intensive to extensive. Intensive: there are very few texts taken very seriously. Extensive: a lot of texts taken more lightly. This is by no means accepted by everybody, but I actually think it makes a lot of sense when you consider how the vast majority of people had only one book at home and could read only that one book, which was the Bible, of course. But then you get not only novels but also newspapers, even more importantly.

In a project on that with a Stanford PhD student who was interested in fMRIs and reading, we obviously couldn't do an experiment that would establish whether there was this shift in the eighteenth century. But we were hoping to do an experiment which would tell us whether a reader could read the same text in both an intensive and an extensive way, and whether that would engage different regions of the brain. We immediately ran into the problem of how you can have extensive reading, which is relaxed reading, absent-minded, in a machine that makes this hammering noise.

That is a constraint that really can stop you, or it can stimulate further thinking. But in the future, as the machines become less noisy, it might be possible to read longer stretches of text and to follow brain activity with much greater accuracy. You can imagine that the neurosciences will become an invaluable ally of studies of reading.

HEISE: I can see that as one part of it, but I'm still surprised that you would point to that as the main approach. I would have thought that a sociological approach would be the first one because fMRI is also, among other things, fairly expensive. So you're only ever going to be able to examine very limited numbers of readers, whereas you could conceivably do a more quantitative version of the work that Janice Radway started doing with her research on the romance, using surveys and focus groups on reading.

MORETTI: I have done a little bit of that myself, circulating libraries and so on for the *Atlas of the European Novel*. I can speak only for myself: one deterrent is that it takes an enormous amount of work and time, and the results are not always very interesting. Academic life at every level, from students to professors, has been increasingly dominated by short-term results, grant writing. You need a longer horizon to embark on those projects. This may be one of the reasons why that hasn't happened. The fMRIs give you information about something we really know very little about. What you are saying is a completely different thing, and I think it actually has, or potentially may have, a digital development – market data and so on. And there are now ways of figuring out where people underline or emphasize annotating their digital texts. So you can have the same book read by ten thousand people: what do they comment on?

HEISE: So is there a role for crowdsourcing in computational criticism in the future?

MORETTI: There is, but there are two problems. One is that crowdsourcing can be either unremunerated or remunerated. When it's remunerated, it's very exploitative – people are paid very little. It is very hard to pay them a lot if you need thousands of readers, so I don't like to go that way. The other, unremunerated way works when people have a personal interest in something, but then you get a crowd of people who have a personal interest and a lot of time to spend declaring their interest. So it becomes a very strangely biased sample of readership, and that can lead to very odd conclusions. It would probably be easy to get people to annotate Jane Austen, for example, but they would be the Jane Austen fans. This would tell you a lot about a subset of the reading population, but potentially very little about Jane Austen. So you end up studying the sample *per se* rather than the sample as indicative of a larger volume of data.

HEISE: To get around that, one would have to really do a scientific sociological survey over the phone, interview two thousand people – none of whom might have read Jane Austen!

MORETTI: Which would be an interesting result in itself.

Models of literary history

HEISE: I'm really interested in your use of, on the one hand, a biological model to think about the evolution of literary forms, aesthetic forms perhaps more generally, and on the other hand, the Marxist emphasis on market forces. *The Bourgeois* refers to Lukács and the conception of the literary work as a resolution to some problem in the culture; how does that square with the market model? Is the assumption that the market picks out the things that provide the best resolutions to these underlying problems?

MORETTI: Yes.

HEISE: That seems to me not all that plausible because of the way in which the publishing industry selects certain works. Some marketing campaigns for certain books result in huge sales; others don't. So what the publishing industry picks out isn't always what readers pick out. But in cases where the two do square, is the underlying assumption that the market, between the publishing industry and the readers, does pick out the literary forms that provide the best answers to these underlying cultural questions? And is that then what propels the evolutionary model?

MORETTI: You're basically right – not so much the publishing industry, about which I have never done much work. For me, the market is mostly a shorthand for the large proportion of readers or buyers that determine the success of certain writers' forms. And, yes, basically my idea is that there are rival forms or rival versions of the same forms that get published more or less simultaneously, and then there are a large number of readers who decide that they would rather read Scott than Jane Porter when they want a historical novel. Because Scott's form provides a better resolution to certain contradictions? That's a big leap, of course, and at that point, you have to do the analysis and show what the supposed large contradiction is that the form addresses, and one has to prove why Scott's solution is liked better.

For me, anyway, the insistence on at least addressing the issue of what makes a form better has something to do with the fact that I didn't want to give simply an ideological answer. Scott is preferred because he's more conservative, which could also be the opposite: because he's more liberal. So for me, the ideological component is clearly always there, but there has to also be a place for the technical component in the choice – meaning how a book is written, how a plot is held together.

HEISE: How does that work across boundaries of language and nation? I'm thinking of the important role that, say, Seix Barral played in the Latin American boom, publishing novels that often could not yet be published in their original countries at the time and so playing a crucial role in bringing about the 1970s boom. Or the crucial role that Heinemann has played in bringing African literature to a European readership. I'm reducing the concept of "market forces" to the publishing industry for the moment. But then the next question is, why were these novels so popular with a European audience? So books that were written to address the cultural contradictions of one culture find themselves accidentally also addressing those of another?

MORETTI: Heinemann is a very good example. I was very struck by a study by an American sociologist, Wendy Griswold, who pointed out that the African novels published by Heinemann had overwhelmingly a village setting. The African novels published, say, in Nigeria had overwhelmingly an urban setting. Heinemann's books dealt with large mythical issues; the locally published ones were romance or crime fiction. In this sense, clearly the Heinemann series was solving the problem of how to perceive Africa for a Western audience, whereas the publishers in Nigeria were solving the problem of how to represent their country for the local audience. So this is a good case.

But in this case, you have really two separate series of books, whereas in the case of the Latin American boom it's the same series of books. And here, I really don't know. I can imagine why *One Hundred Years of Solitude* could be both extraordinarily successful in Latin America and in Western Europe for slightly different reasons. In Western Europe, magic realism acts as a sort of anesthetic vis-à-vis the guilt of imperialism, whereas in Latin America, it's a sense of liberation, of freedom. I suspect that maybe in the West, these novels were read more for the magic and in Latin America more for the realism. This has a certain conceptual elegance, though I'm not sure it's true!

But it is a perfectly good question that arises within comparative literature.

HEISE: It also arises with literary history. Why is it that texts that were written at a certain time get selected again or continuously later on? In comparative literature, how do we figure out what the different impulses or questions are that these texts respond to, and how do contemporary audiences hit back upon the solutions of the past? How do those get reselected from the archives of the past?

MORETTI: They're not reselected. They are selected once, and the archive is really never reopened. There have been some selective reopenings – women writers republished, for example. But by and large, the archive is thousands and tens of thousands and hundreds of thousands of texts – once you fall off the limelight, it's for good. For most texts, it's forever. So it's just inertia, but still, this doesn't answer the question, why does the inertia continue rather than stopping altogether with certain texts?

HEISE: Right. And it brings up another question with regard to that interface of the biological model and the market model. What role do changing media technologies play in that? One argument you could make about changing forms of the novel in the twentieth century is that in some ways, the novel had to recalibrate itself when film became dominant in the 1920s, and it had to recalibrate itself yet again when television became the dominant medium in the 1950s.

MORETTI: That is another case of competition of loosely comparable forms for the same attention span. People have two or three hours to devote to entertainment. Are they going to pick film, a TV series, a novel? It's not the competition between gothic novels and historical novels, but I would address it, more or less, with the same conceptual tool box. It seems to me to be a more complex case of the previous scenarios, competition among forms.

HEISE: One could argue that some of the more experimental forms of the postmodern novel certainly can be explained in terms of the novel really not being the main narrative medium anymore. That the more standard and perhaps more obviously ideologically inflected narratives get relayed in film and in television, and so the novel suddenly finds itself with its hands free, so to speak, able to do things for much more niche audiences but also having to reinvent itself, as one of its main functions has migrated to a different medium.

MORETTI: Which in a sense would be a second act of what happened to poetry already in the second half of the nineteenth century. Poetry became much more adventurous than the normal form, both in the nineteenth century and in the moment of high modernism. Why? Because it had its hands freer.

Geographies and genres

HEISE: In geographical terms, comparative literature has had a strong East-West axis, the Far East and Europe and North America. There's also been the transatlantic axis, and postcolonial work has functioned with a global North-global South axis. Comparative literature is now expanding into literatures that don't neatly fit into any of these – Eastern European and Arabic literatures, for example. In this expanded context, where do the theoretical paradigms for comparative literature come from? The question's been around since the 1990s. As the comparative literature canon of objects of study has expanded, one of the complaints was for a long time that the theoretical paradigms have nevertheless remained adamantly Western, and in fact European and Euro-American in a fairly narrow sense. In your research, where do the theoretical paradigms come from?

MORETTI: I've always been struck by the question, how do concepts change? They change if they're challenged, and I've always been struck by how timid, for instance, Sinologists are in challenging the normative idea of the novel from the West. That's a completely comparable tradition, and morphologically very different.

Now, in one study I've done of Chinese novels, I've tried to use some concepts elaborated by Sinologists, but in the absence of concepts that really challenge the way we study narrative, I will use the concepts I know – this is inevitable. But if a strong concept shows up, like magical realism, that was unthinkable in terms of Western categories, either you come up with a better concept or you have to use it. So this change has to happen. It has to happen in a polemical way.

You were mentioning earlier what doesn't fit neatly into North-South or East-West coordinates. I think that's important for two reasons. One is that one of the types of studies that comparative literature most needs is macroregional studies, in which Latin America has been successful. But, for instance, Arabic, Scandinavian, Eastern European are all regions that are supranational, and it would be important to have a much better sense of all these. It's not infinite, but there are several regions of this kind, sub-Saharan Africa and Central Asia maybe. This would be empirically very important; it has nothing to do, of course, with area studies.

The second is: what comparative literature still lacks, it seems to me, is an intellectual stage, an intellectual moment comparable to what happened in, say, historical sociology, with books like Perry Anderson's *Lineages of the Absolutist State* or Barrington Moore's *Social Origins of Dictatorship and Democracy*. What we need are studies, possibly on a world scale, that work with a matrix of concepts – say, play or drama or literature or narrative or lyric or whatever other categories one wants to use – and ask: what are the four or six main cultural, formal, political features that contribute to the making of, say, novels, and how do they change in different areas of the world and different eras? In this way, the analysis of various literatures, historical or geographical, is simultaneously a conceptual readjustment. It's really a systematic comparison rather than just a study of differences, which is the inevitable starting point. This is a way of making sense of differences by creating a unitary scheme for them. A unitary scheme doesn't have to come from the West. It has to be a model – I'm completely indifferent as to where it comes from.

This has happened extremely seldom in comparative literature, it seems to me. I know there are some moments like, for instance, in Auerbach's chapter on realism in *Mimesis*. It's all on French literature, and then he has a few pages in which he explains why he doesn't have German texts or English texts or Russian texts. That is a way of doing it. In that case, it's not really full-fledged comparison – it's sketched out. This kind of systematic comparison has happened too rarely.

HEISE: One issue in ecocriticism that I think is also a question for comparative literature is the nonliterary. There are plenty of novelists and poets who write on environmental issues between circa 1960 and the present. But when you look at the works that actually had social impact, they tend to be, in both literature and film, nonfiction: Rachel Carson's *Silent Spring* or Al Gore's *An Inconvenient Truth*, to pick two milestones. So whatever claims you might want to make about the power of literature to transform the cultural imagination, in reality it's the documentary mode that's proven more transformative. You've dealt with nonliterary texts in one of your new pieces, the Bankspeak one, where you analyze the reports of the World Bank. What do you think is the role of the nonliterary for comparative literature?

MORETTI: I think the nonliterary archives are going to be a really important test case for what we can contribute in terms of the analysis of cultures. After all, that's what cultural studies was trying to do initially in the 1990s. There are all of these discourses that we can look at. And also, it would be important, I imagine – not in the case of World Bank reports but in other cases like journalism – to rethink the issue of the shifting boundaries between the literary and the nonliterary.

In general – and this is something that I became convinced of very early on in my life in the early 1970s, when I was studying literature, and I was engaged almost full-time in politics: I don't think literature can change things. I've always been skeptical about the political impact of literary works, aesthetic works in general. There are exceptional cases in which a spark can detonate. Say *Guernica*, the painting.

HEISE: Or *The Jungle*, or *Uncle Tom's Cabin*. Or Edward Bellamy's *Looking Backward*, all of which *were* really socially important. But it's just a handful of examples.

MORETTI: But by and large, when there are aesthetic activities that are designed to produce pleasure and they're successful in producing pleasure, that pleasure is not an activist emotional pleasure. I have no argument against pleasure, unless it's exploitative, but it's not a revolutionary virtue. It's not a transgressive virtue. It's clearly quietist, in a sense. So that's one of the paradoxes of great literature; you can say, "My God, this is fantastic," but the fantastic doesn't change the world.

HEISE: For nonliterary texts, I've found myself going back to narrative – narratology broadly conceived, which built originally on fictional texts and then developed into a more general theory of narrative. Elements of genre theory and narrative theory seem to be most useful when you start to think about narrative beyond literature.

MORETTI: I've gone in a completely parallel direction back to linguistics and social linguistics and corpus linguistics because that's more germane to digital humanities. Also the analysis of grammar and syntax – you can use it for literature, but you can use it for anything. Literature departments in the 1980s cut the connection with linguistics, which had been so important in the previous twenty years, and now, thirty years later, the panorama of linguistics has completely changed. It's a very interesting panorama, especially when it comes to corpus linguistics and so on, because it mixes systematic linguistic theory with empirical findings, and that's quite fascinating. And indeed, linguists usually use four categories within corpus linguistics: conversation; news; academic prose; and fiction. Fiction is the most confused of the four, but it's really the literary within a universe of discourses.

HEISE: You've already mentioned a couple of the areas that you see as possibilities for comparative literature. Any other research questions or outlines that might be ways comparative literature might want to go or that it might see itself forced to go in the next ten years?

MORETTI: Rethinking the meaning of the past. What is the significance of the past? This is a much broader question, of course. This is a period in which enrollments in the humanities are falling, which means that interest in the humanities is falling. Simplifying a bit, if we take literature and history as the two pillars of the humanities, they're both disciplines that are fundamentally devoted to the study of the past. So we have to make the past interesting in a new way. At bottom, I think it's this. The past has to be reimagined.

Works cited

Anderson, Perry. *Lineages of the Absolutist State*. London: New Left Books, 1974. Print.

Auerbach, Erich. 1946. *Mimesis: The Representation of Reality in Western Literature*. Trans. Willard R. Trask. Princeton: Princeton UP, 2003. Print.

Beecroft, Alexander. "World Literature without a Hyphen: Towards a Typology of Literary Systems." *New Left Review* 54 (2008): 87–100. Print.

Bellamy, Edward. 1888. *Looking Backward 2000–1887*. Ed. Matthew Beaumont. Oxford: Oxford UP, 2009. Print.

Braudel, Fernand. "Histoire et sciences sociales: La longue durée." *Annales: Histoires, Sciences Sociales* 13.4 (1958): 725–53. Print.

Carson, Rachel. 1962. *Silent Spring: Fortieth Anniversary Edition*. Boston: Mariner, 2002. Print.

Engelsing, Rolf. "Die Perioden der Lesergeschichte in der Neuzeit: Das statistische Ausmass und die soziokulturelle Bedeutung der Lektüre." *Archiv für Geschichte des Buchwesens* 10 (1970): 945–1002. Print.

Griswold, Wendy. *Bearing Witness: Readers, Writers, and the Novel in Nigeria*. Princeton: Princeton UP, 2000. Print.

An Inconvenient Truth. Dir. Davis Guggenheim. Perf. Albert Gore. Paramount: 2006. Film.

Moore, Barrington. *Social Origins of Dictatorship and Democracy: Lord and Peasant in the Making of the Modern World.* Boston: Beacon Press, 1966. Print.

Moretti, Franco. *Atlas of the European Novel 1800–1900.* London: Verso, 1999. Print.

———. *The Bourgeois: Between History and Literature.* London: Verso, 2013. Print.

———. "Conjectures on World Literature." *New Left Review* 1 (2000): 54–69. Print.

Moretti, Franco, and Dominique Pestre. "Bankspeak: The Language of World Bank Reports." *New Left Review* 92 (2015): 75–99. Web. 8 June 2016.

Sinclair, Upton. 1906. *The Jungle.* N.p.: Enhanced Media, 2014. Kindle edn.

Stowe, Harriet Beecher. *Uncle Tom's Cabin: Or Life among the Lowly.* Edinburgh: Adam and Charles Black, 1853. Web. 8 June 2016. http://purl.galileo.usg.edu/ugafax/PS2954xU5.

Zwicker, Jonathan E. *Practices of the Sentimental Imagination: Melodrama, the Novel, and the Social Imaginary in Nineteenth-Century Japan.* Cambridge, MA: Harvard UP, 2006. Print.

Platforms of the imagination
Stages of electronic literature
Mexico 2015

Susana González Aktories and María Andrea Giovine Yáñez

Platforms of the Imagination: Stages of Electronic Literature Mexico 2015 (www.plataformasdelaimaginacion.mx) was conceived by a small group of comparatists at the National Autonomous University of Mexico (UNAM) to address emerging reading and writing practices in the digital cultures that we all inhabit and share. Digital technologies are expanding the ways in which we all read, write, teach, and study literary texts, often blurring the distinctions between literature and other expressive media. The study of electronic literatures in comparative literature curricula is apt, given that e-lit is constituted by artistic languages, media, and expressive traditions *in relation* – relations that require comparative attention on the part of both its audience and its critics. Our study group agreed that it was time to move the discussion from our classrooms into open public spaces. So *Platforms of the Imagination* grew into a series of "e-literature" exhibitions and events in eight arts and cultural venues across Mexico City over a three-month period, from October 2015 to January 2016. Our aim was to place electronic literature at the center of the cultural agenda of prestigious Mexican institutions by presenting pieces that were original, born-digital creations – that is, not remediated from a previous analog device, such as a book or printed text. Some of the pieces were commissioned by us, which meant that their premiere was to a live audience on a large scale, as museum pieces to be experienced and manipulated by their creators and users (readers, viewers, and listeners).

Platforms' concurrent exhibitions and events featured an array of e-literatures and a discussion of their modes of communication and distribution: graphic literatures, sound poetics to emphasize the integration of visual and auditory forms of expression, and an array of other technological avant-gardes. A principal issue in each of the exhibitions was, inevitably, the difference between "literature" and "e-literature": the latter is *not* simply "adapted" or "remediated" from print into digital form but rather conceived, developed, and presented as a digital artifact, always in contact with other expressive forms (e.g., visual art, video, voice, instrumental music, rhythm, and performance). In fact, e-lit exploits its capacity to integrate distinct artistic languages so as to create aesthetic experiences that are often interactive, unstable, open to revision and addition. In a certain sense, the creator is a performer, enacting a digital text with words, sounds, images, and sometimes tactile and olfactory content. In short, we may think of e-literature as textual artifacts – literary, yes, but now a hybrid, mixed medium.

All the pieces that were presented in the different exhibits deserve to be mentioned. Take, for instance, *Mis movimientos mexicanos*, a work by Seoul-based artists who call themselves Young-hae Chang Heavy Industries (yhchang.com) that was specifically created for *Platforms of the Imagination*. It is a narrative text, ironic and humorous, with the typography that is the trademark of YHCHI: a visual arrangement of letters and words that moves to the accompaniment of original music, creating a synesthesic reading effect. Another interesting work is *Between Page and Screen* (betweenpageandscreen.com) by Amaranth Borsuk and Brad Bouse, a book consisting of geometrical patterns that have to be read through a webcam so that the texts appear on the screen, showing the interdependence between the book and the computer. At the Palacio de Bellas Artes, the Mexican digital artist Eugenio Tisselli presented *La tiranía del código* (Tyranny of the Code), a video that addresses implicitly the continuities and discontinuities between contemporary digital avant-gardes and "traditional" Russian avant-garde art, which was concurrently in exhibition. At the Centro de Cultura Digital, the sound artist and musician Alexander Bruck discussed a piece by Jan Robert Leegte from his series *Random Selection Objects* as a musical score, and there were two other visual digital installations by Jan Robert Leegte. Another piece that is important to mention is the *IP Poetry* (ip-poetry.findelmundo.com.ar) project by Gustavo Romano, which creates poetry based on searches of the Internet in real time. Robots connected to the Internet convert the found texts into prerecorded sounds of a human voice reciting phonemes. The different search topics and their programmed sounds create the images, structure, and meaning of the poems.

A geopolitical question inherent in the study of e-literature is whether to translate one of its communicative levels – namely, the textual language. Since e-literature circulates in English, we felt the importance of making a curatorial point by showing that, despite its dominance, this language was not the only choice: in fact, very valuable pieces of electronic literature are written in Spanish and other languages. Moreover, considering that e-literature is also about decoding, we wanted to highlight the fact that the use of various languages also gives pieces their particular identity. Consequently, our selection included artists from France, the Netherlands, the United States, Spain, Korea, Argentina, and Mexico, among other countries. For obvious reasons we privileged pieces in Spanish by Mexican, Argentinian, and Spanish artists, and also translated some of the commissioned texts into Spanish, with the authors' approval.

Clearly e-literature represents a major shift in literary aesthetics and creative processes because it will almost always be collaborative work. The author becomes a conceptual creator dependent on the possible synergies of interacting media and the participation of programmers, sound engineers, and digital designers, among others. Whether the future of comparative literature as a discipline includes e-literature is as yet undecided, but we would miss an opportunity were we to ignore its challenges to traditional literary, and literary critical, categories: genre, period, narrative structure, meter, rhyme, voice, and tone, not to mention grammar, syntax, phonetics, and style. With the challenges of this new textuality in mind, we designed a literal "platform" to harbor multiple activities in eight different venues, each focused on digital developments in "literary" production. *Platforms* gradually came to include the following events; we list the venues for those who know these major arts institutions in Mexico City:

- A series of preliminary talks under the title of "Multiple Textualities" at the UNAM Bookstore, with the support of the Publications Department of the UNAM;
- An international symposium at the Centro Cultural Universitario (cultura. unam.mx), with lectures by invited artists from five countries, and critics and scholars both national and international;
- Three museum exhibitions: the Universum-Museo de las Ciencias (universum. unam.mx): *Literatura electrónica: Escenarios híbridos* (Electronic Literature: Hybrid Scenarios); the Centro Cultural Universitario Tlatelolco (tlatelolco. unam.mx): *Literatura electrónica: Política y cuerpo en el presente digital* (Electronic Literature: Politics and the Body in the Digital Present); and the Centro de Cultura Digital (centroculturadigital.mx): *Selecciones como objetos* (Selections as Objects);
- A world premiere at the Palacio de Bellas Artes (palacio.bellasartes.gob.mx): *La tiranía del código* (The Tyranny of the Code), by the Mexican digital artist Eugenio Tisselli;
- Two programs (described earlier) related to post-Internet works at Casa del Lago (casadellago.unam.mx) and the Centro de Cultura Digital (centroculturadigital.mx). "Post-Internet" refers to the engagement of material objects taken from the digital context and located in the "physical" world;
- A round table with invited artists at the Museo Universitario del Chopo (chopo.unam.mx);
- A printed catalogue with textual and visual documentation of the entire program.[1]

Laboratory of extended literatures and other materialities (lleom)

Below, we address the immense organizational challenges of this project, and the commensurate advantages of partnering with diverse cultural institutions to draw attention to what might otherwise seem merely "academic." We will also consider how this kind of multi-institutional outreach might be replicated, and to what ends, by comparative literature programs in other universities. And finally, we will mention our growing enrollments in comparative literature at the UNAM, and consider whether and how enrollments have been affected by our programmatic focus on emerging practices of electronic literatures and digital cultures.

Platforms of the Imagination had its origin in a small working group called *laboratory of extended literatures and other materialities* (http://lleom.net). Five comparatists met for the first time in August 2013 with the purpose of promoting the study of hybrid artistic processes and products (digital and nondigital), with literary and media studies as a starting point. *Lleom*'s focus has consistently been on technological and digital media and their tools; our activities have included traditional formats, such as seminars, lectures, and round tables, and also more experimental contexts, such as sound walks, conversation walks, handmade editions, and performances and interventions in museums. *Lleom* has facilitated opportunities for faculty and students to collaborate with national and international digital and sound artists, visual artists, and graphic writers, as well as scholars and critics working in and on these new hybrid media. We have been gratified by the generous support of Mexican institutions – some part of the UNAM and some not. In the fall of 2014, we began to plan an e-literature exhibition in a public venue.

How a small group carried out a big project

We approached the director of the Museum del Palacio de Bellas Artes, one of the most important museums in Mexico City, whose director was already programming an exhibition on the Russian avant-garde for October 2015. The connection of contemporary e-literatures with the Russian avant-garde seemed possible and promising. A natural link was the Institute of Bibliographical Research at the UNAM, whose director immediately supported the idea of an e-lit exhibition as integral to the study of book history. This contact allowed us to connect to the Centro Cultural Universitario Tlatelolco and several other UNAM institutions spread around the city: museums, cultural centers, and cultural areas in historic buildings owned by the university. Astonishingly, all of the directors wanted to be involved, in part because they were as interested as we were in learning more about the new technologies. This broad participation required that we redefine our strategic plan according to the specific profile and needs of each institutional participant, and ascertain how their participation would be articulated within the overall project. On the basis of this institutional support, we organized three exhibitions, a symposium, and travel and honoraria for five artists from Mexico and abroad, as well as presentations in a variety of venues designed to engage diverse audiences.

Resonances and responses

Looking back, we are still amazed that a small team of comparatists with a clear vision of the needs and interests of the interdisciplinary digital community could get financial and artistic support from so many Mexican cultural institutions. With such broad institutional involvement, our events received ample media coverage, which in turn assured good-sized audiences for the exhibitions and events. We have long been aware of the need for intellectual programming that includes public participation, and we offer *Platforms of the Imagination* as a possible model for other comparative projects. By taking our "academic" questions into the public sphere, and more particularly into visual arts spaces, we enriched our own understanding of emerging forms of e-literature, as did our students and a public wanting to know more about these new areas of literary practice. Collaborations with arts and other cultural institutions, whether inside the university or outside, will always amplify the discussion of "academic" subjects by including interlocutors who aren't in our classes but who are glad to be included, and who often have very interesting things to contribute. Furthermore, with enrollments declining in some humanistic disciplines, it behooves us to speak beyond of the walls of academia, and let the public know what comparatists are doing across many areas of inquiry.

We acknowledge our privileged situation at the UNAM for such a venture. The UNAM is the oldest university in Latin America, established in 1551; with a significant interruption in the second half of the nineteenth century, it reopened in 1910 on the eve of the Mexican Revolution. It is also the largest university in Latin America by every measure: students, faculty, and facilities. The *rector* (chancellor) of the UNAM is appointed by the president of the Republic, and the university is referred to without irony as the "Máxima Casa de Estudios." UNAM has important buildings throughout the historic center of Mexico City, many of which are used as arts and educational spaces, and the Ciudad Universitaria (University City) in the south of the city also has museum spaces, including the new University Museum of Contemporary Art (MUAC). We recognize that not all universities have such resources, but collaborative programs need not be as multifaceted as ours turned out to be. Collaboration with a single public arts organization should be enough to create the kind of intellectual energy and student involvement generated by *Platforms*. Through this particular project we were able to organize a series of events that centrally emphasized the richness of e-literature but were also concerned with core topics of comparative literature in general, such as materiality, virtuality, sound and visual poetry, experimentalisms, and avant-gardes. This project, in our context, helped us to remember that literature is a dynamic field, and it is not only possible but also to a certain extent natural to link literature with science, technology, and other humanistic areas, such as book history. Another important discovery for us was all that can be achieved when taking literature from its accustomed spaces into museums and galleries. Curating is very much like editing and one of the futures of comparative literature.

In fact, enrollments in the UNAM's Comparative Literature graduate program (we have no undergraduate program) are growing, and though it would be impossible to say whether our recent focus on digital technologies and e-literature has anything to do with this growth, we do know that our students are enthusiastic participants in the programming of *lleom*, as well as other types of alternative cultural groups working in public forums. Our intention is to continue to include courses on new literary modes alongside our more traditional seminars, and consider how to maintain the public conversation begun with *Platforms of the Imagination*.

Note

1 These events and exhibitions are described in more detail on *Platforms*' website. Reading through the descriptions provides an informal overview of the current status and forms of e-literature and their combined media (www.plataformasde laimaginacion.mx).

Beyond the human

Comparative literature and the environmental humanities

Ursula K. Heise

From ecocriticism to the environmental humanities

Ecocriticism and the environmental humanities form part of an array of new interdisciplinary areas that have emerged across the humanities and qualitative social sciences over the last two decades (see Heise, "Introduction," this volume). The story of ecocriticism – the study of texts, images, and films that construct and reflect humans' interactions with natural environments and with nonhuman species – is usually told as a development from an original focus on mostly British and American literatures of the last two hundred years to a much broader comparatist spectrum of literatures and periods. During its first decade, ecocritical research engaged above all with US-American traditions of nonfiction nature writing (from Henry David Thoreau and Susan Fenimore Cooper to Wendell Berry and Annie Dillard), nature poetry, and Native American literature, as well as with British Romantic nature poets and their successors. Comparatist impulses transformed the field after the turn of the millennium in a variety of directions, multiplying its objects of study and the range of theoretical perspectives brought to bear on them. Americanist ecocritics working outside the United States – for example, in Germany, Japan, and Taiwan – started out with their own approaches to classical authors, such as Thoreau, Edward Abbey, or Gary Snyder, and then worked to link their findings to the literatures of their own countries and to collaborate with specialists in these traditions.

Postcolonial ecocritics, from the mid-2000s onward, drew new attention to the convergences between colonial oppression and ecological degradation, to the unequal distribution of resources and risks, and in some cases, to First-World environmentalists' complicity in perpetuating conditions of socioeconomic injustice. In the process, they refocused part of the field's energy on the literatures of sub-Saharan Africa, the Caribbean, India, and Latin America.[1] At the same time, theoretically oriented ecocritics connected environmental analysis with theories of displacement, diaspora, nomadism, hybridization, *mestizaje*, globalization, and cosmopolitanism that had gained momentum in literary studies since the 1990s (Buell, "Ecoglobalist Affect"; Heise, *Sense of Planet* Ch. 1). Even more recently, researchers focusing on East Asian literatures have developed ecocriticism in the contexts of Chinese, Korean, Japanese, and Taiwanese literature.[2] With a history of more than twenty years, a US-based professional organization that numbers over 1,500 members, and more than half a dozen sister organizations in other parts of the world, ecocriticism has outgrown the profile of an "emergent" disciplinary formation. In a sense, then, ecocriticism exemplifies the diffusion of comparatist assumptions and perspectives into other fields of literary study that Haun Saussy portrayed as characteristic of comparative literature in 2004 (Saussy 3–5).

But telling the story of ecocriticism as the victory of comparatism and transnational collaboration simplifies its history and current status. The emphasis on growth, expansion, and increased diversity can take on overtones of disciplinary turf war and triumphalism as easily as of deepened knowledge. A more interesting story about the encounter between comparative literature and ecocriticism involves not so much the victory of comparatism as ideas and developments that challenge literary studies in their usual form. The first of these challenges has been the emphasis, from about 2010 onward, on a new matrix usually called "environmental humanities" (or "ecological humanities," in Australia) that seeks to connect environmentally oriented research across a variety of disciplines in the humanities and social sciences: environmental philosophy, environmental history, environmental literary studies, environmental anthropology, cultural geography, communication and media studies, gender studies, urban studies, and religious studies. The possibility for such an interdisciplinary vision arose from several factors. Environmental perspectives had, after several decades of struggle, established themselves successfully enough in disciplines such as history, literature, and philosophy that researchers could afford to look past departmental boundaries at their shared goals. And the interdisciplinary field of "environmental studies," institutionalized since the 1960s at many universities around the world, had usually not given much space to the humanities.

But more importantly, shortfalls in public communication about environmental crises – especially in the case of climate change – prompted many environmentalist activists and even scientists to think more deeply about questions of culture, language, and narrative. The environmental historian Sverker Sörlin has observed:

> Our belief that science alone could deliver us from the planetary quagmire is long dead. For some time, hopes were high for economics and incentive-driven new public management solutions. However, after the 20 years since the Rio Conference in 1992 . . . we must again determine pathways to sustainability. It seems this time that our hopes are tied to the humanities.
>
> (788)

What is at stake in this turn is not merely a closer analysis of what are often referred to as "the human dimensions of environmental crisis" in the policy-speak of NGOs and international institutions. Rather, as they explore local, national, regional, and global cultures of environmentalism, environmental humanists seek to redefine ecological crises that are often approached as primarily scientific, technological, and policy questions – pollution, biodiversity loss, and global warming, for example – as challenges of social justice and cultural difference (see Neimanis, Åsberg, and Hedrén; Rose et al.).

For comparative ecocritics, the emergence of the environmental humanities has opened up an enormously rich and varied field of exchanges with anthropologists, geographers, and historians. But as literary scholars have brought their expertise in narrative and rhetoric to bear on this expanded field, they have also confronted three challenges that affect not just ecocriticism but also the future of comparatist literary study more broadly: the challenge of nonfiction, the tensions between the concept of the Anthropocene and posthumanist theories, and the challenge of the nonhuman.

The challenge of nonfiction

In 2010, Djelal Kadir approached me in his role as one of the editors of the *Routledge Companion to World Literature* for a contribution on world literature and the environment. With David Damrosch's definition of world literature as literary texts that circulate beyond their context of origin in mind, I planned to focus on the text that is often claimed to have started the US-American environmentalist movement as well as similar movements around the world: Rachel Carson's *Silent Spring* (1962), a work of nonfiction that is often praised for its literary qualities. Retracing the itinerary of this book across languages and countries, I thought, would highlight the importance of nonfiction prose and documentary film for environmental thought and activism, but would also demonstrate how such works circulate in ways that fit the definition of world literature.

But the more I researched translation dates and read histories of the emergence of environmental movements in a variety of countries and regions, the more I was overcome by a sense of unease. True, *Silent Spring* was translated into most major European languages within a decade of its publication and was known to many West European environmentalists by the 1970s. And some of its translations into other languages did resonate with local environmental struggles: the 1969 Japanese translation, for example, with the unfolding disaster of mercury poisoning in Minamata and growing concern over environmental and household toxins that crystallized in such fictional works as Ariyoshi Sawako's *Compound Pollution* (複合汚染; *Fukugō osen*, 1975). But the work that was mentioned most frequently in histories and autobiographies chronicling the emergence of environmental awareness and activism across a variety of regions turned out to be not *Silent Spring* but *The Limits to Growth*, Donella and Dennis L. Meadows's report to the Club of Rome (1972). World literature? A hard case to make. Whatever the merits of *The Limits to Growth* may be, literary storytelling is not one of them, and I found myself the closest I had ever come to the experience of a failed lab experiment. With the submission deadline looming, I decided to focus my essay on a more conventional argument instead, the interleaving of ecological and cultural misunderstandings in four recent novels from different parts of the world.

This case study in failure points to one of the difficulties in the otherwise successful encounter of environmentalism and comparative literature. Environmental movements in many parts of the world have been inspired and energized by texts and films: writings ranging from those of Mohandas Gandhi and Thoreau to those of Carson and Vandana Shiva; films from Bernhard Grzimek's *Serengeti darf nicht sterben* (Serengeti Must Not Die, 1959) to Al Gore's *An Inconvenient Truth* (2006); and television series from Félix Rodríguez de la Fuente's *El hombre y la tierra* in the 1960s to the BBC's *Blue Planet* (2006). But these television series and films are documentaries, and the texts are nonfiction prose. That doesn't mean that literary analysis cannot shed light on them – quite the contrary: Lawrence Buell's work is often credited with opening up an entire canon of nonfiction nature writing to literary analysis and thereby making it part of the American literature canon. But this particular type of nonfiction writing about nature is not as common in other cultural traditions as it is in the United States, and when literary critics turn to the analysis of popular science publications, travel writing, newspaper and magazine articles, and documentary films across a variety of cultures, their work shifts from a focus on the literary and the aesthetic to modes of analyses that overlap with those common in studies of media and communication.

This may be an obvious step to take if we consider attention to nonfiction as simply the latest development in the expansion of literary studies to a wide variety of textual, visual, and other objects that began with cultural studies in the 1980s. And if we approach nonfiction works as another means of manifesting cultural concerns about nature, different from literary approaches in their rhetorical strategies, affect, and audiences, but not in the underlying concerns, they become an indispensable part of comparative ecocriticism.[3] Nonfiction prose nevertheless challenges the usual disciplinary parameters of comparative literature, though it does so unevenly. While the study of some national traditions and historical eras has included religious and philosophical writings, travel narratives, or essays, literary theory and analysis still tend to focus on those genres that are understood to have an explicit aesthetic dimension. The prominence of nonfictional and documentary modes in environmental arts and letters, as well as in some of the other new research areas, such as medical humanities and food studies, challenges comparatists to articulate the specificity of their work programmatically within broader frameworks of rhetoric, narrative theory, communication, and media analysis that also include neighboring disciplines such as film studies, communication studies, and media studies.

Between the Anthropocene and posthumanisms

One of the most salient dimensions of comparatist ecocritical analysis, obviously, is its attention to the role of linguistic and cultural differences in communities' engagement with global ecological crises that range from toxification to biodiversity loss and climate change (see Wenzel, this volume). As I have shown elsewhere, comparatist ecocritics have interpreted this engagement in divergent ways: while Karen Thornber, for example, emphasizes similarities of environmentalist thinking that cut across national, linguistic, and cultural borders, postcolonial ecocritics such as Rob Nixon tend to emphasize the overarching structures of socioeconomic inequality that expose communities in the global South to greater and more varied risks than those in global North (Heise, "Globality" and "Comparative Ecocriticism"). And while environmentalist policies and projects initiated by conservation organizations in the global North are sometimes themselves understood as part and parcel of neocolonial strategies of intrusion and domination, as Shiva has argued, Marisol de la Cadena and Jorge Marcone have highlighted new environmentalisms in Latin America that blend indigenous cosmologies with progressive philosophies that originally emerged in Europe and North America ("Stone Guests"). Under the umbrella of the environmental humanities, comparatists as well as environmental anthropologists, environmental historians, and cultural geographers have contributed to this work.

At a more theoretical level, the debate about cultural difference and convergence in the confrontation with ecological crises has crystallized around the notion of the Anthropocene, originally proposed by the ecologist Eugene Stoermer in the 1980s and popularized by him and the atmospheric scientist Paul Crutzen starting in 2000 as a way of understanding humans' transformative impact on global ecosystems ("The Anthropocene"; "Geology of Mankind"). In a by now classic essay, the postcolonial historian Dipesh Chakrabarty interpreted the concept of the Anthropocene and one of its ecological manifestations, global climate change, as invitations to reconsider the role of foundational differences in humanistic and social-scientific theories – whether they be differences of class, gender, race, or geopolitical power – and to envision the human species as a whole as an agent of historical change. A new form of universalism is necessary in this context, Chakrabarty argued, even if this universalism can be envisioned only negatively, in terms of what it is not, if it is to avoid the error of past universalisms – generalizing the characteristics of one particular culture as the universal yardstick of the human, with dire consequences for those judged to fall short of this measure ("Climate of History").

The controversy that erupted between Chakrabarty and his critics over the necessity of such a new universalism helps to situate the different ways in which comparatist approaches have inflected environmental analyses and generated the divergent emphases on cross-cultural similarity and difference in recent work. I have argued that even if we accept Chakrabarty's challenge of conceiving the human species as a new kind of agent, what the human means cannot be considered a biological given in this context, but must be carefully assembled from the analysis of social and cultural differences. There is no freeway from ecological crisis to human universalism that does not have to retrace the byways and detours of difference, and the comparatist perspective retains its crucial importance in this context (Heise, *Imagining Extinction*, Ch. 6).

The challenge of the nonhuman

But if comparatism remains vital for the environmental humanities, what difference does the environmental perspective make for comparative literature? Beyond

298 Ursula K. Heise

a new attention to the material – specifically, ecological – foundations of comparatism, from the economic structures that enable the circulation of world literature to the carbon footprint of the international airplane trips that often function like merit badges in the discipline, recent work in the environmental humanities challenges us to reconsider the centrality of the human.[4] A wide range of theories that one might classify under the label "posthumanism" are inviting us to reconsider human existence, intentionality, and agency as only part of networks that also include other modes of being and agency.

Some of these theories are of recent vintage, while others date back to the 1980s; some have emerged from environmentalism proper, others from a broader consideration of nonhuman agents; some of them focus on systems, some on machines, others on objects, yet others on animals. But they share the goal of rethinking the centrality of human agency – especially that of the liberal humanist subject of the Enlightenment, and in this respect they stand in palpable tension with the centrality of human agency in debates surrounding the Anthropocene. Actor-network theory as it has been developed by Bruno Latour, Michel Callon, and John Law since the 1980s foregrounds "heterogeneous" social networks that consist of human and nonhuman, animate and inanimate agents that relate to each other in material as well as semiotic ways. Niklas Luhmann's brand of systems theory sees individuals and societies as systems that operate in each other's environments rather than individuals as part of societies. A variety of "new materialisms" proposed by Karen Barad, Stacy Alaimo, Serenella Iovino, and Serpil Oppermann, among others, have sought to redefine human minds and bodies as "transcorporeal" vectors (Alaimo, *Bodily Natures*) in relations and material flows that constitute the human subject in and through ecological networks. Jane Bennett's new vitalism, in somewhat similar but not explicitly environmentalist fashion, explores the vibrant agency of matter. Objects make an appearance mostly by way of their human relations and significance in Bill Brown's thing theory, whereas object-oriented ontology (OOO) as proposed by Graham Harman, Levy Bryant, Quentin Meillassoux, and Timothy Morton seeks to free objects from such "correlationism" and to explore them on their own terms, even as OOO also emphasizes that objects will ultimately always remain withdrawn from human knowledge. Human-animal studies as pioneered by Jacques Derrida, Giorgio Agamben, Roberto Esposito, Donna Haraway, and Cary Wolfe have questioned the foundational distinction between human and animal along with its political implications (see Ortiz Robles, this volume), and even more recent work in plant studies by such anthropologists as Matthew Hall and Eduardo Kohn has formulated analogous doubts about the category of the plant. Under the labels of multispecies ethnography, etho-ethnology, or zooanthropology, anthropologists working in Australia, Western Europe, and North America such as Eben Kirksey, Stefan Helmreich, and Anna Tsing, have proposed a new approach to analyzing what we normally understand as *human* societies and cultures as, in reality, multispecies assemblages (see de Gennaro, this volume).

This somewhat indiscriminate enumeration is not meant to minimize the differences and even incompatibilities between some of these strands of thought – new materialists and object-oriented ontologists, for example, have little sympathy for each other's foundational assumptions. But it *is* meant to suggest some of the breadth and variety in reconceptualizations of the human that have been undertaken across the humanities and social sciences over the last thirty years. Through ecocriticism and the environmental humanities, some of this body of thought is now reshaping comparatist work, complementing comparatists' traditional interest in linguistic, cultural, and other differences between humans with a layer of inquiry that focuses on the relationships between humans, other species, and the inanimate world. Social and economic stratifications as well as cultural conventions work to produce these relationships differently in different places – but the more-than-human world also produces human differences in a variety of ways, as new work in the environmental humanities is beginning to show. The comparatism of the future will have to engage with both vectors of production. Rethinking concepts such as culture, community, politics, language, meaning, memory, narrative, rights, and self beyond their purely human implications represents one of the most enthralling tasks for comparatists in years to come, but also an important challenge to the way in which literary and cultural studies are currently understood.

Notes

1 For a sample of this work, see DeLoughrey et al.; Forns-Broggi; Handley; Huggan and Tiffin; Marcone, "De retorno" and "Jungle Fever"; Marzec; Mukherjee; Nixon; O'Brien.
2 See the contributions of Estok and Kim; Shirane; Thornber; and Yuki, among many others.
3 Rob Nixon's *Slow Violence and the Environmentalism of the Poor*, for example, moves seamlessly back and forth between fictional and nonfictional texts.
4 Jennifer Wenzel delivered a brilliant presentation on the different understandings of the global in the "world" of world literature and the "planet" in environmental thought at the ACL(x) conference at Penn State University in September 2013 (see also Moraru, this volume).

Works cited

Alaimo, Stacy. *Bodily Natures: Science, Environment, and the Material Self.* Bloomington: Indiana UP, 2010. Print.
Bennett, Michael. "Anti-Pastoralism, Frederick Douglass, and the Nature of Slavery." *Beyond Nature Writing: Exploring the Boundaries of Ecocriticism.* Ed. Karla Armbruster and Kathleen R. Wallace. Charlottesville: University of Virginia Press, 2001. 195–210. Print.
Buell, Lawrence. "Ecoglobalist Affects: The Emergence of U.S. Environmental Imagination on a Planetary Scale." *Shades of the Planet: American Literature as World Literature.* Ed. Wai Chee Dimock and Lawrence Buell. Princeton: Princeton UP, 2007. 227–48. Print.
———. *The Future of Environmental Criticism: Environmental Crisis and Literary Imagination.* Oxford: Blackwell, 2005. Print.

Cadena, Marisol de la. "Indigenous Cosmopolitics in the Andes: Conceptual Reflections beyond 'Politics'." *Cultural Anthropology* 25.2 (2010): 334–70. Print.

Carson, Rachel. *Silent Spring: Fortieth Anniversary Edition*. 1962. Boston: Houghton Mifflin, 2002. Print.

Chakrabarty, Dipesh. "The Climate of History: Four Theses." *Critical Inquiry* 35 (2009): 197–222. Print.

Crutzen, Paul J. "Geology of Mankind." *Nature* 415 (3 January 2002): 23. Print.

Crutzen, Paul J., and Eugene F. Stoermer. "The 'Anthropocene'." *Global Change Newsletter* 41 (2000): 17–18. Print.

DeLoughrey, Elizabeth M., Renée K. Gosson, and George B. Handley, eds. *Caribbean Literature and the Environment: Between Nature and Culture*. Charlottesville: U of Virginia P, 2005. Print.

Estok, Simon C., and Won-Chung Kim, eds. *East Asian Ecocriticisms: A Critical Reader*. New York: Palgrave Macmillan, 2013. Print.

Forns-Broggi, Roberto. *Nudos como estrellas: ABC de la imaginación ecológica en nuestras Américas*. Lima: Nido de Cuervos, 2012. Print.

Handley, George. *New World Poetics: Nature and the Adamic Imagination of Whitman, Neruda, and Walcott*. Athens: U of Georgia P, 2007. Print.

Heise, Ursula K. "Comparative Ecocriticism in the Anthropocene." *Komparatistik* (May 2014): 19–33. Print.

———. "Globality, Difference, and the International Turn in Ecocriticism." *PMLA* 128.3 (2013): 636–43. Print.

———. *Imagining Extinction: The Cultural Meanings of Endangered Species*. Chicago: U of Chicago P, 2016. Print.

———. *Sense of Place and Sense of Planet: The Environmental Imagination of the Global*. New York: Oxford University Press, 2008. Print.

Huggan, Graham, and Helen Tiffin. *Postcolonial Ecocriticism: Literature, Animals, Environment*. London: Routledge, 2010. Print.

Latour, Bruno. *War of the Worlds: What about Peace?* Trans. Charlotte Bigg. Ed. John Tresch. Chicago: Prickly Paradigm Press, 2002. Print.

Marcone, Jorge. "De retorno a lo natural: La serpiente de oro, la 'novela de la selva' y la crítica ecológica." *Hispania: Journal of the American Association of Teachers of Spanish and Portuguese* 81 (1998): 299–308. Print.

———. "Jungle Fever: Primitivism in Environmentalism, Rómulo Gallegos's *Canaima*, and the Romance of the Jungle." *Primitivism and Identity in Latin America: Essays on Art, Literature, and Culture*. Ed. Erik Camayd-Freixas and José Eduardo González. Tucson: U of Arizona P, 2000. 157–72. Print.

———. "The Stone Guests: *Buen Vivir* and Popular Environmentalisms in the Andes and Amazonia." *The Routledge Companion to the Environmental Humanities*. Ed. Jon Christensen, Ursula K. Heise, and Michelle Niemann. London: Routledge, 2017. 227–235. Print.

Marzec, Robert P. *An Ecological and Postcolonial Study of Literature: From Daniel Defoe to Salman Rushdie*. New York: Palgrave Macmillan, 2007. Print.

Meadows, Donella, Dennis L. Meadows, and Jørgen Randers. *Beyond the Limits: Confronting Global Collapse, Envisioning a Sustainable Future*. Post Mills, VT: Chelsea Green, 1992.

Meadows, Donella, Dennis L. Meadows, Jørgen Randers, and William W. Behrens III. *The Limits to Growth: A Report for the Club of Rome's Project on the Predicament of Mankind*. New York: Universe, 1972.

Meadows, Donella, Jørgen Randers, and Dennis L. Meadows. *Limits to Growth: The 30-Year Update*. White River Junction, VT: Chelsea Green, 2004.

Mukherjee, Upamanyu Pablo. *Postcolonial Environments: Nature, Culture and the Contemporary Indian Novel in English*. Houndmills: Palgrave Macmillan, 2010. Print.

Neimanis, Astrida, Cecilia Åsberg, and Johan Hedrén. "Four Problems, Four Directions for Environmental Humanities: Toward Critical Posthumanities for the Anthropocene." *Ethics and the Environment* 20.1 (2015): 67–97. Web. 15 Jan. 2015.

Nixon, Rob. *Slow Violence and the Environmentalism of the Poor*. Cambridge, MA: Harvard UP, 2011. Print.

O'Brien, Susie. "Articulating a World of Difference: Ecocriticism, Postcolonialism and Globalization." *Canadian Literature* 170–1 (2001): 140–58. Print.

Rose, Deborah Bird, Thom van Dooren, Matthew Chrulew, Stuart Cooke, Matthew Kearnes, and Emily O'Gorman. "Thinking Through the Environment, Unsettling the Humanities." *Environmental Humanities* 1 (2012): 1–5. 1 July 2013. Web. 15 Jan. 2015. www.environmentalhumanities.org

Saussy, Haun. *Comparative Literature in an Age of Globalization*. Baltimore: Johns Hopkins UP, 2006. Print.

Shirane, Haruo. *Japan and the Culture of the Four Seasons: Nature, Literature, and the Arts*. New York: Columbia UP, 2012. Print.

Shiva, Vandana. "The Greening of the Global Reach." *Global Ecology: A New Arena of Conflict*. Ed. Wolfgang Sachs. London: Zed Books, 1993. 149–56. Print.

Sörlin, Sverker. "Environmental Humanities: Why Should Biologists Interested in the Environment Take the Humanities Seriously?" *BioScience* 62 (2012): 788–9. Print.

Thornber, Karen. *Ecoambiguity: Environmental Crises and East Asian Literature*. Ann Arbor: U of Michigan P, 2012. Print.

Yuki, Masami. *Tabi no houe* [The Hearth of Contemporary Japanese Women Writers: Ecocritical Approaches to Literary Foodscapes]. Tokyo: Suiseisha, 2012. Print.

Comparative literature and animal studies

Mario Ortiz Robles

(a) A critical cliché

Quoting "a certain Chinese Encyclopedia" called "The Celestial Emporium of Benevolent Knowledge," Jorge Luis Borges offers the following animal taxonomy:

> (a) those that belong to the emperor; (b) embalmed ones; (c) those that are trained; (d) suckling pigs; (e) mermaids; (f) fabulous ones; (g) stray dogs; (h) those included in this classification; (i) those that tremble as if they were mad; (j) innumerable ones; (k) those drawn with a very fine camel's-hair brush; (l) *et cetera*; (m) those that have just broken a flower vase; (n) those that at a distance resemble flies.
>
> (231)

Acknowledging the arbitrariness of this classification, Borges suggests that the attempt to classify the universe is speculative not because the results are inevitably imperfect but because there is no universe in the organic, unifying sense we commonly give that "ambitious word" (231). Yet, far from being useless, Borges's incongruous classification makes visible the difficulties we face when we try to classify large numbers of objects. Indeed, Borges's taxonomy has become a sort of taxono-meme that signifies, more than the impossibility of classification, the inevitability of its imperfection and thus the further affirmation of our need for it as a means to both establish and unsettle the "order of things."

Michel Foucault's celebrated study of the human sciences, *The Order of Things* (1966), in fact opens with an extended meditation on the psychosomatic effects of Borges's taxonomy: an "uneasiness that makes us laugh" (xviii). For Foucault, the uneasiness we feel when we read Borges's taxonomy is hard to shake off because it makes visible, as an uncanny double, the "pure experience of order," a primary state anterior to words, perceptions, and gestures that is made manifest in the various practical modalities of classification (xviii). But in our own historical context, in which the place of the more humanistic of the human sciences within the current order of knowledge is contested, Borges's taxonomy gives rise to an altogether different sort of laughter. By unsettling the distinction that we routinely make between living and nonliving, human and nonhuman, real and imagined, literal and literary animals, Borges's taxonomy raises the more troubling prospect that our attempts to classify the multiplicity of the living under the rubric of the "animal" are themselves something of a literary enterprise.

(b) Literary animals

Everyone knows that animals frequently appear in literature and that literature, from its inception, has used animals in a variety of imaginative and figural registers. A historical classification of animals in literature – a properly literary history of animals – would include all sorts of imaginary creatures, fabulous beasts, and improbable chimeras as well as talking and nontalking animals that are recognizably "real"; it would not, that is, look very different from Borges's taxonomy. Borges's fictional taxonomy thus invites us to entertain the possibility that animals are themselves fictional; that the entity we call "animal" cannot be conceived apart from its literariness; that animals, in short, are a literary invention. It might seem scandalous to make such a claim in a social context in which animal suffering is all too real, in an ecological context in which species are going extinct at an unprecedented rate, in a disciplinary context in which the biological sciences reign supreme, and in an ideological climate in which the theory of evolution is still, for some, little more than a fiction.

Yet, to assert that animals are a literary invention is to draw attention to the logic of classification whereby the systematic accounting of the living also amounts to a categorical appropriation of nature in which the "pure experience of order" is also an ordering of humans' mastery over the natural world. In Linnaeus's *Systema Naturae* (1735), for instance, humans occupy a privileged position that falls just outside the categories under which all other animals are subsumed. Linnaean classification, as Harriet Ritvo has noted, constituted the "invention of tradition" among naturalists keen on proclaiming the triumph of science over nature, but it was also an invention in the more literal sense that it assigned, with the use of Latinate binomials, a unique position to individual animals and plants within a comprehensive system (*Platypus* 15). Codified, standardized, regulated, and continually updated, Linnaeus's Latin nomenclature is still in use today, providing the literary critic with a veritable cabinet of philological curiosities in which are mingled place names, proper names, trivial names, "epithets," and various forms of morphological, physiological, and etiological stand-ins for taxon and type that make the task of classifying a new species an elaborate exercise in interpretative stylistics.

(c) Anthropos

After visiting Lascaux, the cave system in the Dordogne that contains some of oldest human-created images of animals, Picasso is reported to have said, "They've invented everything!" Picasso may have been talking about artistic technique, but, read literally, his observation encourages us to consider the extent to which animal representations are implicated in our invention of the entity we call the "animal." If the first metaphor was animal, as John Berger has argued, then the invention of the animal is also the invention of the human since to construct an animal metaphor is to compare ourselves to other animals in order to establish what we hold in common with them and what we don't (9). The fact that the earliest surviving traces of the act of figuration by humans involve animals – the paintings found at the Chauvet cave in present-day France, painted some thirty-five thousand years ago, are ten thousand years older than those at Lascaux – suggests that the comparison between humans and animals is the comparison that structures all subsequent comparisons.

To depict animals is to take stock of difference, the differences among the animals depicted, but also the differences obtaining between the animals depicted and those that depict them. The comparison between animals and humans can thus be said to be the condition of possibility of representation and, to the extent that comparison gives rise to metaphor, it is also the condition of possibility of literature itself since literature is the giving of wing to metaphor. In theory, comparison is a two-way street when it comes to metaphor since it operates on the basis of chiasmic similarity (beauty is truth; truth beauty), but, in practice, one of the terms of comparison tends to be favored over the other: the vehicle modifies the tenor. In anthropomorphism, the ascription of human attributes to nonhuman entities, the favored term is the one that belongs to the one making the comparison.

Unlike metaphor, anthropomorphism operates as a comparison in which the favored term is posited as a given, as the ground for all figures. The term "human" (*anthropos*) in anthropomorphism, as Barbara Johnson puts it, is "epistemologically resolved" (190). This asymmetry may well be inevitable, but it is perhaps inevitable only because it forms the basis of literature's claim to fictionality: the animal fable as the index of literary fabulation, *tout court*. And to the extent that we fashion literature as a uniquely human endeavor (can birds sing of singing?), literature both draws a stark contrast between human and nonhuman animals and, by virtue of its structural anthropomorphism, simultaneously undermines its claims to a figural plasticity of the sort that might allow one to entertain the possibility of an avian song of songs. As Jacques Derrida and others have shown, the history of Western thought proceeds by erecting a strict division between human and nonhuman animals that grants priority to the human by drawing a series of comparisons in which the human is epistemologically resolved: the human is a political animal (Aristotle); an animal with soul (Descartes); a moral animal (Kant); a promising animal (Nietzsche); a time-keeping animal (Heidegger); a lying animal (Lacan); a nude animal (Derrida).

(d) Disciplines of animal studies

Animal studies is a relatively new interdisciplinary field of inquiry concerned with the political, ethical, social, and cultural status of animals. Whether the aim is to expose the exploitation of animals by humans, to advocate for their welfare, or to examine the animality of the human, animal studies asks us to reflect on our inevitable anthropocentrism. The very name of the discipline, as Cary Wolfe has argued, suggests that, in studying animals, we, as humanists, are also reinforcing the division it is meant to unsettle (*Posthumanism* 99). Yet animal studies situates itself in the human/animal divide as a wedge that opens up to scrutiny the history of human-animal relations from different methodological perspectives and distinct epistemological domains. It cannot overcome the distance that separates the human from the nonhuman; it can hope only to map it.

We can trace the beginning of this largely academic enterprise back to the publication of Peter Singer's *Animal Liberation* in 1975, even though the ethical concern over the treatment of animals, as Singer himself notes, dates at least as far back as the late eighteenth century, when Jeremy Bentham brought the issue of animal suffering into political discourse. Singer popularized the term "speciesism" (originally coined by Richard Ryder in 1971) in his influential utilitarian argument against animal discrimination, which has served as the foundation stone for the work of an impressive array of philosophers, including Tom Regan, Mary Midgley, Thomas Nagel, Alasdair MacIntyre, Cora Diamond, Martha Nussbaum, Matthew Calarco, Brian Massumi, and Paola Cavalieri, among others. Animal rights discourse has gained less traction among continental philosophers, for whom the question of the animal has a longer intellectual tradition but a more recent moment of critical self-reflection. The work of Derrida, Gilles Deleuze, Félix Guattari, and Giorgio Agamben, among others, represents a less overtly pragmatic, if no less political, engagement than that of Anglo-American philosophy with the conceptual categories that have made not only possible but also even permissible the manipulation of animals by humans.

The issue of animal manipulation is of course not only of philosophical interest; historians, anthropologists, environmentalists, psychologists, legal scholars, geographers, economists, artists, musicologists, and literary critics alike have made vigorous interventions in the field of animal studies over the course of the last two decades in the effort to understand the social, cultural, legal, and ethical implications of human-animal relations. These disciplines in the humanities and the humanistic social sciences do not aim to displace or supplant the biological sciences as the principal purveyors of knowledge about the animal world, but rather seek to supplement the scientific study of animals by offering new perspectives on a set of assumptions about our knowledge of animals that often lead to their instrumentalization.

(e) Literature of the world

As Franco Moretti accurately notes, "we do not *know* what world literature is" ("Evolution" 399). Nevertheless, we can posit four constructs to which the term "world literature" can be applied. The first is archival: the sum total of literary texts written in the world up to the present. The second is conceptual: it refers to the critical enterprise that seeks to account for this vast corpus. The third is canonical: it groups those exceptional works of literature that have been deemed to speak beyond the local circumstances of their production and thus to belong not to specific cultures but to humanity as a whole. The fourth is referential: those works that make specific reference to the world (as urban literature refers to the city or nature poetry to nature).

When they don't conflate them, recent debates on the fate of world literature tend to emphasize one of the first three senses of the term. The fourth sense of the term is yet to be adequately theorized. This is surprising since all literature, no matter how seemingly abstracted from the real, is always referential in nature and thus eminently *of* the world. If we take literally the referential ambition implied by the term "world literature" – a term that, to be worth its conceptual salt, ought to be "universal" in scope (as the standard translations of Goethe's *Weltliteratur* into the Romance languages suggest: *littérature universelle, literatura universal, letteratura universale*) – then the problem of world literature becomes one of figuration. Borges is of course right to point out that the universe, that "ambitious word," does not have an adequate referent in reality (it is, in this sense, a catachresis) and thus cannot be reliably classified (231). ("Planetarity" is Gayatri Spivak's preferred term for this impossible figure [72–3].)

But, as ecocriticism has taught us, the worldliness of the world's literatures – a referential structure that encompasses languages, peoples, and regions to be sure, but also biomes, ecosystems, and the myriad habitats that sustain the vast multiplicity of the living – can be accessed, can *only* be accessed, through literary figuration. Awareness of the relation between "place" and "planet," as Ursula Heise argues, involves an imaginative exercise that is textually transacted, a form of figuration made all the more urgent by the persistence of ecological provincialism in the face of environmental events that put us at risk of global catastrophe. This does not mean that world literature must refer explicitly and exclusively to the globe, the planet, the world (see Moraru, this volume) – literature is surely that which can refer to anything at all – but it does mean that in order to grasp the wordliness of world literature and situate its place in the world, we need to analyze the rhetorical means by which it reaches for the universe (whatever it might be), precisely because it is, as Borges notes, an "ambitious word." Indeed, the impossibility of representing the universe is what ought to give the concept of world literature purchase on the critical practice of comparison: world literature as the impossible chronicle of the Anthropocene.

(f) Representing animals

The representation of animals is as old as representation itself, but it is only relatively recently that the question of animal representativeness – the rights of animals, broadly construed – has become part of our discourse about animals. Human-animal relations, as Ritvo and other historians have shown, underwent a radical transformation at the end of the eighteenth century when animals became significant primarily as "objects of human manipulation" (*Animal Estate* 2). From the traditional use of animals in sacrifice and ritual, hunting and fishing, transport and labor, the development of zoological, biological, ethological, and, more recently, genetic forms of knowledge has permitted the technological exploitation of animals at an unprecedented scale. The growth and acceleration of animal manipulation by humans over the last two hundred years have led to a paradox of representation: on the one hand, animals have disappeared from view as a result of increased urbanization and the development of technologies for meat production and animal experimentation that tend to place animals out of the public eye; on the other, animals have never been as visible as they are today through a broad range of cultural practices – including zoos, circuses, natural history museums, nature shows on television, and nature writing – that attempt to portray animals "as they really are."

Accompanying this paradoxical history of visibility and invisibility is the history of the attempt to grant animals a degree of legal and political representativeness. The legislative history of animal protections begins in the British Parliament with the passage of the Act to Prevent the Cruel and Improper Treatment of Cattle (also known as Martin's Act) in 1822. The first private organization devoted to the prevention of cruelty to animals, the Society for the Prevention of Cruelty to Animals (SPCA), was founded in 1824. The scope and applicability of animal protection laws as well as the proliferation of animal rights advocacy organizations have considerably expanded since then, with most so-called advanced democracies having embraced some form of animal welfare legislation and animal rights activist networks now operating around the world.

The parallel development of these two histories – the acceleration of animal manipulation in visible and invisible forms and the slow accretion of animal rights through public and private means – offers grounds for suggesting that the relation between them is one of cause and effect. The need to regulate the human mistreatment of animals occurs when it exceeds the state's capacity to control it; the persistence of animal mistreatment, in turn, prompts calls for abolishing it; commercial and institutional interests then resist regulation in the name of social progress. But, described in these terms, the causal relation between these parallel histories can also be understood as just one more instance of the endless tug-of-war that characterizes parliamentary capitalism. And to understand the relation in this way is in fact to grant no representation to animals themselves. Animals, as Marx famously wrote of small peasant proprietors, "cannot represent themselves, they must be represented" (347). The confusion between the representation of animals in culture (*Darstellung*) and their political representation (*Vertretung*) condemns them to a form of spectacle that, in animating the animal ("Disney" might stand as a shorthand for this process), hides the more excruciating spectacle of the nonsacrificial putting-to-death of the animal. As Wolfe puts it, "[W]e are all, after all, potentially animals before the law" (*Before the Law* 105).

(g) Wild child

Agamben calls the discursive apparatus that produces an ontological difference between human and animal the "anthropological machine." For Agamben, the anthropological machine creates a "zone of indifference" or "state of exception" within which the articulation of the relation between human and animal, human and nonhuman, speaking animal and nonspeaking animal takes place on the basis of inside/outside inversions (37). The modern version of the anthropological machine animalizes the human by isolating the nonhuman within the human. Beginning at the end of the eighteenth century, this animal-within-the-human becomes the focus of a new form of governmental rationalization whereby the state assumes responsibility for the care of its population's life. The animalization of the human under "biopower," Foucault's name for this new political dispensation, not only entails the statistical capture of life processes among the population (e.g., birth rates, life expectancy, infant mortality, illness) but also includes the creation of pseudobiological categories, such as race, that now become the markers of difference within a population.

The premodern anthropological machine, in contrast, humanizes the animal by producing quasi-human figures that occupy an ambiguous place within the chain of being since they are considered animals in human form: the slave, the barbarian, the foreigner, the *enfant sauvage* or *Homo ferus* (Agamben 30). The two anthropological machines operate in symmetrical fashion using the same basic procedure: the establishment of an empty signifier – what Agamben calls "bare life" – that is neither human nor animal but nevertheless serves in its emptiness to keep the human separate from the nonhuman. In its two versions, the anthropological machine creates, on the basis of false or empty comparisons, hybrid figures whose function is not the blurring but the reaffirmation of categorical differences.

(h) Elective affinities

The discipline of "comparative zoology" is largely a fiction. It was invented in 1850 by Louis Agassiz, one of Darwin's most implacable foes, for the purpose of showing how natural classification approaches the Mind of the Creator. Agassiz, an accomplished biologist working in Switzerland, was invited to deliver the Lowell Lectures in Boston in 1845. The lectures, titled "On the Plan of Creation in the Animal Kingdom," pointed to recent findings in comparative anatomy, embryology, and paleontology that suggested that coherent relations of similarity among animal species could not be explained by material necessity alone (Winsor 2). Patterns of similarity, for Agassiz, were evidence of a planning mind, evidence for what we might now refer to as intelligent design. By investing with a spiritual message the findings obtained using the comparative method, Agassiz was able to persuade Harvard's administration to appoint him to a new professorship. From this position, Agassiz created a new field of study, "comparative zoology," and, in 1859, founded an institution that would be both the center and the instrument of this field, "The Museum of Comparative Zoology."

The spectacular failure of his enterprise as an intellectual endeavor in the wake of Darwin's description of evolution did not seriously challenge the method he refined: classification. To define natural groupings of species instead of simply describing them became a permanent feature of the natural historical repertoire, however misguided his own goals were in implementing it as a method. In his

1857 *Essay on Classification*, Agassiz argues that classification seeks patterns in the geographic distribution of species: a feature is homologous when the resemblance expresses deep-seated structural "affinities"; a feature is called analogous when the resemblance pertains to function rather than affinity (24–5). Despite his belief in the direct divine creation of species, his scientific practice as well as his program for the future direction of natural history was perfectly consonant with those of most of his professional peers. Agassiz parted ways with his peers, however, in insisting that evidence of thought, planning, and design was patently visible in the correlations among species that he and his colleagues were discovering. The museum that he built as a kind of fortress against the theory of evolution no longer shares its founding vision, but the specific methodology that it meant to exhibit through the organization of its collection survives. The aim of the museum, then as now, was to provide material for scientific research based on the exploration of several dimensions of comparison. "The education of a naturalist," he wrote, "now consists chiefly in learning how to compare" (*Methods* 4).

(i) On the origin of literary species

The comparative study of literature is intertwined at its origins with the comparative study of animals by virtue of methodological affinities. Whether the method begets the object of study or the object of study the method is not entirely clear since the use of comparison in comparative literature is based on an analogy between literary forms (meters, figures, plots, genres) and biological forms (vertebrae, organs, species, genera) that seems to suspend their differences in "nature." This analogy can be traced at least as far back as Aristotle, who famously compares a well-constructed plot to a beautiful living creature in the *Poetics*: "Just in the same way . . . as a beautiful whole made up of parts, or a beautiful living creature, must be of some size, but a size to be taken in by the eye, so a story or plot must be of some length, but of a length to be taken in by the memory" (1451a).

Aristotle's analogy, which bears comparison with Borges's taxonomy in its attention to scale and perception, makes visible an intrinsic feature of comparison that, though seemingly obvious, is oddly absent from traditional accounts of the origins of comparative literature: its interdisciplinarity. To compare plots to living organisms does not exactly advance the cause of science: literature is not only an unreliable source of knowledge of the natural world but also an unworthy institutional partner in an age in which so-called STEM subjects overshadow the humanities. But to compare animals to texts could well advance the cause of literary studies by providing a new purchase on what comparison might signify for students of literature around the world without making its practice archaic, vestigial, or, worse, extinct. We may yet learn something about the nature of the discipline of comparative literature by attending to its constitutive figuration as the *literarization* (the making literary) of animal comparison. Without a reconsideration of its literariness comparative literature could go the way of comparative zoology: a museum housing the fossilized remains of a discipline.

(j) Literary evolution

The first theory of comparative literature to appear in English, Hutcheson Macaulay Posnett's *Comparative Literature*, a volume he wrote in 1886 for a prestigious series of scientific monographs, was also the first to use evolutionary science to explain the "secrets of literary workmanship" (86). For Posnett, comparative literature offers a general theory of literary evolution that follows the social history of literature as it passes through stages of inception, development, culmination, and decline. More than one hundred years after it was first proposed by Posnett, the view that literary history functions as literary evolution finds expression in two very different contemporary versions: one which compares literature and evolution by means of analogy and one which compares them as two members of the same set.

Moretti's innovative use of an evolutionary model involves an account of the development, success, and ultimate extinction of specific novelistic genres in a cultural environment he suggestively calls the "slaughterhouse of literature." For Moretti, Darwin's evolutionary tree provides a good explanatory model for representing the diversity and complexity of literary forms and, especially, for tracing their transformation over time. But Moretti is not wedded to this particular analogy; he is ready to use other abstract models (maps, graphs, world-systems) to explain the literary field as a whole. In contrast, other exponents of literary Darwinism, such as Joseph Carroll, read evolution literally, arguing that the adaptive advantage of storytelling selects for specific features expressed in the themes and forms familiar to students of literature but now explained by the literary cognitive capacity developed over time in humans (54). Jonathan Kramnick is right, of course, in arguing that this literal form of literary evolution may tell us little more than that humans tell stories, which we already know (345). Yet something else seems to be at stake in this type of analysis.

By exalting humans' capacity to tell stories, the sociobiological view of literary evolution tends to reaffirm the strict division between humans and animals in such a way that it restores the hierarchical difference that the theory of evolution was meant to upend in the natural world. Analogy, it turns out, is a better guide for thinking about difference and diversity in nature than scientific literalism is for thinking about form and function in literary ecologies.

(k) Anything is possible

Elizabeth Costello, J.M. Coetzee's character in *Elizabeth Costello*, suggests that literature, unlike philosophy, is uniquely equipped to posit a different way of being-in-the-world (96). The sympathetic imagination – the ability literature grants us to embody the lives of others – allows us to see the world from the perspective of an animal. Referring to Thomas Nagel, who famously argued in his 1974 essay "What Is It Like to Be a Bat?" that we are restricted in our ability to know what it is like to be a bat *for* the bat, Costello suggests that there are no bounds to what we are able to imagine in literature. If nothing else, literature is a discourse that knows no bounds – a discourse in which anything is possible. The animals in Kafka's stories, for instance, may not act exactly like real animals (what kind of "vermin" is Gregor Samsa anyway?), but, in giving voice to the experiences we might imagine they have, Kafka is asking us to put ourselves in their place.

We could say, more generally, that talking animals – animals that are conspicuously literary – make visible literature's capacity to imagine other lives. Talking animals might be said in this regard to be the emblems of literature's literarity. And, even if Nagel were right, who is to say that animals don't in fact talk and might one day tell us what it is like to be an animal *for* the animal? Literature is that place where we await the animal's response. It will probably be a very long wait, but refusing to listen attentively for the animal's talk would in the meantime do little to reinvigorate comparative literature's signature protocol of reading literature in its original language. Imagine what it would be like to be a translator of dolphin or a reader of gnu.

(1) The elephant in the room

Like the proverbial elephant, literature cannot be grasped in its entirety by any one of its practitioners. To judge by the studied indifference with which we regard the findings of those working immediately outside our circles of influence, there is little hope that literary critics will ever agree as to the size, shape, and texture of the elephant we are groping in the dark. Rather than feeling anxious about this state of affairs, we might consider making a virtue of this unavoidable uncertainty by learning to live with the provisional, partial, and incomplete accounts of the literary elephant enabled by any one of our preferred reading protocols, whether distant, close, medium, surface, symptomatic, or what-have-you.

In the animal sciences, it would be absurd to expect that the anatomical description of an elephant would invalidate the biophysical description of the sodium-channel physiology of the elephant's cardiac muscle, just as it would be presumptuous to suggest that elephant ethology is somehow divorced from its habitat or that the history of the ivory trade has had no impact on the population dynamics of the species. Different elephant scientists use different protocols to study different elephants, but they all operate under the reasonable assumption that one set of findings will corroborate, or at least not discredit, other sets of findings.

In contrast, different comparatists employ different reading protocols to study different types of literature, but we don't always operate under the assumption that our findings are compatible with those produced by other comparatists. Our findings are incompatible neither because our methods are flawed nor because we do not have one single method to rival the so-called scientific method, but because we do not always agree on what it is that we are comparing when we compare literature. Learning to live in the dark, therefore, not only involves accepting methodological promiscuity (a plausible definition of being "comparative") but also entails allowing for different species of the literary – literary elephants, for instance – to imprint their memories on our ways of doing criticism.

(m) Futures of comparative literature

There is already a considerable body of work in literary studies that treats the representation of literary species. Scholars such as Wolfe, Erica Fudge, Ron Broglio, Susan Crane, Anat Pick, David Clark, Colleen Boggs, Kari Weil, Carrie Rohman, Susan McHugh, Nicole Shukin, Ivan Kreilkamp, and Akira Mizuta Lippit, among others, have explored the complex entanglements of human and animals as they come to be processed in textual form. To the extent that their work is about animals, they are all already comparatists in practice, if not always in name. The future of comparative literature might well depend on the opening up of the categories it employs to classify its work (period, language, nationality) to the possibility of an animal perspective that would, in enjoining us to read differently, also make us think differently about literature and about comparison. What would it be like to construct a literary geography based on the migratory patterns of songbirds instead of the walking itineraries of those who sing of them? Or else imagine a literary history based on the comparison of the literary habitats of the Siberian tiger, the Andean puma, and the Iberian lynx instead of the literary habits of their captors?

   Animal studies, of course, is not the only way to pry open the traditional categories of comparative literature. Other recent interdisciplinary initiatives – environmental humanities, disability studies, queer theory, biopolitics, food studies, and digital humanities, among others – force upon comparative literature a new set of conceptual and aesthetic resources with which to revitalize the terms of comparison – point of view, agency, matter, affect, otherness, diversity – and redraw the shape of the literary. The work of classification would not cease, of course, but it would need to adapt to a new intellectual environment in order to make room for those discourses that have heretofore found no branch on which to perch in the tree of literary genealogy.

(n) Gato por liebre

The rhetorical coherence of the human/animal divide relies on the fact that we are habituated to naturalize catachresis as metaphor: we posit an entity – say, the "animal" – and then we accord it the consistency of a metaphorical concept. When Derrida coins the awkward neologism "animot" to draw attention to the fact that humans use a single word ("mot") to name all animals ("animaux"), he is also suggesting that the term "animals" is a figure of speech we use to name the vast multiplicity of the living, as though we had the right, in doing so, to determine the fate of the world (41).

   To erase the difference between humans and animals (the rhetorical logic of "rights") will not undo the coherence of this figure; rather, we must insist that difference is what there is: humans are as different from "suckling pigs" as "stray dogs" are from "those that at a distance resemble flies." These "animots" invite comparison not because they are members of the same set but because they are incongruent. Already living in that strange literary biome inhabited by animots that roam outside in the nature-text, comparative literature might yet be that discipline that learns to read difference differently.

Works cited

Agamben, Giorgio. *The Open: Man and Animal.* Trans. Kevin Attell. Stanford: Stanford UP, 2004. Print.

Agassiz, Louis. *Essay on Classification.* 1857. Ed. Edward Lurie. Cambridge: Harvard UP, 1962. Print.

———. *Methods of Study in Natural History.* 4th ed. Boston: Ticknor and Fields, 1868. Print.

Aristotle. *Poetics. The Complete Works of Aristotle Volume Two.* Ed. Jonathan Barnes. Princeton: Princeton UP, 1984. Print.

Berger, John. *About Looking.* New York: Vintage, 1980. Print.

Borges, Jorge Luis. "John Wilkins' Analytical Language." *Collected Fictions.* Ed. and trans. Eliot Weinberger. New York: Penguin, 1999. 229–32. Print.

Carroll, Joseph. "Three Scenarios for Literary Darwinism." *New Literary History* 41.1 (2010): 53–67. Project Muse. Web. 9 Feb. 2010.

Coetzee, J. M. *Elizabeth Costello.* New York: Penguin, 2003. Print.

Derrida, Jacques. *The Animal That Therefore I Am.* Ed. Marie-Louise Mallet. Trans. David Wills. New York: Fordham UP, 2008. Print.

Foucault, Michel. *The History of Sexuality: An Introduction.* 1978. Trans. Robert Hurley. Vol. 1. New York: Vintage, 1990. Print.

———. *The Order of Things.* 1966. New York: Vintage, 1994. Print.

Heise, Ursula K. *Sense of Place and Sense of Planet.* Oxford: Oxford UP, 2008. Print.

Johnson, Barbara E. *Persons and Things.* Cambridge: Harvard UP, 2008. Print.

Kramnick, Jonathan. "Against Literary Darwinism." *Critical Inquiry* 37.2 (2011): 315–47. Web. 8 Dec. 2011.

Marx, Karl. "The Eighteenth Brumaire of Louis Bonaparte." 1852. *Karl Marx: Selected Writings.* 2nd ed. Ed. David McLellan. Oxford: Oxford UP, 2000. 329–55. Print.

Moretti, Franco. "Evolution, World-Systems, *Weltliteratur.*" 2006. *The Princeton Sourcebook in Comparative Literature.* Ed. David Damrosch, Natalie Melas, and Mbongiseni Buthelezi. Princeton: Princeton UP, 2009. 399–409. Print.

———. "The Slaughterhouse of Literature." *MLQ* 61.1 (March 2000): 207–27. Print.

Nagel, Thomas. "What Is It Like to Be Bat?" *The Philosophical Review* 83.4 (1974): 435–50. Web. 9 Dec. 2011.

Posnett, Hutcheson Macaulay. *Comparative Literature.* London: Kegan Paul, 1886. Print.

Ritvo, Harriet. *The Animal Estate.* Cambridge: Harvard UP, 1989. Print.

———. *The Platypus and the Mermaid.* Cambridge: Harvard UP, 1997. Print.

Singer, Peter. *Animal Liberation.* 1975. New York: Ecco, 2002. Print.

Spivak, Gayatri Chakravorty. *Death of a Discipline.* New York: Columbia UP, 2003. Print.

Winsor, Mary P. *Reading the Shape of Nature.* Chicago: U of Chicago P, 1991. Print.

Wolfe, Cary. *Before the Law.* Chicago: U of Chicago P, 2013. Print.

———. *What Is Posthumanism?* Minneapolis: U of Minnesota P, 2010. Print.

Multispecies stories, subaltern futures

Mara de Gennaro

"Species interdependence is a well-known fact – except when it comes to humans."
When Anna Tsing writes this in one of a series of essays that look to diverse matsutake mushroom forests around the world to show that "human nature is an
interspecies relationship," she joins a small but growing number of anthropologists and artists for whom the influential interdisciplinary work of animal studies has not yet gone far enough (Tsing, "Unruly" 144). For these multispecies
ethnographers, what is needed is not simply a recognition of nonhuman agents
still on the margins of current discourse on animality, whether plants, microor-
ganisms, or less charismatic animals belonging to "unloved species."[1] What most
animates these scholars, from Tsing and her Matsutake Worlds Research Group
to Deborah Bird Rose studying Aboriginals and their wild dingo "kin," to Eben
Kirksey and his Multispecies Salon, is the work of understanding the intricate,
continually fluctuating relationships and interdependencies of humans and nonhumans in highly variable cultures and ecosystems.

If writings on animality in the last decade have rightly broken long-
unquestioned habits of philosophizing about some undifferentiated abstraction
called "the animal" (e.g., Derrida 32), they have rarely altogether avoided charac-
terizing members of particular nonhuman species as biological and transcultural
constants, such that for the purposes of animal advocacy, theoretical reflection,
and literary-critical analysis, a dog is a dog is a dog is a dog. Consequently, it is
often difficult to tell from essays that profess to be "posthumanist" how exactly
to proceed in the absence of familiar human-animal divides once we have finished
identifying their defects and urging their demolition, or what a critical approach
might look like that "begins with relationships rather than with an essence of the
agents in question" (Lestel 64).[2]

Multispecies ethnography changes that by revealing just how bound we continue to be, across disciplines, by a preoccupation with the human as center and
subject and by an allegiance to humanist paradigms of agency and value. The
durable humanism we keep nominally casting off continues – perhaps all the
more so because we think of it as already cast off – to obscure the environmental
and interspecies relations that make the stories we tell about ourselves possible,
even as we mostly banish those relations from our stories. Multispecies ethnographies give a different view, or multiplicity of views, with narrators traveling from

one field of relations to another and showing, through both closely observed and serially juxtaposed localities, stories of seemingly idiosyncratic human actions to be entwined within much larger ecological, legal, economic, and political stories of how power and value get distributed. At a time when many in comparative literary studies have shifted away from postcolonial critical approaches to what can seem politically gentler and more optimistic globalist approaches, multispecies ethnography's engagement with postcolonial theories of subalternity not only extends those theories to spheres beyond the merely human but also suggests work that we in literary studies still might do to recognize exercises of agency we have not adequately credited as such.

Gleaning stories

Tsing's innovative techniques in narrating her early fieldwork in Indonesia exemplified a new trend in anthropology of defining fieldwork as "travel encounters," with consequences for destabilizing conventional distinctions not only between "dwelling" and "traveling" but also, by extension, between academic ethnography and travel literature, as James Clifford argued in his well-known book *Routes.* "Her account historicizes both her own and her subjects' practices of dwelling and traveling, deriving her knowledge from specific encounters between differently cosmopolitan, gendered individuals, not cultural types" (68). Ethnographies such as Tsing's, "presented as stories rather than as observations and interpretations," substituted a self-implicating field of relations for the conventionally distanced and exoticized "field as an other *place*" (68).

Multispecies ethnography builds on the "reflexive turn" in late twentieth-century anthropology in which disciplinary self-critique became a focal point of ethnographic texts marked by heightened narratorial self-consciousness. Anthropology reinvented itself "by means of literary therapy applied to its primary genre form"; this therapy involved introducing "a literary consciousness to ethnographic practice by showing various ways in which ethnographies can be read and written" (Marcus 428, 442 n2). The phrase "literary therapy" points to the redemptive functions of narrative in multispecies ethnography, whose focus on "the embodied, situated, kinetic and narratival nature of place" leads from stories of humans to "stories enacted and expressed by multiple species" (van Dooren and Rose 2). Thom van Dooren and Rose, for example, challenge the assumption that city-dwelling penguins and flying foxes in Australia are "out of place" by showing how they impart meaning to the urban spaces they inhabit. Recognizing them as "narrative subjects" whose stories matter – to themselves and to the city around them – has the larger purpose of giving their human neighbors an incentive to ask in earnest, "What would it mean to really share a place?" (van Dooren and Rose 2–3). In his book *Flight Ways*, van Dooren continues what he calls the "ethical work" of telling stories, this time the stories of birds living "at the edge of extinction" (9). With a theoretical framework grounded in readings of Holocaust narratives and testimonies, van Dooren tells the stories of plastic-consuming albatrosses, endangered Indian vultures, urban penguins, captive cranes, and nearly extinct Hawaiian crows so as to make these "disappearing others thick on the page," awakening in turn his readers' "genuine care and concern" (9). Rose expresses a similar hope in *Wild Dog Dreaming* that "a narrative emerging from extinctions" might impress on readers the urgency of a relational ethics that learns from wild dingoes and the Aboriginal people who identify with them: "Perhaps voices from the death space *will speak* to us" (146).

   With its aspiration to tell stories that stir readers to notice and take seriously the environmental imprints and creative interventions of living beings considered marginal, multispecies ethnography holds promise for broadening the scope of interdisciplinary discussions about subaltern agency and representation. Even so, it must contend with enduring problems of voice and power that have long been matters of dispute in those discussions. In their essay-manifesto, "Tactics of Multispecies Ethnography," Kirksey, Craig Schuetze, and Stefan Helmreich question Bruno Latour's proposal to bring nonhumans into the democratic political process by assigning "human spokespeople" to represent them. Citing historian Timothy Mitchell's playful reformulation of Gayatri Spivak's famous question "Can the subaltern speak?" as "Can the mosquito speak?," they compare the difficulties of speaking for and with other species to those we face when representing other people and cultures. Given these problems of representation, Kirksey, Schuetze, and Helmreich suggest that ethnographers attend less to trying to speak for nonhumans, and more to examining what it means for humans to live with them.[3]

   Taking inspiration from Donna Haraway's theorizations of living with nonhumans in *The Companion Species Manifesto* and *When Species Meet*, multispecies ethnographers explore how humans are defined by the many ways we relate to our nonhuman companions, with "companions" ranging, in Haraway's terms, from dogs to "rice, bees, tulips, and intestinal flora" (*Companion* 15). Haraway's colorful accounts of interspecies meetings and companionships have also frequently been enlisted in the field of human-animal studies to contest anthropocentrism and presumptions of human exceptionalism (cf. *PMLA*'s special section on animal studies in 2009), but multispecies ethnography tends to encompass multiple interspecies relationships and their ecological significance, with humans rarely prominent and never independent. This dramatic repositioning of the human resonates with "Can the Mosquito Speak?," Mitchell's study of political and economic impacts of malarial mosquitos in World War II–era Egypt. Mitchell's essay asks whether and in what ways "the very possibility of the human, of intentionality, of abstraction depends on, at the same time that it overlooks, nonhuman elements" which "appear merely physical, secondary, and external" (29). Not overlooking the constitutive interdependencies of humans and nonhumans means interrogating "what kinds of hybrid agencies, connections, interactions, and forms of violence are able to portray their actions as history, as human expertise overcoming nature" (53).

   Tsing's stories of wild mushrooms ask similar questions and highlight the connection between noticing what is chronically overlooked and pursuing social justice. Tsing's call for us to look down and take note of the "cosmopolitan

transactions" of a forest floor's "underground city" of fungi reveals an altogether unexpected discrepant cosmopolitanism (Tsing, "Arts"; Clifford 36). She
continues:

> In agribusiness plantations, we coerce plants to grow without the assistance
> of other beings, including fungi in the soil . . . We maim and simplify crop
> plants until they no longer know how to participate in multispecies worlds.
> One of the many extinctions our development projects aim to produce is
> the cosmopolitanism of the underground city. And almost no one notices,
> because so few humans even know of the existence of that city. Yet a good
> many of those few who do notice fungi love them with a breathless passion.
>
> ("Arts")

Two familiar features of Tsing's otherwise unpredictable essays on matsutake
appear together here: an affective language used to describe diverse responses to
mycorrhizal mushrooms that resist cultivation and grow wild in damaged landscapes, offering themselves up to be harvested in socially, culturally, and eco-
logically disparate circumstances; and a sharp condemnation of the values and
methods of agriculture. Unabashed assertions of emotional states by Tsing and
other multispecies ethnographers further dramatize and even radicalize innovations from anthropology's reflexive turn. When Tsing claims that "there is a
new science studies afoot" whose "key characteristic is multispecies love," she
advances a vision of making oneself by turning toward what differs from oneself.
New ethnographic writing such as Tsing's and Rose's levels distinctions between
professional and amateur by turning its lens on the feeling, learning, empathizing
presence of the writer, for whom passion and affection are strong emotions that
do not cloud her judgment but rather allow her to see what is valuable about the
stories she is gathering.

Kirksey, Schuetze, and Helmreich liken the process of gathering stories to
gleaning in the field, "a form of trespassing that makes use of excess."[4] "If Clifford Geertz famously described 'The Anthropologist as Author,' perhaps it
is time to move beyond an individualistic model of innovation to think about the
anthropologist as editor who gleans narratives and ideas from others" (Kirksey
loc. 489–90, 707n73). Tsing's research method similarly entails traveling from
one forest to another and foraging for stories as her human subjects forage for
mushrooms. This method and the resulting forms of her ethnographic accounts
differ from those that grow out of an anthropologist's usual long immersion
into a region. Her essay "Blasted Landscapes," for example, an environmental
history of four matsutake forests in southwestern China, the eastern Cascades,
Finland, and Japan, uses a comparative approach to recount a transnational story
of how environments were damaged either gradually (by deforestation) or suddenly and cataclysmically (by the nuclear explosion at Chernobyl). Such damaged
landscapes can, under the right conditions, become fertile sites for unlikely interspecies encounters between matsutake mushrooms, which grow only in nutrient-
poor soils, and the often displaced, disempowered people for whom mushroom

harvesting is an attractive livelihood. Neither individualized human protagonists nor generalized human collectivities are positioned as central to the stories in "Blasted Landscapes," and yet Tsing's intricate histories of local matsutake worlds and their eco-cosmopolitan relations give a vivid sense of how these histories have shaped, and been shaped by, human lives.

Comparing entanglements

Another word very often recurs in multispecies ethnographies: "entanglement." With the burgeoning of transnational approaches to literary studies over the last decade and more, the metaphors we favor for challenging inequality have changed. In *Globalectics*, Ngũgĩ wa Thiong'o asks us to imagine works of litera-ture and orature as points on a globe where "there is no one center; any point is equally a center" and all the points are "balanced and related to one another by the principle of giving and receiving" (8, 61). Shu-mei Shih also advocates a "relational method" of comparison, arguing that "relational comparison is not a center-periphery model, as the texts form a network of relations from wherever the texts are written, read, and circulated" (96). Spatial figures of globes and networks have helped us to address and diminish the (usually European) ethno-centrism that too often endures in even well-intentioned uses of center-periphery models of literary relation.

Entanglement, a term that otherwise disparate multispecies ethnographers use frequently and for the most part consistently, is a more complicated rhetori-cal figure, and one that could provoke a more robust dialogue between literary studies and anthropology. If "entanglement" is surely the single most pervasive rhetorical figure in multispecies ethnography, it has recently begun to appear in literary criticism as well, notably in Rey Chow's *Entanglements, or Transmedial Thinking about Capture*. Compared to the relatively consistent use of the term in multispecies ethnography, Chow's entanglements, like those of the stories that interest her, are more indefinite and migratory. This matters because it is precisely the postcolonial field's long-standing exploration and valorization of the indefi-nite and migratory – the textual and discursive deviations, absences, and silences that need to be searched out and valued as sources of insight for institutionalized generalizations about the human to begin to lose their authority – whose reach multispecies ethnographers such as Tsing seek to extend. Tsing is explicit about this in her recent book, where she argues that in the sciences there persists too pervasive a sense of science as a "translation machine" in which "the elements of science come together into a unified system of knowledge and practice" (*Mush-room* 217). To recognize and learn from the periodic "eruption of difference" in transnational practices of research, "science studies needs postcolonial theory," especially its very different sense of translation as a messy process that "shows us misfits as well as joins" (217). A translational practice alert to "misfits," or scholarly convergences that signal areas of "incoherence and incompatibility," is one that, we would expect, would subject its own language of relationality to a comparably fraught interpretive practice.

Some version of the word "tangle" (including "entangled" or "entanglement") appears eighty-six times in *The Multispecies Salon*. When Rose writes of
"the entangled quality of life on earth" (*Wild* 50), van Dooren of "avian entanglements" and "multispecies entanglements" (4), and Haraway of "tangled species" (*When Species Meet*), there is usually an implication that to be entangled is to
be unavoidably connected and interdependent with another, or with many others. Van Dooren defines an "attentiveness to entanglements" as an understanding
of species "as vast intergenerational lineages, interwoven in rich patterns of co-
becoming with others" (2). Rose often uses variants of "entangled" and "connected" interchangeably, as when she writes that "as creatures enmeshed within
the connectivities of Earth life, there is no ultimate isolation; we are thoroughly
entangled" (*Wild* 44). Not emphasized in these uses, though not precluded
either, is the association of states of entanglement with states of captivity – with
all the restricted freedom and potential terror that this implies.[5] To be entangled
is not the same as to be connected, as Tsing highlights when she refers to "the
various webs of domestication in which we humans have entangled ourselves"
("Unruly" 144). To be entangled is, potentially at least, to be trapped.

For all the figurative language and exaltations of narrative that make multispecies ethnography so lively and irreverent, the field could benefit from engaging
more deeply with the literary as such – words' multiple and competing resonances
and narrative's divergent conceptions of identity and possibilities for action. For a
modeling of this we can turn to literary criticism concerned with related themes.
Chow's fluid analysis of the now coalescent, now divergent significations of
"trap," "entanglement," "captivity," and "captivation" is more elaborate than
I can capture here (pun intended). It is worth considering, though, how one of
her central insights can work together with multispecies ethnography to illuminate the action of T. C. Boyle's short story "Thirteen Hundred Rats."

"To be captivated is to be captured by means other than the purely physical,
with an effect that is, nonetheless, lived and felt as embodied captivity" (47).
Chow and Julian Rohrhuber, co-author of this chapter of *Entanglements*, offer
this definition after having contemplated cultural anthropologist Alfred Gell's
theorization of abduction as a means "to depict the contingency of agency in
situations in which agency can only be grasped as effect, as the outcome of interactions between agents who or which are seeking to realize their life projects
through their relations with others" (41). This perspective leads Chow and
Rohrhuber to stories of captivation and identification, including *Madame Bovary*.
For them, "Emma's state of captivation" with a fantasy world of romantic eroticism and luxury goods is "like a virulent parasite that has gradually overtaken its
host" (51). The received idea that Emma is "trapped" in a dull, loveless marriage
in a dull, provincial town is not what interests Chow and Rohrhuber, but rather
that her state of captivation "tangles up" the very opposition between being
trapped and being free because it is a state of being both and neither: of being
trapped by an all-consuming desire for an illusion that will destroy her, and of
being free from the sense of identification with material reality that would prevent her from engulfing herself in the fantasy she desires, and ultimately chooses,

over life itself. Captivation is thus a form of psychic captivity that brings with it pleasure and "a terrifying kind of freedom" (56).

T. C. Boyle's "Thirteen Hundred Rats," which appeared in the *New Yorker* in 2008, can seem a parable of multispecies entanglements, but if so, its entanglements are at once the entanglements of ethnography and of comparative literature. In the voice of a neighbor, Boyle tells the story of a grieving widower named Gerard who adopts a Burmese python only to let it die when he becomes entranced with the rat he buys to feed it, with terrible consequences for Gerard, the rat, and the other rats he buys to keep it company. Like Emma's captivation with romance, Gerard's grief is so consuming as to seem parasitical: "A quick search around the house, everything a mess (and here the absence of Marietta bit into him, down deep, like a parasitical set of teeth), the drawers stuffed with refuse, dishes piled high, nothing where it was supposed to be." Gerard's parasite confines him as Emma's does her, but it also frees him (in the course of overwhelming him) from any sense of obligation he would ordinarily have to conform to the values of what Boyle portrays as an extraordinarily circumscribed and homogeneous "village" community which has, the narrator claims proudly, "we like to think, a closeness and uniformity of outlook that you wouldn't find in some of the newer developments." And yet this "real community," as the narrator conceives of it, can think of no way to help Gerard other than suggesting he get a dog, while the pet trade is shown to operate purely for profit, with no regulations or reliable measures in place that would protect animals from consumers unable to care for them, such as Gerard ("Hell, no – I mean, I'll sell you all I've got if that's what you want, and everything else, too. You want gerbils? Parakeets? Albino toads? I'm in business, you know – pets for sale. This is a pet shop, *comprende?*").

"It takes a village" is an ironic subtext of this story set in an unnamed village where care, both intraspecies and interspecies, is so direly needed and so frequently denied. In this way, "Thirteen Hundred Rats" accords with multispecies ethnographies that educate readers about human beings' neglected and disavowed relations with other species, and that encourage us to make wiser, more farsighted choices about how to interact with them. But Boyle's story, like Chow's readings of stories in *Entanglements*, has narrative tools at its disposal that enable it to delve into complexities of feeling, identification, and agency that rarely come to the surface in the ethnographic stories and assertions of affect considered earlier. The force of Gerard's parasitical grief, no less than the narrator's faltering struggle to identify with it and account for the "choices" that followed from it, derives in part from its illustration that to be human is to be "entangled" with others in Rose's sense of being interconnected and interdependent. But its force derives too from its illustration that to be human is to be entangled in the more precise sense of being caught and confined – in our own captivated perceptions. That we are caught thus is precisely why collaborative and multidirectional efforts to make us recognize ourselves as defined by relationships only partly within our control are so important, but it is also why this recognition is so hard to come by and so difficult to act on.

A new interdisciplinary collaboration between multispecies ethnography and comparative literature will ideally be as unpredictable as any unprecedented interdisciplinary collaboration can be. It will be a collaboration between ethnographers who press us to recognize the chronically overlooked and disavowed relational agency of innumerable human-nonhuman convergences, and literary critics and writers who press us to recognize what is not immediately comprehensible or generalizable in the stories of such convergences, but that is no less moving or edifying for eluding us.

Notes

1 See Rose and van Dooren's "Guest Editors' Introduction" to a special issue of *Australian Humanities Review* titled "Unloved Others: Death of the Disregarded in the Time of Extinctions." There are in turn many references to "unloved species" and "unloved others" in *The Multispecies Salon* anthology. Hermit crabs inundated by oil in the Deepwater Horizon spill in 2010, for example, without either "an economic benefit or a cuteness factor," were "unloved" – "outside centralized biopolitical regimes" and "largely beyond the political, economic, and affective calculus of most Americans" (Kirksey et al., kindle locations 837, 842, 891).

2 French philosopher Dominique Lestel's mostly untranslated work on ethology is productive to read together with multispecies ethnography, partly because of the emphasis both place on personhood as "a relational narrative process" in which multispecies interactions are fundamentally constitutive (Lestel 64). An important figure in what Brett Buchanan, Jeffrey Bussolini, and Matthew Chrulew have called an "ethological revolution," Lestel is one of several European philosophers, along with Vinciane Despret and Roberto Marchesini, whose revisionist writing on animality and multispecies relationality is just beginning to reach Anglophone readers (see Buchanan et al. 1).

3 Indeed, a weakness of some multispecies ethnographers is their occasional lapses into overidentification with the nonhuman subjects they want to defend, so that they ascribe to them thoughts and motives that are far from clear (see, e.g., Rose 131).

4 For a film roughly contemporary with anthropology's reflexive turn that is itself highly reflexive, and that probes the theme of gleaning and scavenging practices so as to chronicle multispecies interdependencies on the margins of what is noticed and valued, see Agnès Varda's avant-garde documentary, *Les glaneurs et la glaneuse*.

5 To be clear, Rose does repeatedly acknowledge violent forms of interspecies connection: "To be alive is to know that one's life is dependent on the deaths of others" (26); "To live in the world, to live in connectivity, is always to be living in proximity to death as well as to life, to cause death as well as to nurture life" (142). My point is that her metaphorical uses of "entanglement" do not characteristically call attention to the word's implications of violence, or to its potential power as a metaphor.

Works cited

Animal Studies. Spec. issue of *PMLA* 124.2 (2009): 361–69, 472–575. Web. 21 May 2015.

Boyle, T. Coraghessan. "Thirteen Hundred Rats." *The New Yorker* 7 July 2008. Web. 4 Mar. 2015.

Buchanan, Brett, Jeffrey Bussolini, and Matthew Chrulew. "General Introduction: Philosophical Ethology." *Philosophical Ethology I: Dominique Lestel.* Spec. issue of *Angelaki: Journal of the Theoretical Humanities* 19.3 (2014): 1–3. Web. 18 May 2015.

Chow, Rey, and Julian Rohrhuber. "On Captivation: A Remainder from the 'Indistinction of Art and Nonart'." *Entanglements, or Transmedial Thinking about Capture.* By Rey Chow. Durham: Duke UP, 2012. 31–57. Print.

Clifford, James. *Routes: Travel and Translation in the Late Twentieth Century.* Cambridge: Harvard UP, 1997. Print.

Derrida, Jacques. *The Animal That Therefore I Am.* Ed. Marie-Louise Mallet. Trans. David Wills. New York: Fordham UP, 2008. Trans. of *L'animal que donc je suis.* Paris: Galilée, 2006. Print.

Geertz, Clifford. *Works and Lives: The Anthropologist as Author.* Stanford: Stanford UP, 1988. Print.

Les glaneurs et la glaneuse. Dir. Agnès Varda. Zeitgeist, 2000. DVD.

Haraway, Donna J. *The Companion Species Manifesto: Dogs, People, and Significant Otherness.* Chicago: Prickly Paradigm P, 2003. Print.

———. *When Species Meet.* Minneapolis: U of Minnesota P, 2007. Print.

Kirksey, Eben, ed. *The Multispecies Salon.* Durham: Duke UP, 2014. Kindle.

Kirksey, Eben, and Stefan Helmreich. "The Emergence of Multispecies Ethnography." *Cultural Anthropology* 25.4 (2010): 545–687. Web. 30 May 2015.

Kirksey, Eben, Craig Schuetze and Stefan Helmreich. "Introduction: Tactics of Multispecies Ethnography." *The Multispecies Salon.* Ed. Eben Kirksey. Durham: Duke UP, 2014. Kindle.

Kirksey, Eben, Nicholas Shapiro and Maria Brodine. "Hope in Blasted Landscapes." *The Multispecies Salon.* Ed. Eben Kirksey. Durham: Duke UP, 2014. Kindle.

Latour, Bruno. *Politics of Nature: How to Bring the Sciences into Democracy.* Cambridge: Harvard UP, 2004. Print.

Lestel, Dominique. "Like the Fingers of the Hand: Thinking the Human in the Texture of Animality." Trans. Matthew Chrulew and Jeffrey Bussolini. *French Thinking about Animals.* Ed. Louisa Mackenzie and Stephanie Posthumus. East Lansing: Michigan State UP, 2015. 61–73. Print.

Marcus, George E. "The Legacies of *Writing Culture* and the Near Future of the Ethnographic Form: A Sketch." *Cultural Anthropology* 27.3 (2012): 427–45. Web. 30 May 2015.

Mitchell, Timothy. "Can the Mosquito Speak?" *Rule of Experts: Egypt, Techno-Politics, Modernity.* Berkeley: U of California P, 2002. 19–53. Print.

Ngũgĩ wa Thiong'o. *Globalectics: Theory and the Politics of Knowing.* New York: Columbia UP, 2012. Print.

Rose, Deborah Bird. *Wild Dog Dreaming: Love and Extinction.* Charlottesville: U of Virginia P, 2011. Print.

Rose, Deborah Bird, and Thom van Dooren. "Introduction." *Australian Humanities Review* 50 (2011). Web. 30 May 2015.

Shih, Shu-mei. "Comparison as Relation." *Comparison: Theories, Approaches, Uses.* Ed. Rita Felski and Susan Stanford Friedman. Baltimore: Johns Hopkins UP, 2013. 79–98. Print.

Spivak, Gayatri Chakravorty. "Can the Subaltern Speak?" *Marxism and the Interpretation of Culture.* Ed. Cary Nelson and Lawrence Grossberg. Urbana: U of Illinois P, 1988. 271–313. Print.

Tsing, Anna. "Arts of Inclusion, or, How to Love a Mushroom." *Australian Humanities Review* 50 (2011). Web. 25 May 2015.

———. "Blasted Landscapes (and the Gentle Arts of Mushroom Picking)." *The Multispecies Salon.* Ed. Eben Kirksey. Durham: Duke UP, 2014. n.p. Kindle.

———. *The Mushroom at the End of the World: On the Possibility of Life in Capitalist Ruins.* Princeton: Princeton UP, 2015. Print.

———. "Unruly Edges: Mushrooms as Companion Species." *Environmental Humanities* 1 (2012): 141–54. Web. 25 May 2015.

van Dooren, Thom. *Flight Ways: Life and Loss at the Edge of Extinction.* New York: Columbia UP, 2014. Print.

van Dooren, Thom, and Deborah Bird Rose. "Storied-Places in a Multispecies City." *Humanimalia: A Journal of Human/Animal Interface Studies* 3.2 (2012): 1–27. Print.

Climate change

Jennifer Wenzel

One could focus this entry on the thematic by surveying literary texts "about" climate change, a body of writing now steadily accumulating, along with greenhouse gases in the atmosphere and oceans. Contemporary novels – particularly speculative fiction – would feature prominently, but a longer historical view would consider earlier moments of climate anxiety, like those of nineteenth-century European colonial scientists who linked deforestation to dessication, or the Arctic melting commemorated in Eleanor Anne Porden's 1818 poem *The Arctic Expeditions* (Grove; Johns-Putra).

An "Anthropocene literature" poses challenges to *periodization* because of the term's implicit dual designation of (1) what some argue is a new geological epoch that eclipsed the Holocene, whether at the dawn of agriculture, with European colonialism, with the invention of the steam engine in 1784, or with the "Great Acceleration" in the mid-twentieth century, and (2) the recent explosion of discussion across the disciplines about this epochal shift. In 2000, Eugene Stoermer and Paul Crutzen coined "Anthropocene" to mark how human activity had transformed the geophysical processes of the planet. This belated recognition of changes that may have been centuries or even millennia in the making has inspired revisionist histories of the Enlightenment and modern democracy as shaped by their dominant energy regimes, with coal having different implications for sociopolitical organization than oil (Chakrabarty; Mitchell). Literary history could be similarly reperiodized (Yaeger et al.). In the twentieth century, modernism aimed to "make it new," while the twenty-first century grapples with the unprecedented (Garrard).

More profoundly, the disjunctive time scales of climate change transcend historical periods and resist literary representation. Over millions of years, dead creatures fossilized into fuels that humans have consumed within a few centuries, with implications for life on Earth for millennia to come. These dilations of the narrative logic of cause and effect are temporal and spatial: climate change promises a future anterior (future inferior?) of changes yet-to-come that will have been effected by carbon emitted long ago and far away from its most extreme effects.

Such processes of attritional harm that elude apprehension and representation constitute "slow violence," argues Rob Nixon, whose work anchored the past decade's emergence of postcolonial ecocriticism. Nixon describes human vulnerability to environmental harm as "unevenly universal" (65) – another pithy formulation that should indicate the necessity of comparison and transnational thinking as literary studies confront climate change. Comparative literature under the sign of CO_2 is part of the environmental humanities, an emergent interdisciplinary formation that works against the diminishment of the humanities in the culture at large at the very moment when the human-as-species is recognized as a geological force. With the rise of market-friendly sustainability discourse as a response to environmental crisis, the environmental humanities urge dwelling critically and reflexively within problems and questions, rather than rushing toward "solutions." Comparatists can grasp the ideological work that literature does all the time, regardless of whether we want it to, while also resisting the instrumentalization of the aesthetic as merely a "useful," pliable, and predictable tool for environmental consciousness-raising.

With renewed confidence and urgency, the discipline can imagine alternatives to the obsolete futures promised by progress narratives unwittingly premised on access to unlimited cheap energy; it can help break through what Imre Szeman calls the "impasse" of "know[ing] where we stand with respect to energy" and climate, yet being unable to take action at the scale and scope necessary to produce adequate change (Yaeger et al. 324). But even if transforming cultural narratives is a challenge our discipline is well suited to address, the built environments, infrastructures, and energy regimes in which scholarship occurs pose a chastening constraint: a materialist analysis attuned to carbon (as well as capital and class) reveals that book publishing is the fourth-largest industrial source of greenhouse gas emissions, and the digital – like Crusoe's Friday – leaves a footprint that is anything but virtual (LeMenager 50).

Works cited

Chakrabarty, Dipesh. "The Climate of History: Four Theses." *Critical Inquiry* 35 (2009): 197–222. Print.

Garrard, Greg. "Towards an Unprecedented Ecocritical Pedagogy." Web. 3 Feb. 2014. https://www.academia.edu/4136119/Towards_an_Unprecedented_Ecocritical_Pedagogy

Grove, Richard. *Green Imperialism: Colonial Expansion, Tropical Island Edens and the Origins of Environmentalism.* Cambridge: Cambridge UP, 1995. Print.

Johns-Putra, Adeline. "Reading Climate Change Historically: Eleanor Anne Porden's Arctic Expeditions." Association for the Study of Literature and Environment Tenth Biennial Conference, University of Kansas, Lawrence. 30 May 2013. Presentation.

LeMenager, Stephanie. "Petro-Melancholia: The BP Blowout and the Arts of Grief." *Qui Parle: Critical Humanities and Social Sciences* 19.2 (2011): 25–56. Print.

Mitchell, Timothy. *Carbon Democracy: Political Power in the Age of Oil.* New York: Verso, 2013. Print.

Nixon, Rob. *Slow Violence and the Environmentalism of the Poor.* Cambridge, MA: Harvard UP, 2011. Print.

Yaeger, Patricia. "Editor's Column: Literature in the Ages of Wood, Tallow, Coal, Whale Oil, Gasoline, Atomic Power, and Other Energy Sources." *PMLA* 126 (2011): 305–26. Print.

Facts and figures

Comparative literature in the United States

Facts and figures

Compiled by the ACLA and Corinne Scheiner

Undergraduate programs and degrees in comparative literature

To establish the 2014 cohort of institutions that grant a BA in comparative literature, the report includes (Figure 17):

1 Institutions that reported completions in comparative literature to the IPEDS (Integrated Post-secondary Education Data System), maintained by the NCES (National Center for Education Statistics), the US government's depository of higher education data, which gathers information about students' graduating majors and programs of study in a given academic year in any year during the period under review (including those that reported "0");
2 institutions that informed the MLA in 2013 that they offered comparative literature at the undergraduate level in the form of a major, minor, concentration, or courses, and that, per their websites, provided students the opportunity to receive a BA in comparative literature.

Given that IPEDS does not collect data on institutions outside the United States, the 2014 totals include only those programs in the United States. The 2005 totals include programs outside the United States, so there is actually a slightly higher increase in programs than the graphs indicate. Figures 18 and 19 indicate the percentage of undergraduates earning degrees from comparative literature departments versus national language and literature departments.

Graduate programs and degrees in comparative literature

The data in Figures 20 and 21 were collected in spring and summer 2014. They reflect the overall size of graduate programs in comparative literature by total number of students enrolled and the number of funded students accepted, on average, from 2010–2013.

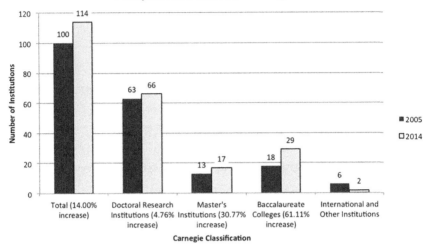

Number of Institutions Offering Undergraduate Comparative Literature Degrees

Figure 17 Number of institutions offering undergraduate comparative literature degrees.
Source credit: Corinne Scheiner.

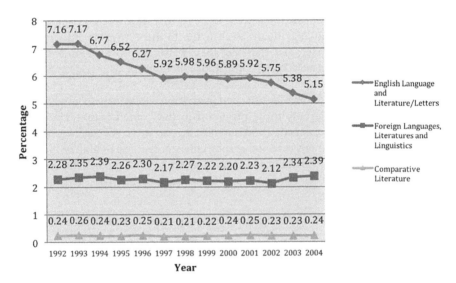

Percentage of BAs in Comparative Literature, 1992-2004

Figure 18 Percentages of total BAs awarded in English Language and Literature/
Letters (all subfields); Foreign Languages, Literatures, and Linguistics (all
subfields); and Comparative Literature at institutions that award BAs in
Comparative Literature, 1992–2004.
Source credit: Corinne Scheiner.

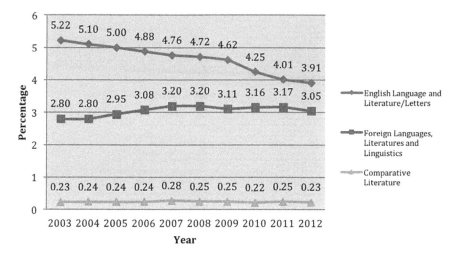

Figure 19 Percentages of total BAs awarded in English Language and Literature/Letters (all subfields); Foreign Languages, Literatures, and Linguistics (all subfields); and Comparative Literature at institutions that award BAs in Comparative Literature, 2003–2012. Note that the percentages for 2003 and 2004 differ in Figures 18 and 19 due to different constructions of the cohort.

Source credit: Corinne Scheiner.

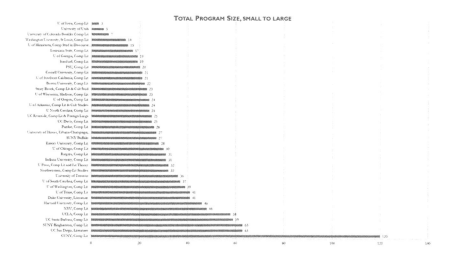

Figure 20 Size of graduate programs in comparative literature by total number of students enrolled 2010–2013.

Source credit: ACLA. https://stateofthediscipline.acla.org/sites/default/files/images/figure4.jpg

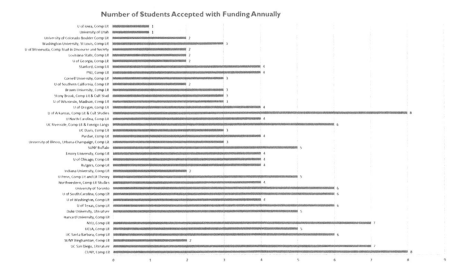

Figure 21 Average number of students accepted with funding in graduate programs in comparative literature, 2010–2013.

Source credit: ACLA. https://stateofthediscipline.acla.org/sites/default/files/images/figure5.jpg

The American Comparative Literature Association (ACLA) convention

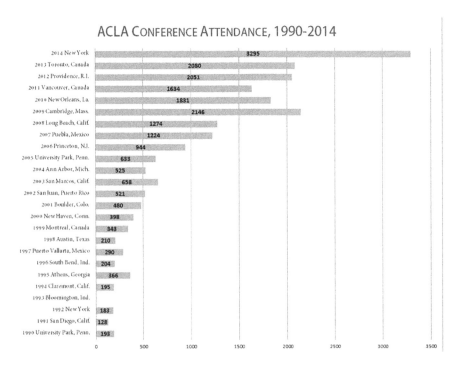

Figure 22 Total number of ACLA annual conference attendees, 1990 2014. (Data not available for 1993.)

Source credit: ACLA. https://stateofthediscipline.acla.org/sites/default/files/images/figure6.jpg

Index

higher 112, 115–16, 193, 329–32;
undergraduate 14–15, 19, 62, 220,
225, 259
Egypt 162–3, 188, 193n1, 197–8, 316
eighteenth century 37, 77, 92–6, 184,
305–8, 324; 1740s 95; in Europe
92–6, 145, 230, 275, 277
electronic literature 248–56, 285–9;
see also digital literature
El Salvador 166
emotion 64–5, 79–90, 113–14,
147–54, 244, 282, 317; *see also* affect,
feeling
empire 72, 102, 167, 179–84, 188,
228; Protestant 185; Catholic 185;
Chinese 150, 228; European 33–4;
global 127, 129; Ottoman 34, 94;
see also imperialism
empiricism 73, 75
Encyclopedia of Postcolonial Studies 179,
195–6
energy 49, 324–5; regimes 50, 324–5
England 93–5, 135, 150, 182, 184
English: African writing in 209, 225–6;
culture 153; degrees 330–31;
departments 19, 112, 211, 216,
224, 227; in digital humanities and
literature 273–4, 286; as dominant
language 22, 108, 120, 183, 196;
language 39, 55–7, 192, 204, 207;
literary criticism 191; literature 19,
25, 40, 109, 135, 219n3; professors
61; sonnet 217; spoken 73, 222; state
33; texts 5, 274, 282; translation 22,
62–3, 108–9, 157, 159, 216
Enlightenment 88, 93, 167, 298, 324;
European 143, 145–53
environmental humanities 6, 158,
274–5, 293–9, 312, 325; *see also*
ecocriticism
environmentalism 293–5, 297–8
environmental studies 294
epistemology 13, 15, 79–90, 124–28,
216–17, 220, 304–5
eroticism 92–6, 101, 319; homo- 93,
101
Ertürk, Nergis 141–4
essence 44, 64–5, 114, 146, 314;
civilizational 191; of a nation 134,
217
essentialism 171
ethics 71, 80, 84, 90, 129–30, 315–16
Ethiopia 207
ethnicity 129, 151, 228
ethnic strife 208

ethnic studies 5, 229
ethnocentrism 36, 43, 318
ethnography 55, 113; and the literary
315; multispecies 298, 314–21
Eubanks, Charlotte 270–2
Eurocentrism 34, 75, 192, 222, 318;
of comparative literature 4, 103,
156–60, 172, 188, 192, 218, 224; of
world literature 61, 134, 234, 210
Europe 35–47, 61–8, 78, 171, 224,
274–81, 297; and Arabic 187–92,
193n3; and Asia 148, 156–8, 160n2,
160n3, 160n6; early modern 93–4;
East and Central 4, 36–47, 51–8,
58n1, 281; eighteenth-century 92,
145; and Latin America 175–85, 279;
medieval 33–4; seventeenth-century 92,
95; Western 39, 51, 93, 95, 210, 298
European languages 35–47, 160n1,
295; non- 22, 39, 160n2
European literatures 35–47, 137–8,
156, 160n1, 175, 179, 192; diffusion
outside Europe 26, 36; East and
Central 4, 36–47, 51–8, 58n1, 281
evolution 303, 308–10; cultural 42;
literary 176, 278–80, 310
exoticism 101–2, 112, 115, 136, 158,
199, 227, 315
expressionism 37–8
extinction: literary 310; narratives of
315–16; of nonhuman species 303,
315–17

Facebook 71–3, 206
Fanon, Frantz 81, 83, 86–90, 195,
200, 259
Farsi 89
feeling 12, 64–5, 75, 79–90, 113,
147–8, 244–5, 320; *see also* affect,
emotion
feminist: movements 102, 190; studies
98; theory 21, 37, 92–6, 98
fiction 49–50, 283; *see also* novel, short
story
figure 44–5, 63, 87, 134–9, 185,
303–12, 318–19
film 20, 38, 101–2, 179, 280, 282;
documentary 295–6; studies 6–7, 19,
216, 296
finance 22, 131, 162–3
Finland 317
Finney, Gail 19–23
First World 51, 293
folklore 26, 42, 44
food studies 5–7, 296, 312